Also by G. Scott Thomas

History

Presidential Election Record Book 2020
Counting the Votes
A New World to Be Won
Advice From the Presidents
The United States of Suburbia
The Pursuit of the White House

Demographics

Micropolitan America
The Rating Guide to Life in America's Fifty States
Where to Make Money
The Rating Guide to Life in America's Small Cities

Sports

The Best (and Worst) of Baseball's Modern Era
Leveling the Field

DREAMTOWNS

DREAMTOWNS

THE 209 SMALL TOWNS WHERE YOU CAN LIVE YOUR BEST LIFE

G. SCOTT THOMAS

 NIAWANDA BOOKS

Dreamtowns: The 209 Small Towns Where You Can Live Your Best Life

Copyright © 2021 by G. Scott Thomas

Niawanda Books
949 Delaware Road
Buffalo, NY 14223

Printed in the United States of America

First Edition
10 9 8 7 6 5 4 3 2 1

CONTENTS

DREAMTOWNS

Chapter 1

THINKING SMALL

The Covid-19 pandemic spelled doom for Jillian Chernofsky's business. She was certain of that.

Chernofsky owns Creekside Chalets, a resort that offers upscale lodging in the high peaks near Salida, Colorado, a three-hour drive southwest of Denver. The Covid shutdown in March cut off her flow of tourists as the ski season wound down, and the prospects for the rest of 2020 appeared grim.

Chernofsky endured a couple of difficult months, then detected an unanticipated upswing. Her mood brightened considerably by the end of the year. "Our revenue for 2020 is up 25% over 2019," she said excitedly. "We're seeing the highest occupancy in four years. This is the busiest we've ever been."

Creekside Chalets benefited from a trend that experts had failed to predict. Residents of Denver and other Western hubs were temporarily flocking to the Rocky Mountains to escape urban congestion and the corresponding danger of Covid contagion. They preferred sparsely settled communities where they could live safely and work remotely. The telltale sign, said Chernofsky, was the first question that most of her visitors asked. They weren't interested in her resort's amenities. They wanted to know about the quality of her internet service.

The same influx was noted in small towns and rural areas across the country, often with lasting consequences. Many of the newcomers were doing more than renting cabins for a few months. They were putting down roots.

Redfin, a real-estate brokerage, reported a 115% increase in online searches for homes outside of metropolitan areas in March 2020, the month when the nation began feeling the impact of the Covid shutdown. "America's urban cities have boomed over the last few decades for their density of amenities, entertainment, innovation, and jobs," said Taylor Marr, Redfin's lead economist. "But this pandemic has forced us to close down those benefits and has shined a bright light on one of the historic downsides of density — the possibility for spread of disease."

The Harris Poll put the question directly to more than 2,000 Americans in early May: "Has the Covid-19 crisis caused you to consider moving to a less densely populated area of the country?" More than a quarter of the survey's participants said yes, including 39% of those who lived in big cities and 23% who had suburban addresses.

Many of Harris's respondents, of course, were engaging in wishful thinking. They fantasized about owning a larger home in a smaller community, yet they were in no condition to make the move. They possessed unbreakable ties to their current cities, or they lacked the money to transfer their families, or they were unable to work remotely. They were destined to stay put.

But others began to act on the impulse. Economists had believed that the housing market would suffer a Covid-related slowdown in 2020, yet it confounded them by accelerating. U.S. home sales soared to a 14-year high, powered by buyers in search of bigger houses that would more easily accommodate remote work. "The pandemic prompted many of them to leave big cities for suburbs or smaller towns, while record-low borrowing rates made the decision to trade up easier," explained the *Wall Street Journal*.

Emory McLeod was among these pandemic movers, leaving Philadelphia in October 2020 for the bucolic charms of Ithaca in the Finger Lakes country of Upstate New York. "Ithaca's just more Covid-friendly," she said. "Everything's a little more spread out, there's fewer people, it's quieter, and that is less anxiety-producing when you do have to go out into public." Brittany McCreary and her husband followed suit in December, slipping away from Chicago to buy their first home, a stone farmhouse in Pennsylvania. "It's totally because of the pandemic," she said. "We're glad we're not renting anymore. We always wanted to buy."

Price was a key motivation for thousands of these Covid-era migrants. The median home value in Chicago — the midpoint price for all of the city's housing units — was $245,300 as of 2019, according to a study released by the U.S. Census Bureau in December 2020. That was 52% higher than the corresponding figure of $161,600 for York, Pennsylvania, the area where the McCrearys found their new home. Disparities were even larger in other parts of the country, especially when California was involved. Median home values had soared by 2019 to $1,002,900 in San Jose, $883,600 in San Francisco, $606,600 in Los Angeles, and $565,700 in San Diego.

Housing costs in major cities, it's true, have been unreasonably stiff for decades. Homeowners might have grumbled, yet they unhappily accepted a steep mortgage as the access fee for the benefits of metropolitan life. The nation's very best jobs — those with the largest paychecks and the greatest power — were held to a considerable extent by the occupants of urban office towers.

Until the pandemic.

Covid-19 revealed that a substantial proportion of white-collar jobs could be done remotely. Executives and their subordinates shifted to their home offices, or they plopped computers onto kitchen counters, dining room tables, or card tables in spare rooms. Most found it surprisingly easy to stay abreast of their work. Researchers Jonathan Dingel and Brent Neiman concluded that 37% of all U.S. jobs can be done entirely at home, and the shares are even higher in technologically savvy places such as San Jose (51%), Washington (50%), and Austin (46%). "These jobs typically pay more than jobs that cannot be done at home, and account for 46% of all U.S. wages," Dingel and Neiman determined.

Working at home was initially viewed as a temporary phenomenon — an emergency stopgap — but thinking changed as the pandemic droned on. Twitter announced on May 12, 2020, just two months after the initial Covid shutdown, that it would extend the option indefinitely. "If our employees are in a role and situation that enables them to work from home," said a Twitter spokesperson, "and they want to continue to do so forever, we will make that happen." Facebook CEO Mark Zuckerberg chimed in nine days later, saying that he now expected half of his company's 48,000 employees to be working from home over the next decade.

"The stage is set for a major exodus from Silicon Valley," concluded *U.S. News and World Report*. San Jose and San Francisco, home to tens of thousands of Twitter and Facebook employees, were the only major U.S. cities with median home values in excess of $800,000. It was easy to imagine thousands of tech workers fleeing to cheaper environments, where they could work from home and actually deposit money into savings accounts.

But the implications were larger than that. Other companies followed suit by loosening their remote-work policies, freeing millions of employees — in theory, at least — to indulge their dreams of small-town life. "We're preparing for a seismic demographic shift toward smaller cities," said Redfin CEO Glenn Kelman. "Prior to this pandemic, the housing affordability crisis was already driving people from large cities to small. Now, more permissive policies around remote work and a rising wariness about close quarters will likely accelerate that trend."

The result, as 2020 played out and 2021 dawned, was a surge in inquiries about homes for sale in small towns. No place, no matter how isolated, seemed immune. Not even Maine, tucked deep into the nation's northeastern corner. The Maine Association of Realtors discovered that 33% of the state's homebuyers in 2020 came from out of state, a substantial increase from 25% the previous year.

"We already knew Maine was popular. More than 32 million people visit between Memorial Day and Labor Day," said Aaron Bolster, the association's president. But these weren't visitors; they were buyers. And they were continuing to purchase as he spoke, even though it was the midst of the frigid, snowy winter of 2021. Bolster shrugged. "They typically don't come at this time of year," he admitted. "But in a pandemic, it's a safe place to be."

Dreaming of Small Towns

Covid-19, of course, isn't the only factor at play. Americans have never really been fond of crowded urban areas, a sentiment that dates back to the nation's earliest years.

"I view large cities as pestilential to the morals, the health, and the liberties of man," declared Thomas Jefferson, who contended that agriculture was the ideal profession, the true path to a noble life. Jefferson preferred the relative peace and quiet of Monticello, his estate southeast of Charlottesville, Virginia, though his political career often drew him to New York, Philadelphia, and other urban centers. He never saw their virtues. "The mobs of great cities," he asserted, "add just so much to the support of pure government as sores do to the strength of the human body."

The nation reflected Jefferson's views for nearly a century and a half. A majority of Americans lived in rural areas until 1920. Cities edged into the lead after World War I, but only because the Census Bureau generously bestowed urban status on towns with populations as small as 2,500. Rural America didn't truly begin to lose its grip until the onset of the Second World War, which triggered the creation of millions of manufacturing jobs in big cities, in turn attracting a stream of workers off of farms. The share of Americans who resided in rural areas still stood at 43% in 1940, but it plummeted to 36% in 1950, then to 30% in 1960.

Yet the rural impulse continued to beat in the hearts of most Americans, even after the nation assumed an urban character. The Gallup Poll asked in 1949 who was happier, a farmer or a city dweller. The results were unexpectedly lopsided:

- Farmer, 65%
- City dweller, 21%

The rural residents surveyed by Gallup in 1949 voted overwhelmingly in favor of farm life, no surprise there. But so did 55% of the respondents who lived in cities, many of whom had undoubtedly been lured by industrial paychecks from the farms or small towns where they grew up.

Their nostalgia was understandable. But it did not diminish, even as the decades rolled by and the nation's urban orientation solidified:

1978: The U.S. Department of Housing and Urban Development surveyed more than 7,000 Americans, asking them to identify the best place to raise children. Most of the participants lived in metropolitan areas, yet nearly half chose small towns as the ideal location for child-rearing. Only 12% picked big cities.

1985: The Gallup Poll asked if people dreamed about moving away from their current communities. Fully 41% in cities with more than 1 million residents said they wanted out. Only 27% in rural areas expressed similar dissatisfaction.

1992: The Harris Poll invited Americans to rate their hometowns. The pollsters divided respondents into two categories: city dwellers and those living anywhere else (including suburbs, small towns, and rural areas). Only 60% of urban residents gave their cities positive grades for overall quality of life, while 79% in the latter group were favorable about their communities. The gap was even wider when Harris asked about the conditions for raising a family: 50% positive in cities, 81% elsewhere.

2001: The Gallup Poll asked participants to choose between six potential residences. Rural areas, favored by 35%, were the most popular location. Big cities, picked by just 8%, received the lowest score.

Gallup dusted off the latter question for an end-of-year survey in December 2020, nine months after the Covid-19 shutdown had brought life to a crawl across America. The results were remarkably similar to those from 19 years earlier. None of the answers varied by more than five percentage points between 2001 and 2020, essentially falling within the poll's four-point margin of error.

"If you could live anywhere you wished," asked Gallup's interviewers in the final month of 2020, "where would you prefer to live?" Rural areas again drew about a third of all votes, while another third was split between towns and small cities, the other two low-scale options on the list:

- Rural area, 31%
- Town, 17%
- Small city, 16%
- Suburb of big city, 16%
- Big city, 11%
- Suburb of small city, 9%

The contradiction couldn't have been more obvious. All of the polls between 1949 and 2020 were conducted in a nation where a sizable majority of residents had congregated in urban areas — the share exceeded 80% by 2019 — yet every single survey detected a strong preference for life in rural areas and small towns.

Economic and technological constraints had prevented most urbanites from packing their belongings into moving vans in prior years. But 2020's pandemic changed the calculus, coupling the heightened health concerns in big cities with a newfound ability to work at home. The stage was finally set for disaffected city dwellers to follow their dreams.

Drawing the Lines

The aim of this book is to pinpoint the small town (or towns) where you can live your best life. But what exactly is the population range for such a community?

The U.S. Census Bureau started wrestling with that question in the late 19th century. It began designating places as urban or rural in 1880, initially setting the cutoff at 8,000. Any community with more than 8,000 residents was classified as urban. Everything else was rural. That threshold proved to be too stringent, so the bureau sliced it to 4,000, then to 2,500. The latter figure, adopted in 1900, remains in effect today.

This urban-rural dichotomy was sufficient prior to World War II, when the landscape was dotted by cities and towns, neatly separated by farmland, forests, and other open spaces. But the situation grew complicated after millions of veterans returned from the European and Pacific theaters. They all wanted homes of their own, and the construction industry happily met the demand. Only 114,000 houses had been built across America in 1944, but the annual figure soared past 1.2 million by 1947 and kept climbing. Subdivisions began springing up everywhere, often in fields far from urban business districts. The suburbanization of America was underway.

The U.S. Bureau of the Budget noted this new development pattern — the ceaseless construction activity, the steady migration from cities to newborn suburbs, the blurring of urban and suburban boundaries — and it devised a statistical concept in 1949 to track the emerging way of life. It created the "metropolitan area," defining a single zone that was economically interdependent, consisting of a central city and its surrounding suburbs. The Census Bureau soon followed the Bureau of the Budget's lead and began collecting data at the metropolitan level.

But some demographers were unhappy with the imprecision of the metropolitan concept. Each metro area was assembled at the county level. If a specific county, taken as a whole, was deemed to be "closely economically integrated" with the central city, the entire county was added to the metro, even if much of the county's land was occupied by decidedly nonmetropolitan farms and small towns. The New York City metro, as defined in 1950, encompassed 17 counties, including distant rural expanses of eastern Suffolk County on Long Island and Middlesex and Somerset counties in New Jersey.

So the Census Bureau — in pursuit of greater precision — introduced a second innovation in 1950, the "urbanized area." Its definition deemed city and county lines to be irrelevant. Demographers started in a central city and worked outward block by block until they reached a designated limit of urban growth. They acted as if they were gazing upon the urbanized area from an airplane, viewing the city and its suburbs as a single community, and they classified it as such.

That was the major difference between the two concepts. The boundaries of a metropolitan area were artificially confined to county lines, while those of an urbanized area reflected the actual conditions on the ground. It was entirely possible that a single metro area might include several urbanized areas, provided that each of the latter was surrounded by a belt of land that was sparsely populated or completely undeveloped.

Public reactions were diametric. Business executives, marketers, politicians, and journalists embraced the metropolitan area, which was easy to understand. Everybody, after all, knew the name of his or her county. The urbanized area, on the other hand, was almost completely ignored, in part because it seemed too complicated. The only definitive maps of urbanized boundaries were buried in the dusty repositories of the Census Bureau.

The bureau continues to generate reams of data for both designations to the present day, with a couple of enhancements. There currently are 384 metropolitan areas, each centered around a city with at least 50,000 residents and encompassing all economically connected counties. A second level of mini-metros — one of the aforementioned tweaks — was added in 2000. These "micropolitan areas," which are focused on cities with populations of 10,000 to 49,999, are similarly constructed of counties. There are 543 micros today.

An urbanized area, as currently defined, must bring together at least 50,000 residents in "a densely settled core of census tracts and/or census blocks that meet minimum population density requirements." A total of 486 areas qualify under those stipulations. The Census Bureau added a new group — the second enhancement — in 2000. Each "urban cluster" is a cohesive community with 2,500 to 49,999 residents, a smaller version of the urbanized area. There currently are 3,087 clusters.

There's no need to go any further with this digression into demographic history. Let's return instead to the question that began this section: What exactly is a small town? Is it a metropolitan area that falls below a specified population limit? Or a micropolitan area within a certain size range? Or an urbanized area or urban cluster that meets certain criteria?

There is no specific answer. The Census Bureau says that any community with at least 2,500 residents is urban, but it doesn't go beyond that. Any decisions about big, medium, and small are left to the beholder. Which means, in this case, that the final choice is mine.

So here's the guiding principle for this book: Forget all about metropolitan and micropolitan areas. We'll deal with the layout of America as it actually exists, not as an artificial reconstruction on a county-by-county basis. A small town will be defined as an urbanized area or urban cluster — a cohesive, self-contained community — that has at least 5,000 and no more than 199,999 residents.

That's a broad sweep — broad enough to encompass widely divergent opinions about size. If you're living in an urban canyon in Manhattan or Chicago, an urbanized area such as Deltona, Florida (population: 199,388), Huntington, West Virginia (199,300), or Spartanburg, South Carolina (197,110), might seem small enough. But if your ideal is a town that has a compact business district and a limited number of houses, you might be happy going as small as Byron, Minnesota (5,004), Grangerland, Texas (5,003), or Kaplan, Louisiana (also 5,003). All of these places — from Deltona to Kaplan — can be found in this book.

The Strengths of America's Small Towns

We'll be examining a total of 2,084 urbanized areas and urban clusters, but let's not use those terms from this point forward. Let's just call them small towns, since that's exactly what they are.

A few of these places, such as Deltona, Huntington, and Spartanburg, are focal points of metropolitan areas — small metros, to be sure, but metros nonetheless. Hundreds more are tucked on the fringes of metropolitan areas named after bigger cities. And the remainder — the vast majority of America's small towns — are located in micropolitan areas or rural counties.

It's important to remember, regardless of the variation in their geographic settings, that all 2,084 small towns share these two key characteristics:

• They have populations between 5,000 and 199,999.
• They are freestanding communities, surrounded by belts of lightly settled or completely open land. That's true even of small towns commonly considered to be suburbs, such as Charlestown, Indiana (outside Louisville), East Aurora, New York (Buffalo), and Lee's Summit, Missouri (Kansas City). All of them meet the federal guidelines for inclusion here.

Your interest in America's small towns is undoubtedly based on their reputed ability to offer your family a superior quality of life. And that's where this book comes in. It's designed to guide you through the tangle of hundreds upon hundreds of possible relocation targets, drilling down to the towns that best meet your needs.

But you shouldn't launch such an extensive search without fully understanding what lies ahead. So let's begin by examining the collective strengths and weaknesses of small towns, matching them against the nation's biggest cities. If you consider the results to be generally favorable, then (and only then) will it make sense for you to continue.

I have chosen to designate the 50 largest urbanized areas — sorry, that term again — as major urban hubs. They range in size from New York (18.75 million residents) to Hartford (923,000). Major hubs contain a total of 150.8 million Americans, nearly half of the nation's population, though they cover just 1.3% of the total land area. (An important note: I will sometimes refer to major hubs as big cities, but it's important to remember that each hub is more than just its central city. It also encompasses all suburbs within the flow of continuous development, the zone that appears from the air to be a single metropolis.)

Here's an alphabetical list.

Major Urban Hubs

Atlanta, GA
Austin, TX
Baltimore, MD
Boston, MA
Bridgeport, CT
Buffalo, NY
Charlotte, NC
Chicago, IL
Cincinnati, OH
Cleveland, OH
Columbus, OH
Dallas, TX
Denver, CO
Detroit, MI
Hartford, CT
Houston, TX
Indianapolis, IN
Jacksonville, FL
Kansas City, MO
Las Vegas, NV
Los Angeles, CA
Louisville, KY
Memphis, TN
Miami, FL
Milwaukee, WI
Minneapolis, MN
Nashville, TN
New Orleans, LA

New York, NY
Oklahoma City, OK
Orlando, FL
Philadelphia, PA
Phoenix, AZ
Pittsburgh, PA
Portland, OR
Providence, RI
Raleigh, NC
Richmond, VA
Riverside, CA
Sacramento, CA
St. Louis, MO
Salt Lake City, UT
San Antonio, TX
San Diego, CA
San Francisco, CA
San Jose, CA
Seattle, WA
Tampa, FL
Virginia Beach, VA
Washington, DC

America's 2,084 small towns cover a total of 32,822 square miles, coming reasonably close to the 45,202 square miles collectively taken up by the 50 major hubs. But there is a massive disparity in population, as you would expect. Nearly three times as many people live in major hubs (150.8 million) than in small towns (54.8 million).

Let's compare the two sides, beginning with six factors that tilt in favor of smaller communities.

1. Room to Breathe

Small towns are less crowded. That goes without saying, right? It's certainly one of the reasons why you find yourself attracted to small-town life.

If you quickly divide population by land area, using the numbers a few paragraphs back, you'll see that 3,336 people are packed into each square mile of a major hub. That's twice as crowded as the 1,670 per square mile in a small town.

But those are simply averages. Densities are much worse in many of the biggest cities, such as Los Angeles (7,224 per square mile), San Francisco (6,748), San Jose (6,295), and New York (5,435). Five other hubs pack more than 4,000 people into each square mile, putting them above the Census Bureau's official threshold for urban crowding.

Nearly three-quarters of all small towns (1,514 of 2,084) have fewer than 2,000 people per square mile. About a tenth of them — a total of 204 — are so sparsely settled that their densities fall below 1,000. The least crowded of all is Interlachen, Florida, with just 506 people per square mile.

But density tells only part of the story. Keep in mind that every community in this book — big and small — is defined by the outer limits of its growth. A major hub covers 904 square miles on average, dwarfing the 16 square miles needed for a typical small town. Where do you think you'll find it easier to escape to the great outdoors?

2. Ease of Movement

It's much simpler to commute or run errands in a small town. The equation couldn't be more direct: Less crowding equals more freedom of movement.

Covid-19 may have changed America's commuting patterns forever, but pre-pandemic measurements can still tell us a great deal about the relative ease of getting to the office or the grocery store or the park on the other side of town.

The Census Bureau annually asks workers to report their typical commuting times, specifically the number of minutes it takes to get from home to worksite. The most recent survey identified Washington, D.C., as the nation's worst horror story. A total of 404,000 Washington workers require more than an hour to make the one-way journey, while another 532,000 burn 40 to 60 minutes. That puts more than a third of Washington's commuters (36.8%) above the 40-minute threshold. Only 24.0% of them get to work in less than 20 minutes.

The latter is the measurement used by this book. If you can complete your rush-hour trip in fewer than 20 minutes, it can be assumed that your other travels around town will be equally carefree. Relatively few city dwellers, sad to say, are familiar with such joy. Only 32.8% of all workers in the 50 major hubs are able to meet the 20-minute standard.

Getting around is much less of a hassle in America's small towns, where a strong majority of all workers (58.3%) travel from home to place of employment in 19 minutes or less. The figure exceeds 75% in 363 towns — and rises to the unfathomable heights above 90% in 14 commuting paradises.

3. Economic Balance

Americans have never been more aware of the chasm that divides the nation's haves and have-nots. The Covid shutdown coincided with a summer of racial unrest and a presidential campaign of unusual vehemence. Those three factors collectively inspired today's ongoing debate about the dangers of inequality.

There are two ways to quantify the problem. The first is to focus on the very peak: The top 5% of America's wage earners, according to the Census Bureau, receive 23.3% of the nation's total income. The second way is to divide earners into five groups of equal size. The 20% with the largest paychecks get 51.6% of all U.S. income, while the 20% with the smallest checks are given just 3.1%.

No part of the country is immune to this dilemma, though the gap does vary according to size. The top 5% of all earners receive more than a quarter of total income in three major hubs: Bridgeport (28.2%), Miami (26.5%), and New York (25.3%). The average for all 50 hubs is 23.2%, essentially mirroring the figure for the entire country.

Financial inequality is less pronounced in small towns, where the top 5% draw an average of 20.7% of total income, two and a half points below the big-city benchmark. Local figures fall below 20% in more than half of all small towns (1,126 of 2,084), which means the 5% with the highest paychecks in those communities get less than a fifth of local income. Only one of the 50 major hubs, Riverside, is below 20%.

4. Affordability

It's no easy thing to measure the cost of living in a specific locality, but the U.S. Bureau of Economic Analysis (BEA) has made the attempt. It devised an index with a bureaucratically intimidating name — regional price parities (RPP) — to gauge any variation in personal expenses from one area to the next.

The bureau collects price quotes across the country for a wide array of goods and services, then generates an RPP index for each state and metropolitan area. The national average is fixed precisely at 100.0, with all other figures calculated from that base. The highest RPP for any metro is San Francisco's 134.5, indicating that it's 34.5% more expensive than the typical American community. The cheapest metro is Beckley, West Virginia, at 77.8, signifying that it's 22.2% less costly than the U.S. average.

This is useful information. Let's say you live in State College,

Pennsylvania, which just happens to have an RPP of exactly 100.0, and a company in San Francisco has offered you a job. You make $50,000 a year in State College, but you would have to obtain a 34.5% raise in San Francisco — all the way up to $67,250 — simply to retain the same buying power.

There's only one problem. The Bureau of Economic Analysis computes RPPs for the few dozen metropolitan areas that also are classified as small towns, such as Beckley and State College, yet it ignores all communities below the metro level. That leaves out the vast majority of places in this book.

So how do we quantify the cost of living in small towns? BEA has given us a rough indication, a separate index that encompasses the vast nonmetropolitan portion of America, including micropolitan areas, outlying small towns, and rural counties. This collective nonmetro RPP is 86.8, which is 13.2% cheaper than the national average. And it's vastly less expensive than the RPPs for some of the country's biggest cities: 35.5% less than San Francisco, 30.9% less than New York, 26.9% less than Los Angeles, and 26.1% less than Washington.

5. A Place of Your Own

The goal of home ownership is more easily attained in small towns, a point directly linked to the previous attribute, affordability. Homes tend to cost less in small towns, so they can be purchased more easily. Simple as that.

The typical owner-occupied home in the 50 major hubs is valued at $326,100, based on the Census Bureau's latest estimates. Individual figures, of course, can be dramatically higher. I previously noted the four California cities where median home values exceed $500,000, led by San Jose's virtually incomprehensible $1,002,900. (Keep in mind that a median is a midpoint. Half of San Jose's prices are even higher!) Five other hubs have medians in excess of $400,000: Washington, New York, Boston, Seattle, and Bridgeport.

And what about the 2,084 small towns? Their median home value, taken collectively, is $188,800. That's 42% cheaper than the corresponding figure for big cities, an immense discount.

More than three-quarters of the nation's small towns (a total of 1,623) have median home values below $200,000. A quarter (553) have medians under $100,000. Big cities can't match these statistics. The price of a typical home is lower than $200,000 in only a third of urban hubs (16 of 50). Not a single one is below Buffalo's $144,300.

6. Resilience

The residents of small towns are more resilient.

How is it possible to make such a claim? The U.S. Census Bureau paved the way in 2020 by devising a resilience index. Its aim, according to an official statement, was "to measure the ability of a population to absorb, endure, and recover from the impacts of disasters, including weather-related and disease-related hazard events such as Covid-19."

We'll delve more deeply into the particulars in the next chapter, but suffice it to say that the index assesses each resident for 11 characteristics that might reduce his or her ability to bounce back from adversity. The persons in each locality are then divided into three groups — those with no risk factors (most resilient), those with one or two factors (moderately resilient), and the remainder with three or more factors (least resilient).

Big cities do not perform well on the resilience index. Only 14.2% of the residents of the 50 major hubs are classified as having no risk factors. Eight cities fall below 10% on the scale, including New York, Los Angeles, Miami, and San Francisco.

Small towns are considerably more resilient, with a quarter of their residents (24.9%) carrying no risk. Nearly a fifth of these communities — 411 of 2,084 — have scores of 32% of better. Not a single big city does better than Raleigh's 31.6%.

And These Are the Weaknesses

There is a flip side, of course. Small towns are blessed with several advantages, as we have just seen, but they are also saddled with deficiencies. I focused on six of the former, so it seems fair to balance the ledger by examining six of the latter.

1. Slow Growth

You might consider this to be an attribute. Their very smallness is what attracts you to small towns. You don't want to relocate to a place that is expanding rapidly, given the danger that it might eventually become as congested as the big city you dream about leaving.

Fair enough. But keep in mind that growth — steady, manageable growth — is essential to a town's development. "Each time someone moves to your community, that is economic growth," says Kurt Schindler, a Michigan State University senior educator. "That person is a new customer. They buy food and services, patronize local businesses, get their car fixed, attend activities, invite others to visit them, and more."

And that's not all. These newcomers also enhance the tax base — facilitating the maintenance and improvement of local services — and they infuse the community with fresh ideas from the outside world. So growth, provided that it's kept at a reasonable pace, is definitely a good thing.

The population of the 50 major hubs grew by 3.9% between 2014 and 2019, the five-year period immediately preceding the pandemic. Austin, Charlotte, and Raleigh led the pack with growth rates in excess of 10% — perhaps a bit too rapid for some tastes — but most cities were comfortably below 7%. Only six hubs suffered population declines.

Small towns were considerably more sluggish over the 2014-2019 span, posting a collective population increase of just 1.8%. There were notable exceptions — 169 towns exceeded growth rates of 10% — but they were vastly outweighed by the communities that shrank. Close to half of America's small towns (955 of 2,084) had fewer residents in 2019 than five years earlier. That is not a recipe for longterm prosperity.

2. Aging Population

Residents of small towns tend to be older. This isn't a case of age discrimination. It's simply a fact of demographic life, an ingredient in the decline that was noted above. If an area has an excess of senior citizens and a paucity of young adults, its prospects for growth are dim.

People who have reached the age of 65 deserve thanks for helping to build and sustain their communities. But most of them have given up the reins. They no longer are the driving forces in their towns. Young adults between the ages of 25 and 39, on the other hand, represent the future. They're establishing careers, forming relationships, and starting families.

Seniors are more commonly found in America's small towns (accounting for 16.3% of their residents) than in major hubs (14.0%). The balance tips the other way for young adults, who are more strongly represented in big cities (22.2% of their total population) than in small towns (19.8%).

The disparity becomes more striking if we convert raw numbers to ratios. Major hubs contain 33.5 million persons in the 25-39 age group and 21.1 million in the 65-plus cohort, which works out to 159 young adults for every 100 seniors. The corresponding ratio for small towns is much tighter: 10.8 million residents between their mid-20s and late 30s, compared to 8.9 million who have passed their 65th birthdays. That yields only 121 young adults per 100 seniors.

3. Less Diversity

You know the stereotype. White is supposedly the dominant color in most small towns — white Victorian homes, white picket fences, white residents. It's a cliché, of course, yet it contains a kernel of racial reality. Big cities are rapidly diversifying, but most small towns are behind the demographic curve.

Fewer than half of all big-city residents (49.1%) were classified as white by the Census Bureau in 2019, compared to two-thirds (67.2%) of the people who live in small towns. Cincinnati and Pittsburgh are the only urban hubs that are more than 75% white, but over half of all small towns (1,118 of 2,084) exceed that threshold.

An arcane statistic dramatizes the difference. The Gini-Simpson racial diversity index determines the likelihood that two randomly selected persons would come from different racial groups. The index for the 50 major hubs is 67.2%, indicating that two of every three random draws would yield a racial mix. The corresponding Gini-Simpson number for the 2,084 small towns is just 51.1%.

So what? Sociological studies have concluded that diverse communities are more likely than homogeneous places to grow and prosper. "Diversity enhances creativity," says Katherine Phillips, a Columbia Business School professor. "It encourages the search for novel information and perspectives, leading to better decision making and problem solving." A substantial number of America's small towns are missing out on these benefits.

4. Education Imbalance

Many of America's finest universities are located in small towns, ranging from elite Ivy League schools, such as Cornell University (Ithaca, New York) and Dartmouth College (Lebanon-Hanover, New Hampshire), to an array of prestigious public schools, including Iowa State University (Ames), Pennsylvania State University (State College), the University of Colorado (Boulder), the University of Mississippi (Oxford), and Washington State University (Pullman).

The professors employed by these schools, of course, are highly educated.

The same is true of the entrepreneurs who flock to college towns to harness the local brainpower. Both groups elevate the educational profiles of their communities. Take Boulder, Colorado, for instance. More than three-quarters of Boulder's working-age adults (76.6%) hold bachelor's degrees, and 36.6% also have master's, doctoral, and/or professional degrees. Those figures dwarf the corresponding national averages for bachelor's (33.5%) and advanced (12.3%) degrees.

But Boulder is uncommon. Slightly more than a quarter of the working-age residents of a typical small town, 26.2%, hold bachelor's degrees. That's roughly seven percentage points below the national benchmark and nearly 14 points beneath the average for major hubs, 40.1%.

Approximately 7.1 million small-town residents between the ages of 25 and 64 have degrees from four-year colleges. If those communities were able to match the big-city graduation rate of 40.1%, that total would soar to 10.8 million. The resulting disparity — a shortage of 3.7 million college-educated adults — puts America's small towns at a disadvantage.

5. Internet Shortcomings

Technology workers are perfectly situated to work from home. They have all the necessary skills and equipment. But can they get reliable connections to the internet? That's an issue for their communities to address. "Broadband availability is a no-brainer when it comes to attracting tech workers, of course, and state and local governments should invest freely in the infrastructure needed to support a high-tech workforce," advises *U.S. News and World Report.*

Not everybody has gotten the message. It can be difficult to secure a dependable broadband connection in many small towns and rural areas. We've all seen the nationwide maps displayed in ads for mobile providers. They shade most of the country in bold colors (regions with reliable service), yet they still contain sizable pockets of white (dead zones), especially in the West.

Three-quarters of all households in major hubs (74.6%) have broadband internet subscriptions, which is almost eight points better than the collective rate of 66.8% for small towns. Memphis is plagued with the weakest high-speed access of any big city, with just 60.5% of its households connected. But more than a third of all small towns (735 of 2,084) do worse than that, and 275 have broadband rates lower than 50%.

6. Fewer Top-Level Jobs

Two of the previously mentioned weaknesses — sluggish growth rates and insufficient numbers of college-educated workers — have put a damper on the job markets in many small towns. If you intend not to work from home, but prefer to seek employment in your new community, you might be disappointed by the lack of appealing opportunities.

Four letters dramatize the difference: MBSA. This acronym stands for "management, business, science, and the arts," a category in which the Census Bureau gathers a broad array of white-collar jobs. Positions in the MBSA sector run the gamut from chief executive officers to professors, engineers to writers, and lawyers to doctors. Most of these jobs require college educations — often advanced degrees — and most also pay quite well.

America's 50 major hubs contain 31.8 million MBSA jobs, accounting for 42.1% of their collective workforce of nearly 75.6 million employees. Five big cities are so heavily oriented toward white-collar work that more than half of their jobs fall under the MBSA umbrella: San Jose, Washington, Raleigh, San Francisco, and Boston.

But only one-third of small-town positions (33.3%) fit into the MBSA classification: 8.2 million out of 24.6 million. That falls well short of the average for major hubs, leaving a gap of almost nine percentage points.

Making a Choice

So that's the scorecard — six appealing strengths of small towns, countered by six troubling weaknesses. You and millions of fellow Americans are currently weighing the balance, trying to decide if this is the time to escape the big-city rat race for a calmer, safer small-town life.

Lending Tree, an online loan marketplace, is closely monitoring this trend. "The changing landscape caused by the Covid-19 pandemic, coupled with a new freedom to work from home, has led to some speculation that people will migrate *en masse* from cities to less expensive towns," admits a report issued by Lending Tree in December 2020. The study then ticks off the attributes and drawbacks of small towns, including some of the points delineated in this chapter.

Its conclusion? The move might make sense, but you're the only one who knows for certain, and you shouldn't make the final decision lightly. "Would-be movers should carefully assess the pros and cons as they consider whether or not to pack their bags and relocate," says Lending Tree.

And that, of course, is precisely what this book is for.

It's time to begin my case-by-case examination of America's small towns. The ultimate aim is to point you to your ideal community — the place where you can establish your future and fulfill your dreams.

Chapter 2
THE TESTS

We all learn the drill by the time we reach first grade. The teacher exercises undisputed authority. She or he holds forth from the front of the classroom, posing questions, initiating discussions, and making assignments. The children listen, take notes, and essentially do whatever is required of them. The teacher periodically uses a time-honored tool — the test — to quantify each student's academic progress.

It isn't a perfect system — no exam can measure a pupil's comprehension of a topic with 100% accuracy — yet it generally works well. If a test touches on the important aspects of a subject, it is likely to yield meaningful results, bestowing the highest grades upon the best students.

This book follows the same principle. I have collected a wide array of data — 24 statistics in all — for each of the nation's 2,084 small towns. These stats have been channeled into 12 tests, each of which is designed to answer a specific question about the local quality of life:

1. Character: Does the town have a distinct spirit and personality?

2. Stability: Is the social structure firmly grounded?

3. Growth: Is the town expanding at a healthy pace?

4. Education: Are local adults well-educated?

5. Jobs: Does the job market offer a good mix of appealing opportunities?

6. Business: Are entrepreneurs playing an important role?

7. Money: Are residents able to comfortably support themselves and their families?

8. Housing: Is home ownership easily affordable for most residents?

9. Health: Is the health care system strong and effective?

10. Diversions: Is the town blessed with a vibrant mix of stores and restaurants?

11. Internet: Is broadband internet access easily obtained?

12. Proximity: Are big cities close enough to be reached with relative ease?

Each test is fueled by two statistics, which count equally toward the final score. Other stats could always be added, I suppose, just as additional questions could always be tacked onto a calculus or history test in school. But my aim was to emulate what teachers do with their tests — touch on the high points of each subject without getting too complicated — and I believe that mission has been accomplished.

The Fine Print

A few housekeeping matters should be addressed before I turn to the 12 tests themselves. I need to explain a bit more about town names, sources of statistics, and the method of generating the rankings. It won't take long, but you can skip ahead if you're not particularly interested in the fine print.

Names

Things can get awfully complicated when the government starts naming urbanized areas and urban clusters. Way too many hyphens are involved. If you scan the Census Bureau's list, you'll see that most entries are named after a single community, though you'll also find such three-headed monstrosities as the Sebastian-Vero Beach South-Florida Ridge, Florida, Urbanized Area and the Shenandoah-Mahanoy City-Frackville, Pennsylvania, Urban Cluster.

I have shortened each multipart name to that of the first town alone, yielding Sebastian and Shenandoah in the instances above. Their stats, of course, still apply to their entire areas. If you're interested in the boundaries of any of the places covered in this book, do a web search for "census urban area reference maps," and you'll see the lines that were drawn in 2010 (and that remain in force today).

Sources

The statistics that fueled my rankings came from official sources, primarily the five-year version of the Census Bureau's 2019 American Community Survey, which was released in December 2020. The ACS provided the numbers for 15 of the 24 parts. Most of the remaining data came from additional Census Bureau programs and two other federal agencies, the Bureau of Economic Analysis and the Bureau of Labor Statistics. All of those numbers were also released in 2020. A list of sources can be found in the final section of this book.

The statistics from the ACS were generated specifically for urbanized areas and urban clusters, so they precisely match the boundaries of the 2,084 small towns. Stats for the other nine parts were collected at the county level. I recalibrated them according to the location of each small town. If a community sits entirely within a single county, it received that county's rates and percentages. But if a town sprawls into two or more counties, its stats were based on weighted averages. Let's say that two-thirds of a town's residents live in County A, with the other third in County B. The resulting averages gave twice as much weight to A's numbers than to B's.

Scoring

Each community's statistics were compared against the averages for all 2,084 small towns. Above-average performances received positive scores (known as z-scores), while below-average results got negative marks. Z-scores larger than plus-3.291 or smaller than minus-3.291 were capped at those respective figures, preventing unusual outliers from skewing the results. Why such strangely precise limits? Because exactly 0.1% of all scores fell outside the capped range.

The z-scores for both parts of each test were added, then converted to a 100-point scale. The community with the best combined z-score in a given category was pegged at 100.0 points, the worst at 0.0 points. Points for all other towns were based on their relative positions between top and bottom.

The final step, of course, was to add the 12 test scores for each community. The places blessed with ideal mixtures of desirable characteristics — the towns, in other words, that offer the best quality of life — naturally emerged with the most points. We'll reveal their names in the next chapter, but let's check the test results first.

The following pages contain summaries of all 12 tests. Each breakdown begins with an overview that restates the question being addressed and reveals the two statistical components. Next are discussions of Parts A and B, each concluding with four numbers — the best, 90th percentile, median, and worst performances. Names of the communities with the best and worst stats are shown in parentheses, unless more than five towns are tied. The 90th percentile is included because it's a good measure of quality — it's the stat that outperforms 90% of all entries — and the median is another name for the 50th percentile. Each breakdown wraps up with an explanation of the final results and a list of the test's top 20 finishers. Scores on the 100-point scale are shown in parentheses.

Test No. 1: Character

Overview

Question: Does the town have a distinct spirit and personality?
Parts: (A) Resilience. (B) Short commutes.

Part A: Resilience

I noted in Chapter 1 that the Census Bureau has developed a new index to measure a community's ability "to absorb, endure, and recover" from disasters, whether a natural calamity such as a hurricane or a health emergency such as a pandemic. Records for each resident have been assessed for 11 risk factors, including age, poverty, disabilities, overcrowding, and various physical ailments. The fewer the risk factors, the more resilient a person is presumed to be. Part A focuses on the share of residents deemed to have the greatest resilience, those burdened with no risk factors at all.

Best: 49.9% (Waconia, MN)
90th: 34.4%
Median: 26.7%
Worst: 2.9% (Lake Los Angeles, CA)

Part B: Short Commutes

Commuting grew more difficult during the decade prior to Covid-19, as traffic worsened in the nation's major hubs. The Census Bureau says the typical American worker spent 25.1 minutes traveling from home to work in 2009, an average that increased to 26.0 minutes by 2014, then to 27.6 minutes by 2019. The latter figure translates to 28 full workdays of commuting per year, greatly cutting into the time that workers can spend in their home communities. Part B is based on the percentage of small-town commuters blessed with the easiest trips from home to worksite in 2019, taking less than 20 minutes. (Those who work at home are not included in these calculations.)

Best: 94.4% (Worland, WY)
90th: 79.4%

Median: 59.7%
Worst: 2.3% (Wedgefield, FL)

Test No. 1 Results

Sioux Center (population: 6,685) has served as a regional hub for agribusiness for more than a century. It's tucked away in the corn and soybean country of northwestern Iowa, less than a 30-minute drive from South Dakota, fewer than 45 minutes from Minnesota, about an hour from Nebraska. The capital city of its own state, Des Moines, is distant by comparison, roughly four hours away. The people of Sioux Center consequently learned long ago to fend for themselves, propelling them to first place in the Character test. Sioux Center is the only small town in America where more than 40% of the residents have been graded as totally resilient (40.8% in its case) and more than 80% of the workers enjoy short commutes (84.9%). Two other Midwestern towns are the runners-up on this test: Carroll, Iowa (about 130 miles southeast of Sioux Center), and Thief River Falls in northwestern Minnesota.

Top 20 for Character

1. Sioux Center, IA (100.0)
2. Carroll, IA (99.9)
3. Thief River Falls, MN (97.0)
4. Los Alamos, NM (96.4)
5. Nantucket, MA (96.1)
6. Sidney, MT (95.7)
7. McPherson, KS (95.2)
8. Pierre, SD (94.2)
9. Pella, IA (93.8)
10. Wayne, NE (93.2)
11. Orange City, IA (93.1)
12. Algona, IA (92.7)
13. Sidney, NE (92.4)
14. Greencastle, IN (91.5)
15. Monroe, WI (91.2)
16. Decorah, IA (91.0)
17. Richfield, UT (90.8)
18. Wahpeton, ND (90.7)
19. Madison, SD (90.3)
20. Creston, IA (90.1)

Test No. 2: Stability

Overview

Question: Is the social structure firmly grounded?
Parts: (A) Living with two parents. (B) Occupied homes.

Part A: Living With Two Parents

About 23% of U.S. children live in single-parent households, and a majority appear to be prospering. Yet experts say children are better off under the same roof as both parents. "If we don't acknowledge that, we're being delusional," says Ian Rowe, the former CEO of a network of charter schools. The Annie E. Casey Foundation, which issues an annual report on America's children, adds: "Kids growing up in households with two parents in a low-conflict marriage tend to have better health, greater access to health care, and fewer emotional or behavioral problems." Part A looks at the percentage of children under the age of 18 who live in two-parent households.
  Best: 95.8% (Orange City, IA)
  90th: 76.0%
  Median: 60.3%
  Worst: 11.7% (Marion, SC)

Part B: Occupied Homes

Any city saddled with abandoned buildings is in trouble. More than 10% of the housing units in two of America's poorest urban hubs, Memphis and New Orleans, are classified by the Census Bureau as vacant. And the situation isn't much better in big cities such as Baltimore, Cleveland, Detroit, and St. Louis, all with vacancy rates between 8% and 10%. "Major costs stem from increased crime and arson generated from abandoned properties," says urban economist Aaron Klein. Part B puts a positive spin on the numbers, checking the percentage of housing units that are occupied.
  Best: 100.0% (10 towns)
  90th: 96.7%
  Median: 91.7%
  Worst: 66.7% (Marlin, TX)

Test No. 2 Results

Let's be honest. Stability comes more easily to affluent communities, and Belterra, Texas, is definitely affluent. It's situated a short drive west of

Austin, an ideal location for commuters carting large paychecks from the state's capital city. Belterra's median household income ($155,917) is the highest for any of the nation's 2,084 small towns, and it does equally well in the Stability test, taking first place. Fully 93.7% of Belterra's children live with both parents, fifth best on that part of the test. And 99.1% of its homes are occupied, translating to a microscopic vacancy rate of just 0.9%. Only three other small towns exceed 90% for two-parent households and 99% for occupied homes — and they happen to be the test's three runners-up: Eagle Mountain South, Utah; Johnstown, Colorado; and Johnson Lane, Nevada.

Top 20 for Stability

1. Belterra, TX (100.0)
2. Eagle Mountain South, UT (99.0)
3. Johnstown, CO (98.6)
4. Johnson Lane, NV (97.8)
5. Rancho Murieta, CA (97.6)
6. Stansbury Park, UT (97.3)
7. Vail, AZ (96.5)
8. Vistancia, AZ (96.4)
9. White Rock, NM (96.2)
10. Ruckersville, VA (95.2)
11. Breckenridge, CO (94.9)
12. Oakland, TN (94.6)
13. Gypsum, CO (93.9)
14. Zimmerman, MN (93.8)
15. Roxborough Park, CO (93.6)
16. Purcellville, VA (92.9)
17. Sioux Center, IA (92.6)
18. Pecan Plantation, TX (92.3)
19. Mukwonago, WI (92.2)
20. Santaquin, UT (91.7)

Test No. 3: Growth

Overview

Question: Is the town expanding at a healthy pace?
Parts: (A) Population growth. (B) Economic growth.

Part A: Population Growth

The equation is simple, according to Moody's chief economist Mark Zandi. "Economic growth," he says, "is driven by a combination of productivity and population, the number of workers." That's why it's important for even the smallest town to welcome a steady stream of new residents. The economic alternative is unattractive. "Fewer people means fewer homes (purchased), fewer cars, fewer vacations," says Zandi. That's the danger currently facing the United States. The national population increased by just 0.2% in 2020, its slowest rise in more than a century. Part A takes a longer view, focusing on small-town population changes during the five-year period prior to the pandemic, 2014 to 2019.

Best: 60.2% (World Golf Village, FL)
90th: 9.0%
Median: 0.4%
Worst: -34.3% (Mecca, CA)

Part B: Economic Growth

Gross domestic product — commonly known as GDP — may seem an arcane stat. But many economists revere its ability to assign a dollar figure to an area's output of goods and services. "GDP is an accurate indicator of the size of an economy, and the GDP growth rate is probably the single best indicator of economic growth," says *Investopedia*, an online financial guide. Paul Samuelson, a Nobel Prize-winning economist, ranked GDP "among the great inventions of the 20th century." The U.S. Bureau of Economic Analysis historically calculated GDP only for the nation as a whole, but it now reaches down to counties. Part B reflects small-town GDP growth rates between 2014 and 2019.

Best: 457.0% (Pecos, TX)
90th: 23.5%
Median: 8.7%
Worst: -35.4% (Robinson, IL)

Test No. 3 Results

Archer Lodge, North Carolina, is nicely positioned for expansion. It sits a half-hour's drive east of Raleigh, which is one of the nation's fastest-growing major hubs. Austin and Charlotte were the only big cities that exceeded Raleigh's growth rate of 10.9% between 2014 and 2019. Much of its development is spilling over into nearby Johnston County, including Archer Lodge. The town's population shot up by 22.5% during the 2014-2019 span, and its gross domestic product ballooned more than twice as rapidly (49.7%) over the same period. No other small town combined population growth above 20% with economic growth greater than 40%, giving Archer

Lodge the top score on the Growth test. Runner-up Lake Conroe Eastshore, Texas, came the closest to meeting both standards. It easily topped the first with a population increase of 28.1%. Yet its economic growth of 36.7%, though impressive, fell short of the threshold.

Top 20 for Growth

1. Archer Lodge, NC (100.0)
2. Lake Conroe Eastshore, TX (96.0)
3. Kermit, TX (95.7)
4. Manor, TX (94.8)
5. World Golf Village, FL (94.5)
6. Anna, TX (92.5)
7. Artesia, NM (91.0)
8. Tea, SD (90.7)
9. Wellington, CO (90.5)
10. Star, ID (90.0)
11. Poinciana Southwest, FL (88.9)
12. Carlsbad, NM (88.2)
13. Midland, TX (87.7)
14. Four Corners, FL (87.4)
15. Phelan, CA (87.2)
16. Lake Norman of Catawba, NC (86.5)
17. Heber, UT (86.3)
18. Johnstown, CO (86.2)
19. Ocala Estates, FL (86.0)
19. Santaquin, UT (86.0)

Test No. 4: Education

Overview

Question: Are local adults well-educated?
Parts: (A) High school graduates. (B) College graduates.

Part A: High School Graduates

The importance of education can be emphasized in two ways. One is to quote experts, such as the Organization for Economic Cooperation and Development: "Basic cognitive skills...are probably the most important longterm determinant of economic growth and thus of the longterm prosperity of a society." The second is to compare incomes. The median paycheck for America's high school dropouts was $608 per week in late 2020, compared to $781 for workers who didn't leave the classroom until picking up their diplomas. Graduating from high school therefore brings an average pay hike of 28%. Part A examines the percentage of small-town residents (between the ages of 25 and 64) who are high school grads.

Best: 100.0% (Belterra, TX; Sun City Hilton Head, SC; White Rock, NM)
90th: 95.4%
Median: 88.9%
Worst: 23.9% (Mecca, CA)

Part B: College Graduates

America's brightest workers supposedly flock to two places — tech hubs such as Silicon Valley and Seattle, or glittering giants such as New York and Los Angeles. Or so we're told. The truth is that many of the nation's smartest communities are small towns centered on prestigious colleges. Highly educated workers are attracted by the impressive wages and stability offered by these schools, which are called "anchor institutions" by University of Vermont economist Jane Kolodinsky. "You don't expect them to close," she says. "They are part of the fabric of the community." Part B analyzes the percentage of small-town working-age adults (25 to 64) who hold bachelor's degrees.

Best: 76.6% (Boulder, CO)
90th: 39.2%
Median: 20.4%
Worst: 1.1% (Mecca, CA)

Test No. 4 Results

The affluence of Belterra, Texas, was noted in the summary for Test No. 2, but it bears repeating. The typical Belterra household draws an annual income of $155,917, encompassing money received by all members. If we narrow the focus to individual employees, Belterra's fulltime workers earn an average of $116,476. Both figures rank highest in their respective categories for all 2,084 small towns, confirming the well-documented link between income and education. All of Belterra's adults have high school diplomas, and nearly three-quarters (73.3%) hold bachelor's degrees, elevating it to first place on the Education test. What's its secret? Belterra isn't a college town or tech center, but it's within commuting distance of Austin, a major hub that fulfills both roles. No other small town exceeds 99% for high school graduates and 72% for college grads, though runner-up White Rock, New Mexico, made the best run with respective rates of 100% and 70.2%.

Top 20 for Education

1. Belterra, TX (100.0)
2. White Rock, NM (99.7)
3. Evergreen, CO (98.4)
4. Aspen, CO (98.3)
5. Crozet, VA (97.3)
6. Boulder, CO (96.6)
6. Davis, CA (96.6)
8. Ames, IA (96.4)
9. Pullman, WA (96.2)
10. Lafayette, CO (96.1)
11. Los Alamos, NM (95.6)
12. Vail, CO (95.4)
13. Vermillion, SD (94.8)
14. State College, PA (94.5)
15. Ithaca, NY (94.2)
16. Gunnison, CO (94.0)
17. Canton, NY (93.7)
18. Twin Rivers, NJ (93.5)
19. Park City, UT (93.2)
20. Waconia, MN (93.1)

Test No. 5: Jobs

Overview

Question: Does the job market offer a good mix of appealing opportunities?

Parts: (A) MBSA workers. (B) Private-sector job growth.

Part A: MBSA Workers

I discussed this acronym in the previous chapter. MBSA is the Census Bureau's shorthand for "management, business, science, and the arts." A 2020 study by the Economic Innovation Group concluded that a healthy MBSA sector is a hallmark of America's most prosperous metropolitan areas. "They have high-paying white-collar jobs that employ a lot of people, and they're some of the ones that rise to the top," says Kenan Fikri, EIG's research director. Small towns can also benefit, of course, and Part A looks at the percentage of local jobs that fit under the MBSA umbrella.

Best: 75.1% (White Rock, NM)
90th: 41.0%

Median: 29.7%
Worst: 4.7% (Mecca, CA)

Part B: Private-Sector Job Growth

Private-sector employment — the number of workers who hold non-government jobs — is a basic, yet important, economic indicator. Consider how it tracked the national ebb and flow during the past decade and a half. The Great Recession triggered the loss of 7.9 million private-sector jobs across the country between 2007 and 2010. A protracted rebound followed, adding 20.4 million positions to private-sector payrolls from 2010 to 2019. But Covid-19 wiped out eight million of those jobs during the single year of 2020. Part B focuses on the five years leading up to the pandemic (2014-2019), calculating small-town gains or losses of private-sector jobs.

Best: 199.6% (Pecos, TX)
90th: 17.2%
Median: 5.0%
Worst: -37.1% (Zapata, TX)

Test No. 5 Results

This is getting a bit monotonous, isn't it? Belterra, Texas, previously reached the head of the class on the Stability and Education tests, and now it takes first place on the Jobs exam. Belterra's performances on both parts of this test were predictably excellent — 60.7% MBSA employment and 29.4% private-sector job growth — though other small towns did better. Belterra ranks seventh for its distribution of white-collar jobs and no better than 27th for its five-year increase in employment. Its strength is its balance, since no other small town excelled on both parts of the test. Belterra is the sole entrant to exceed 60% on the MBSA side and 20% in private-sector job growth. The two runners-up — Paloma Creek South, Texas, and Buckhead (Bryan County), Georgia — both aced the growth part, but fell a bit short on MBSA employment.

Top 20 for Jobs

1. Belterra, TX (100.0)
2. Paloma Creek South, TX (98.8)
3. Buckhead (Bryan County), GA (98.2)
4. World Golf Village, FL (97.4)
5. Boerne, TX (91.4)
6. Jefferson, GA (90.8)
7. Purcellville, VA (88.9)

8. Vistancia, AZ (88.1)
9. White Rock, NM (88.0)
10. Los Alamos, NM (87.8)
11. Summit Park, UT (87.4)
12. Heber, UT (86.9)
13. Rancho Murieta, CA (86.6)
14. Spring Hill, TN (86.4)
15. Crozet, VA (86.2)
16. Roxborough Park, CO (85.8)
17. Davis, CA (85.7)
18. Snoqualmie, WA (84.4)
19. Lafayette, CO (83.8)
20. Twin Rivers, NJ (83.6)

Test No. 6: Business

Overview

Question: Are entrepreneurs playing an important role?
Parts: (A) Small business growth. (B) Self-employed workers.

Part A: Small Business Growth

"Small businesses are the engine of our economic progress," says President Joe Biden. "They are the glue in the heart and soul of our community." Economists agree, though they caution that many members of this sector were struggling even before Covid. "Small businesses and entrepreneurs drive America's economy, but the environment they operate in is far from level," says Philip Gaskin, vice president of the Kauffman Foundation, who specifically cites the challenges confronting owners in small towns. The nation has 7.7 million small businesses, defined as employers with fewer than 100 employees. Part A checks the pre-pandemic change in the number of small businesses, using 2013-2018 data, the latest figures available.

Best: 59.5% (Pecos, TX)
90th: 11.0%
Median: 1.9%
Worst: -18.2% (Zapata, TX)

Part B: Self-Employed Workers

You've undoubtedly read about workers who struggle to survive in the "gig economy." They juggle short-term jobs and freelance assignments, often finding it difficult to make ends meet. The upside for many, it seems, is that they aren't tied to a desk. But freedom doesn't have to come at such a cost. Millions of self-employed workers earn comfortable livings, with dentists, doctors, lawyers, chiropractors, and IT specialists leading the way. Average self-employment pay for the first two occupations is well above $100,000. The other three are just a few thousand below that threshold. Self-employment is a key indicator of entrepreneurship, so Part B examines the percentage of small-town workers who fit the definition.

Best: 26.9% (Sedona, AZ)
90th: 10.9%
Median: 6.2%
Worst: 0.0% (Whiteriver, AZ)

Test No. 6 Results

The entrepreneurial spirit is alive and well in Santa Rosa Beach, sprawling along the Gulf of Mexico about 60 miles east of Pensacola, Florida. All of the necessary ingredients are there — brisk population growth (8.1% in the past five years), a vigorous job market (up 24.8% between 2014 and 2019), and the magnetic attraction of Santa Rosa's towering sand dunes and sunny beaches. An endless flow of tourists, coupled with the local population upswing, have increased the demand for shops, restaurants, bars, and related services. The number of small businesses in Santa Rosa Beach consequently grew by 29.0% over the past half-decade, while the share of self-employed workers sits at 23.2%. In no other small town are both figures above 20%, which is why Santa Rosa Beach ranks first on the Business test. A close runner-up is Rigby, Idaho, located nearly a mile above sea level and about 270 miles east of Boise.

Top 20 for Business

1. Santa Rosa Beach, FL (100.0)
2. Rigby, ID (99.6)
3. Boerne, TX (95.9)
4. Lake Conroe Westshore, TX (93.3)
5. Bend, OR (92.6)
6. Woodcreek, TX (90.5)
7. Nantucket, MA (89.4)
8. Orangetree, FL (87.7)
9. Granite Shoals, TX (87.6)
10. Heber, UT (87.3)
11. Salida, CO (86.3)
12. St. George, UT (85.0)

13. Lake Conroe Eastshore, TX (84.1)
14. Park City, UT (82.6)
15. Incline Village, NV (82.3)
16. Lake Arrowhead, CA (80.5)
17. Big Bear City, CA (78.9)
18. Vineyard Haven, MA (78.6)
19. Colorado City, AZ (78.4)
20. Marble Falls, TX (78.0)

Test No. 7: Money

Overview

Question: Are residents able to comfortably support themselves and their families?

Parts: (A) Median annual earnings. (B) Living in poverty.

Part A: Median Annual Earnings

Income and earnings are not the same thing. The U.S. Census Bureau recognizes 42 sources of income, beginning with wages and proceeding to such arcane categories as low-energy assistance, "regular contributions from persons not living in the household," and the fungible value of Medicaid. Earnings are much easier to define, consisting solely of the money paid by employers to their employees. Annual earnings for fulltime U.S. workers reached a median of $49,041 in 2019, which means that half were above that mark, and half were below. Part A compares the median earnings for fulltime workers living in each small town.

Best: $116,476 (Belterra, TX)
90th: $52,491
Median: $40,580
Worst: $21,747 (Rio Bravo, TX)

Part B: Living in Poverty

The federal government's definition of poverty is variable. The Census Bureau has established an income threshold of $13,300 for a single person under age 65, for example, while a family of four has been given a line of $25,926. Any household that falls short of its threshold is considered to be in poverty. The national poverty rate was 14.4% in 2019, though it tended to be higher in small communities. "Not only are rural children more likely to be poor, but they also are more likely than urban children to live in areas with high rates of poverty," said a University of Wisconsin study in 2020. Part B matches small-town poverty rates for the year prior to the pandemic.

Best: 0.9% (Byron, MN)
90th: 7.7%
Median: 16.7%
Worst: 49.1% (Rio Bravo, TX)

Test No. 7 Results

Say hello yet again to Belterra, Texas, which previously won top honors on the Stability, Education, and Jobs exams. Belterra's victory on the Money test was almost preordained. Its residents benefit from the strongest educational base in any small town, which leads to the best array of employment opportunities, which brings the largest paychecks. Median earnings for fulltime workers are pegged at $116,476 in Belterra, putting it 13.7% ahead of White Rock, New Mexico, the only other small town to reach six figures ($102,451). Poverty rates are microscopic in both places: 2.2% in Belterra, 2.4% in White Rock. That makes them the only communities with earnings higher than $90,000 and poverty rates lower than 4%, which is why they occupy the top two slots in the final standings.

Top 20 for Money

1. Belterra, TX (100.0)
2. White Rock, NM (99.7)
3. Eureka, MO (99.5)
3. Roxborough Park, CO (99.5)
5. Purcellville, VA (98.8)
6. Chesapeake Beach, MD (97.6)
7. Waconia, MN (97.3)
8. Rancho Murieta, CA (97.2)
9. Mountain House, CA (96.9)
10. Livermore, CA (96.8)
11. Snoqualmie, WA (96.6)
12. Lake of the Pines, CA (96.5)
13. Los Alamos, NM (96.4)
14. Evergreen, CO (96.3)
14. Jefferson Township North, NJ (96.3)
14. Leonardtown, MD (96.3)
17. Twin Rivers, NJ (96.2)
18. Half Moon Bay, CA (96.0)
19. Aledo, TX (95.1)
20. Buckhead (Bryan County), GA (95.0)

Test No. 8: Housing

Overview

Question: Is home ownership easily affordable for most residents?
Parts: (A) Home ownership. (B) Monthly housing costs.

Part A: Home Ownership

"There is an emotional side to home ownership, particularly in the United States. It's often baked into people's vision of the future or part of the American dream," says Tom Figgatt, president of Portolan Financial in New Orleans. There's a practical consideration, too, as noted by a recent report from the U.S. Government Accountability Office. "Owning a home," says GAO, "has been one of the primary ways Americans built wealth and financial security." Economists grew concerned when the national rate of home ownership bottomed out at 62.9% in 2016, but it rebounded to 67.9% by mid-2020. Part A examines the percentage of small-town homes occupied by their owners.

Best: 97.6% (Jupiter Farms, FL)
90th: 74.6%
Median: 61.1%
Worst: 4.0% (Fort Polk, LA)

Part B: Monthly Housing Costs

Houses have become unaffordable for a substantial number of big-city residents. San Francisco offers an extreme example. A federal study detected a 69% increase between 2010 and 2018 in San Francisco homeowners who earn more than $150,000 a year. But the ownership rate dropped sharply for those below that income level. Yet prices continue to rise in Covid-era America. Zillow estimated that the total value of U.S. homes grew by $2.5 trillion in 2020. Where does that leave most potential buyers? Part B looks at the percentage of a typical small-town worker's monthly earnings that would be needed to pay the median costs of local home ownership (mortgage, taxes, insurance, and utilities).

Best: 7.1% (Whiteriver, AZ)
90th: 18.1%
Median: 24.5%
Worst: 59.3% (Lahaina, HI)

Test No. 8 Results

Sun City Hilton Head, South Carolina, is an urban cluster with a population of 13,430, comfortably fitting this book's definition of a small town. But it's an uncommon place, a community for seniors about 15 miles northwest of its seaside namesake, Hilton Head Island, itself a small town. Sun City Hilton Head was planned by Del Webb, the same company that built the original Sun City retirement community in Arizona. Its typical resident is 72.1 years old. Equally notable is its outstanding inventory of homes, which vaults Sun City Hilton Head to first place on the Housing test. No other small town can say that more than 93% of its housing units are occupied by their owners and that its monthly housing expenses consume less than 30% of individual earnings. White Rock, New Mexico, is the runner-up here.

Top 20 for Housing

1. Sun City Hilton Head, SC (100.0)
2. White Rock, NM (95.7)
3. Rainbow Lakes Estates, FL (95.5)
4. Sugarmill Woods, FL (93.4)
5. Denver City, TX (93.0)
6. Fairfield Glade, TN (91.6)
7. Kermit, TX (91.4)
8. Zuni Pueblo, NM (89.7)
9. Lake Placid, FL (88.1)
10. Diamondhead, MS (87.9)
11. Ocean View, DE (87.5)
12. Sahuarita, AZ (86.8)
13. Galliano, LA (86.4)
14. Gramercy, LA (85.7)
15. Dorr, MI (85.5)
16. Lady Lake, FL (85.0)
17. Hot Springs Village, AR (84.8)
18. Portage, PA (84.5)
19. Sullivan City, TX (84.3)
20. Carmi, IL (84.0)

Test No. 9: Health

Overview

Question: Is the health care system strong and effective?
Parts: (A) Health care workers. (B) Fair or poor health.

Part A: Health Care Workers

Many small-town residents have only limited access to doctors and hospitals, greatly restricting their medical options. Rural communities often "face inequities that result in worse health care than that of urban and suburban residents," says the Association of American Medical Colleges. The root cause is usually financial. An inadequate local economic base is incapable of supporting a wide range of medical services. "As income and wealth increase or decrease, so does health," says data analyst Amanda Jovaag. Part A assesses the size of small-town medical sectors, calculating the percentage of all local workers who are employed in health care.

Best: 28.4% (Blountstown, FL)
90th: 13.4%
Median: 9.4%
Worst: 0.0% (Page, AZ)

Part B: Fair or Poor Health

An ideal way to assess the health of a community's residents is simply to ask how they feel, which is precisely what the Behavioral Risk Factor Surveillance System (BRFSS) does. It conducts more than 400,000 interviews across the country each year, asking respondents to grade their health on a scale that runs from excellent or very good to fair or poor. "Self-assessed health status is a more powerful predictor of mortality and morbidity than many objective measures of health," says the Centers for Disease Control and Prevention, which oversees BRFSS. Part B compares the share of residents in each small town who characterize their health as fair or poor.

Best: 8.1% (Roxborough Park, CO)
90th: 12.5%
Median: 17.1%
Worst: 41.0% (Crystal City, TX)

Test No. 9 Results

Two words make it clear why Rochester, Minnesota, is the top-rated small town on the Health test — Mayo Clinic. The world-renowned medical complex, which W.W. Mayo founded in Rochester in 1889, is now rated by *U.S. News and World Report* as America's best hospital for overall quality of service. It also ranks first in the nation for six different specialties. Nearly a quarter of Rochester's workers (22.2%) are employed in the medical field, while only 10.0% of its residents classify their health as fair or poor, the two lowest levels on the scale. No other small town sits above 20% for medical employment and below 15% for people with health problems. The runner-up on this test clearly enjoys spillover benefits from the Mayo Clinic's presence. Byron, Minnesota, is located just 10 miles west of Rochester.

Top 20 for Health

1. Rochester, MN (100.0)
2. Byron, MN (99.3)
3. Fergus Falls, MN (92.9)
4. Crozet, VA (88.8)
5. Marshfield, WI (88.4)
6. Gowanda, NY (87.2)
7. Port Townsend, WA (86.5)
8. Northern Cambria, PA (85.7)
9. Greenville, PA (84.9)
10. Kasson, MN (84.5)
11. Glenwood, IA (83.4)
12. Lee, MA (83.1)
13. Detroit Lakes, MN (82.9)
14. Sun City Hilton Head, SC (82.2)
15. New Lexington, OH (81.3)
16. Breese, IL (80.9)
17. Lake Monticello, VA (80.5)
18. Tea, SD (80.4)
19. Lebanon, NH (79.9)
20. Monticello, IL (79.7)

Test No. 10: Diversions

Overview

Question: Is the town blessed with a vibrant mix of stores and restaurants?

Parts: (A) Stores per 10,000. (B) Restaurants per 10,000.

Part A: Stores Per 10,000

Covid-19 dramatically altered America's retail landscape. It spurred a sudden burst in the popularity of online shopping, and it pushed malls closer to extinction. Yet it did not lessen America's acquisitive spirit. U.S. retail sales in January 2021, one of the pandemic's darkest periods, soared 7.4% above the same month in 2020. The downtowns of small communities are well-positioned to benefit from this zest for shopping, according to a 2020 Brookings Institution study. It lauds "the ability to walk from store to store, the proximity of business owners to each other." Part A takes the number of retail establishments in each small town and expresses it as a ratio per 10,000 residents.

Best: 139.3 (Nantucket, MA)
90th: 47.0
Median: 33.3
Worst: 11.3 (six towns)

Part B: Restaurants Per 10,000

Americans love to eat out, but they temporarily lost the chance during the Covid-19 shutdown. U.S. restaurant sales plummeted from $65 billion in February 2020 to $30 billion in April, as sit-down establishments struggled to adjust to a takeout world. The sector rebounded above $50 billion by June, a sign of the public's attachment. "The hospitality we are missing during our national quarantine was invented by people who wanted to serve others and make them happy. The desire to create those connected experiences is not going away," says Nick Kokonas, the founder of Tock, a restaurant reservation system. Part B presents the ratio of small-town restaurants per 10,000 residents.

Best: 89.3 (Nantucket, MA)
90th: 25.3
Median: 17.9
Worst: 3.3 (Lake Butler, FL)

Test No. 10 Results

There was no suspense about the final results. The famed tourist island of Nantucket, Massachusetts, took first place in both Part A and Part B, a double victory that hadn't occurred on any of the previous nine exams. That made it the inevitable winner of the Diversions test. Nantucket, located about 30 miles off the coast of Cape Cod, has evolved to meet the needs of hordes of visitors who arrive by ferry and plane each summer. It offers a wealth of shopping and dining opportunities, as evidenced by its respective ratios of 139.3 stores and 89.3 restaurants per 10,000 residents. Those figures are respectively 12% and 24% better than the numbers for any other small town. Just one other community — runner-up Aspen, Colorado — has a retail ratio above 120 and a restaurant ratio above 70.

Top 20 for Diversions

1. Nantucket, MA (100.0)
2. Aspen, CO (99.9)
3. Manteo, NC (99.8)
4. Vineyard Haven, MA (99.7)
5. Kill Devil Hills, NC (99.6)
6. Breckenridge, CO (99.5)
6. Silverthorne, CO (99.5)
8. Galax, VA (99.2)
9. Sturgeon Bay, WI (99.1)
10. Moab, UT (99.0)
11. Jackson, WY (98.9)
12. Gunnison, CO (98.7)
13. Basalt, CO (98.6)
14. Big Pine Key, FL (98.5)
14. Key Largo, FL (98.5)
14. Key West, FL (98.5)
14. Marathon, FL (98.5)
18. Steamboat Springs, CO (98.1)
19. Hailey, ID (98.0)
20. Park City, UT (97.9)
20. Summit Park, UT (97.9)

Test No. 11: Internet

Overview

Question: Is broadband internet access easily obtained?
Parts: (A) Broadband subscriptions. (B) Smartphone access.

Part A: Broadband Subscriptions

Online access, once considered a luxury, is now a necessity. The Pew Research Center conducted a poll in the midst of the Covid shutdown, asking Americans if they were relying on the internet. A majority of 53% called it "essential," while another 34% described it as "important." Mick Bates, a West Virginia state legislator, says all households must have access to the internet. "It's essential for schooling. It's essential for business," he says. "It's essential for health care. You can't get a Covid vaccine unless you go on the frigging internet and register." Part A looks at the percentage of small-town households that subscribe to broadband internet services.

Best: 95.1% (Roxborough Park, CO)
90th: 76.8%

Median: 64.5%
Worst: 13.1% (Tuba City, AZ)

Part B: Smartphone Access

The smartphone magnifies the power of the internet, enabling online access not only in the home or office, but absolutely everywhere. It has become such an important tool that economists now talk about the "smartphone economy." But millions of rural Americans and low-income city residents are unable to participate because of weak online signals and steep phone costs. "If we can encourage the diffusion of these powerful information technologies across broader sections of the economy, we can spread the benefits of...higher productivity," says Bret Swanson, a visiting fellow at the American Enterprise Institute. Part B analyzes the percentage of small-town households that have access to smartphones.

Best: 96.2% (Corona de Tucson, AZ)
90th: 84.9%
Median: 74.7%
Worst: 24.2% (Kayenta, AZ)

Test No. 11 Results

There's no reason to worry about online connections in Roxborough Park, Colorado, which is tucked into the foothills about 20 miles south of Denver. Its median household income of $134,555 is the third-highest among all 2,084 small towns, suggesting that nearly all of its residents can afford home internet service and smartphones. And its proximity to a major hub guarantees access to reliable wireless signals. Those two factors explain why broadband subscriptions are almost universal (95.1%) in Roxborough Park, and smartphones are nearly as common (92.7%). No other small town exceeds 92.5% on both parts of the Internet test, giving Roxborough Park a smooth path to first place in the standings. Runner-up Vistancia, Arizona, does three and a half points worse in broadband services (91.6%), but actually surpasses Roxborough Park on the smartphone side (94.5%).

Top 20 for Internet

1. Roxborough Park, CO (100.0)
2. Vistancia, AZ (99.3)
3. Corona de Tucson, AZ (99.2)
4. Mountain House, CA (98.9)

5. Discovery Bay, CA (98.8)
6. Belterra, TX (98.6)
7. Buckhead (Bryan County), GA (95.8)
8. Truckee, CA (95.0)
9. Spring Hill, TN (93.8)
10. Snoqualmie, WA (93.7)
11. Jupiter Farms, FL (93.2)
12. Spout Springs, NC (92.5)
13. Havelock, NC (92.4)
14. Santa Rosa Beach, FL (92.2)
15. World Golf Village, FL (91.9)
16. Middletown, DE (91.6)
17. Archer Lodge, NC (91.5)
18. Eagle Mountain South, UT (91.0)
19. Paloma Creek South, TX (90.4)
20. Manor, TX (90.0)

Test No. 12: Proximity

Overview

Question: Are big cities close enough to be reached with relative ease?
Parts: (A) Major hub miles. (B) Major or mid-major miles.

Part A: Major Hub Miles

Big cities may not be the greatest places to live, but they're loads of fun to visit. The 50 major hubs possess the necessary resources for cultural activities and sports franchises that couldn't survive in small towns. And they feature specialty stores and restaurants unavailable in areas with fewer people. The key is to live close enough for occasional sojourns, as Florida developer David Pelletz explained. "People are looking to have access to big cities, but still get a small town," he said in 2005 after completing a residential project outside Tampa. Part A measures the air mileage from each town to the nearest major hub. (See Chapter 1 for the list of hubs.)
Best: 10 (Waterbury, CT)
90th: 34
Median: 88
Worst: 2,473 (Kekaha, HI)

Part B: Major or Mid-Major Miles

The 50 major hubs are all very large — running from 900,000 residents to almost 19 million — but sometimes you're not looking to visit a city that big. You don't want to see a world-class orchestra or a major-league ballclub. All you want is a nice weekend of shopping and dining in a urban setting. The next 50 urbanized areas — let's call them mid-major hubs — fit those needs perfectly. Mid-majors can be as large as Tucson (population: 873,164) and Honolulu (837,258), or as small as Chattanooga (401,675) and Boise (394,355). Part B checks the air mileage from a small town to the closest hub, whether major or mid-major.

Best: 10 (Kuna, ID; Waterbury, CT)
90th: 26
Median: 64
Worst: 1,524 (Fairbanks, AK)

Test No. 12 Results

Waterbury, Connecticut, is not a major hub, though it sits extremely close to one. Waterbury is just 10 air miles north of the Bridgeport urbanized area, based on coordinates supplied by the U.S. Census Bureau. (The actual cities of Waterbury and Bridgeport are farther apart, but the ring of development around Bridgeport extends well inland from Long Island Sound, greatly reducing the distance.) You might not think of Bridgeport (official name: Bridgeport-Stamford) as a hub, but its urbanized area is the 47th largest in America with a population of 946,200. Residents of Waterbury can dash in and out with relative ease, and they're also within 100 miles of three other major hubs (New York, Providence, and Hartford) and five mid-majors. Waterbury consequently earns the top score on the Proximity test. Two other small towns in Connecticut — Danbury and Lake Pocotopaug — are the runners-up. (The latter is tied with Manor, Texas, for third place.)

Top 20 for Proximity

1. Waterbury, CT (100.0)
2. Danbury, CT (99.5)
3. Lake Pocotopaug, CT (99.1)
3. Manor, TX (99.1)
5. Charlestown, IN (98.7)
5. East Aurora, NY (98.7)
5. Lago Vista, TX (98.7)
5. Lee's Summit, MO (98.7)
9. Rancho Murieta, CA (98.1)
9. Smithfield, VA (98.1)
11. Paloma Creek South, TX (97.9)

12. Johnstown, OH (97.7)
13. Eagle Mountain South, UT (97.5)
14. Archer Lodge, NC (97.3)
14. Canby, OR (97.3)
14. Darbydale, OH (97.3)
14. Eureka, MO (97.3)
14. Harrison, OH (97.3)
14. Lockport, NY (97.3)
14. Mukwonago, WI (97.3)
14. Ramona, CA (97.3)
14. Roxborough Park, CO (97.3)

Chapter 3
THE WINNERS

The tests have been administered, the scores have been totaled, and the standings have been determined. The whole process has most likely planted a single question in your mind, the question that most Americans would ask.

Who is No. 1?

I would argue that this book is about something more than that. The subhead on the cover promises to introduce you to "the 209 small towns where you can live your best life." There's no reason to believe that the No. 1 community will be your quintessentially perfect match. It might be outside the section of the country you prefer, or in a climate you don't enjoy, or too far from (or too close to) a big city, or simply too expensive for your tastes, not to mention your wallet.

The idea here is to introduce you to an array of attractive places, allowing you to sift through their relative merits as you eventually winnow down to the town of your dreams — your very own Dreamtown.

More about that concept in a moment. But let's slake your initial curiosity by introducing the small town at the pinnacle of the national standings, as well as the 24 runners-up.

The Top 25

The two highest-rated small towns in America are ski resorts, and several others in the top 25 are mountain or ocean retreats. These places are saturated in money, a benefit that elevates any community in any quality-of-life study. The interconnection of education, employment, and income is so solid that any town blessed with all three is guaranteed to do well.

But don't be mistaken. Money is not the sole criterion for admission to the top 25, nor is it even an essential ingredient. It's true that the median household income (MHI) in seven communities listed below exceeds $125,000, which is twice the U.S. norm of $62,043. But it's equally true that the MHI in eight of these 25 highly rated towns ls lower than $90,000, including two places that dip very near the national benchmark.

And remember this, too. These are only 25 of the 209 Dreamtowns. You'll soon be awash in facts and figures for the entire group, which is considerably more diverse (both financially and geographically) than this short list of leaders. You might be intrigued — and rightly so — by some of the communities you meet in the following rundown, but keep an open mind for the other options that lie ahead.

1. Summit Park, Utah

A 2019 *Bloomberg* roundup conceded that Aspen, Colorado, and Jackson Hole, Wyoming, have higher profiles as ski towns. "But if you're actually looking to buy a home and care about convenience as well as luxury," *Bloomberg* said, "then Utah's Summit Park region may be the best option." This popular destination for skiers, snowshoers, hikers, and mountain bikers — located 20 miles east of Salt Lake City — is America's top-rated small town, thanks to its record of broad-based excellence. Summit Park ranked among the top 3% of all 2,084 towns on eight of the 12 tests, peaking at 11th place for Jobs and 20th for Diversions.

2. Park City, Utah

A short jaunt down the road — either eight or 12 miles, depending on your choice of routes — whisks you from the nation's No. 1 small town to its closest competitor. Park City was founded in the 19th century as a mining center, but evolved into a winter sports resort after World War II. Its Victorian downtown, a remnant of those mining days, is now on the National Register of Historic Places. Park City is also famed as the base for Robert Redford's Sundance Institute, which hosts an international film festival. Its best test rankings were 14th for Business and 19th for Education.

3. Belterra, Texas

You undoubtedly remember this community from the previous chapter. Belterra, hailed by *Texas Monthly* as "the ideal of small-town living just outside the Austin metropolis," won first-place honors on four separate tests: Stability, Education, Jobs, and Money. No other town notched multiple wins; No. 1 ratings on the remaining eight exams were split among eight different places. So why isn't Belterra the top small town in America? Inconsistency. It slipped badly enough on a few tests — dipping as low as 1,641st place for Health and 1,856th for Character — to fall below Summit Park and Park City in total points.

4. World Golf Village, Florida

Its name tells the story. The builders of World Golf Village picked a site south of Jacksonville in the 1990s, envisioning a resort centered on world-class courses. But they shifted gears after being inundated with requests for permanent housing. "We changed immediately," said developer Jim Davidson. "No more resort, no more. We went pure, hardcore residential." Yet golf remains important. Novelist Steve Berry lived in World Golf Village for a decade. "Its location was perfect," he said of his home, "right on the first tee." The town notched a pair of top 10 test scores: fourth for Jobs and fifth for Growth.

5. Roxborough Park, Colorado

Red sandstone formations cast stark shadows on the terrain south of Denver. They're the chief drawing card for Colorado's Roxborough State Park and a distinctive characteristic of the nearby community with the same name. Archaeological digs in the park have found evidence of life dating back to 11,500 B.C., including the remains of 24 Columbian mammoths. The town, on the other hand, is as modern as it could possibly be. It earned the nation's best score on the Internet test, and it also took third place on the Money exam.

6. Nantucket, Massachusetts

White settlers arrived on Nantucket a century before the American Revolution, establishing it as a whaling hub. The island, located 30 miles off the coast of Cape Cod, was prominent in Herman Melville's 1851 seafaring classic, *Moby-Dick*. But the whale trade vanished long ago. Nantucket is now a prime tourist destination, jammed with warm-weather visitors. "Although Nantucket is primarily a summer destination," writes journalist Ann Binlot, "during the fall, it's a quiet island escape within driving distance from New York." No small town outperformed Nantucket on the Diversions test. It also finished fifth for Character and seventh for Business.

7. Evergreen, Colorado

Denver calls itself the Mile High City. Evergreen, just 19 air miles to the west, soars even higher to an elevation of 7,200 feet. "It appears unassuming from the road, but exit here and wind your way into town, and you'll find a quaint town with both mountain and lake activities," says travel writer Amy Sward. Evergreen trumpets its "mountain-town feeling" as a major attribute, promising easy access to golf courses, hiking trails, and lakes. Another impressive strength is brainpower, certified by Evergreen's rank of No. 3 on the Education test. It also finished 14th on the Money exam.

8. Heber, Utah

There's a small disconnect. Locals call their community Heber City, yet the Census Bureau's urban cluster is simply named Heber. This book makes a rule of following the bureau's lead, so Heber it is. The town is tucked away in Utah's Heber Valley, framed by mountain ranges about 15 miles southeast of Park City. "Heber City is the kind of place where the scenery is so magnificent that it's almost distracting," raves Expedia, which reserved a spot for Heber on its list of America's most beautiful towns. The best test ranks were 10th for Business and 12th for Jobs.

9. Vistancia, Arizona

Vistancia sprouted early in the 21st century northwest of Phoenix, surrounded by foothills of the Sonoran Desert. It welcomes residents of all ages, unlike some nearby developments that are restricted to senior citizens. The town is located in the West Valley, an area that historically trailed the pace of growth in Phoenix and its eastern suburbs, but now is rapidly expanding itself. John Burns Real Estate Consulting, an executive housing firm, has named Vistancia one of the nation's 50 best master-planned communities. It took second place on the Internet test and eighth for both Stability and Jobs.

10. Buckhead (Bryan County), Georgia

Mention Buckhead, and many listeners believe you're referring to the upscale neighborhood north of midtown Atlanta. But the focus here is on a lesser-known Georgia namesake. The urban Buckhead is located in Fulton County, while the small town is 250 miles to the southeast. The Census Bureau has parenthetically attached Bryan County to the latter name to avoid confusion. The smaller Buckhead bills itself as being "nestled among Georgia's salt marshes." The Atlantic Ocean is indeed just a few miles away, and Savannah is only a half-hour's drive. Buckhead (Bryan County) did best on the tests for Jobs (third place) and Internet (seventh).

11. Lafayette, Colorado

Lafayette initially thrived as a coal-mining town, but the industry spiraled into a terminal decline after World War II. The community was saved by two factors — a stroke of good timing and a fortuitous location. The end of the war triggered America's great suburban boom, as young families spread out from major cities in search of homes and land. Lafayette is just 21 miles north of the urban hub of Denver and 11 miles east of the college town of Boulder. It attracted newcomers from both, while retaining a separate identity. Lafayette's best results were 10th on the Education exam and 19th for Jobs.

12. Purcellville, Virginia

A few of the top 25 small towns are of recent vintage, such as No. 9 Vistancia, which has yet to celebrate its 20th birthday. At the opposite end of the timeline is Purcellville, located in Virginia's horse and wine country northwest of Washington. The town, initially settled in 1764, long served as a hub for farmers, but has recently attracted a stream of newcomers. "The challenge," writes a local historian, "is to accept this change without the town losing its historic identity and those everyday, small-town amenities." Purcellville made the top 10 on two tests, finishing fifth for Money and seventh for Jobs.

13. Aspen, Colorado

Journalist Bryan Hood calls Aspen an "unapologetically ostentatious winter wonderland for one-percenters," and who could disagree? Four local ski resorts attract the wealthy from both coasts. Many of these elites maintain homes in this picturesque town, tucked into the Roaring Fork Valley of the Rocky Mountains, roughly a four-hour drive west of Denver. The typical house in Aspen is valued above $650,000. Those who find a way to afford the lifestyle reap the benefits. "It's a peaceful retreat in every season," says travel writer Sarah Kuta. Aspen finished second on the Diversions test and fourth for Education.

14. Spring Hill, Tennessee

Spring Hill was primarily a livestock center until General Motors came calling in the mid-1980s. GM created Saturn Corp. to beat back the rising tide of Japanese automotive imports, and it chose a site 30 miles south of Nashville for Saturn's manufacturing facility. Saturn disappeared in 2010, but GM retains a sizable operation in Spring Hill. Its impact is reflected in the town's meteoric growth from 989 residents in 1980 to a current population of 40,314. The greatest local strengths, as reflected by test results, are Internet (ninth place on that exam) and Jobs (14th place).

15. Bend, Oregon

Welcome to the biggest small town in the top 25. Bend's population of 101,737 is about 7,300 above Lafayette, Colorado, at 94,416. The other communities in this rundown are all below 50,000, and 12 of the remaining 23 are below 10,000. Bend sprawls across the foothills of the Cascade Mountains, making it a popular destination for hiking and rafting. "The Deschutes River is packed so full of rafts on a weekend that you could walk across the river and not get your feet wet," says local photographer James Parsons. Bend is economically strong, as shown by test ranks of fifth for Business and 26th for Jobs.

16. St. Simons, Georgia

St. Simons Island is a popular tourist attraction on Georgia's Atlantic coast. It's ringed by sandy beaches and salt marshes, while its namesake town occupies the middle ground. This is one of the biggest of the Sea Islands, which extend from Cape Hatteras, North Carolina, to the northern extremities of Florida. Readers of *Conde Nast Traveler* annually elect St. Simons as one of the 10 best U.S. islands for vacationers. It finished among the top 50 small towns on four of this book's tests, reaching its peak on the Education (22nd place) and Jobs (31st) exams.

17. Tea, South Dakota

This community in southeastern South Dakota has two distinctions. Tea is tied with three other small towns — two called Ada, one Lee — for the shortest name. And it might have the strangest origin story. The U.S. Post Office Department asked local officials in the late 1800s to submit 10 possible names. The town fathers came up with nine, then took a tea break, which inspired their final nominee. Guess which name the officials in Washington picked? Tea ranked eighth on the Growth test — its population shot up from 786 in 1990 to 5,129 today — and it was 18th for Health.

18. Snoqualmie, Washington

A clarification is in order. This is not Washington's infamous Snoqualmie Pass, which averages more than 30 feet of snow per year. (Yes, 30 *feet*.) This is a separate town 25 miles northwest of the pass and a half-hour drive east of Seattle. It receives less than a foot of snow annually. Timber once was Snoqualmie's major industry, but visitors are drawn today by its scenery, which was featured on David Lynch's TV series, *Twin Peaks*. A recent surge of development has pushed the population up to 24,383. Snoqualmie excelled on the Internet (10th place) and Money (11th) tests.

19. Archer Lodge, North Carolina

A few settlers sensed this area's charms prior to the Civil War. The number of antebellum residents was never large, though sufficient to establish a masonic lodge. The latter's legacy endures in the name of Archer Lodge, a 30-minute car trip from Raleigh. The town had only 795 residents as late as 2000, and it wasn't incorporated until 2010. But its location on the eastern fringe of the Raleigh area — North Carolina's fastest-growing belt — has sparked development. Archer Lodge now has a population of 17,895, earning first place on the Growth test. It also finished 14th for Proximity.

20. Crozet, Virginia

Give it a French twist. Say kroh-ZAY, not kroh-ZET. This unusual name was bestowed on a railroad stop 15 miles west of Charlottesville. Farms and orchards across Virginia's Piedmont region would ship their crops to Crozet, where trains collected produce for distant markets. But those days are long gone. Crozet has evolved into a bedroom community for Charlottesville, as well as a gateway to the Blue Ridge Mountains. The Crozet Greenway Tunnel opened in 2020, allowing bikers and hikers to travel a mile *under* the mountains. Two of this book's tests brought Crozet outstanding results — fourth place for Health, fifth for Education.

21. White Rock, New Mexico

White Rock is located 10 miles southeast of Los Alamos, which is embedded in American history as the birthplace of the atomic bomb. The

Los Alamos National Laboratory remains the largest employer in the area, and many of its engineers and technicians choose to live in White Rock. "It's a fabulous place to raise kids, it is an active community, and it's a super safe place," says Amy Regan, an electrical engineer who moved there with her husband 30 years ago. White Rock earned runner-up honors on three separate tests, finishing second for Education, Money, and Housing.

22. Lake Conroe Eastshore, Texas

A massive drought struck the Houston area in the 1950s, accentuating the need for an alternate supply of water. State officials proposed a 21,000-acre reservoir, which was named Lake Conroe upon its completion in 1973. Upscale housing developments sprouted along the wooded shoreline in rapidly expanding Montgomery County, and the Census Bureau eventually identified three urban clusters. Lake Conroe Eastshore is concentrated on the eastern side, as you would expect, though it paradoxically includes a bit of the western shore, too. Its best test ranks were second place for Growth and 13th for Business.

23. Vineyard Haven, Massachusetts

Martha's Vineyard and Nantucket both emerged as whaling hubs, then evolved into upscale tourist islands. A key difference is distance. Vineyard Haven, the main town on Martha's Vineyard, sits just seven miles from the Massachusetts mainland, while Nantucket is 30 miles off. Vineyard Haven is crowded with rich and famous tourists in the summer, though the pace is slower in other seasons. "Fall is the prize; the thick, hazy air of summer is gone, yet it is still warm enough for a swim well into October," says fulltime resident Mike Benjamin. Vineyard Haven took fourth place on the Diversions test, 18th on the Business exam.

24. Byron, Minnesota

This book's population threshold is 5,000, a standard Byron barely meets. Its current headcount, according to the Census Bureau, is 5,004. The smallest community in the top 25 retains strong links to the surrounding farmland in southeastern Minnesota. A grain elevator towers over the rail line that runs through town. Yet Byron also benefits from being within commuting distance of Rochester, Minnesota, the nation's top-rated small town on the Health test. Byron took runner-up honors in the same category — easily its best performance — and it finished in the top 100 on five other tests.

25. Breckenridge, Colorado

Breckenridge bills itself as the altitude champion among American ski towns, and it makes a strong case with a Rocky Mountain elevation of 9,600 feet. Long winters are par for the course, with annual snowfall exceeding 300 inches. Denver is just a 90-minute drive away, and the overall vibe is more relaxed than in Aspen and other upscale resorts. Travel writer Amy Piper calls Breckenridge "a casual mountain town that highlights outdoor activities." Hiking and biking are popular in months when the flakes aren't flying. Breckenridge's top test ranks were sixth for Diversions and 11th for Stability.

High Honors

Now to the concept that underpins this entire book.

A Dreamtown is defined as any small town that outperformed more than 90% of its competitors in the quality-of-life rankings — that is, any community that finished no lower than 209th out of the 2,084 on the master list. (Nobody is actually credited with 209th place, as you'll see. That's because two towns are tied for 208th.)

Students understand the importance of scoring in the 90s on a test or an assignment. A mark of 90 is generally the threshold — the cutoff point — for the desired grade of A. That, in turn, is the best way to think of the 209 Dreamtowns. They endured 12 strenuous tests and scored above the cutoff of 90%. They have distinguished themselves as Grade-A small towns.

The communities that we visited in the previous section — the top 25 — all carry the Dreamtown label, of course, but they are far from alone. Another 184 small towns across the country, all blessed with outstanding qualities, have earned the same elite designation.

Dreamtowns offer something for everyone. They're as large as Olympia, Washington (population: 194,812), and Santa Cruz, California (an even 170,000), and as small as Johnson Lane, Nevada (5,052), and Byron, Minnesota (5,004). They're scattered across all four sections of the country, with 29 Dreamtowns located in the East, 49 in the Midwest, 50 in the South, and 81 in the West. And they can be found in 40 of the 50 states, with especially strong concentrations in Colorado (home to 22 Dreamtowns), California (16), Minnesota (16), Texas (14), and Utah (12).

The next chapter will offer a full page of facts and figures for each Dreamtown, providing more than enough data to fuel your search for the ideal place to live. Here, for now, is a rundown of these highly rated communities. Each town is followed in parentheses by the points it earned on the 12 tests.

Dreamtowns

1. Summit Park, UT (949.7)
2. Park City, UT (935.0)
3. Belterra, TX (926.4)
4. World Golf Village, FL (904.1)
5. Roxborough Park, CO (882.4)
6. Nantucket, MA (877.4)
7. Evergreen, CO (875.9)
8. Heber, UT (870.1)
9. Vistancia, AZ (866.0)
10. Buckhead (Bryan County), GA (865.2)
11. Lafayette, CO (865.1)
12. Purcellville, VA (861.5)
13. Aspen, CO (857.0)
14. Spring Hill, TN (850.9)
15. Bend, OR (850.8)
16. St. Simons, GA (849.4)
17. Tea, SD (842.3)
18. Snoqualmie, WA (841.3)
19. Archer Lodge, NC (840.9)
20. Crozet, VA (839.9)
21. White Rock, NM (837.6)
22. Lake Conroe Eastshore, TX (837.5)
23. Vineyard Haven, MA (836.5)
24. Byron, MN (832.8)
25. Breckenridge, CO (828.6)
26. Wellington, CO (826.0)
27. Silverthorne, CO (823.4)
28. Los Alamos, NM (822.7)
29. Boerne, TX (822.1)
30. Waconia, MN (820.5)
31. Vail, CO (818.5)
32. Lake of the Pines, CA (817.0)
33. Rochester, MN (816.0)
34. Steamboat Springs, CO (814.5)
35. Lake Conroe Westshore, TX (812.8)
36. Rancho Murieta, CA (811.6)
37. Boulder, CO (809.1)
38. Jupiter Farms, FL (808.2)

39. Truckee, CA (808.0)
40. Portsmouth, NH (807.9)
41. Lewes, DE (807.8)
42. Aledo, TX (806.7)
43. Kennebunk, ME (805.0)
44. Paloma Creek South, TX (804.6)
45. Hood River, OR (802.7)
46. Salida, CO (802.6)
47. Sun City Hilton Head, SC (801.6)
48. Hampstead, NC (799.6)
49. Eagle Mountain South, UT (799.5)
50. Mauldin, SC (799.3)
51. Woodcreek, TX (797.8)
52. Chelsea, MI (797.6)
53. Ocean View, DE (797.0)
54. Whitefish, MT (796.6)
55. Port Townsend, WA (796.4)
56. Pawleys Island, SC (795.6)
57. Jackson, WY (795.4)
58. Johnstown, CO (795.1)
59. Woodland Park, CO (794.7)
60. Manor, TX (794.2)
61. Fernandina Beach, FL (794.1)
62. South Lyon, MI (793.4)
62. Spirit Lake, IA (793.4)
64. Mandeville, LA (791.0)
65. Ruckersville, VA (790.9)
65. Stansbury Park, UT (790.9)
67. Eureka, MO (790.3)
68. Saratoga Springs, NY (790.1)
69. Hudson, WI (789.9)
70. Santa Rosa Beach, FL (789.6)
71. Ocean Pines, MD (788.1)
72. Basalt, CO (787.0)
73. Rigby, ID (785.2)
74. Lake Pocotopaug, CT (784.9)
75. Kill Devil Hills, NC (782.8)
76. Estes Park, CO (781.5)
77. New Bremen, OH (780.3)
77. Orange City, IA (780.3)
79. Orangetree, FL (779.6)
80. Manteo, NC (779.3)
81. Santaquin, UT (777.8)
82. Platte City, MO (777.1)

83. Mukwonago, WI (776.8)
84. Jefferson Township North, NJ (776.1)
85. St. George, UT (775.7)
86. Lee's Summit, MO (775.6)
87. Lebanon, NH (774.7)
87. Mountain House, CA (774.7)
89. Bozeman, MT (774.5)
90. Firestone, CO (773.6)
90. Twin Rivers, NJ (773.6)
92. Vail, AZ (772.6)
93. Lake Norman of Catawba, NC (772.4)
94. Oregon, WI (771.4)
95. St. Augustine, FL (770.6)
96. Frankenmuth, MI (770.1)
97. Gunnison, CO (769.6)
98. Corona de Tucson, AZ (768.2)
99. Half Moon Bay, CA (767.7)
99. Lake Monticello, VA (767.7)
101. Williamsburg, VA (767.6)
102. Anacortes, WA (766.8)
102. Livermore, CA (766.8)
104. Star, ID (766.4)
105. Decorah, IA (765.3)
106. Fairview, TN (765.1)
107. Pella, IA (763.7)
108. Carroll, IA (760.8)
109. West Point, NY (759.4)
110. Daphne, AL (759.1)
111. Oxford, MS (758.9)
112. Warwick, NY (758.8)
113. Middletown, DE (758.3)
114. Johnson Lane, NV (758.2)
115. Anna, TX (757.2)
116. Traverse City, MI (756.3)
117. Charlottesville, VA (756.1)
117. Prairie du Sac, WI (756.1)
119. Marysville, OH (755.8)
120. Westminster, MD (754.8)
121. Birch Bay, WA (754.4)
122. Delano, MN (754.1)
122. Lago Vista, TX (754.1)
124. Petaluma, CA (753.8)
125. Forney, TX (753.3)
126. Sturgeon Bay, WI (753.2)

127. Mount Horeb, WI (752.3)
128. Moab, UT (751.3)
129. Sioux Center, IA (751.2)
130. Sedona, AZ (751.1)
131. Gypsum, CO (750.5)
132. Eaton, CO (750.4)
133. Canyon Lake, TX (749.8)
133. McPherson, KS (749.8)
135. Leonardtown, MD (749.5)
136. Chester, NY (748.8)
137. Frederick, MD (748.3)
138. Hilton Head Island, SC (748.0)
139. Buffalo, MN (746.9)
140. Pecan Plantation, TX (746.7)
141. Lake of the Woods, VA (746.2)
142. Eagle, CO (745.4)
143. Mount Vernon, IA (745.2)
144. Astoria, OR (745.0)
145. Edwards, CO (744.9)
146. Lindstrom, MN (744.6)
147. Chesapeake Beach, MD (744.5)
148. Logan, UT (743.7)
149. Monticello, IL (743.5)
150. Alexandria, MN (743.4)
151. Bellingham, WA (743.1)
152. Pinehurst, NC (742.5)
152. Red Hook, NY (742.5)
154. Davis, CA (742.0)
155. Auburn, CA (741.7)
156. Big Pine Key, FL (741.0)
157. Key Largo, FL (740.4)
157. Olympia, WA (740.4)
159. Iowa City, IA (738.8)
160. Forest Lake, MN (738.5)
161. Discovery Bay, CA (737.9)
162. Seaside, OR (737.7)
163. Cedar City, UT (737.6)
164. Lake Mills, WI (737.1)
165. Longmont, CO (736.5)
166. Colchester, CT (736.2)
167. Southold, NY (736.1)
168. Breese, IL (735.9)
169. Kuna, ID (735.7)
170. Santa Cruz, CA (735.5)

171. Burlington, VT (735.3)
172. Petoskey, MI (735.0)
173. East Aurora, NY (734.9)
174. Morro Bay, CA (734.7)
174. Moscow, ID (734.7)
176. Goodrich, MI (734.5)
177. Bishop, CA (734.4)
178. Monticello, MN (734.2)
179. Belle Plaine, MN (733.9)
179. Brunswick, ME (733.9)
181. Incline Village, NV (732.8)
182. Midland, MI (732.1)
183. Coeur d'Alene, ID (731.6)
183. South Deerfield, MA (731.6)
185. New Prague, MN (729.8)
186. Plumas Lake, CA (729.7)
187. Colby, KS (729.2)
188. Corvallis, OR (729.1)
189. Zimmerman, MN (728.9)
190. Dorr, MI (728.5)
191. Oak Island, NC (728.3)
192. Jordan, MN (728.2)
192. Murfreesboro, TN (728.2)
194. Ephraim, UT (727.7)
194. Morehead City, NC (727.7)
196. Redmond, OR (727.4)
197. Solvang, CA (727.1)
198. Cambria, CA (727.0)
198. Fredericksburg, VA (727.0)
198. Northfield, MN (727.0)
201. Weatherford, TX (726.7)
202. Belgrade, MT (726.4)
203. Brunswick, MD (726.3)
204. New Ulm, MN (726.0)
204. State College, PA (726.0)
206. Kasson, MN (725.8)
207. Idaho Falls, ID (725.2)
208. Nephi, UT (725.0)
208. Silverton, OR (725.0)

Just Off the Pace

You should be able to find a compelling community — or, more likely, several of them — on the list of 209 Dreamtowns. But if you prefer to widen your search, there is a second option.

A total of 313 small towns have been designated as Honorable Mentions. They failed to reach the Dreamtowns threshold of 90%, but they did outperform at least 75% of the nation's 2,084 small towns, which means they still have plenty to offer. You'll find them in the overall standings between 210th and 521st place. (There's a tie for the latter.)

Towns designated as Honorable Mentions can be found in 44 states, with the greatest concentrations in California (home to 25), Wisconsin (also 25), Minnesota (16), Iowa (15), and Washington (14).

Here is the full rundown, with point totals in parentheses.

Honorable Mentions

210. Durango, CO (724.3)
211. Estrella, AZ (724.2)
211. St. Helena, CA (724.2)
213. Clear Lake, IA (723.9)
214. Pocono Woodland Lakes, PA (723.8)
215. Danbury, CT (723.7)
216. Diamondhead, MS (723.5)
217. Waterloo, IL (723.3)
218. Camarillo, CA (723.1)
218. Easton, MD (723.1)
220. Columbus, WI (722.9)
220. Placerville, CA (722.9)
222. Brandon, SD (722.5)
222. Sugarmill Woods, FL (722.5)
224. Williamston, MI (722.3)
225. Livingston, MT (722.0)
225. New Freedom, PA (722.0)
227. Arlington, TN (721.9)
228. Rio Vista, CA (721.7)
229. Villas, NJ (721.6)
230. Wedgefield, FL (721.4)
231. Holland, MI (720.6)
231. Lynden, WA (720.6)
231. Owatonna, MN (720.6)
234. Gilroy, CA (720.5)
235. Jefferson, GA (720.3)
235. West Bend, WI (720.3)
237. Lake Geneva, WI (720.1)
238. Fredericksburg, TX (719.7)
239. Indianola, WA (719.1)

240. Sandy, OR (718.9)
240. Springs, NY (718.9)
242. Mammoth Lakes, CA (718.8)
242. Marshfield, WI (718.8)
244. Indianola, IA (718.7)
245. Kalispell, MT (718.4)
246. Winterset, IA (718.2)
247. Marana West, AZ (717.9)
248. Sequim, WA (717.3)
248. Wayne, NE (717.3)
250. Ames, IA (717.2)
250. Marble Falls, TX (717.2)
252. Canby, OR (716.7)
253. Stevens Point, WI (716.3)
254. Spring Hill, KS (716.2)
255. Granite Shoals, TX (715.6)
256. Milan, MI (715.5)
257. Mahomet, IL (715.4)
258. Stewartville, MN (715.1)
259. Lake Wildwood, CA (714.3)
260. Sahuarita, AZ (713.6)
261. Yankton, SD (713.5)
262. Shady Side, MD (713.2)
263. Eudora, KS (713.1)
264. Arroyo Grande, CA (712.8)
265. Wendell, NC (712.7)
266. Ithaca, NY (712.6)
267. Ellensburg, WA (712.5)
268. Hastings, MN (712.4)
268. Morgantown, WV (712.4)
270. New Richmond, WI (712.3)
271. Milton, VT (712.1)
271. Stanwood, WA (712.1)
273. Effingham, IL (712.0)
273. Forestville, CA (712.0)
275. Baldwin, WI (711.5)
276. Kearney, MO (710.4)
277. Prescott Valley, AZ (710.1)
278. Laconia, NH (710.0)
279. Le Mars, IA (709.2)
280. Camano, WA (709.0)
280. Lee, MA (709.0)
282. Lowell, MI (708.9)
283. Leadville, CO (708.2)

283. Paso Robles, CA (708.2)
285. Winchester, VA (708.1)
286. Cedar Rapids, IA (707.4)
286. Port Clinton, OH (707.4)
288. Grass Valley, CA (707.2)
289. Slidell, LA (707.1)
290. Lebanon, TN (706.9)
291. Rock Hill, SC (706.3)
292. Colville, WA (706.1)
293. Marysville, WA (705.8)
294. St. Joseph, IL (705.7)
295. Columbia, MO (705.3)
295. Jasper, IN (705.3)
295. North Branch, MN (705.3)
298. Concord, NH (705.0)
298. Spearfish, SD (705.0)
300. Beaufort, SC (704.5)
300. Manchester, MD (704.5)
302. Hailey, ID (704.3)
303. Seville, OH (703.5)
304. New Castle, CO (703.4)
305. Lake City, MN (702.9)
306. Chardon, OH (702.8)
307. Sebastian, FL (702.7)
308. Lawrence, KS (702.2)
309. Cody, WY (702.0)
309. Waverly, IA (702.0)
311. Honeoye Falls, NY (701.9)
312. Yulee, FL (701.8)
313. Pottstown, PA (701.2)
314. Edgerton, WI (700.7)
315. Hurricane, UT (700.6)
315. Sonora, CA (700.6)
317. Monroe, WI (700.5)
318. Willard, MO (700.0)
319. Columbus, IN (699.7)
320. Emmitsburg, MD (699.5)
321. Brookings, SD (699.4)
321. Carbondale, CO (699.4)
323. Oakland, TN (699.3)
323. Washington, MO (699.3)
325. Sonoma, CA (699.0)
326. Long Neck, DE (698.9)
327. Eau Claire, WI (698.8)

327. Moapa Valley, NV (698.8)
329. Seward, NE (698.5)
330. Dandridge, TN (698.4)
330. Evansville, WI (698.4)
332. Holdrege, NE (698.3)
333. River Falls, WI (697.8)
334. Pocatello, ID (697.3)
335. Pagosa Springs, CO (697.1)
336. Lexington Park, MD (696.9)
336. Silver Lakes, CA (696.9)
338. Mankato, MN (696.7)
339. Albany, OR (696.5)
340. Sioux Falls, SD (696.2)
341. Byron, IL (695.9)
342. San Luis Obispo, CA (695.8)
343. Canton, NY (695.6)
343. Missoula, MT (695.6)
343. Sandpoint, ID (695.6)
346. Plymouth, WI (695.2)
347. Brevard, NC (695.1)
348. Baker City, OR (695.0)
348. Baraboo, WI (695.0)
348. La Crosse, WI (695.0)
351. Pleasant Hill, MO (694.9)
352. Wausau, WI (694.4)
353. Jackson, CA (694.2)
354. Wamego, KS (693.8)
355. North Port, FL (693.7)
356. Midland, TX (693.6)
357. Helena, MT (693.5)
358. Glens Falls, NY (693.4)
359. Middlebury, VT (693.3)
360. Thurmont, MD (693.0)
361. Alachua, FL (692.6)
362. York, NE (692.1)
363. Long Beach, MD (691.7)
363. St. Francis, MN (691.7)
365. Lebanon, IN (690.9)
366. Kearney, NE (690.8)
367. Hutchinson, MN (690.6)
368. St. Peter, MN (690.4)
369. Smithfield, VA (690.0)
370. Bloomington, IL (689.9)
370. Elkhorn, WI (689.9)

370. Village of Oak Creek (Big Park), AZ (689.9)
373. Pratt, KS (689.8)
374. Orwigsburg, PA (689.7)
374. Rathdrum, ID (689.7)
376. Simi Valley, CA (689.5)
377. Highland, IL (689.4)
378. Flagstaff, AZ (689.0)
378. Tremonton, UT (689.0)
380. Bloomington, IN (688.9)
380. St. Cloud, MN (688.9)
382. Columbia Falls, MT (688.8)
382. Tonganoxie, KS (688.8)
384. Ottawa, OH (688.7)
385. Celina, OH (688.5)
386. Butler, PA (688.3)
387. Dubuque, IA (688.2)
387. Lake Delton, WI (688.2)
389. Charles Town, WV (688.1)
390. Bastrop, TX (688.0)
391. Fergus Falls, MN (687.6)
391. Rincon, GA (687.6)
391. Sanger, TX (687.6)
394. Versailles, KY (687.5)
395. Franklin, NJ (687.2)
396. Sheridan, WY (686.8)
397. Manchester, NH (686.4)
397. Spring Hill, FL (686.4)
399. Oak Harbor, WA (686.1)
400. Marathon, FL (686.0)
400. Oxford, OH (686.0)
402. Findlay, OH (685.6)
403. Grove City, PA (685.5)
404. Rancho Calaveras, CA (685.3)
405. Dallas, OR (685.1)
405. Fairmont, MN (685.1)
407. Cheyenne, WY (685.0)
408. Lander, WY (684.5)
409. El Dorado, KS (683.9)
409. Watertown, SD (683.9)
411. Granbury, TX (683.3)
411. Grinnell, IA (683.3)
411. North Brookfield, MA (683.3)
414. Morris, IL (683.1)
415. Newberg, OR (683.0)

416. Fairfield, IA (682.7)
416. Grantsville, UT (682.7)
416. Reedsburg, WI (682.7)
419. Algona, IA (682.5)
420. Jerseyville, IL (682.4)
421. Keene, NH (682.2)
422. Walden, NY (682.0)
423. Richfield, UT (681.5)
424. Leesburg, FL (681.1)
425. South Lake Tahoe, CA (681.0)
426. South Haven, MI (680.9)
427. Auburn, AL (680.8)
427. Janesville, WI (680.8)
427. Tooele, UT (680.8)
427. Twin Falls, ID (680.8)
431. Mystic Island, NJ (680.7)
431. Newport, OR (680.7)
431. Norman, OK (680.7)
434. Bonadelle Ranchos, CA (680.6)
434. Evanston, WY (680.6)
436. Springfield, IL (680.2)
437. Waldorf, MD (680.1)
438. Madison, SD (679.8)
439. Cambridge, MN (679.7)
440. Chico, CA (679.3)
441. Lafayette, IN (679.2)
442. Holly, MI (679.1)
442. Lady Lake, FL (679.1)
444. Rice Lake, WI (678.9)
445. Columbia City, IN (678.6)
445. Geneva, NY (678.6)
447. Lexington, VA (678.5)
447. Mascoutah, IL (678.5)
447. Titusville, FL (678.5)
450. Everson, WA (678.4)
450. Newfane, NY (678.4)
452. Dover, NH (678.2)
453. Vermillion, SD (678.1)
454. St. Marys, PA (677.9)
455. Sheboygan, WI (677.7)
456. Nevada, IA (677.6)
457. Canon City, CO (677.4)
457. Independence, IA (677.4)
459. Corning, NY (677.0)

460. Burlington, WI (676.8)
460. Spencer, IA (676.8)
462. Lindale, TX (676.7)
463. Franklin, NC (676.6)
464. Pullman, WA (676.0)
464. Washington, NJ (676.0)
466. Hastings, MI (675.9)
467. Batesville, IN (675.1)
467. St. Helens, OR (675.1)
469. Athens, GA (675.0)
470. Newark, OH (674.8)
470. Wauseon, OH (674.8)
472. Fort Atkinson, WI (674.5)
473. Litchfield, MN (674.3)
474. Escalon, CA (674.2)
474. Orrville, OH (674.2)
476. Duluth, MN (674.0)
477. Mason City, IA (673.9)
478. Winder, GA (673.8)
479. Blair, NE (673.7)
479. Mount Vernon, WA (673.7)
481. Kingston, NY (673.5)
482. Saw Creek, PA (673.4)
482. Wooster, OH (673.4)
484. Columbia, TN (673.2)
485. Yelm, WA (673.1)
486. Spout Springs, NC (672.9)
487. Warner Robins, GA (672.6)
488. Clifton Springs, NY (672.5)
489. Spartanburg, SC (672.4)
490. Braidwood, IL (672.3)
490. Granite Falls, WA (672.3)
492. Laramie, WY (672.1)
492. Montrose, CO (672.1)
494. Brainerd, MN (672.0)
495. Angola, IN (671.8)
495. Greeley, CO (671.8)
497. St. Marys, OH (671.4)
498. Carlsbad, NM (670.9)
498. Crawfordville, FL (670.9)
500. Pittsfield, MA (670.8)
501. Anderson, SC (670.7)
501. Keystone Heights, FL (670.7)
501. Lake Holiday, IL (670.7)

504. Medford, OR (670.5)
505. Lincoln City, OR (670.4)
506. Cloverdale, CA (670.1)
506. Johnstown, OH (670.1)
508. Rhinelander, WI (669.9)
509. Boulder City, NV (669.7)
510. Columbus, NE (669.6)
511. Barre, VT (669.4)
511. Warsaw, IN (669.4)
513. Santa Fe, NM (669.3)
514. Cape Girardeau, MO (669.2)
515. Redding, CA (668.8)
515. Vacaville, CA (668.8)
517. Blacksburg, VA (668.6)
518. Georgetown, KY (668.5)
519. Butner, NC (668.4)
520. Richmond, MI (668.0)
521. Lynchburg, VA (667.9)
521. Pierre, SD (667.9)

Rest of the Pack

The two elite designations — Dreamtowns and Honorable Mentions — have been bestowed on only 522 of America's 2,084 small towns. Three-quarters remain unaccounted for, a total of 1,562 communities.

I don't intend to go into their rankings here. It's more important, I think, to proceed directly to the heart of the matter, a close examination of America's 209 Dreamtowns. But if you wish to peruse the quality-of-life standings from top to bottom, as well as an alphabetical list by state, turn to the final chapter.

Chapter 4
THE DREAMTOWNS

Welcome to this book's longest chapter (by far). It runs nearly 230 pages, yet it doesn't contain much text. Most of its space is devoted not to sentences and paragraphs, but to detailed scorecards for all 209 Dreamtowns.

Each scorecard provides a wide range of data — a total of 62 statistics — for a specific small town. Dig deeply into these numbers, and you'll begin to comprehend the relative strengths and weaknesses of every elite community from No. 1 Summit Park, Utah, to the pair tied for 208th place, Nephi, Utah, and Silverton, Oregon.

Any Dreamtown would be an outstanding place to live — it outscored 90-plus percent of the other 2,083 small towns, didn't it? — but you're looking for more than just a high test score. You're seeking the very best fit for you and your family. This chapter gives you the statistical tools to weigh the possibilities and narrow your choices, setting the stage for the final three steps in your quest — targeted research, in-person visits, and the ultimate selection of your very own Dreamtown.

Outperforming Everybody

You might be raring to go, all set to pack the moving van. Small-town life is exactly what you've been hoping for. If so, skip directly to the scorecards.

Or perhaps you're still on the fence, uncertain that you would benefit from making the leap, despite everything we've discussed up to this point. Perhaps you're not yet convinced of the collective superiority of America's Dreamtowns.

Let me make the case.

You'll remember that we tallied the collective strengths and weaknesses of small towns in Chapter 1. There were six of each.

Here, once again, are the strengths:

1. Room to breathe
2. Ease of movement
3. Economic balance
4. Affordability
5. A place of your own
6. Resilience

All 2,084 small towns, taken as a group, outperform the 50 major urban hubs when the six qualities above are measured statistically. (You'll recall that major hubs, which I also call big cities, actually encompass cities and suburbs that are blended in continuous belts of metropolitan development.)

The same advantages exist when we narrow the focus to Dreamtowns. I'm not going to belabor the numbers, but it's fair to say that the collective stats for America's 209 elite towns are considerably better than the corresponding figures for the nation's 50 biggest cities in the same six categories. No shock there.

But something else *is* surprising. Dreamtowns completely erase more than half of the weaknesses of small towns, surpassing the major hubs in four of six instances. Let's revisit those weaknesses one by one:

1. Slow growth: The population of the typical small town increased by only 1.8% between 2014 and 2019, far behind the 3.9% rate for big cities. But the 209 Dreamtowns grew at a brisk (yet manageable) pace of 6.4%, putting the major hubs in the shade.

2. Aging population: This is one of two cases where big cities retain an advantage. Their ratio of 159 young adults per 100 senior citizens is more promising than the identical ratios for Dreamtowns and all small towns, 121 per 100.

3. Less diversity: Here's the other victory for major hubs. Their diversity index — the likelihood that two randomly selected persons would come from different racial groups — is 67.2%. The index drops to 51.1% for all small towns and just 37.0% for Dreamtowns.

4. Education imbalance: Big cities have a massive lead over small towns in the share of working-age adults holding bachelor's degrees: 40.1% vs. 26.2%. But the figure soars to 44.6% for Dreamtowns, actually putting them four and a half points ahead of the major hubs.

5. Internet shortcomings: Broadband subscriptions are more common in big cities (74.6% of all households) than in small towns (66.8%). Yet Dreamtowns again prove the exception to the rule, with a subscription rate of 77.9%.

6. Fewer top-level jobs: Occupations classified as MBSA (management, business, science, and the arts) account for 42.1% of all jobs in the 50 major hubs, dwarfing the 33.3% distribution in the 2,084 small towns. But the 209 Dreamtowns outshine both sides with a robust MBSA share of 44.4%.

The logical conclusion is that Dreamtowns offer the best of both worlds. They share the strengths of other small towns, yet eliminate most of the weaknesses. And that's not all. The balance tilts even more heavily toward Dreamtowns when we cite a few additional strengths:

• **New homes:** More than a quarter of all housing units in Dreamtowns (28.0%) have been built since 2000. That's far more impressive than the inventory of new homes in major hubs (17.1%).

• **Big homes:** A house with four or more bedrooms is a substantial structure, don't you think? The share of homes fitting that size classification is 26.1% in Dreamtowns, compared to 22.2% in big cities.

• **Working from home:** Dreamtowns joined the WFH revolution before it became trendy. Fully 7.1% of workers in the 209 elite towns were home-based as of 2019, a year before Covid struck. The work-from-home share in big cities was just 5.5%.

• **Less poverty:** The poverty rate for Dreamtowns (10.3%) is roughly two points lower than the corresponding rate for major hubs (12.5%).

• **Family stability:** A two-adult household isn't the only formula for a happy and successful childhood, yet it does seem to improve the odds. The percentage of children living under the same roof as both parents is almost 10 points higher in Dreamtowns (74.9%) than in big cities (65.4%).

• **Better health:** Fewer adults suffer from fair or poor health in Dreamtowns (13.5%) than in big cities (16.1%).

• **More diversions:** Dreamtowns hold surprising advantages in a pair of entertainment-related measures. They beat big cities in the ratios of stores per 10,000 residents (37.6 vs 30.9) and restaurants per 10,000 (23.3 vs 22.1).

Case closed.

Individual Strengths

The numbers in the previous section were collective. They identified the strengths of all 209 Dreamtowns *as a group*.

But you're naturally interested in these elite communities as separate entities. That's why this chapter concludes with 209 individual scorecards, and it's also why you should pay attention to this particular section.

The following list is divided by 24 subheads, corresponding to the 24 statistics that fueled the book's 12 tests. Each Dreamtown is listed under the stat that marked its best performance, based on its rank among all 2,084 small towns.

Subheads are displayed in the same order that the tests and their parts were unveiled in Chapter 2, with Dreamtowns presented alphabetically underneath. Each town is followed by its overall rank in parentheses — and then by the three statistical categories in which it received its best ranks.

Let's use the first town below, Belle Plaine, Minnesota, as an example. It ranks 179th in the overall standings. The Census Bureau has determined that 42.3% of Belle Plaine's residents carry no risk factors, which is the nation's 10th best score for resilience. That's the town's highest rank in any category, so it's featured under the Resilience subhead. Belle Plaine's two runner-up performances are 13th for private-sector job growth and 30th for fair or poor health.

The advantages of this list are obvious. If you deem certain characteristics to be important, you can quickly identify the towns that possess those qualities. Just remember that the list doesn't necessarily show the strongest communities for a given stat, but the towns that did better in that particular category than any other. (If you would prefer to see the leaders on a particular test, flip back to the top 20 charts in Chapter 2.)

Two other occurrences should be noted. The first is the existence of several ties in the category rankings, such as the five Dreamtowns that share first place for occupied homes. (All have 100% rates.) The second is the fact that nine towns have identical top ranks in two categories. Each is preceded by an asterisk and featured under the first subhead that applies.

Resilience

Belle Plaine, MN (179) — Resilience (10), private-sector job growth (13), and fair or poor health (30).

Buffalo, MN (139) — Resilience (8), fair or poor health (38), and high school graduates (112).

Fairview, TN (106) — Resilience (10), private-sector job growth (24), and small business growth (84).

Hudson, WI (69) — Resilience (7), fair or poor health (9), and high school graduates (73).

Lindstrom, MN (146) — Resilience (28), fair or poor health (45), and high school graduates (100).

Marysville, OH (119) — Resilience (3), median annual earnings (78), and major hub miles (90).

Monticello, MN (178) — Resilience (4), occupied homes (30), and fair or poor health (38).

New Prague, MN (185) — Resilience (26), fair or poor health (45), and living with two parents (50).

Saratoga Springs, NY (68) — Resilience (31), MBSA workers (47), and fair or poor health (55).

Sioux Center, IA (129) — Resilience (21), living with two parents (33), and short commutes (75).

Waconia, MN (30) — Resilience (1), fair or poor health (2), and living in poverty (11).

Zimmerman, MN (189) — Resilience (2), occupied homes (18), and home ownership (32).

Short Commutes

Carroll, IA (108) — Short commutes (29), resilience (36), and self-employed workers (36).

Living With Two Parents

Eaton, CO (132) — Living with two parents (16), economic growth (44), and small business growth (47).

Ephraim, UT (194) — Living with two parents (53), population growth (84), and small business growth (84).

Gypsum, CO (131) — Living with two parents (6), restaurants per 10,000 (25), and stores per 10,000 (29).

New Bremen, OH (77) — Living with two parents (12), living in poverty (15), and high school graduates (26).

Orange City, IA (77) — Living with two parents (1), high school graduates (19), and resilience (21).

*Pecan Plantation, TX (140) — Living with two parents (9), home ownership (9), and MBSA workers (45).

Prairie du Sac, WI (117) — Living with two parents (68), major or mid-major miles (74), and occupied homes (87).

Rancho Murieta, CA (36) — Living with two parents (4), median annual earnings (7), and major hub miles (9).

Vail, AZ (92) — Living with two parents (7), population growth (15), and median annual earnings (25).

Occupied Homes

Delano, MN (122) — Occupied homes (1), high school graduates (7), and resilience (8).

Estes Park, CO (76) — Occupied homes (56), fair or poor health (91), and self-employed workers (95).

Fernandina Beach, FL (61) — Occupied homes (67), population growth (74), and private-sector job growth (92).

Jordan, MN (192) — Occupied homes (1), resilience (10), and private-sector job growth (13).

*Kuna, ID (169) — Occupied homes (1), major or mid-major miles (1), and smartphone access (39).

Plumas Lake, CA (186) — Occupied homes (16), high school graduates (19), and smartphone access (19).

Ruckersville, VA (65) — Occupied homes (1), population growth (16), and living in poverty (38).

Stansbury Park, UT (65) — Occupied homes (13), living in poverty (17), and major hub miles (21).

Wellington, CO (26) — Occupied homes (1), population growth (11), and home ownership (17).

Population Growth

Anna, TX (115) — Population growth (12), smartphone access (26), and small business growth (56).

Hampstead, NC (48) — Population growth (25), private-sector job growth (48), and small business growth (54).

Lake Conroe Eastshore, TX (22) — Population growth (19), small business growth (42), economic growth (61), and self-employed workers (61).

Lake Norman of Catawba, NC (93) — Population growth (14), major hub miles (62), and occupied homes (87).

Murfreesboro, TN (192) — Population growth (74), major hub miles (75), and small business growth (86).

World Golf Village, FL (4) — Population growth (1), smartphone access (9), and MBSA workers (14).

Economic Growth

Bellingham, WA (151) — Economic growth (37), broadband subscriptions (116), and college graduates (174).

Birch Bay, WA (121) — Economic growth (37), median annual earnings (93), and population growth (118).

Idaho Falls, ID (207) — Economic growth (115), small business growth (175), and living with two parents (177).

McPherson, KS (133) — Economic growth (14), short commutes (18), and resilience (129).

High School Graduates

*Belterra, TX (3) — High school graduates (1), median annual earnings (1), and broadband subscriptions (2).

Breese, IL (168) — High school graduates (11), health care workers (66), and living in poverty (81).

Decorah, IA (105) — High school graduates (16), living with two parents (72), and stores per 10,000 (79).

Gunnison, CO (97) — High school graduates (5), restaurants per 10,000 (12), and occupied homes (18).

Kennebunk, ME (43) — High school graduates (11), college graduates (41), and broadband subscriptions (46).

Monticello, IL (149) — High school graduates (81), MBSA workers (83), and health care workers (101).

Mount Horeb, WI (127) — High school graduates (17), major or mid-major miles (25), and living in poverty (46).

Mount Vernon, IA (143) — High school graduates (51), living in poverty (70), and college graduates (71).

Northfield, MN (198) — High school graduates (128), college graduates (130), and fair or poor health (161).

Sun City Hilton Head, SC (47) — High school graduates (1), home ownership (5), and monthly housing costs (22).

Vail, CO (31) — High school graduates (10), college graduates (22), and restaurants per 10,000 (25).

*White Rock, NM (21) — High school graduates (1), MBSA workers (1), and median annual earnings (2).

Woodland Park, CO (59) — High school graduates (26), major or mid-major miles (41), and fair or poor health (45).

College Graduates

Boulder, CO (37) — College graduates (1), MBSA workers (13), and broadband subscriptions (33).

Bozeman, MT (89) — College graduates (30), high school graduates (35), and private-sector job growth (52).

Corvallis, OR (188) — College graduates (23), MBSA workers (42), and broadband subscriptions (87).

Davis, CA (154) — College graduates (2), MBSA workers (6), and median annual earnings (24).

Frankenmuth, MI (96) — College graduates (45), high school graduates (51), and median annual earnings (52).

Iowa City, IA (159) — College graduates (27), MBSA workers (58), and health care workers (108).

Lebanon, NH (87) — College graduates (18), MBSA workers (26), and restaurants per 10,000 (78).

Moscow, ID (174) — College graduates (36), high school graduates (61), and MBSA workers (86).

Oxford, MS (111) — College graduates (21), small business growth (39), and smartphone access (57).

Pinehurst, NC (152) — College graduates (75), MBSA workers (103), and high school graduates (199).

State College, PA (204) — College graduates (16), MBSA workers (17), and living with two parents (86).

Whitefish, MT (54) — College graduates (28), population growth (33), and living with two parents (36).

MBSA Workers

Charlottesville, VA (117) — MBSA workers (23), college graduates (33), and restaurants per 10,000 (43).

Crozet, VA (20) — MBSA workers (5), living in poverty (6), and college graduates (7).

Daphne, AL (110) — MBSA workers (70), college graduates (99), and private-sector job growth (121).

Lafayette, CO (11) — MBSA workers (11), college graduates (12), and broadband subscriptions (13).

Lake Mills, WI (164) — MBSA workers (78), fair or poor health (123), and broadband subscriptions (133).

Leonardtown, MD (135) — MBSA workers (3), median annual earnings (8), and college graduates (57).

Los Alamos, NM (28) — MBSA workers (2), median annual earnings (3), and college graduates (10).

Mandeville, LA (64) — MBSA workers (69), median annual earnings (102), and college graduates (104).

Midland, MI (182) — MBSA workers (106), college graduates (145), and high school graduates (153).

Olympia, WA (157) — MBSA workers (118), broadband subscriptions (144), and median annual earnings (145).

South Deerfield, MA (183) — MBSA workers (33), high school graduates (66), and college graduates (89).

Twin Rivers, NJ (90) — MBSA workers (10), college graduates (11), and median annual earnings (11).

Williamsburg, VA (101) — MBSA workers (54), college graduates (70), and broadband subscriptions (114).

Private-Sector Job Growth

Belgrade, MT (202) — Private-sector job growth (52), small business growth (61), and fair or poor health (63).

Boerne, TX (29) — Private-sector job growth (6), small business growth (10), and self-employed workers (41).

Canyon Lake, TX (133) — Private-sector job growth (11), small business growth (27), and home ownership (94).

Heber, UT (8) — Private-sector job growth (5), living with two parents (19), and small business growth (22).

Small Business Growth

Bend, OR (15) — Small business growth (17), private-sector job growth (27), and self-employed workers (44).

Cedar City, UT (163) — Small business growth (15), private-sector job growth (19), and economic growth (72).

Coeur d'Alene, ID (183) — Small business growth (76), population growth (145), and occupied homes (150).

Forney, TX (125) — Small business growth (36), population growth (42), home ownership (43), and smartphone access (43).

Logan, UT (148) — Small business growth (71), living with two parents (77), and smartphone access (84).

Nephi, UT (208) — Small business growth (88), smartphone access (119), and occupied homes (184).

Redmond, OR (196) — Small business growth (17), private-sector job growth (27), and economic growth (56).

Rigby, ID (73) — Small business growth (13), economic growth (25), and self-employed workers (27).

Santa Rosa Beach, FL (70) — Small business growth (3), self-employed workers (6), and broadband subscriptions (14).

Santaquin, UT (81) — Small business growth (17), private-sector job growth (22), and occupied homes (30).

St. Augustine, FL (95) — Small business growth (22), private-sector job growth (42), and economic growth (77).

St. George, UT (85) — Small business growth (5), private-sector job growth (16), and economic growth (59).

*Tea, SD (17) — Small business growth (2), fair or poor health (2), and living in poverty (14).

Weatherford, TX (201) — Small business growth (33), population growth (152), and smartphone access (194).

Woodcreek, TX (51) — Small business growth (11), private-sector job growth (27), and self-employed workers (65).

Self-Employed Workers

Anacortes, WA (102) — Self-employed workers (102), median annual earnings (143), and economic growth (159).

Cambria, CA (198) — Self-employed workers (5), living with two parents (8), and broadband subscriptions (57).

Hilton Head Island, SC (138) — Self-employed workers (80), smartphone access (103), and broadband subscriptions (116).

Hood River, OR (45) — Self-employed workers (55), economic growth (71), and restaurants per 10,000 (72).

Incline Village, NV (181) — Self-employed workers (14), smartphone access (78), and broadband subscriptions (84).

Lake Conroe Westshore, TX (35) — Self-employed workers (29), small business growth (42), and median annual earnings (56).

Lewes, DE (41) — Self-employed workers (59), home ownership (60), and MBSA workers (67).

Morro Bay, CA (174) — Self-employed workers (61), restaurants per 10,000 (127), and occupied homes (139).

Oak Island, NC (191) — Self-employed workers (61), population growth (62), and high school graduates (153).

Pawleys Island, SC (56) — Self-employed workers (19), population growth (72), and occupied homes (76).

Port Townsend, WA (55) — Self-employed workers (4), health care workers (43), and short commutes (57).

Salida, CO (46) — Self-employed workers (22), restaurants per 10,000 (34), and stores per 10,000 (39).

Sedona, AZ (130) — Self-employed workers (1), MBSA workers (151), and median annual earnings (169).

Southold, NY (167) — Self-employed workers (19), major or mid-major miles (55), and median annual earnings (156).

St. Simons, GA (16) — Self-employed workers (16), college graduates (24), and living with two parents (28).

*Vineyard Haven, MA (23) — Self-employed workers (3), stores per 10,000 (3), and restaurants per 10,000 (8).

Median Annual Earnings

Bishop, CA (177) — Median annual earnings (79), restaurants per 10,000 (124), and short commutes (144).

Brunswick, MD (203) — Median annual earnings (68), fair or poor health (73), and home ownership (108).

Chelsea, MI (52) — Median annual earnings (28), living in poverty (29), occupied homes (30), and college graduates (30).

Chesapeake Beach, MD (147) — Median annual earnings (15), resilience (23), and living in poverty (23).

Chester, NY (136) — Median annual earnings (18), broadband subscriptions (70), and major or mid-major miles (74).

Colchester, CT (166) — Median annual earnings (39), major hub miles (42), and major or mid-major miles (55).

Frederick, MD (137) — Median annual earnings (42), MBSA workers (56), and broadband subscriptions (73).

Half Moon Bay, CA (99) — Median annual earnings (13), MBSA workers (32), and major hub miles (32).

Lake of the Pines, CA (32) — Median annual earnings (17), living in poverty (35), and self-employed workers (44).

Livermore, CA (102) — Median annual earnings (9), broadband subscriptions (22), and MBSA workers (40).

*Mountain House, CA (87) — Median annual earnings (4), smartphone access (4), and broadband subscriptions (5).

Petaluma, CA (124) — Median annual earnings (32), occupied homes (45), and broadband subscriptions (77).

Purcellville, VA (12) — Median annual earnings (6), MBSA workers (18), and living in poverty (20).

Snoqualmie, WA (18) — Median annual earnings (5), broadband subscriptions (11), and smartphone access (17).

Solvang, CA (197) — Median annual earnings (22), self-employed workers (49), and broadband subscriptions (91).

Warwick, NY (112) — Median annual earnings (33), living in poverty (82), and high school graduates (100).

Living in Poverty

Byron, MN (24) — Living in poverty (1), fair or poor health (12), and health care workers (13).

Eureka, MO (67) — Living in poverty (2), major hub miles (12), and median annual earnings (20).

Firestone, CO (90) — Living in poverty (27), smartphone access (32), and occupied homes (35).

Johnstown, CO (58) — Living in poverty (5), living with two parents (13), and occupied homes (23).

Kasson, MN (206) — Living in poverty (20), resilience (30), and fair or poor health (35).

Pella, IA (107) — Living in poverty (35), resilience (71), and living with two parents (74).

Spring Hill, TN (14) — Living in poverty (8), smartphone access (13), and broadband subscriptions (16).

Home Ownership

Dorr, MI (190) — Home ownership (11), major or mid-major miles (25), and high school graduates (94).

Goodrich, MI (176) — Home ownership (45), broadband subscriptions (66), and median annual earnings (88).

Jefferson Township North, NJ (84) — Home ownership (7), median annual earnings (12), and broadband subscriptions (37).

Johnson Lane, NV (114) — Home ownership (5), living with two parents (15), and occupied homes (27).

Jupiter Farms, FL (38) — Home ownership (1), broadband subscriptions (9), and living with two parents (20).

Lake Monticello, VA (99) — Home ownership (25), MBSA workers (37), and population growth (39).

Lake of the Woods, VA (141) — Home ownership (3), occupied homes (49), population growth (82), and living in poverty (82).

Ocean View, DE (53) — Home ownership (20), population growth (30), and self-employed workers (65).

Orangetree, FL (79) — Home ownership (4), self-employed workers (26), and living in poverty (32).

Monthly Housing Costs

[none]

Health Care Workers

Rochester, MN (33) — Health care workers (4), fair or poor health (12), and MBSA workers (33).

Silverton, OR (208) — Health care workers (16), occupied homes (76), and economic growth (120).

Fair or Poor Health

Auburn, CA (155) — Fair or poor health (30), major hub miles (62), and private-sector job growth (89).

Brunswick, ME (179) — Fair or poor health (18), college graduates (125), and MBSA workers (141).

Burlington, VT (171) — Fair or poor health (9), college graduates (46), and MBSA workers (60).

Evergreen, CO (7) — Fair or poor health (2), college graduates (9), and median annual earnings (10).

Forest Lake, MN (160) — Fair or poor health (6), resilience (16), and living in poverty (70).

Longmont, CO (165) — Fair or poor health (91), economic growth (123), and college graduates (143).

New Ulm, MN (204) — Fair or poor health (69), living in poverty (140), and home ownership (167).

Portsmouth, NH (40) — Fair or poor health (9), college graduates (48), and resilience (52).

*Roxborough Park, CO (5) — Fair or poor health (1), broadband subscriptions (1), and home ownership (2).

South Lyon, MI (62) — Fair or poor health (45), median annual earnings (59), and living in poverty (75).

Westminster, MD (120) — Fair or poor health (25), median annual earnings (38), and major hub miles (50).

Stores Per 10,000

Alexandria, MN (150) — Stores per 10,000 (64), resilience (84), and short commutes (216).

Aspen, CO (13) — Stores per 10,000 (2), college graduates (5), and restaurants per 10,000 (5).

Big Pine Key, FL (156) — Stores per 10,000 (13), restaurants per 10,000 (15), and smartphone access (103).

Colby, KS (187) — Stores per 10,000 (12), short commutes (47), and living with two parents (48).

Jackson, WY (57) — Stores per 10,000 (6), restaurants per 10,000 (32), and college graduates (35).

Key Largo, FL (157) — Stores per 10,000 (13), restaurants per 10,000 (15), and self-employed workers (16).

Kill Devil Hills, NC (75) — Stores per 10,000 (5), restaurants per 10,000 (7), and self-employed workers (10).

Manteo, NC (80) — Stores per 10,000 (4), restaurants per 10,000 (6), and population growth (18).

*Nantucket, MA (6) — Stores per 10,000 (1), restaurants per 10,000 (1), and short commutes (5).

Petoskey, MI (172) — Stores per 10,000 (18), restaurants per 10,000 (35), and occupied homes (49).

Sturgeon Bay, WI (126) — Stores per 10,000 (10), restaurants per 10,000 (11), and fair or poor health (98).

Traverse City, MI (116) — Stores per 10,000 (60), fair or poor health (123), and restaurants per 10,000 (186).

Restaurants Per 10,000

Astoria, OR (144) — Restaurants per 10,000 (19), stores per 10,000 (40), and self-employed workers (214).

Breckenridge, CO (25) — Restaurants per 10,000 (2), stores per 10,000 (8), and living with two parents (18).

Eagle, CO (142) — Restaurants per 10,000 (25), stores per 10,000 (29), and smartphone access (73).

Edwards, CO (145) — Restaurants per 10,000 (25), smartphone access (27), and stores per 10,000 (29).

Moab, UT (128) — Restaurants per 10,000 (10), short commutes (12), and stores per 10,000 (19).

Morehead City, NC (194) — Restaurants per 10,000 (98), stores per 10,000 (101), and self-employed workers (115).

Ocean Pines, MD (71) — Restaurants per 10,000 (9), stores per 10,000 (34), and self-employed workers (64).

Seaside, OR (162) — Restaurants per 10,000 (19), stores per 10,000 (40), and self-employed workers (247).

Silverthorne, CO (27) — Restaurants per 10,000 (2), stores per 10,000 (8), living with two parents (45), and fair or poor health (45).

Spirit Lake, IA (62) — Restaurants per 10,000 (24), self-employed workers (37), and high school graduates (43).

Steamboat Springs, CO (34) — Restaurants per 10,000 (22), stores per 10,000 (24), and broadband subscriptions (42).

Broadband Subscriptions

Buckhead (Bryan County), GA (10) — Broadband subscriptions (7), private-sector job growth (12), and smartphone access (15).

Discovery Bay, CA (161) — Broadband subscriptions (4), smartphone access (5), and median annual earnings (14).

Fredericksburg, VA (198) — Broadband subscriptions (51), median annual earnings (116), and MBSA workers (146).

Middletown, DE (113) — Broadband subscriptions (6), MBSA workers (25), and median annual earnings (41).

Red Hook, NY (152) — Broadband subscriptions (25), college graduates (43), and MBSA workers (74).

Vistancia, AZ (9) — Broadband subscriptions (3), smartphone access (7), and living with two parents (11).

Smartphone Access

Aledo, TX (42) — Smartphone access (14), living in poverty (17), and median annual earnings (27).

Basalt, CO (72) — Smartphone access (10), self-employed workers (11), and restaurants per 10,000 (14).

Corona de Tucson, AZ (98) — Smartphone access (1), broadband sub-scriptions (8), and living in poverty (9).

Eagle Mountain South, UT (49) — Smartphone access (6), occupied homes (13), and living with two parents (14).

Park City, UT (2) — Smartphone access (10), college graduates (14), and stores per 10,000 (20).

Platte City, MO (82) — Smartphone access (28), resilience (41), and high school graduates (43).

Summit Park, UT (1) — Smartphone access (3), college graduates (8), and MBSA workers (16).

Truckee, CA (39) — Smartphone access (2), occupied homes (11), and broadband subscriptions (31).

Major Hub Miles

Archer Lodge, NC (19) — Major hub miles (12), home ownership (14), and broadband subscriptions (18).

East Aurora, NY (173) — Major hub miles (5), major or mid-major miles (16), and MBSA workers (30).

Lago Vista, TX (122) — Major hub miles (5), major or mid-major miles (16), and living in poverty (32).

Lake Pocotopaug, CT (74) — Major hub miles (3), major or mid-major miles (13), and fair or poor health (19).

Lee's Summit, MO (86) — Major hub miles (5), major or mid-major miles (16), and MBSA workers (47).

Manor, TX (60) — Major hub miles (3), population growth (10), and major or mid-major miles (13).

Mukwonago, WI (83) — Major hub miles (12), fair or poor health (19), and living in poverty (32).

Santa Cruz, CA (170) — Major hub miles (21), median annual earnings (29), and major or mid-major miles (55).

Major or Mid-Major Miles

Mauldin, SC (50) — Major or mid-major miles (7), broadband subscriptions (51), and population growth (84).

Oregon, WI (94) — Major or mid-major miles (16), living in poverty (35), and high school graduates (48).

Paloma Creek South, TX (44) — Major or mid-major miles (3), MBSA workers (15), and small business growth (17).

Star, ID (104) — Major or mid-major miles (3), population growth (13), and small business growth (71).

West Point, NY (109) — Major or mid-major miles (3), living in poverty (23), and broadband subscriptions (35).

Digging Into the Data

Now to the real meat of this chapter. The following pages contain scorecards for all 209 Dreamtowns. Communities are shown in alphabetical order.

The listings tend to be self-explanatory, but it never hurts to have a key. One special point should be noted at the start: The final 24 entries on each town's scorecard are the statistics that generated its test scores. A star (★) denotes any instance where one of those stats is ranked in the top 10% — 209th place or better — among all 2,084 small towns in that category.

Score and ranks: The town's total score in points, followed by its ranks among all small towns in the nation, region (East, South, Midwest, or West), and state. The percentile is the percentage of other U.S. small towns that the given community outranks.

Closest major hub: The major hub that is nearest the town, followed by the distance in air miles. (Major hubs are defined as the nation's 50 biggest cities.)

Tests: The town's scores on the book's 12 tests. The maximum score on any test is 100 points; the minimum is zero.

Basic stats: The population and population density (per square mile) of the town, based on the boundaries of its urbanized area or urban cluster. Also listed are the percentage of residents who were born in another state or country, the percentage of local housing units that have been built since 2000, and the percentage of all units that have at least four bedrooms.

Race: The percentages of residents who are classified as white, black, Hispanic, Asian, or Native American. (Percentages won't add to 100% because other racial groups are not listed.) The diversity index indicates the likelihood that two randomly selected residents would be of different races.

Household income ladder: The annual incomes of local households at six different levels, known as percentiles. A household is defined as persons who share the same house, apartment, condominium, or trailer, regardless of whether they are related by blood or marriage. Household income encompasses all money received from 42 sources (such as salaries, welfare, and Social Security) by all members of the household in a calendar year. A percentile is the percentage of local households that fall below a certain income. The income at the 95th percentile, for example, exceeds the incomes of 95% of local households. The income at the 50th percentile is the median. (The Census Bureau does not report specific household incomes in excess of $250,000. Such instances are listed here as ">$250,000.")

Home value ladder: The values of local owner-occupied homes at three different levels, known as percentiles. A percentile is the percentage of local homes that fall below a certain value. The value at the 75th percentile, for example, exceeds the values of 75% of local owner-occupied homes. The value at the 50th percentile is the median. (The Census Bureau does not report specific home values in excess of $2 million. Such instances are listed here as ">$2,000,000.")

Resilience: The percentage of residents who are not burdened with any of 11 risk factors enumerated by the Census Bureau.

Short commutes: The percentage of workers who commute from home to work in less than 20 minutes. The figure does not include those who work at home.

Living with two parents: The percentage of children under the age of 18 who live in two-parent households.

Occupied homes: The percentage of housing units that have residents, regardless of whether those persons are owners or renters.

Population growth: The change in population between 2014 and 2019.

Economic growth: The change in local gross domestic product between 2014 and 2019.

High school graduates: The percentage of working-age adults (25 to 64) who hold high school diplomas.

College graduates: The percentage of working-age adults (25 to 64) who hold bachelor's degrees.

MBSA workers: The percentage of local jobs that are classified by the Census Bureau as occupations in management, business, sciences, and the arts.

Private-sector job growth: The change in non-government employment between 2014 and 2019.

Small business growth: The change in the number of small businesses between 2013 and 2018, the latest figures available. A small business is defined as an employer with fewer than 100 employees.

Self-employed workers: The percentage of workers who own businesses, thereby functioning as their own bosses.

Median annual earnings: The median earnings for fulltime employees in a given year. Earnings are defined as wages paid by employers to their employees. A median is a midpoint, with half of local workers being paid more, and the other half being paid less.

Living in poverty: The percentage of local residents who live in households whose incomes fall below the Census Bureau's poverty threshold.

Home ownership: The percentage of housing units (houses, apartments, condominiums, and trailers) that are occupied by their owners.

Monthly housing costs: The percentage of a typical worker's monthly earnings that would be needed to pay the median costs of local home ownership (mortgage, taxes, insurance, and utilities).

Health care workers: The percentage of all local workers who are employed in health care.

Fair or poor health: The share of residents who characterize their health as fair or poor.

Stores per 10,000: The number of local retail establishments, expressed as a ratio per 10,000 residents.

Restaurants per 10,000: The number of local restaurants and bars, expressed as a ratio per 10,000 residents.

Broadband subscriptions: The percentage of households that subscribe to broadband internet services.

Smartphone access: The percentage of households that have access to smartphones.

Major hub miles: The air mileage from the town to the nearest major hub. (Major hubs are defined as the nation's 50 largest urbanized areas, all with populations greater than 900,000.)

Major or mid-major miles: The air mileage from the town to the nearest major or mid-major hub, whichever is closest. (Mid-major hubs are defined as the nation's 51st to 100th urbanized areas in size. Their populations range roughly between 400,000 and 900,000.)

Aledo, Texas

Score ....*806.7 points*
National rank ....*42 of 2,084*
Percentile...*98.03%*
South rank .... *13 of 745*
Texas rank.. *5 of 173*
Closest major hub ....*Dallas, 40 air miles*

TESTS
1. Character...47.1
2. Stability..76.2
3. Growth...47.4
4. Education...84.8
5. Jobs..70.4
6. Business...62.3
7. Money..95.1
8. Housing..69.9
9. Health..59.7
10. Diversions..21.8
11. Internet 82.3
12. Proximity..89.7

BASIC STATS
Population.. 6,063
Density 1,293.6
Born out of state 30.0%
Homes built since 2000............................48.2%
4 or more bedrooms 46.5%

RACE
Whites...86.4%
Blacks 0.3%
Hispanics..8.0%
Asians..0.8%
Native Americans 1.6%
Diversity index...24.6%

HOUSEHOLD INCOME LADDER
95th percentile .... >$250,000
80th percentile $201,667
60th percentile $141,833
50th percentile $119,267
40th percentile $97,031
20th percentile $61,389

HOME VALUE LADDER
75th percentile $348,900
50th percentile $267,100
25th percentile $180,500

CHARACTER
Resilience...32.1%
Short commutes 22.7%

STABILITY
Living with two parents .... 79.6% (★)
Occupied homes..94.1%

GROWTH
Population growth.......................................8.2%
Economic growth 0.5%

EDUCATION
High school graduates .... 96.8% (★)
College graduates .... 53.1% (★)

JOBS
MBSA workers..................................... 52.3% (★)
Private-sector job growth 6.7%

BUSINESS
Small business growth .... 22.1% (★)
Self-employed workers 6.8%

MONEY
Median annual earnings...............$69,219 (★)
Living in poverty....................................3.0% (★)

HOUSING
Home ownership.............................. 87.5% (★)
Monthly housing costs 30.3%

HEALTH
Health care workers.................................. 10.2%
Fair or poor health...................................13.8%

DIVERSIONS
Stores per 10,000...25.9
Restaurants per 10,000................................13.9

INTERNET
Broadband subscriptions 76.2%
Smartphone access .... 93.1% (★)

PROXIMITY
Major hub miles... 40
Major or mid-major miles................................ 40

Alexandria, Minnesota

Score ....743.4 points
National rank .... 150 of 2,084
Percentile...92.85%
Midwest rank.. 32 of 622
Minnesota rank .... 7 of 53
Closest major hub ....Minneapolis, 120 air miles

TESTS
1. Character.................................89.6
2. Stability..................................74.7
3. Growth....................................42.5
4. Education................................62.5
5. Jobs..52.4
6. Business..................................41.5
7. Money.....................................64.2
8. Housing...................................56.2
9. Health.....................................65.8
10. Diversions.............................57.3
11. Internet.................................61.1
12. Proximity...............................75.6

BASIC STATS
Population...............................17,831
Density....................................1,201.8
Born out of state.......................22.9%
Homes built since 2000.............22.8%
4 or more bedrooms..................29.9%

RACE
Whites.......................................93.6%
Blacks..0.5%
Hispanics...................................2.7%
Asians..0.5%
Native Americans......................0.4%
Diversity index..........................12.3%

HOUSEHOLD INCOME LADDER
95th percentile.....................$184,506
80th percentile.....................$107,735
60th percentile......................$72,469
50th percentile......................$58,734
40th percentile......................$47,103
20th percentile......................$25,632

HOME VALUE LADDER
75th percentile.....................$291,800
50th percentile.....................$192,700
25th percentile.....................$135,300

CHARACTER
Resilience.............................. 37.2% (★)
Short commutes........................79.1%

STABILITY
Living with two parents.............72.4%
Occupied homes........................95.9%

GROWTH
Population growth......................2.3%
Economic growth.......................6.1%

EDUCATION
High school graduates..............94.4%
College graduates.....................29.1%

JOBS
MBSA workers............................35.4%
Private-sector job growth..........7.1%

BUSINESS
Small business growth...............1.5%
Self-employed workers...............9.1%

MONEY
Median annual earnings.........$46,612
Living in poverty.......................8.1%

HOUSING
Home ownership.......................63.0%
Monthly housing costs...............25.8%

HEALTH
Health care workers...................11.6%
Fair or poor health....................12.8%

DIVERSIONS
Stores per 10,000.................... 59.3 (★)
Restaurants per 10,000..............20.8

INTERNET
Broadband subscriptions..........69.9%
Smartphone access....................77.3%

PROXIMITY
Major hub miles............................120
Major or mid-major miles.............120

Anacortes, Washington

Score ....*766.8 points*
National rank ....*102 of 2,084*
Percentile...*95.15%*
West rank...*43 of 471*
Washington rank...*3 of 44*
Closest major hub ....*Seattle, 72 air miles*

TESTS
1. Character................................59.6
2. Stability....................................72.4
3. Growth....................................58.6
4. Education................................72.3
5. Jobs...60.4
6. Business..................................59.1
7. Money.....................................72.0
8. Housing...................................55.3
9. Health.....................................61.1
10. Diversions..............................47.2
11. Internet 64.7
12. Proximity................................84.1

BASIC STATS
Population................................17,806
Density 1,876.5
Born out of state 58.7%
Homes built since 2000............20.3%
4 or more bedrooms 18.5%

RACE
Whites.......................................89.0%
Blacks...0.5%
Hispanics...................................4.4%
Asians...2.8%
Native Americans 0.7%
Diversity index..........................20.4%

HOUSEHOLD INCOME LADDER
95th percentile $247,943
80th percentile $134,205
60th percentile $86,829
50th percentile $71,848
40th percentile $57,125
20th percentile $31,452

HOME VALUE LADDER
75th percentile $591,600
50th percentile $410,400
25th percentile $308,400

CHARACTER
Resilience...................................25.8%
Short commutes 59.3%

STABILITY
Living with two parents 69.5%
Occupied homes.......................95.7%

GROWTH
Population growth....................5.6%
Economic growth .... 25.5% (★)

EDUCATION
High school graduates 95.1%
College graduates .... 40.2% (★)

JOBS
MBSA workers.......................41.1% (★)
Private-sector job growth 9.3%

BUSINESS
Small business growth 6.8%
Self-employed workers ....13.2% (★)

MONEY
Median annual earnings...............$54,906 (★)
Living in poverty........................8.6%

HOUSING
Home ownership.......................66.9%
Monthly housing costs 29.0%

HEALTH
Health care workers................11.2%
Fair or poor health....................14.5%

DIVERSIONS
Stores per 10,000......................41.1
Restaurants per 10,000.............24.2

INTERNET
Broadband subscriptions 74.0%
Smartphone access 77.9%

PROXIMITY
Major hub miles.........................72
Major or mid-major miles............72

Anna, Texas

Score .... *757.2 points*
National rank .... *115 of 2,084*
Percentile *94.53%*
South rank .... *35 of 745*
Texas rank .... *9 of 173*
Closest major hub .... *Dallas, 46 air miles*

TESTS
1. Character.......................27.5
2. Stability..........................73.6
3. Growth............................92.5
4. Education.......................61.7
5. Jobs.................................66.5
6. Business.........................46.6
7. Money.............................67.4
8. Housing..........................56.3
9. Health.............................63.6
10. Diversions....................31.7
11. Internet.........................79.8
12. Proximity......................90.0

BASIC STATS
Population........................15,415
Density...........................2,204.7
Born out of state...............46.9%
Homes built since 2000............73.5%
4 or more bedrooms................31.2%

RACE
Whites................................63.5%
Blacks................................13.4%
Hispanics..........................16.8%
Asians..................................5.1%
Native Americans..............0.2%
Diversity index.................54.8%

HOUSEHOLD INCOME LADDER
95th percentile.....................$191,614
80th percentile....................$126,936
60th percentile....................$105,837
50th percentile......................$89,922
40th percentile......................$72,231
20th percentile......................$39,582

HOME VALUE LADDER
75th percentile.....................$241,300
50th percentile.....................$202,300
25th percentile.....................$151,500

CHARACTER
Resilience...........................17.9%
Short commutes................22.6%

STABILITY
Living with two parents...................80.5% (★)
Occupied homes.............................92.4%

GROWTH
Population growth............................34.0% (★)
Economic growth............................30.1% (★)

EDUCATION
High school graduates.............................89.3%
College graduates.....................................34.8%

JOBS
MBSA workers..38.0%
Private-sector job growth...............20.5% (★)

BUSINESS
Small business growth....................19.0% (★)
Self-employed workers.................................2.3%

MONEY
Median annual earnings.......................$50,236
Living in poverty...8.5%

HOUSING
Home ownership.......................................73.6%
Monthly housing costs............................32.4%

HEALTH
Health care workers.................................11.5%
Fair or poor health..................................13.7%

DIVERSIONS
Stores per 10,000..28.8
Restaurants per 10,000.............................19.8

INTERNET
Broadband subscriptions.......................75.2%
Smartphone access...........................91.6% (★)

PROXIMITY
Major hub miles...46
Major or mid-major miles..............................35

Archer Lodge, North Carolina

Score ....840.9 points
National rank .... 19 of 2,084
Percentile...99.14%
South rank .... 7 of 745
North Carolina rank... 1 of 65
Closest major hub ....Raleigh, 18 air miles

TESTS
1. Character.................................43.2
2. Stability.................................79.0
3. Growth...................................100.0
4. Education...............................76.6
5. Jobs.......................................69.5
6. Business.................................52.8
7. Money....................................82.6
8. Housing..................................74.9
9. Health....................................51.2
10. Diversions.............................22.3
11. Internet.................................91.5
12. Proximity...............................97.3

BASIC STATS
Population.................................17,895
Density......................................886.7
Born out of state.......................51.6%
Homes built since 2000.............70.2%
4 or more bedrooms.................39.9%

RACE
Whites.......................................76.5%
Blacks...9.2%
Hispanics...................................9.8%
Asians..1.2%
Native Americans......................0.3%
Diversity index.........................39.6%

HOUSEHOLD INCOME LADDER
95th percentile.....................>$250,000
80th percentile.......................$154,792
60th percentile.......................$111,632
50th percentile.........................$98,406
40th percentile.........................$85,276
20th percentile.........................$49,936

HOME VALUE LADDER
75th percentile.......................$320,400
50th percentile.......................$242,300
25th percentile.......................$184,700

CHARACTER
Resilience..................................31.3%
Short commutes........................17.9%

STABILITY
Living with two parents.............74.4%
Occupied homes.................. 97.5% (★)

GROWTH
Population growth................. 22.5% (★)
Economic growth.................. 49.7% (★)

EDUCATION
High school graduates.......... 95.6% (★)
College graduates................ 44.8% (★)

JOBS
MBSA workers........................ 44.0% (★)
Private-sector job growth......16.3%

BUSINESS
Small business growth.......... 13.8% (★)
Self-employed workers.............7.3%

MONEY
Median annual earnings...............$62,839 (★)
Living in poverty.......................6.0% (★)

HOUSING
Home ownership.................. 90.5% (★)
Monthly housing costs............28.1%

HEALTH
Health care workers...................9.3%
Fair or poor health...................16.7%

DIVERSIONS
Stores per 10,000.......................27.5
Restaurants per 10,000..............13.3

INTERNET
Broadband subscriptions................ 86.3% (★)
Smartphone access........... 92.0% (★)

PROXIMITY
Major hub miles.....................18 (★)
Major or mid-major miles.......18 (★)

Aspen, Colorado

Score ....*857.0 points*
National rank .... *13 of 2,084*
Percentile..*99.42%*
West rank.. *8 of 471*
Colorado rank .... *4 of 47*
Closest major hub .... *Denver, 107 air miles*

TESTS
1. Character................................74.7
2. Stability................................62.2
3. Growth................................53.7
4. Education................................98.3
5. Jobs................................62.3
6. Business................................70.6
7. Money................................73.1
8. Housing................................45.9
9. Health................................61.0
10. Diversions................................99.9
11. Internet 77.4
12. Proximity................................77.9

BASIC STATS
Population................................ 8,460
Density 1,853.6
Born out of state 78.5%
Homes built since 2000................................22.6%
4 or more bedrooms 19.4%

RACE
Whites................................87.5%
Blacks................................0.0%
Hispanics................................5.9%
Asians................................4.1%
Native Americans 0.0%
Diversity index................................22.9%

HOUSEHOLD INCOME LADDER
95th percentile ....>$250,000
80th percentile $162,074
60th percentile $105,777
50th percentile $84,388
40th percentile $67,195
20th percentile $38,320

HOME VALUE LADDER
75th percentile ....>$2,000,000
50th percentile $656,600
25th percentile $257,400

CHARACTER
Resilience................................27.1%
Short commutes .... 82.4% (★)

STABILITY
Living with two parents 73.8%
Occupied homes................................88.7%

GROWTH
Population growth................................6.9%
Economic growth 14.1%

EDUCATION
High school graduates .... 98.6% (★)
College graduates .... 72.5% (★)

JOBS
MBSA workers................................ 49.8% (★)
Private-sector job growth 0.3%

BUSINESS
Small business growth 4.6%
Self-employed workers .... 20.9% (★)

MONEY
Median annual earnings................................$54,353 (★)
Living in poverty................................7.0% (★)

HOUSING
Home ownership................................59.0%
Monthly housing costs................................31.6%

HEALTH
Health care workers................................8.3%
Fair or poor health................................ 10.6% (★)

DIVERSIONS
Stores per 10,000................................124.6 (★)
Restaurants per 10,000................................70.6 (★)

INTERNET
Broadband subscriptions 71.6%
Smartphone access .... 91.7% (★)

PROXIMITY
Major hub miles................................107
Major or mid-major miles................................107

Astoria, Oregon

Score ....745.0 points
National rank .... 144 of 2,084
Percentile...93.13%
West rank.. 54 of 471
Oregon rank .... 3 of 45
Closest major hub ....Portland, 74 air miles

TESTS
1. Character...................................64.9
2. Stability....................................70.3
3. Growth.....................................44.4
4. Education.................................59.1
5. Jobs..56.4
6. Business...................................50.8
7. Money......................................57.0
8. Housing....................................40.4
9. Health......................................64.4
10. Diversions..............................94.0
11. Internet 59.6
12. Proximity...............................83.7

BASIC STATS
Population................................14,060
Density 1,544.4
Born out of state 57.1%
Homes built since 2000..............9.3%
4 or more bedrooms 14.7%

RACE
Whites..81.5%
Blacks 0.7%
Hispanics 10.4%
Asians...1.5%
Native Americans 0.3%
Diversity index.........................32.1%

HOUSEHOLD INCOME LADDER
95th percentile....................$166,426
80th percentile......................$98,550
60th percentile......................$62,730
50th percentile......................$51,616
40th percentile......................$42,222
20th percentile......................$25,276

HOME VALUE LADDER
75th percentile....................$334,500
50th percentile....................$256,200
25th percentile....................$193,500

CHARACTER
Resilience...................................25.1%
Short commutes 70.2%

STABILITY
Living with two parents 68.7%
Occupied homes........................94.9%

GROWTH
Population growth.....................-1.6%
Economic growth 18.4%

EDUCATION
High school graduates 92.3%
College graduates 27.7%

JOBS
MBSA workers...........................32.9%
Private-sector job growth 15.0%

BUSINESS
Small business growth 5.2%
Self-employed workers 10.8%

MONEY
Median annual earnings.......$41,937
Living in poverty.......................10.5%

HOUSING
Home ownership.......................53.9%
Monthly housing costs..............32.8%

HEALTH
Health care workers.................12.5%
Fair or poor health...................14.7%

DIVERSIONS
Stores per 10,000......................67.7 (★)
Restaurants per 10,000..............49.9 (★)

INTERNET
Broadband subscriptions 71.0%
Smartphone access 75.1%

PROXIMITY
Major hub miles................................ 74
Major or mid-major miles................ 74

Auburn, California

Score ....741.7 points
National rank .... 155 of 2,084
Percentile...92.61%
West rank.. 59 of 471
California rank .... 9 of 145
Closest major hub .... Sacramento, 24 air miles

TESTS
1. Character.................................48.0
2. Stability..................................70.8
3. Growth....................................50.6
4. Education................................59.8
5. Jobs..67.4
6. Business..................................67.1
7. Money.....................................68.8
8. Housing...................................49.6
9. Health.....................................63.2
10. Diversions..............................38.1
11. Internet.................................65.8
12. Proximity...............................92.5

BASIC STATS
Population..............................34,950
Density..................................1,308.1
Born out of state....................32.4%
Homes built since 2000...........12.3%
4 or more bedrooms................18.1%

RACE
Whites.....................................80.8%
Blacks.......................................0.4%
Hispanics................................12.7%
Asians.......................................2.2%
Native Americans.....................0.3%
Diversity index........................32.9%

HOUSEHOLD INCOME LADDER
95th percentile....................$216,084
80th percentile....................$132,460
60th percentile.....................$82,651
50th percentile.....................$65,529
40th percentile.....................$50,067
20th percentile.....................$24,160

HOME VALUE LADDER
75th percentile....................$553,800
50th percentile....................$421,500
25th percentile....................$308,900

CHARACTER
Resilience................................21.3%
Short commutes.......................50.1%

STABILITY
Living with two parents...........69.6%
Occupied homes.......................94.8%

GROWTH
Population growth....................-0.1%
Economic growth............ 25.3% (★)

EDUCATION
High school graduates.............92.2%
College graduates....................28.7%

JOBS
MBSA workers..........................37.6%
Private-sector job growth............... 22.1% (★)

BUSINESS
Small business growth.................... 13.6% (★)
Self-employed workers................... 12.9% (★)

MONEY
Median annual earnings...............$56,004 (★)
Living in poverty......................12.6%

HOUSING
Home ownership.......................64.5%
Monthly housing costs.............32.1%

HEALTH
Health care workers...................9.1%
Fair or poor health............... 10.6% (★)

DIVERSIONS
Stores per 10,000.......................32.0
Restaurants per 10,000..............22.8

INTERNET
Broadband subscriptions.........70.9%
Smartphone access...................81.1%

PROXIMITY
Major hub miles..........................24 (★)
Major or mid-major miles.........24 (★)

Basalt, Colorado

Score .... *787.0 points*
National rank .... *72 of 2,084*
Percentile *96.59%*
West rank .... *31 of 471*
Colorado rank .... *14 of 47*
Closest major hub .... *Denver, 116 air miles*

TESTS
1. Character.........................47.4
2. Stability..........................75.8
3. Growth............................69.4
4. Education........................60.2
5. Jobs................................54.5
6. Business..........................76.4
7. Money.............................66.9
8. Housing...........................37.1
9. Health..............................47.0
10. Diversions.......................98.6
11. Internet...........................77.4
12. Proximity........................76.3

BASIC STATS
Population.....................10,167
Density.........................2,536.7
Born out of state................70.6%
Homes built since 2000.............29.7%
4 or more bedrooms.................27.7%

RACE
Whites..............................63.2%
Blacks...............................1.4%
Hispanics.........................34.6%
Asians...............................0.3%
Native Americans.....................0.0%
Diversity index...................48.1%

HOUSEHOLD INCOME LADDER
95th percentile ....>$250,000
80th percentile....................$150,838
60th percentile....................$107,271
50th percentile.....................$85,530
40th percentile.....................$73,024
20th percentile.....................$43,356

HOME VALUE LADDER
75th percentile $823,500
50th percentile $588,400
25th percentile $405,600

CHARACTER
Resilience.........................30.1%
Short commutes.....................27.9%

STABILITY
Living with two parents 75.7%
Occupied homes......................95.3%

GROWTH
Population growth............... 16.7% (★)
Economic growth...................17.7%

EDUCATION
High school graduates 82.4%
College graduates .... 42.0% (★)

JOBS
MBSA workers.......................34.2%
Private-sector job growth 11.1%

BUSINESS
Small business growth 8.1%
Self-employed workers .... 21.6% (★)

MONEY
Median annual earnings $50,615
Living in poverty.....................9.3%

HOUSING
Home ownership.....................69.0%
Monthly housing costs.............45.0%

HEALTH
Health care workers...................4.3%
Fair or poor health............. 11.9% (★)

DIVERSIONS
Stores per 10,000..............82.6 (★)
Restaurants per 10,000.......51.1 (★)

INTERNET
Broadband subscriptions 69.3%
Smartphone access .... 93.3% (★)

PROXIMITY
Major hub miles..............................116
Major or mid-major miles...........116

Belgrade, Montana

Score ....726.4 points
National rank ....202 of 2,084
Percentile...90.35%
West rank...78 of 471
Montana rank ....3 of 19
Closest major hub ....Salt Lake City, 357 air miles

TESTS
1. Character...50.8
2. Stability..83.6
3. Growth..60.3
4. Education..63.9
5. Jobs...64.4
6. Business..59.3
7. Money..62.0
8. Housing...50.5
9. Health..55.5
10. Diversions.....................................67.0
11. Internet...67.3
12. Proximity.......................................41.8

BASIC STATS
Population.................................14,889
Density.......................................1,434.7
Born out of state.......................45.6%
Homes built since 2000...........47.5%
4 or more bedrooms.................22.5%

RACE
Whites...93.0%
Blacks..0.0%
Hispanics.......................................4.5%
Asians..0.0%
Native Americans.......................1.9%
Diversity index..........................13.3%

HOUSEHOLD INCOME LADDER
95th percentile....................$146,980
80th percentile.....................$111,545
60th percentile......................$77,232
50th percentile......................$67,096
40th percentile......................$52,655
20th percentile......................$30,836

HOME VALUE LADDER
75th percentile....................$299,700
50th percentile....................$248,600
25th percentile....................$190,200

CHARACTER
Resilience.......................................22.4%
Short commutes..........................52.2%

STABILITY
Living with two parents...................81.8% (★)
Occupied homes..............................97.3% (★)

GROWTH
Population growth.........................5.1%
Economic growth.....................29.4% (★)

EDUCATION
High school graduates.............93.2%
College graduates......................32.4%

JOBS
MBSA workers..............................32.2%
Private-sector job growth..............25.4% (★)

BUSINESS
Small business growth.....................18.4% (★)
Self-employed workers.................7.5%

MONEY
Median annual earnings.........$45,095
Living in poverty............................8.8%

HOUSING
Home ownership.......................69.5%
Monthly housing costs.............34.5%

HEALTH
Health care workers....................6.8%
Fair or poor health.........................11.2% (★)

DIVERSIONS
Stores per 10,000.............................53.1 (★)
Restaurants per 10,000....................32.1 (★)

INTERNET
Broadband subscriptions.........69.6%
Smartphone access....................83.4%

PROXIMITY
Major hub miles...............................357
Major or mid-major miles............292

Belle Plaine, Minnesota

Score ....*733.9 points*
National rank ....*179 of 2,084*
Percentile...*91.45%*
Midwest rank..*40 of 622*
Minnesota rank ....*10 of 53*
Closest major hub ....*Minneapolis, 34 air miles*

TESTS

1. Character..............................67.6
2. Stability................................61.9
3. Growth.................................47.7
4. Education.............................59.3
5. Jobs.....................................67.1
6. Business...............................50.8
7. Money..................................67.1
8. Housing................................65.8
9. Health...................................70.9
10. Diversions............................18.2
11. Internet 66.7
12. Proximity.............................90.8

BASIC STATS

Population.............................. 6,447
Density 2,491.1
Born out of state 18.3%
Homes built since 2000..........43.2%
4 or more bedrooms 36.9%

RACE

Whites...................................91.5%
Blacks.....................................1.9%
Hispanics 2.9%
Asians.....................................3.3%
Native Americans 0.0%
Diversity index.......................16.0%

HOUSEHOLD INCOME LADDER

95th percentile $166,719
80th percentile $116,938
60th percentile.......................$90,598
50th percentile.......................$78,919
40th percentile.......................$63,193
20th percentile.......................$40,750

HOME VALUE LADDER

75th percentile $251,600
50th percentile $216,000
25th percentile $178,000

CHARACTER

Resilience................................ 42.3% (★)
Short commutes 33.8%

STABILITY

Living with two parents 60.9%
Occupied homes......................93.2%

GROWTH

Population growth......................-1.6%
Economic growth .... 23.9% (★)

EDUCATION

High school graduates 95.1%
College graduates 24.3%

JOBS

MBSA workers........................29.0%
Private-sector job growth ....32.8% (★)

BUSINESS

Small business growth 6.6%
Self-employed workers 10.1%

MONEY

Median annual earnings $49,479
Living in poverty..........................8.1%

HOUSING

Home ownership.............................. 85.7% (★)
Monthly housing costs 32.4%

HEALTH

Health care workers...................11.8%
Fair or poor health.............................. 10.6% (★)

DIVERSIONS

Stores per 10,000......................21.7
Restaurants per 10,000................13.7

INTERNET

Broadband subscriptions 74.7%
Smartphone access 79.4%

PROXIMITY

Major hub miles............................34 (★)
Major or mid-major miles..............................34

Bellingham, Washington

Score ....*743.1 points*
National rank ....*151 of 2,084*
Percentile...*92.80%*
West rank..*57 of 471*
Washington rank.. *5 of 44*
Closest major hub ....*Seattle, 91 air miles*

TESTS
1. Character...63.7
2. Stability...76.3
3. Growth..71.4
4. Education...72.4
5. Jobs..57.7
6. Business...51.2
7. Money..56.3
8. Housing...38.0
9. Health..61.3
10. Diversions.......................................40.6
11. Internet 73.5
12. Proximity...80.7

BASIC STATS
Population.......................................125,076
Density 2,604.6
Born out of state..............................50.5%
Homes built since 2000.....................20.9%
4 or more bedrooms 17.5%

RACE
Whites..79.2%
Blacks...1.2%
Hispanics 9.2%
Asians..5.3%
Native Americans 1.2%
Diversity index................................36.0%

HOUSEHOLD INCOME LADDER
95th percentile......................$194,485
80th percentile......................$113,190
60th percentile........................$73,586
50th percentile........................$58,432
40th percentile........................$46,750
20th percentile........................$23,052

HOME VALUE LADDER
75th percentile......................$490,200
50th percentile......................$359,000
25th percentile......................$261,000

CHARACTER
Resilience..27.4%
Short commutes 62.7%

STABILITY
Living with two parents 72.2%
Occupied homes............................. 96.8% (★)

GROWTH
Population growth................................7.9%
Economic growth............................. 41.6% (★)

EDUCATION
High school graduates 94.6%
College graduates .... 40.9% (★)

JOBS
MBSA workers.....................................37.1%
Private-sector job growth 11.2%

BUSINESS
Small business growth 9.7%
Self-employed workers 8.7%

MONEY
Median annual earnings......................$48,240
Living in poverty................................17.1%

HOUSING
Home ownership................................53.1%
Monthly housing costs...........................34.2%

HEALTH
Health care workers...............................9.8%
Fair or poor health............................. 12.5% (★)

DIVERSIONS
Stores per 10,000..................................36.1
Restaurants per 10,000.......................22.2

INTERNET
Broadband subscriptions .... 79.9% (★)
Smartphone access 82.4%

PROXIMITY
Major hub miles.......................................91
Major or mid-major miles...............................91

Belterra, Texas

Score ....926.4 points
National rank ....3 of 2,084
Percentile...99.90%
South rank ....1 of 745
Texas rank..1 of 173
Closest major hub ....Austin, 19 air miles

TESTS
1. Character................................40.4
2. Stability.................................100.0
3. Growth...................................73.5
4. Education...............................100.0
5. Jobs.......................................100.0
6. Business.................................72.5
7. Money....................................100.0
8. Housing..................................71.9
9. Health....................................40.9
10. Diversions...........................32.4
11. Internet 98.6
12. Proximity.............................96.2

BASIC STATS
Population................................5,335
Density 1,519.1
Born out of state....................58.9%
Homes built since 2000...........90.9%
4 or more bedrooms 68.4%

RACE
Whites.....................................72.7%
Blacks......................................4.3%
Hispanics 12.4%
Asians......................................4.2%
Native Americans 0.0%
Diversity index.......................44.8%

HOUSEHOLD INCOME LADDER
95th percentile ....>$250,000
80th percentile ....>$250,000
60th percentile $173,803
50th percentile $155,917
40th percentile $133,827
20th percentile $74,510

HOME VALUE LADDER
75th percentile $516,300
50th percentile $434,600
25th percentile $358,800

CHARACTER
Resilience......................................25.7%
Short commutes 26.4%

STABILITY
Living with two parents ....93.7% (★)
Occupied homes.................................99.1% (★)

GROWTH
Population growth............................15.7% (★)
Economic growth ....26.8% (★)

EDUCATION
High school graduates ....100.0% (★)
College graduates ....73.3% (★)

JOBS
MBSA workers.....................................60.7% (★)
Private-sector job growth ....29.4% (★)

BUSINESS
Small business growth ....25.3% (★)
Self-employed workers 9.0%

MONEY
Median annual earnings............$116,476 (★)
Living in poverty...................................2.2% (★)

HOUSING
Home ownership...............................89.9% (★)
Monthly housing costs.....................30.2%

HEALTH
Health care workers...............................6.6%
Fair or poor health................................18.0%

DIVERSIONS
Stores per 10,000..................................31.1
Restaurants per 10,000...................18.9

INTERNET
Broadband subscriptions ....94.7% (★)
Smartphone access ....92.1% (★)

PROXIMITY
Major hub miles..19 (★)
Major or mid-major miles........................19 (★)

Bend, Oregon

Score ....*850.8 points*
National rank ....*15 of 2,084*
Percentile..*99.33%*
West rank...*9 of 471*
Oregon rank ....*1 of 45*
Closest major hub ....*Portland, 121 air miles*

TESTS
1. Character......................................72.9
2. Stability.......................................74.8
3. Growth...83.4
4. Education.....................................74.6
5. Jobs...81.2
6. Business.......................................92.6
7. Money 62.5
8. Housing 42.2
9. Health..62.0
10. Diversions...................................54.8
11. Internet 74.3
12. Proximity.....................................75.5

BASIC STATS
Population.....................................101,737
Density 2,561.5
Born out of state 62.0%
Homes built since 2000...................39.8%
4 or more bedrooms 16.0%

RACE
Whites...85.9%
Blacks..0.5%
Hispanics 8.9%
Asians...1.6%
Native Americans 0.5%
Diversity index................................25.3%

HOUSEHOLD INCOME LADDER
95th percentile $234,156
80th percentile $124,291
60th percentile $80,483
50th percentile $66,155
40th percentile $52,736
20th percentile $29,249

HOME VALUE LADDER
75th percentile $522,700
50th percentile $380,400
25th percentile $281,200

CHARACTER
Resilience...29.6%
Short commutes 73.4%

STABILITY
Living with two parents 70.8%
Occupied homes................................96.5%

GROWTH
Population growth............................ 17.2% (★)
Economic growth .... 38.4% (★)

EDUCATION
High school graduates 95.3%
College graduates .... 42.7% (★)

JOBS
MBSA workers.................................... 42.7% (★)
Private-sector job growth .... 29.4% (★)

BUSINESS
Small business growth .... 24.2% (★)
Self-employed workers .... 15.8% (★)

MONEY
Median annual earnings....................$47,495
Living in poverty.............................. 10.6%

HOUSING
Home ownership................................61.0%
Monthly housing costs..........................35.8%

HEALTH
Health care workers................................10.4%
Fair or poor health...............................13.0%

DIVERSIONS
Stores per 10,000 ....44.7
Restaurants per 10,000....................... 27.9 (★)

INTERNET
Broadband subscriptions .... 77.0% (★)
Smartphone access .... 85.1% (★)

PROXIMITY
Major hub miles....................................121
Major or mid-major miles............................121

Big Pine Key, Florida

Score .... *741.0 points*
National rank .... *156 of 2,084*
Percentile...*92.56%*
South rank .... *44 of 745*
Florida rank .... *7 of 63*
Closest major hub ....*Miami, 126 air miles*

TESTS
1. Character.................................34.7
2. Stability...................................46.0
3. Growth.....................................56.0
4. Education.................................65.4
5. Jobs...52.6
6. Business...................................56.5
7. Money......................................66.3
8. Housing....................................64.9
9. Health......................................48.2
10. Diversions................................98.5
11. Internet...................................77.3
12. Proximity.................................74.6

BASIC STATS
Population................................. 8,710
Density 1,142.9
Born out of state 79.7%
Homes built since 2000............. 16.7%
4 or more bedrooms 4.5%

RACE
Whites.......................................84.0%
Blacks..2.5%
Hispanics 12.2%
Asians..0.6%
Native Americans 0.1%
Diversity index........................... 27.9%

HOUSEHOLD INCOME LADDER
95th percentile .... >$250,000
80th percentile $138,750
60th percentile $90,192
50th percentile $75,220
40th percentile $54,972
20th percentile $32,571

HOME VALUE LADDER
75th percentile $596,900
50th percentile $392,900
25th percentile $295,100

CHARACTER
Resilience..................................15.8%
Short commutes 40.2%

STABILITY
Living with two parents 57.6%
Occupied homes.......................85.9%

GROWTH
Population growth....................7.7%
Economic growth 16.1%

EDUCATION
High school graduates 94.2%
College graduates 32.9%

JOBS
MBSA workers..........................34.8%
Private-sector job growth 8.1%

BUSINESS
Small business growth 5.8%
Self-employed workers .... 12.7% (★)

MONEY
Median annual earnings.......................$50,148
Living in poverty.............................9.4%

HOUSING
Home ownership......................73.2%
Monthly housing costs 25.3%

HEALTH
Health care workers...................8.0%
Fair or poor health.....................16.4%

DIVERSIONS
Stores per 10,000 .... 83.5 (★)
Restaurants per 10,000...................... 50.3 (★)

INTERNET
Broadband subscriptions .... 77.8% (★)
Smartphone access .... 87.4% (★)

PROXIMITY
Major hub miles................................126
Major or mid-major miles...........................126

Birch Bay, Washington

Score ....*754.4 points*
National rank ....*121 of 2,084*
Percentile..*94.24%*
West rank..*47 of 471*
Washington rank...*4 of 44*
Closest major hub ....*Seattle, 105 air miles*

TESTS
1. Character...52.5
2. Stability...68.9
3. Growth...77.1
4. Education..60.3
5. Jobs..53.3
6. Business..59.2
7. Money..73.4
8. Housing...67.2
9. Health..51.7
10. Diversions...40.6
11. Internet...71.9
12. Proximity...78.3

BASIC STATS
Population...14,075
Density 1,123.6
Born out of state.....................................61.3%
Homes built since 2000...........................32.3%
4 or more bedrooms 14.3%

RACE
Whites...81.5%
Blacks...0.7%
Hispanics 6.0%
Asians...6.1%
Native Americans 0.8%
Diversity index...32.6%

HOUSEHOLD INCOME LADDER
95th percentile $245,444
80th percentile $117,641
60th percentile $76,762
50th percentile $66,330
40th percentile $54,801
20th percentile $26,677

HOME VALUE LADDER
75th percentile $412,000
50th percentile $287,700
25th percentile $214,600

CHARACTER
Resilience..27.4%
Short commutes 43.2%

STABILITY
Living with two parents 67.4%
Occupied homes......................................94.6%

GROWTH
Population growth............................ 12.0% (★)
Economic growth.............................. 41.6% (★)

EDUCATION
High school graduates 92.7%
College graduates 28.6%

JOBS
MBSA workers...33.0%
Private-sector job growth 11.2%

BUSINESS
Small business growth 9.7%
Self-employed workers .... 11.8% (★)

MONEY
Median annual earnings...............$59,322 (★)
Living in poverty......................................11.4%

HOUSING
Home ownership.............................. 77.6% (★)
Monthly housing costs............................26.2%

HEALTH
Health care workers...................................6.4%
Fair or poor health............................ 12.5% (★)

DIVERSIONS
Stores per 10,000.....................................36.1
Restaurants per 10,000............................22.2

INTERNET
Broadband subscriptions .... 77.2% (★)
Smartphone access 82.7%

PROXIMITY
Major hub miles..105
Major or mid-major miles............................105

Bishop, California

Score ....*734.4 points*
National rank ....*177 of 2,084*
Percentile..*91.55%*
West rank...*69 of 471*
California rank ....*13 of 145*
Closest major hub ....*Sacramento, 181 air miles*

TESTS
1. Character...67.6
2. Stability...71.4
3. Growth...34.9
4. Education..64.4
5. Jobs..58.0
6. Business..37.1
7. Money..79.0
8. Housing...66.1
9. Health..62.3
10. Diversions...57.6
11. Internet 59.3
12. Proximity...76.7

BASIC STATS
Population.. 9,394
Density 2,208.3
Born out of state 30.6%
Homes built since 2000...........................6.4%
4 or more bedrooms 8.3%

RACE
Whites..62.9%
Blacks...0.4%
Hispanics 19.8%
Asians...2.4%
Native Americans 12.2%
Diversity index.....................................54.9%

HOUSEHOLD INCOME LADDER
95th percentile $176,038
80th percentile $103,386
60th percentile $71,712
50th percentile $60,979
40th percentile $45,465
20th percentile $29,148

HOME VALUE LADDER
75th percentile $420,700
50th percentile $303,000
25th percentile $56,400

CHARACTER
Resilience..22.4%
Short commutes .... 81.4% (★)

STABILITY
Living with two parents 73.4%
Occupied homes....................................93.8%

GROWTH
Population growth.................................-5.8%
Economic growth 12.2%

EDUCATION
High school graduates 92.9%
College graduates 33.4%

JOBS
MBSA workers...................................... 42.1% (★)
Private-sector job growth 5.1%

BUSINESS
Small business growth ....-3.9%
Self-employed workers 10.1%

MONEY
Median annual earnings...............$60,350 (★)
Living in poverty....................................7.1% (★)

HOUSING
Home ownership.....................................63.2%
Monthly housing costs.................... 18.0% (★)

HEALTH
Health care workers 11.7%
Fair or poor health.................................14.6%

DIVERSIONS
Stores per 10,000....................................47.4 (★)
Restaurants per 10,000........................28.4 (★)

INTERNET
Broadband subscriptions 70.1%
Smartphone access 75.4%

PROXIMITY
Major hub miles...181
Major or mid-major miles............................. 84

Boerne, Texas

Score ....*822.1 points*
National rank ....*29 of 2,084*
Percentile...*98.66%*
South rank ....*10 of 745*
Texas rank..*3 of 173*
Closest major hub ....*San Antonio, 24 air miles*

TESTS
1. Character..................59.0
2. Stability...................71.0
3. Growth.....................81.4
4. Education..................70.0
5. Jobs..........................91.4
6. Business...................95.9
7. Money......................66.3
8. Housing....................35.6
9. Health.......................51.5
10. Diversions...............37.9
11. Internet 69.6
12. Proximity................92.5

BASIC STATS
Population........................14,064
Density 2,037.1
Born out of state.................38.0%
Homes built since 2000...........49.9%
4 or more bedrooms 17.1%

RACE
Whites................................69.4%
Blacks...................................1.0%
Hispanics 26.6%
Asians..................................0.6%
Native Americans 0.4%
Diversity index....................44.7%

HOUSEHOLD INCOME LADDER
95th percentile $222,638
80th percentile $134,234
60th percentile.......................$81,411
50th percentile.......................$69,649
40th percentile.......................$57,815
20th percentile.......................$30,115

HOME VALUE LADDER
75th percentile $377,700
50th percentile $280,100
25th percentile $217,200

CHARACTER
Resilience................................27.8%
Short commutes 53.6%

STABILITY
Living with two parents 65.0%
Occupied homes.......................96.6%

GROWTH
Population growth............17.6% (★)
Economic growth ....34.7% (★)

EDUCATION
High school graduates 93.7%
College graduates ....39.2% (★)

JOBS
MBSA workers.......................42.0% (★)
Private-sector job growth ....40.1% (★)

BUSINESS
Small business growth ....27.1% (★)
Self-employed workers ....16.6% (★)

MONEY
Median annual earnings.......................$47,389
Living in poverty................................6.9% (★)

HOUSING
Home ownership.......................50.9%
Monthly housing costs............................34.8%

HEALTH
Health care workers................................7.8%
Fair or poor health.................................14.5%

DIVERSIONS
Stores per 10,000.............................35.3
Restaurants per 10,000.........................20.6

INTERNET
Broadband subscriptions 70.1%
Smartphone access ....85.3% (★)

PROXIMITY
Major hub miles.................................24 (★)
Major or mid-major miles.........................24 (★)

Boulder, Colorado

Score ....*809.1 points*
National rank ....*37 of 2,084*
Percentile..*98.27%*
West rank...*20 of 471*
Colorado rank ....*10 of 47*
Closest major hub ....*Denver, 27 air miles*

TESTS
1. Character...47.5
2. Stability...79.5
3. Growth...56.2
4. Education..96.6
5. Jobs...82.8
6. Business..55.6
7. Money..67.6
8. Housing...40.9
9. Health..57.2
10. Diversions..47.5
11. Internet 85.7
12. Proximity..92.0

BASIC STATS
Population......................................123,965
Density 3,820.4
Born out of state 73.0%
Homes built since 2000...........................12.3%
4 or more bedrooms 24.5%

RACE
Whites..80.7%
Blacks...1.0%
Hispanics 9.7%
Asians..5.2%
Native Americans 0.1%
Diversity index.................................33.5%

HOUSEHOLD INCOME LADDER
95th percentile ....>$250,000
80th percentile $173,123
60th percentile.....................................$95,994
50th percentile.....................................$72,419
40th percentile.....................................$54,659
20th percentile.....................................$25,329

HOME VALUE LADDER
75th percentile......................................$953,800
50th percentile......................................$673,700
25th percentile......................................$435,200

CHARACTER
Resilience...16.1%
Short commutes 61.6%

STABILITY
Living with two parents ....77.9% (★)
Occupied homes.......................................96.5%

GROWTH
Population growth................................3.3%
Economic growth ....26.7% (★)

EDUCATION
High school graduates ....96.9% (★)
College graduates ....76.6% (★)

JOBS
MBSA workers.....................................58.7% (★)
Private-sector job growth 11.6%

BUSINESS
Small business growth 9.5%
Self-employed workers 10.5%

MONEY
Median annual earnings...............$61,500 (★)
Living in poverty...18.8%

HOUSING
Home ownership......................................52.3%
Monthly housing costs.............................31.4%

HEALTH
Health care workers....................................7.7%
Fair or poor health............................ 11.6% (★)

DIVERSIONS
Stores per 10,000..............................36.3
Restaurants per 10,000........................27.4 (★)

INTERNET
Broadband subscriptions ....84.9% (★)
Smartphone access ....89.0% (★)

PROXIMITY
Major hub miles...27 (★)
Major or mid-major miles................................ 27

Bozeman, Montana

Score .... *774.5 points*
National rank .... *89 of 2,084*
Percentile *95.78%*
West rank .... *37 of 471*
Montana rank .... *2 of 19*
Closest major hub .... *Salt Lake City, 351 air miles*

TESTS
1. Character.................................67.5
2. Stability..................................75.2
3. Growth...................................70.2
4. Education...............................92.2
5. Jobs.......................................76.9
6. Business.................................70.8
7. Money....................................51.7
8. Housing..................................29.5
9. Health....................................54.1
10. Diversions.............................67.0
11. Internet.................................77.5
12. Proximity..............................41.9

BASIC STATS
Population..............................49,880
Density..................................2,560.4
Born out of state......................62.9%
Homes built since 2000............34.1%
4 or more bedrooms.................19.1%

RACE
Whites.......................................89.3%
Blacks..0.7%
Hispanics...................................4.1%
Asians..2.2%
Native Americans......................0.7%
Diversity index.........................19.9%

HOUSEHOLD INCOME LADDER
95th percentile.....................$204,547
80th percentile.....................$117,632
60th percentile.......................$69,625
50th percentile.......................$56,002
40th percentile.......................$44,327
20th percentile.......................$23,710

HOME VALUE LADDER
75th percentile.....................$480,100
50th percentile.....................$361,600
25th percentile.....................$265,200

CHARACTER
Resilience..................................22.4%
Short commutes................... 81.2% (★)

STABILITY
Living with two parents.........74.8%
Occupied homes.......................95.3%

GROWTH
Population growth............. 12.3% (★)
Economic growth................ 29.4% (★)

EDUCATION
High school graduates..................... 98.0% (★)
College graduates..................... 57.4% (★)

JOBS
MBSA workers........................ 42.7% (★)
Private-sector job growth.............. 25.4% (★)

BUSINESS
Small business growth.................... 18.4% (★)
Self-employed workers.................... 11.9% (★)

MONEY
Median annual earnings.......................$42,298
Living in poverty............................ 15.9%

HOUSING
Home ownership.............................. 47.3%
Monthly housing costs........................... 37.4%

HEALTH
Health care workers..................................6.3%
Fair or poor health............................ 11.2% (★)

DIVERSIONS
Stores per 10,000............................ 53.1 (★)
Restaurants per 10,000....................... 32.1 (★)

INTERNET
Broadband subscriptions............... 78.3% (★)
Smartphone access........................... 87.3% (★)

PROXIMITY
Major hub miles................................... 351
Major or mid-major miles............................294

Breckenridge, Colorado

Score ....828.6 points
National rank ....25 of 2,084
Percentile..98.85%
West rank... 12 of 471
Colorado rank .... 5 of 47
Closest major hub ....Denver, 60 air miles

TESTS
1. Character.................................75.7
2. Stability..................................94.9
3. Growth...................................65.5
4. Education...............................87.0
5. Jobs.......................................51.6
6. Business.................................54.1
7. Money....................................56.9
8. Housing..................................24.6
9. Health....................................54.7
10. Diversions............................99.5
11. Internet 77.9
12. Proximity..............................86.2

BASIC STATS
Population.............................. 8,061
Density 1,244.4
Born out of state 72.3%
Homes built since 2000.............20.5%
4 or more bedrooms 18.6%

RACE
Whites......................................93.8%
Blacks..0.1%
Hispanics 4.1%
Asians..0.3%
Native Americans 0.0%
Diversity index........................11.8%

HOUSEHOLD INCOME LADDER
95th percentile $203,594
80th percentile $139,417
60th percentile $108,623
50th percentile $90,625
40th percentile $73,607
20th percentile $36,846

HOME VALUE LADDER
75th percentile $750,300
50th percentile $504,700
25th percentile $322,900

CHARACTER
Resilience................................30.2%
Short commutes 76.7%

STABILITY
Living with two parents ....90.4% (★)
Occupied homes.............................98.1% (★)

GROWTH
Population growth..............................8.1%
Economic growth ....31.3% (★)

EDUCATION
High school graduates ....97.5% (★)
College graduates ....53.9% (★)

JOBS
MBSA workers.......................27.7%
Private-sector job growth 16.0%

BUSINESS
Small business growth 5.8%
Self-employed workers ....11.8% (★)

MONEY
Median annual earnings........................$40,073
Living in poverty...................................8.9%

HOUSING
Home ownership......................58.0%
Monthly housing costs.............51.6%

HEALTH
Health care workers..................6.3%
Fair or poor health............................10.9% (★)

DIVERSIONS
Stores per 10,000.............................99.9 (★)
Restaurants per 10,000.......................72.0 (★)

INTERNET
Broadband subscriptions 72.3%
Smartphone access ....91.7% (★)

PROXIMITY
Major hub miles................................. 60
Major or mid-major miles................................ 60

Breese, Illinois

Score .... *735.9 points*
National rank .... *168 of 2,084*
Percentile..*91.98%*
Midwest rank...*36 of 622*
Illinois rank.. *2 of 79*
Closest major hub ....*St. Louis, 44 air miles*

TESTS
1. Character...61.9
2. Stability..74.8
3. Growth..42.2
4. Education..65.7
5. Jobs...57.8
6. Business..24.5
7. Money...66.6
8. Housing...70.4
9. Health...80.9
10. Diversions.....................................41.6
11. Internet 60.5
12. Proximity.......................................89.0

BASIC STATS
Population....................................... 6,140
Density 1,339.7
Born out of state 17.1%
Homes built since 2000............................ 24.2%
4 or more bedrooms 16.8%

RACE
Whites..95.3%
Blacks..0.0%
Hispanics 1.9%
Asians..1.4%
Native Americans 0.1%
Diversity index..................................9.1%

HOUSEHOLD INCOME LADDER
95th percentile $164,230
80th percentile $113,192
60th percentile $76,696
50th percentile $68,232
40th percentile $54,156
20th percentile $24,840

HOME VALUE LADDER
75th percentile $196,600
50th percentile $150,800
25th percentile $109,100

CHARACTER
Resilience.............................. 34.6% (★)
Short commutes 42.3%

STABILITY
Living with two parents 70.9%
Occupied homes.................................... 96.5%

GROWTH
Population growth...............................5.8%
Economic growth ....-2.5%

EDUCATION
High school graduates .... 99.0% (★)
College graduates 27.0%

JOBS
MBSA workers...................................... 43.5% (★)
Private-sector job growth 3.1%

BUSINESS
Small business growth ....-2.2%
Self-employed workers 4.4%

MONEY
Median annual earnings.....................$46,123
Living in poverty...................................5.4% (★)

HOUSING
Home ownership.............................. 80.4% (★)
Monthly housing costs............................25.4%

HEALTH
Health care workers.......................... 15.9% (★)
Fair or poor health.....................................13.0%

DIVERSIONS
Stores per 10,000......................................35.8
Restaurants per 10,000................................23.1

INTERNET
Broadband subscriptions 74.0%
Smartphone access 73.9%

PROXIMITY
Major hub miles...................................... 44
Major or mid-major mileage 44

Brunswick, Maine

Score ....733.9 points
National rank .... 179 of 2,084
Percentile...91.45%
East rank.. 26 of 246
Maine rank .... 2 of 9
Closest major hub ....Boston, 123 air miles

TESTS

1. Character................................71.8
2. Stability..................................66.4
3. Growth...................................47.6
4. Education...............................75.0
5. Jobs.......................................61.7
6. Business.................................42.7
7. Money....................................62.1
8. Housing..................................51.9
9. Health....................................66.4
10. Diversions.............................51.4
11. Internet 61.8
12. Proximity...............................75.1

BASIC STATS

Population...............................29,096
Density 1,182.8
Born out of state 50.6%
Homes built since 2000.............. 11.2%
4 or more bedrooms 15.3%

RACE

Whites......................................90.0%
Blacks..1.6%
Hispanics 3.1%
Asians..2.1%
Native Americans 0.0%
Diversity index......................... 18.7%

HOUSEHOLD INCOME LADDER

95th percentile $193,694
80th percentile $108,752
60th percentile $70,002
50th percentile $55,679
40th percentile $44,105
20th percentile $25,668

HOME VALUE LADDER

75th percentile $285,800
50th percentile $199,800
25th percentile $137,100

CHARACTER

Resilience..................................33.7%
Short commutes 61.7%

STABILITY

Living with two parents 65.0%
Occupied homes........................94.1%

GROWTH

Population growth.......................3.4%
Economic growth 12.0%

EDUCATION

High school graduates 94.5%
College graduates .... 44.3% (★)

JOBS

MBSA workers...................... 43.4% (★)
Private-sector job growth 7.8%

BUSINESS

Small business growth 6.0%
Self-employed workers 7.3%

MONEY

Median annual earnings.......$48,439
Living in poverty....................... 11.8%

HOUSING

Home ownership......................63.3%
Monthly housing costs 29.5%

HEALTH

Health care workers................. 10.0%
Fair or poor health............. 10.3% (★)

DIVERSIONS

Stores per 10,000......................43.5
Restaurants per 10,000....... 26.0 (★)

INTERNET

Broadband subscriptions 74.8%
Smartphone access 74.6%

PROXIMITY

Major hub miles 123
Major or mid-major miles...........123

Brunswick, Maryland

Score ....*726.3 points*
National rank ....*203 of 2,084*
Percentile...*90.30%*
East rank...*28 of 246*
Maryland rank .... *6 of 23*
Closest major hub .... *Washington, 37 air miles*

TESTS
1. Character...34.3
2. Stability...76.8
3. Growth..56.6
4. Education..71.0
5. Jobs..65.9
6. Business..32.9
7. Money..80.2
8. Housing..60.6
9. Health...54.3
10. Diversions...28.7
11. Internet 74.8
12. Proximity...90.2

BASIC STATS
Population.. 9,760
Density 1,465.5
Born out of state.....................................51.8%
Homes built since 2000...........................30.0%
4 or more bedrooms 37.5%

RACE
Whites..80.2%
Blacks..5.9%
Hispanics 7.5%
Asians...1.5%
Native Americans 0.0%
Diversity index..34.5%

HOUSEHOLD INCOME LADDER
95th percentile ....>$250,000
80th percentile $162,633
60th percentile $111,054
50th percentile $87,385
40th percentile $74,550
20th percentile $41,938

HOME VALUE LADDER
75th percentile $383,300
50th percentile $262,000
25th percentile $204,900

CHARACTER
Resilience...25.6%
Short commutes 16.0%

STABILITY
Living with two parents 75.8%
Occupied homes......................................95.8%

GROWTH
Population growth...............................9.8% (★)
Economic growth 12.3%

EDUCATION
High school graduates 94.0%
College graduates .... 40.0% (★)

JOBS
MBSA workers...................................... 43.6% (★)
Private-sector job growth 12.6%

BUSINESS
Small business growth 7.8%
Self-employed workers 2.6%

MONEY
Median annual earnings...............$61,607 (★)
Living in poverty...................................7.1% (★)

HOUSING
Home ownership.............................. 80.0% (★)
Monthly housing costs 33.0%

HEALTH
Health care workers..................................6.5%
Fair or poor health............................. 11.4% (★)

DIVERSIONS
Stores per 10,000 ....27.4
Restaurants per 10,000 ....18.3

INTERNET
Broadband subscriptions .... 78.2% (★)
Smartphone access 84.8%

PROXIMITY
Major hub miles.. 37
Major or mid-major miles............................. 37

Buckhead (Bryan County), Georgia

Score ....*865.2 points*
National rank ....*10 of 2,084*
Percentile..*99.57%*
South rank ....*3 of 745*
Georgia rank ....*1 of 65*
Closest major hub ....*Jacksonville, 114 air miles*

TESTS
1. Character....................................58.6
2. Stability......................................89.4
3. Growth.......................................46.1
4. Education...................................90.8
5. Jobs..98.2
6. Business.....................................67.9
7. Money..95.0
8. Housing......................................64.4
9. Health..53.1
10. Diversions................................27.7
11. Internet....................................95.8
12. Proximity..................................78.2

BASIC STATS
Population................................ 5,434
Density 696.3
Born out of state 68.2%
Homes built since 2000.............55.6%
4 or more bedrooms 67.5%

RACE
Whites..81.6%
Blacks 10.5%
Hispanics 1.9%
Asians...1.6%
Native Americans 0.0%
Diversity index..........................32.1%

HOUSEHOLD INCOME LADDER
95th percentile......................>$250,000
80th percentile.......................$179,649
60th percentile.......................$136,086
50th percentile.......................$119,444
40th percentile.......................$108,097
20th percentile.........................$66,867

HOME VALUE LADDER
75th percentile.......................$399,300
50th percentile.......................$332,800
25th percentile.......................$269,900

CHARACTER
Resilience.............................. 36.7% (★)
Short commutes 31.6%

STABILITY
Living with two parents .... 90.5% (★)
Occupied homes............................ 96.1%

GROWTH
Population growth.............................-4.2%
Economic growth .... 27.3% (★)

EDUCATION
High school graduates .... 96.7% (★)
College graduates .... 58.3% (★)

JOBS
MBSA workers................................ 53.6% (★)
Private-sector job growth .... 32.9% (★)

BUSINESS
Small business growth .... 15.4% (★)
Self-employed workers .... 12.3% (★)

MONEY
Median annual earnings...............$69,429 (★)
Living in poverty..................................3.2% (★)

HOUSING
Home ownership............................. 84.5% (★)
Monthly housing costs 32.8%

HEALTH
Health care workers.............................9.3%
Fair or poor health................................15.8%

DIVERSIONS
Stores per 10,000..............................26.8
Restaurants per 10,000................17.9

INTERNET
Broadband subscriptions .... 89.8% (★)
Smartphone access .... 92.8% (★)

PROXIMITY
Major hub miles................................114
Major or mid-major miles............................102

Buffalo, Minnesota

Score ....746.9 points
National rank .... 139 of 2,084
Percentile...93.37%
Midwest rank.. 28 of 622
Minnesota rank .... 5 of 53
Closest major hub ....Minneapolis, 32 air miles

TESTS
1. Character...72.8
2. Stability...75.9
3. Growth..46.5
4. Education...66.9
5. Jobs..61.9
6. Business...49.5
7. Money...71.4
8. Housing..57.9
9. Health..62.5
10. Diversions......................................27.0
11. Internet 63.5
12. Proximity..91.1

BASIC STATS
Population...................................16,619
Density 1,998.2
Born out of state 22.1%
Homes built since 2000............34.5%
4 or more bedrooms 32.3%

RACE
Whites...96.6%
Blacks..0.6%
Hispanics 1.1%
Asians..0.8%
Native Americans 0.1%
Diversity index.............................6.7%

HOUSEHOLD INCOME LADDER
95th percentile $216,402
80th percentile $120,812
60th percentile $87,863
50th percentile $74,812
40th percentile $55,925
20th percentile $34,293

HOME VALUE LADDER
75th percentile $264,600
50th percentile $203,500
25th percentile $158,500

CHARACTER
Resilience............................... 42.5% (★)
Short commutes 42.4%

STABILITY
Living with two parents .... 76.1% (★)
Occupied homes............................95.2%

GROWTH
Population growth.........................2.5%
Economic growth 12.4%

EDUCATION
High school graduates .... 96.5% (★)
College graduates 31.7%

JOBS
MBSA workers...............................36.7%
Private-sector job growth 16.7%

BUSINESS
Small business growth 9.2%
Self-employed workers 8.3%

MONEY
Median annual earnings.......................$52,175
Living in poverty.....................6.6% (★)

HOUSING
Home ownership.........................72.1%
Monthly housing costs............................30.2%

HEALTH
Health care workers........................9.0%
Fair or poor health............................. 10.8% (★)

DIVERSIONS
Stores per 10,000...............................32.1
Restaurants per 10,000....................14.1

INTERNET
Broadband subscriptions 69.3%
Smartphone access 80.0%

PROXIMITY
Major hub miles...........................32 (★)
Major or mid-major miles..............................32

Burlington, Vermont

Score ....735.3 points
National rank ....171 of 2,084
Percentile...91.84%
East rank.. 24 of 246
Vermont rank .... 1 of 9
Closest major hub ....Boston, 177 air miles

TESTS

1. Character..................................69.0
2. Stability....................................73.8
3. Growth......................................42.8
4. Education.................................82.8
5. Jobs...63.7
6. Business...................................39.7
7. Money......................................61.9
8. Housing...................................35.3
9. Health......................................68.1
10. Diversions.............................55.3
11. Internet 70.9
12. Proximity...............................72.0

BASIC STATS

Population.............................112,751
Density 1,825.6
Born out of state 58.9%
Homes built since 2000 .... 18.2%
4 or more bedrooms 16.1%

RACE

Whites...............................85.6%
Blacks.................................3.3%
Hispanics 3.0%
Asians................................5.2%
Native Americans 0.2%
Diversity index......................26.2%

HOUSEHOLD INCOME LADDER

95th percentile $228,188
80th percentile $126,511
60th percentile.......................$81,247
50th percentile.......................$64,861
40th percentile.......................$52,177
20th percentile.......................$25,669

HOME VALUE LADDER

75th percentile $380,100
50th percentile $287,300
25th percentile $216,600

CHARACTER

Resilience..............................33.8%
Short commutes 56.6%

STABILITY

Living with two parents 67.2%
Occupied homes.................... 97.3% (★)

GROWTH

Population growth.....................2.2%
Economic growth.......................6.9%

EDUCATION

High school graduates 94.0%
College graduates .... 54.4% (★)

JOBS

MBSA workers...................... 48.4% (★)
Private-sector job growth 3.8%

BUSINESS

Small business growth 2.9%
Self-employed workers 7.7%

MONEY

Median annual earnings.......................$51,813
Living in poverty.....................15.2%

HOUSING

Home ownership......................53.3%
Monthly housing costs 36.5%

HEALTH

Health care workers.................. 10.3%
Fair or poor health..................9.9% (★)

DIVERSIONS

Stores per 10,000 .... 49.6 (★)
Restaurants per 10,000...............25.2

INTERNET

Broadband subscriptions .... 77.9% (★)
Smartphone access 81.2%

PROXIMITY

Major hub miles.............................177
Major or mid-major miles...........................124

Byron, Minnesota

Score ....*832.8 points*
National rank ....*24 of 2,084*
Percentile...*98.90%*
Midwest rank...*2 of 622*
Minnesota rank ....*1 of 53*
Closest major hub ....*Minneapolis, 72 air miles*

TESTS
1. Character..67.8
2. Stability...78.0
3. Growth...47.5
4. Education...77.8
5. Jobs...69.4
6. Business...36.9
7. Money...80.7
8. Housing...73.2
9. Health...99.3
10. Diversions..35.7
11. Internet...82.4
12. Proximity..84.1

BASIC STATS
Population.. 5,004
Density 2,110.5
Born out of state 28.9%
Homes built since 2000...........................40.1%
4 or more bedrooms 55.2%

RACE
Whites..94.0%
Blacks..0.0%
Hispanics...2.2%
Asians...2.6%
Native Americans 0.0%
Diversity index....................................11.5%

HOUSEHOLD INCOME LADDER
95th percentile $219,734
80th percentile $150,077
60th percentile $108,500
50th percentile...............................$92,903
40th percentile...............................$70,950
20th percentile...............................$47,863

HOME VALUE LADDER
75th percentile $285,300
50th percentile $211,400
25th percentile $163,000

CHARACTER
Resilience.. 34.9% (★)
Short commutes 51.8%

STABILITY
Living with two parents .... 77.0% (★)
Occupied homes...96.0%

GROWTH
Population growth..............................0.8%
Economic growth 18.0%

EDUCATION
High school graduates .... 97.1% (★)
College graduates .... 44.3% (★)

JOBS
MBSA workers..................................... 49.6% (★)
Private-sector job growth 9.0%

BUSINESS
Small business growth 2.7%
Self-employed workers 6.7%

MONEY
Median annual earnings...............$55,484 (★)
Living in poverty....................................0.9% (★)

HOUSING
Home ownership............................. 87.6% (★)
Monthly housing costs............................27.7%

HEALTH
Health care workers.......................... 19.7% (★)
Fair or poor health................................10.0% (★)

DIVERSIONS
Stores per 10,000................................35.8
Restaurants per 10,000................................18.6

INTERNET
Broadband subscriptions .... 80.5% (★)
Smartphone access .... 90.2% (★)

PROXIMITY
Major hub miles 72
Major or mid-major miles............................ 72

Cambria, California

Score ....*727.0 points*
National rank ....*198 of 2,084*
Percentile...*90.54%*
West rank... *77 of 471*
California rank .... *16 of 145*
Closest major hub ....*San Jose, 131 air miles*

TESTS
1. Character................................46.1
2. Stability..................................87.7
3. Growth...................................26.9
4. Education...............................61.5
5. Jobs......................................58.7
6. Business.................................77.4
7. Money....................................68.3
8. Housing..................................53.7
9. Health....................................51.4
10. Diversions.............................51.0
11. Internet.................................68.4
12. Proximity...............................75.9

BASIC STATS
Population.............................. 5,378
Density.................................1,506.9
Born out of state.......................40.3%
Homes built since 2000............10.3%
4 or more bedrooms..................10.7%

RACE
Whites......................................78.2%
Blacks..0.6%
Hispanics..................................17.9%
Asians...3.0%
Native Americans.......................0.0%
Diversity index..........................35.5%

HOUSEHOLD INCOME LADDER
95th percentile.......................$248,604
80th percentile.......................$124,857
60th percentile........................$90,264
50th percentile........................$71,029
40th percentile........................$55,765
20th percentile........................$33,467

HOME VALUE LADDER
75th percentile........................$894,600
50th percentile........................$663,700
25th percentile........................$497,500

CHARACTER
Resilience..................................16.3%
Short commutes.........................58.7%

STABILITY
Living with two parents.................. 92.7% (★)
Occupied homes........................94.7%

GROWTH
Population growth.....................-12.7%
Economic growth......................14.9%

EDUCATION
High school graduates.............89.5%
College graduates....................34.3%

JOBS
MBSA workers............................40.2%
Private-sector job growth.............8.4%

BUSINESS
Small business growth..................8.2%
Self-employed workers.................. 23.3% (★)

MONEY
Median annual earnings......................$51,932
Living in poverty..........................9.3%

HOUSING
Home ownership............................... 76.3% (★)
Monthly housing costs.............36.2%

HEALTH
Health care workers.......................6.8%
Fair or poor health.........................13.2%

DIVERSIONS
Stores per 10,000.......................39.4
Restaurants per 10,000.........................28.2 (★)

INTERNET
Broadband subscriptions................ 82.7% (★)
Smartphone access......................75.6%

PROXIMITY
Major hub miles............................. 131
Major or mid-major miles..............113

Canyon Lake, Texas

Score ....*749.8 points*
National rank .... *133 of 2,084*
Percentile...*93.66%*
South rank .... *39 of 745*
Texas rank.. *12 of 173*
Closest major hub ....*San Antonio, 27 air miles*

TESTS
1. Character................41.2
2. Stability....................57.2
3. Growth......................57.5
4. Education.................57.3
5. Jobs...........................78.4
6. Business....................70.5
7. Money.......................60.7
8. Housing....................77.6
9. Health.......................55.5
10. Diversions................33.9
11. Internet 68.0
12. Proximity.................92.0

BASIC STATS
Population............................... 5,440
Density 832.4
Born out of state 45.0%
Homes built since 2000...........19.1%
4 or more bedrooms 12.7%

RACE
Whites...................................75.5%
Blacks 0.0%
Hispanics 22.4%
Asians.....................................0.2%
Native Americans 0.2%
Diversity index.....................38.0%

HOUSEHOLD INCOME LADDER
95th percentile $209,924
80th percentile $115,304
60th percentile $73,528
50th percentile $64,073
40th percentile $46,121
20th percentile $24,441

HOME VALUE LADDER
75th percentile $290,500
50th percentile $158,200
25th percentile $68,900

CHARACTER
Resilience................................26.4%
Short commutes 26.0%

STABILITY
Living with two parents 53.6%
Occupied homes.....................93.3%

GROWTH
Population growth......................6.5%
Economic growth 21.6%

EDUCATION
High school graduates 91.8%
College graduates 26.2%

JOBS
MBSA workers...........................36.2%
Private-sector job growth ....35.2% (★)

BUSINESS
Small business growth ....23.6% (★)
Self-employed workers 9.2%

MONEY
Median annual earnings.......................$50,523
Living in poverty.........................15.1%

HOUSING
Home ownership.................80.7% (★)
Monthly housing costs.............20.3%

HEALTH
Health care workers....................9.7%
Fair or poor health........................15.2%

DIVERSIONS
Stores per 10,000..........................30.2
Restaurants per 10,000..................20.6

INTERNET
Broadband subscriptions 72.1%
Smartphone access 82.4%

PROXIMITY
Major hub miles ....27 (★)
Major or mid-major miles.............................27

Carroll, Iowa

Score ....*760.8 points*
National rank .... *108 of 2,084*
Percentile...*94.86%*
Midwest rank.. *19 of 622*
Iowa rank... *5 of 55*
Closest major hub .... *Kansas City, 210 air miles*

TESTS
1. Character...99.9
2. Stability...63.4
3. Growth...40.1
4. Education...66.3
5. Jobs..39.6
6. Business..60.9
7. Money..60.3
8. Housing...66.8
9. Health..63.8
10. Diversions..70.8
11. Internet...52.1
12. Proximity...76.8

BASIC STATS
Population.. 9,794
Density...2,122.7
Born out of state.................................... 19.2%
Homes built since 2000...........................11.2%
4 or more bedrooms................................27.2%

RACE
Whites..95.3%
Blacks..0.2%
Hispanics..4.1%
Asians..0.1%
Native Americans...................................0.0%
Diversity index.......................................9.0%

HOUSEHOLD INCOME LADDER
95th percentile...................................$169,272
80th percentile...................................$104,750
60th percentile.....................................$68,034
50th percentile.....................................$46,972
40th percentile.....................................$35,532
20th percentile.....................................$22,903

HOME VALUE LADDER
75th percentile...................................$202,700
50th percentile...................................$147,800
25th percentile.....................................$98,800

CHARACTER
Resilience... 39.4% (★)
Short commutes .... 88.2% (★)

STABILITY
Living with two parents.........................66.7%
Occupied homes......................................91.9%

GROWTH
Population growth................................-0.7%
Economic growth....................................9.1%

EDUCATION
High school graduates .... 96.5% (★)
College graduates 31.0%

JOBS
MBSA workers..30.7%
Private-sector job growth........................-2.0%

BUSINESS
Small business growth...............................0.2%
Self-employed workers................... 17.2% (★)

MONEY
Median annual earnings........................$44,230
Living in poverty.......................................9.6%

HOUSING
Home ownership......................................68.6%
Monthly housing costs............................20.8%

HEALTH
Health care workers............................... 10.4%
Fair or poor health............................ 12.1% (★)

DIVERSIONS
Stores per 10,000....................................69.0 (★)
Restaurants per 10,000.........................25.3 (★)

INTERNET
Broadband subscriptions 66.5%
Smartphone access 70.9%

PROXIMITY
Major hub miles...210
Major or mid-major miles................................ 70

Cedar City, Utah

Score .... *737.6 points*
National rank .... *163 of 2,084*
Percentile *92.22%*
West rank .... *63 of 471*
Utah rank .... *10 of 20*
Closest major hub .... *Las Vegas, 159 air miles*

TESTS
1. Character	67.2
2. Stability	77.3
3. Growth	63.3
4. Education	64.9
5. Jobs	70.4
6. Business	70.1
7. Money	47.1
8. Housing	47.4
9. Health	51.6
10. Diversions	38.8
11. Internet	70.7
12. Proximity	68.8

BASIC STATS
Population	35,626
Density	2,120.5
Born out of state	43.3%
Homes built since 2000	33.0%
4 or more bedrooms	35.1%

RACE
Whites	83.5%
Blacks	0.7%
Hispanics	10.1%
Asians	0.9%
Native Americans	2.1%
Diversity index	29.1%

HOUSEHOLD INCOME LADDER
95th percentile	$152,343
80th percentile	$95,028
60th percentile	$62,156
50th percentile	$50,270
40th percentile	$40,809
20th percentile	$22,691

HOME VALUE LADDER
75th percentile	$277,900
50th percentile	$212,400
25th percentile	$158,400

CHARACTER
Resilience	22.6%
Short commutes	80.2% (★)

STABILITY
Living with two parents	82.1% (★)
Occupied homes	93.8%

GROWTH
Population growth	5.4%
Economic growth	33.8% (★)

EDUCATION
High school graduates	93.7%
College graduates	33.0%

JOBS
MBSA workers	32.6%
Private-sector job growth	32.1% (★)

BUSINESS
Small business growth	24.7% (★)
Self-employed workers	8.5%

MONEY
Median annual earnings	$40,258
Living in poverty	18.2%

HOUSING
Home ownership	56.6%
Monthly housing costs	28.9%

HEALTH
Health care workers	8.1%
Fair or poor health	14.9%

DIVERSIONS
Stores per 10,000	40.6
Restaurants per 10,000	18.0

INTERNET
Broadband subscriptions	67.3%
Smartphone access	88.2% (★)

PROXIMITY
Major hub miles	159
Major or mid-major miles	159

Charlottesville, Virginia

Score ....756.1 points
National rank .... 117 of 2,084
Percentile..94.43%
South rank .... 36 of 745
Virginia rank... 6 of 41
Closest major hub .... Richmond, 67 air miles

TESTS
1. Character.................................64.5
2. Stability..................................67.9
3. Growth...................................51.0
4. Education................................82.9
5. Jobs.......................................76.5
6. Business..................................42.6
7. Money....................................60.0
8. Housing..................................36.7
9. Health....................................60.7
10. Diversions.............................64.2
11. Internet.................................64.1
12. Proximity...............................85.0

BASIC STATS
Population...............................101,520
Density 2,935.6
Born out of state 54.9%
Homes built since 2000..............22.2%
4 or more bedrooms 20.4%

RACE
Whites....................................67.0%
Blacks 15.4%
Hispanics 6.7%
Asians.....................................7.7%
Native Americans 0.2%
Diversity index.........................51.6%

HOUSEHOLD INCOME LADDER
95th percentile ....>$250,000
80th percentile $138,577
60th percentile $84,106
50th percentile $65,458
40th percentile $51,979
20th percentile $25,718

HOME VALUE LADDER
75th percentile $435,700
50th percentile $301,900
25th percentile $218,700

CHARACTER
Resilience.................................26.2%
Short commutes 66.9%

STABILITY
Living with two parents 66.4%
Occupied homes.......................94.4%

GROWTH
Population growth.....................6.2%
Economic growth......................11.3%

EDUCATION
High school graduates 92.0%
College graduates ....57.2% (★)

JOBS
MBSA workers..........................53.8% (★)
Private-sector job growth 10.8%

BUSINESS
Small business growth 5.7%
Self-employed workers 7.4%

MONEY
Median annual earnings...............$53,019 (★)
Living in poverty.......................18.1%

HOUSING
Home ownership.......................44.6%
Monthly housing costs...............29.9%

HEALTH
Health care workers...................11.7%
Fair or poor health....................15.4%

DIVERSIONS
Stores per 10,000.......................45.3
Restaurants per 10,000...............34.8 (★)

INTERNET
Broadband subscriptions 64.5%
Smartphone access 83.8%

PROXIMITY
Major hub miles........................67
Major or mid-major miles...........67

Chelsea, Michigan

Score .... *797.6 points*
National rank .... *52 of 2,084*
Percentile *97.55%*
Midwest rank .... *5 of 622*
Michigan rank .... *1 of 67*
Closest major hub .... *Detroit, 42 air miles*

TESTS
1. Character 49.3
2. Stability 90.5
3. Growth 55.2
4. Education 90.9
5. Jobs 71.2
6. Business 38.4
7. Money 93.6
8. Housing 61.7
9. Health 60.3
10. Diversions 34.1
11. Internet 63.0
12. Proximity 89.4

BASIC STATS
Population 6,000
Density 1,428.6
Born out of state 29.7%
Homes built since 2000 .... 27.4%
4 or more bedrooms 26.2%

RACE
Whites 94.6%
Blacks 0.8%
Hispanics 1.9%
Asians 0.6%
Native Americans 0.0%
Diversity index 10.4%

HOUSEHOLD INCOME LADDER
95th percentile .... >$250,000
80th percentile $161,913
60th percentile $104,961
50th percentile $82,074
40th percentile $66,833
20th percentile $39,233

HOME VALUE LADDER
75th percentile $296,400
50th percentile $228,700
25th percentile $170,000

CHARACTER
Resilience 25.6%
Short commutes 42.0%

STABILITY
Living with two parents .... 83.8% (★)
Occupied homes .... 98.9% (★)

GROWTH
Population growth 7.7%
Economic growth 14.8%

EDUCATION
High school graduates .... 97.4% (★)
College graduates .... 57.4% (★)

JOBS
MBSA workers .... 50.8% (★)
Private-sector job growth 9.6%

BUSINESS
Small business growth 2.9%
Self-employed workers 7.2%

MONEY
Median annual earnings .... $68,816 (★)
Living in poverty .... 3.7% (★)

HOUSING
Home ownership 69.0%
Monthly housing costs 25.2%

HEALTH
Health care workers 9.0%
Fair or poor health .... 11.9% (★)

DIVERSIONS
Stores per 10,000 .... 29.8
Restaurants per 10,000 .... 21.0

INTERNET
Broadband subscriptions 75.2%
Smartphone access 75.5%

PROXIMITY
Major hub miles 42
Major or mid-major miles 42

Chesapeake Beach, Maryland

Score ....*744.5 points*
National rank .... *147 of 2,084*
Percentile...*92.99%*
East rank.. *20 of 246*
Maryland rank .... *5 of 23*
Closest major hub .... *Washington, 34 air miles*

TESTS
1. Character................................56.6
2. Stability..................................76.9
3. Growth...................................39.3
4. Education...............................71.9
5. Jobs.......................................61.3
6. Business.................................33.6
7. Money....................................97.6
8. Housing..................................65.3
9. Health....................................50.9
10. Diversions............................22.7
11. Internet 77.6
12. Proximity..............................90.8

BASIC STATS
Population.........................24,334
Density............................. 957.5
Born out of state 52.8%
Homes built since 2000............25.3%
4 or more bedrooms 38.6%

RACE
Whites..81.6%
Blacks..8.8%
Hispanics 3.2%
Asians..2.3%
Native Americans 0.2%
Diversity index.........................32.3%

HOUSEHOLD INCOME LADDER
95th percentile .... >$250,000
80th percentile $180,044
60th percentile $127,479
50th percentile $106,745
40th percentile $91,836
20th percentile $51,773

HOME VALUE LADDER
75th percentile $466,600
50th percentile $366,400
25th percentile $286,900

CHARACTER
Resilience........................... 40.5% (★)
Short commutes 19.1%

STABILITY
Living with two parents 73.4%
Occupied homes.................. 96.7% (★)

GROWTH
Population growth........................0.1%
Economic growth.........................5.9%

EDUCATION
High school graduates .... 97.5% (★)
College graduates 36.6%

JOBS
MBSA workers..45.7% (★)
Private-sector job growth 4.4%

BUSINESS
Small business growth 2.6%
Self-employed workers 5.5%

MONEY
Median annual earnings...............$76,250 (★)
Living in poverty...............................3.3% (★)

HOUSING
Home ownership............................... 81.9% (★)
Monthly housing costs............................30.4%

HEALTH
Health care workers..............................5.6%
Fair or poor health............................. 11.8% (★)

DIVERSIONS
Stores per 10,000................................23.3
Restaurants per 10,000................................16.2

INTERNET
Broadband subscriptions .... 82.4% (★)
Smartphone access 84.6%

PROXIMITY
Major hub miles..34 (★)
Major or mid-major miles............................... 34

Chester, New York

Score ....748.8 points
National rank ....136 of 2,084
Percentile...93.52%
East rank.. 18 of 246
New York rank .... 4 of 65
Closest major hub ....New York, 47 air miles

TESTS
1. Character..........................50.9
2. Stability..............................71.1
3. Growth...............................49.9
4. Education..........................61.2
5. Jobs....................................60.3
6. Business............................27.9
7. Money................................94.3
8. Housing.............................55.0
9. Health................................60.3
10. Diversions.......................46.8
11. Internet 79.3
12. Proximity.........................91.8

BASIC STATS
Population............................ 5,670
Density 1,568.9
Born out of state 21.4%
Homes built since 2000............5.1%
4 or more bedrooms 28.4%

RACE
Whites...................................56.1%
Blacks.....................................9.9%
Hispanics 28.1%
Asians.....................................4.0%
Native Americans 0.0%
Diversity index....................59.5%

HOUSEHOLD INCOME LADDER
95th percentile $221,948
80th percentile $142,478
60th percentile $113,037
50th percentile $92,121
40th percentile $67,694
20th percentile $32,539

HOME VALUE LADDER
75th percentile $316,200
50th percentile $232,900
25th percentile $183,000

CHARACTER
Resilience..............................28.4%
Short commutes 38.1%

STABILITY
Living with two parents 74.6%
Occupied homes..................93.2%

GROWTH
Population growth...............3.1%
Economic growth 16.7%

EDUCATION
High school graduates 92.6%
College graduates 29.9%

JOBS
MBSA workers.......................39.7%
Private-sector job growth 10.9%

BUSINESS
Small business growth 5.6%
Self-employed workers 1.8%

MONEY
Median annual earnings..............$73,655 (★)
Living in poverty....................5.7% (★)

HOUSING
Home ownership....................67.5%
Monthly housing costs 29.6%

HEALTH
Health care workers..............11.2%
Fair or poor health................14.9%

DIVERSIONS
Stores per 10,000.....................41.3
Restaurants per 10,000............23.8

INTERNET
Broadband subscriptions ....82.0% (★)
Smartphone access ....86.5% (★)

PROXIMITY
Major hub miles 47
Major or mid-major miles.........20 (★)

Coeur d'Alene, Idaho

Score ....*731.6 points*
National rank ....*183 of 2,084*
Percentile...*91.26%*
West rank..*71 of 471*
Idaho rank .... *5 of 21*
Closest major hub ....*Seattle, 257 air miles*

TESTS
1. Character....................................63.2
2. Stability.......................................73.0
3. Growth..63.1
4. Education....................................58.7
5. Jobs...58.2
6. Business......................................62.6
7. Money...53.7
8. Housing.......................................52.4
9. Health...59.0
10. Diversions.................................43.8
11. Internet 64.5
12. Proximity...................................79.4

BASIC STATS
Population......................................110,484
Density 2,337.5
Born out of state 66.4%
Homes built since 2000...........................33.7%
4 or more bedrooms 24.8%

RACE
Whites...90.2%
Blacks..0.3%
Hispanics 5.0%
Asians..1.0%
Native Americans 1.0%
Diversity index 18.3%

HOUSEHOLD INCOME LADDER
95th percentile $168,872
80th percentile $100,055
60th percentile $65,065
50th percentile $53,924
40th percentile $44,090
20th percentile $25,261

HOME VALUE LADDER
75th percentile $344,700
50th percentile $240,500
25th percentile $170,800

CHARACTER
Resilience.......................................27.2%
Short commutes 62.2%

STABILITY
Living with two parents 66.3%
Occupied homes...............................97.2% (★)

GROWTH
Population growth...........................10.5% (★)
Economic growth.............................21.6%

EDUCATION
High school graduates 93.6%
College graduates 25.5%

JOBS
MBSA workers.................................32.3%
Private-sector job growth ....17.9% (★)

BUSINESS
Small business growth ....16.5% (★)
Self-employed workers 9.7%

MONEY
Median annual earnings.......................$41,050
Living in poverty.............................12.8%

HOUSING
Home ownership..............................65.1%
Monthly housing costs...............................30.2%

HEALTH
Health care workers.......................................9.7%
Fair or poor health........................13.5%

DIVERSIONS
Stores per 10,000...............................37.8
Restaurants per 10,000................................23.6

INTERNET
Broadband subscriptions 70.8%
Smartphone access 79.9%

PROXIMITY
Major hub miles.................................257
Major or mid-major miles...............................27

Colby, Kansas

Score ....729.2 points
National rank ....187 of 2,084
Percentile...91.07%
Midwest rank..43 of 622
Kansas rank .... 2 of 40
Closest major hub .... Denver, 209 air miles

TESTS
1. Character.............................87.6
2. Stability..............................83.4
3. Growth.................................56.3
4. Education.............................49.3
5. Jobs.....................................40.1
6. Business...............................37.3
7. Money..................................57.8
8. Housing...............................57.5
9. Health..................................69.1
10. Diversions..........................72.1
11. Internet 58.0
12. Proximity............................60.7

BASIC STATS
Population.............................. 5,566
Density 1,857.2
Born out of state 34.0%
Homes built since 2000.............2.8%
4 or more bedrooms 31.9%

RACE
Whites.....................................88.4%
Blacks.......................................3.0%
Hispanics 7.1%
Asians.......................................1.2%
Native Americans 0.0%
Diversity index.........................21.2%

HOUSEHOLD INCOME LADDER
95th percentile $149,573
80th percentile $100,655
60th percentile $68,120
50th percentile $56,196
40th percentile $41,429
20th percentile $20,275

HOME VALUE LADDER
75th percentile $163,300
50th percentile $123,000
25th percentile $91,600

CHARACTER
Resilience...............................32.8%
Short commutes .... 87.3% (★)

STABILITY
Living with two parents ....85.4% (★)
Occupied homes.............................95.9%

GROWTH
Population growth............................3.0%
Economic growth .... 27.6% (★)

EDUCATION
High school graduates 90.1%
College graduates 18.6%

JOBS
MBSA workers.......................24.3%
Private-sector job growth 6.8%

BUSINESS
Small business growth 0.6%
Self-employed workers 7.9%

MONEY
Median annual earnings.......................$45,490
Living in poverty.............................13.1%

HOUSING
Home ownership.....................61.8%
Monthly housing costs 24.0%

HEALTH
Health care workers........................... 14.4% (★)
Fair or poor health............................15.0%

DIVERSIONS
Stores per 10,000...................84.3 (★)
Restaurants per 10,000.................23.3

INTERNET
Broadband subscriptions 63.7%
Smartphone access 78.5%

PROXIMITY
Major hub miles.............................209
Major or mid-major miles............203

Colchester, Connecticut

Score ....*736.2 points*
National rank ....*166 of 2,084*
Percentile...*92.08%*
East rank...*22 of 246*
Connecticut rank...*2 of 8*
Closest major hub ....*Hartford, 22 air miles*

TESTS
1. Character.................................47.6
2. Stability..................................67.7
3. Growth...................................36.8
4. Education...............................77.5
5. Jobs..63.2
6. Business.................................30.9
7. Money 86.7
8. Housing..................................55.3
9. Health....................................60.5
10. Diversions.............................42.6
11. Internet 72.4
12. Proximity...............................95.0

BASIC STATS
Population................................. 9,406
Density 642.5
Born out of state....................34.9%
Homes built since 2000............ 13.4%
4 or more bedrooms 19.3%

RACE
Whites................................89.5%
Blacks 2.5%
Hispanics..............................3.7%
Asians...................................2.4%
Native Americans 0.4%
Diversity index................... 19.6%

HOUSEHOLD INCOME LADDER
95th percentile ....>$250,000
80th percentile $153,734
60th percentile $118,487
50th percentile $96,992
40th percentile $76,429
20th percentile $44,032

HOME VALUE LADDER
75th percentile $323,400
50th percentile $244,400
25th percentile $203,200

CHARACTER
Resilience.....................................33.3%
Short commutes 20.7%

STABILITY
Living with two parents 68.6%
Occupied homes..........................93.5%

GROWTH
Population growth.......................-2.1%
Economic growth.........................6.8%

EDUCATION
High school graduates ....97.3% (★)
College graduates ....43.7% (★)

JOBS
MBSA workers.............................48.0% (★)
Private-sector job growth 3.7%

BUSINESS
Small business growth 3.7%
Self-employed workers 3.9%

MONEY
Median annual earnings ....$65,752 (★)
Living in poverty....................................6.3% (★)

HOUSING
Home ownership.........................70.5%
Monthly housing costs 31.3%

HEALTH
Health care workers.....................................8.7%
Fair or poor health............................ 11.4% (★)

DIVERSIONS
Stores per 10,000 ....36.1
Restaurants per 10,000....................23.7

INTERNET
Broadband subscriptions .... 80.9% (★)
Smartphone access 80.7%

PROXIMITY
Major hub miles.......................................22 (★)
Major or mid-major miles.......................19 (★)

Corona de Tucson, Arizona

Score ....*768.2 points*
National rank ....*98 of 2,084*
Percentile..*95.34%*
West rank..*41 of 471*
Arizona rank..*3 of 44*
Closest major hub ....*Phoenix, 127 air miles*

TESTS

1. Character...................................17.0
2. Stability.....................................87.1
3. Growth.......................................59.6
4. Education...................................76.0
5. Jobs..69.5
6. Business.....................................36.2
7. Money..84.0
8. Housing......................................76.3
9. Health..51.3
10. Diversions.................................25.0
11. Internet 99.2
12. Proximity..................................87.0

BASIC STATS

Population................................. 7,714
Density 1,800.2
Born out of state.......................59.4%
Homes built since 2000.............74.9%
4 or more bedrooms 42.0%

RACE

Whites..68.2%
Blacks..3.8%
Hispanics 25.5%
Asians..0.6%
Native Americans 0.5%
Diversity index............................46.8%

HOUSEHOLD INCOME LADDER

95th percentile $212,984
80th percentile $130,244
60th percentile $106,580
50th percentile $95,625
40th percentile $83,839
20th percentile $61,721

HOME VALUE LADDER

75th percentile $284,900
50th percentile $228,100
25th percentile $179,100

CHARACTER

Resilience.....................................16.1%
Short commutes 8.7%

STABILITY

Living with two parents .... 89.7% (★)
Occupied homes..........................95.6%

GROWTH

Population growth........................... 10.5% (★)
Economic growth 15.7%

EDUCATION

High school graduates .... 97.5% (★)
College graduates .... 41.6% (★)

JOBS

MBSA workers.................................. 50.5% (★)
Private-sector job growth 8.0%

BUSINESS

Small business growth 1.4%
Self-employed workers 7.1%

MONEY

Median annual earnings...............$59,947 (★)
Living in poverty....................................2.4% (★)

HOUSING

Home ownership............................. 90.4% (★)
Monthly housing costs...........................27.1%

HEALTH

Health care workers................................9.7%
Fair or poor health................................17.2%

DIVERSIONS

Stores per 10,000................................25.5
Restaurants per 10,000................................16.6

INTERNET

Broadband subscriptions .... 89.0% (★)
Smartphone access .... 96.2% (★)

PROXIMITY

Major hub miles..................................127
Major or mid-major miles.......................23 (★)

Corvallis, Oregon

Score .... *729.1 points*
National rank .... *188 of 2,084*
Percentile *91.02%*
West rank .... *73 of 471*
Oregon rank .... *5 of 45*
Closest major hub .... *Portland, 72 air miles*

TESTS
1. Character.................................63.2
2. Stability...................................73.9
3. Growth....................................52.1
4. Education................................90.3
5. Jobs...72.3
6. Business..................................36.5
7. Money.....................................51.4
8. Housing...................................39.3
9. Health.....................................55.4
10. Diversions.............................33.0
11. Internet 77.6
12. Proximity...............................84.1

BASIC STATS
Population.............................65,803
Density 3,095.4
Born out of state 58.4%
Homes built since 2000............19.6%
4 or more bedrooms 19.1%

RACE
Whites......................................77.4%
Blacks 1.3%
Hispanics 7.8%
Asians.......................................9.2%
Native Americans 0.5%
Diversity index.......................38.5%

HOUSEHOLD INCOME LADDER
95th percentile $210,484
80th percentile $112,244
60th percentile $69,748
50th percentile $54,606
40th percentile $40,972
20th percentile $18,555

HOME VALUE LADDER
75th percentile $428,900
50th percentile $320,400
25th percentile $235,000

CHARACTER
Resilience.....................................23.8%
Short commutes 70.4%

STABILITY
Living with two parents 71.7%
Occupied homes........................95.7%

GROWTH
Population growth.......................4.8%
Economic growth........................16.4%

EDUCATION
High school graduates ....95.9% (★)
College graduates ....58.8% (★)

JOBS
MBSA workers......................................50.4% (★)
Private-sector job growth 11.5%

BUSINESS
Small business growth 4.4%
Self-employed workers 5.7%

MONEY
Median annual earnings.......................$50,701
Living in poverty.............................24.0%

HOUSING
Home ownership.............................46.5%
Monthly housing costs 29.0%

HEALTH
Health care workers.............................8.5%
Fair or poor health...............................13.6%

DIVERSIONS
Stores per 10,000..............................27.7
Restaurants per 10,000................................21.5

INTERNET
Broadband subscriptions ....81.0% (★)
Smartphone access ....85.6% (★)

PROXIMITY
Major hub miles 72
Major or mid-major miles................................ 72

Crozet, Virginia

Score .... *839.9 points*
National rank .... *20 of 2,084*
Percentile *99.09%*
South rank .... *8 of 745*
Virginia rank .... *2 of 41*
Closest major hub .... *Richmond, 77 air miles*

TESTS

1. Character................................43.4
2. Stability...................................71.3
3. Growth....................................43.5
4. Education................................97.3
5. Jobs..86.2
6. Business..................................58.4
7. Money.....................................94.5
8. Housing...................................74.0
9. Health.....................................88.8
10. Diversions..............................31.7
11. Internet..................................67.6
12. Proximity................................83.2

BASIC STATS

Population................................. 6,223
Density 1,783.6
Born out of state 52.7%
Homes built since 2000.............46.8%
4 or more bedrooms 37.1%

RACE

Whites.......................................92.2%
Blacks...2.9%
Hispanics 1.1%
Asians...1.9%
Native Americans 0.0%
Diversity index..........................14.8%

HOUSEHOLD INCOME LADDER

95th percentile $230,800
80th percentile $149,422
60th percentile $105,386
50th percentile $86,897
40th percentile $66,909
20th percentile $37,575

HOME VALUE LADDER

75th percentile $464,100
50th percentile $365,100
25th percentile $262,900

CHARACTER

Resilience..................................31.0%
Short commutes 18.9%

STABILITY

Living with two parents ....76.5% (★)
Occupied homes........................92.6%

GROWTH

Population growth.......................0.8%
Economic growth 11.3%

EDUCATION

High school graduates ....98.0% (★)
College graduates ....70.0% (★)

JOBS

MBSA workers.................................62.9% (★)
Private-sector job growth 13.7%

BUSINESS

Small business growth 10.5%
Self-employed workers ....11.1% (★)

MONEY

Median annual earnings...............$68,011 (★)
Living in poverty................................2.2% (★)

HOUSING

Home ownership................................79.5% (★)
Monthly housing costs............................21.9%

HEALTH

Health care workers........................ 18.2% (★)
Fair or poor health................................12.8%

DIVERSIONS

Stores per 10,000..32.8
Restaurants per 10,000................................17.3

INTERNET

Broadband subscriptions 70.7%
Smartphone access 82.9%

PROXIMITY

Major hub miles...77
Major or mid-major miles.............................77

Daphne, Alabama

Score .... *759.1 points*
National rank .... *110 of 2,084*
Percentile *94.77%*
South rank .... *33 of 745*
Alabama rank .... *1 of 37*
Closest major hub .... *New Orleans, 145 air miles*

TESTS
1. Character................................53.8
2. Stability..................................63.7
3. Growth...................................49.3
4. Education...............................77.3
5. Jobs.......................................77.5
6. Business.................................55.2
7. Money....................................68.7
8. Housing..................................63.7
9. Health....................................57.2
10. Diversions.............................48.8
11. Internet 72.7
12. Proximity...............................71.2

BASIC STATS
Population.................................65,806
Density 1,189.5
Born out of state.......................48.0%
Homes built since 2000.............36.3%
4 or more bedrooms 29.9%

RACE
Whites.......................................79.2%
Blacks..12.8%
Hispanics 4.0%
Asians..1.5%
Native Americans 0.3%
Diversity index..........................35.4%

HOUSEHOLD INCOME LADDER
95th percentile ....>$250,000
80th percentile $138,608
60th percentile $88,362
50th percentile $71,474
40th percentile $56,802
20th percentile $32,681

HOME VALUE LADDER
75th percentile $356,300
50th percentile $232,200
25th percentile $164,400

CHARACTER
Resilience....................................29.8%
Short commutes 39.8%

STABILITY
Living with two parents 73.9%
Occupied homes.........................89.5%

GROWTH
Population growth.......................2.6%
Economic growth 16.8%

EDUCATION
High school graduates 94.8%
College graduates ....46.7% (★)

JOBS
MBSA workers.............................47.7% (★)
Private-sector job growth ....19.4% (★)

BUSINESS
Small business growth ....13.0% (★)
Self-employed workers 8.6%

MONEY
Median annual earnings $52,019
Living in poverty.........................9.0%

HOUSING
Home ownership........................72.5%
Monthly housing costs 25.8%

HEALTH
Health care workers....................12.0%
Fair or poor health.....................17.5%

DIVERSIONS
Stores per 10,000.......................45.1
Restaurants per 10,000...............23.0

INTERNET
Broadband subscriptions 74.4%
Smartphone access ....85.3% (★)

PROXIMITY
Major hub miles.........................145
Major or mid-major miles...........145

Davis, California

Score ....*742.0 points*
National rank ....*154 of 2,084*
Percentile..*92.65%*
West rank..*58 of 471*
California rank ....*8 of 145*
Closest major hub ....*Sacramento, 23 air miles*

TESTS
1. Character..31.9
2. Stability..81.8
3. Growth..53.8
4. Education...96.6
5. Jobs..85.7
6. Business..44.0
7. Money...63.9
8. Housing...28.6
9. Health...51.5
10. Diversions......................................23.6
11. Internet..87.9
12. Proximity..92.7

BASIC STATS
Population...77,252
Density...5,471.5
Born out of state..............................44.1%
Homes built since 2000...................13.4%
4 or more bedrooms........................25.3%

RACE
Whites..53.0%
Blacks...2.0%
Hispanics...14.6%
Asians...24.6%
Native Americans..............................0.4%
Diversity index.................................63.4%

HOUSEHOLD INCOME LADDER
95th percentile...........................>$250,000
80th percentile.............................$168,694
60th percentile...............................$93,567
50th percentile...............................$67,839
40th percentile...............................$50,149
20th percentile...............................$18,281

HOME VALUE LADDER
75th percentile..............................$849,000
50th percentile..............................$658,800
25th percentile..............................$512,400

CHARACTER
Resilience...7.6%
Short commutes...............................54.8%

STABILITY
Living with two parents...................78.3% (★)
Occupied homes..............................97.6% (★)

GROWTH
Population growth...............................4.3%
Economic growth..............................20.4%

EDUCATION
High school graduates......................97.2% (★)
College graduates.............................73.7% (★)

JOBS
MBSA workers....................................62.4% (★)
Private-sector job growth................13.4%

BUSINESS
Small business growth........................7.8%
Self-employed workers.......................6.9%

MONEY
Median annual earnings...............$70,439 (★)
Living in poverty...............................30.7%

HOUSING
Home ownership................................42.4%
Monthly housing costs......................35.0%

HEALTH
Health care workers............................8.8%
Fair or poor health............................15.9%

DIVERSIONS
Stores per 10,000..............................22.2
Restaurants per 10,000.....................17.6

INTERNET
Broadband subscriptions................84.9% (★)
Smartphone access...........................90.3% (★)

PROXIMITY
Major hub miles.................................23 (★)
Major or mid-major miles.................23 (★)

Decorah, Iowa

Score ....*765.3 points*
National rank ....*105 of 2,084*
Percentile...*95.01%*
Midwest rank..*17 of 622*
Iowa rank...*3 of 55*
Closest major hub ....*Minneapolis, 137 air miles*

TESTS
1. Character...91.0
2. Stability..85.2
3. Growth..37.1
4. Education...83.1
5. Jobs..52.2
6. Business...39.7
7. Money..61.4
8. Housing..60.0
9. Health..54.4
10. Diversions..66.7
11. Internet..59.7
12. Proximity..74.8

BASIC STATS
Population.. 8,101
Density 1,568.4
Born out of state 42.6%
Homes built since 2000..............11.3%
4 or more bedrooms 22.6%

RACE
Whites..93.1%
Blacks...2.7%
Hispanics 2.2%
Asians...1.4%
Native Americans 0.1%
Diversity index.............................13.2%

HOUSEHOLD INCOME LADDER
95th percentile $169,705
80th percentile $112,801
60th percentile $75,225
50th percentile $64,028
40th percentile $50,703
20th percentile $25,264

HOME VALUE LADDER
75th percentile $268,300
50th percentile $188,300
25th percentile $140,100

CHARACTER
Resilience..................................35.9% (★)
Short commutes ....83.6% (★)

STABILITY
Living with two parents ....82.8% (★)
Occupied homes......................97.4% (★)

GROWTH
Population growth..........................-0.9%
Economic growth.............................4.5%

EDUCATION
High school graduates ....98.8% (★)
College graduates ....48.5% (★)

JOBS
MBSA workers.................................38.3%
Private-sector job growth 3.1%

BUSINESS
Small business growth 1.5%
Self-employed workers 8.4%

MONEY
Median annual earnings.......................$44,185
Living in poverty..............................8.5%

HOUSING
Home ownership............................70.2%
Monthly housing costs..............27.3%

HEALTH
Health care workers........................7.0%
Fair or poor health............................12.0% (★)

DIVERSIONS
Stores per 10,000.....................57.0 (★)
Restaurants per 10,000......................29.5 (★)

INTERNET
Broadband subscriptions 71.6%
Smartphone access 74.8%

PROXIMITY
Major hub miles.................................137
Major or mid-major miles...........................119

Delano, Minnesota

Score .... *754.1 points*
National rank .... *122 of 2,084*
Percentile *94.19%*
Midwest rank .... *23 of 622*
Minnesota rank .... *4 of 53*
Closest major hub .... *Minneapolis, 25 air miles*

TESTS
1. Character..68.0
2. Stability..86.4
3. Growth..50.0
4. Education..77.4
5. Jobs...60.7
6. Business..48.9
7. Money...74.5
8. Housing...54.1
9. Health...43.9
10. Diversions..27.0
11. Internet...70.8
12. Proximity...92.4

BASIC STATS
Population..................................... 5,503
Density 1,856.6
Born out of state..........................22.9%
Homes built since 2000.............. 29.0%
4 or more bedrooms 42.5%

RACE
Whites...90.7%
Blacks...0.0%
Hispanics 4.3%
Asians...0.3%
Native Americans 0.0%
Diversity index..............................17.3%

HOUSEHOLD INCOME LADDER
95th percentile $203,818
80th percentile $137,449
60th percentile $108,903
50th percentile $89,800
40th percentile $65,295
20th percentile $35,884

HOME VALUE LADDER
75th percentile $297,200
50th percentile $245,700
25th percentile $180,300

CHARACTER
Resilience................................. 42.5% (★)
Short commutes 34.0%

STABILITY
Living with two parents .... 76.8% (★)
Occupied homes............................100.0% (★)

GROWTH
Population growth.............................5.0%
Economic growth 12.4%

EDUCATION
High school graduates .... 99.3% (★)
College graduates .... 40.9% (★)

JOBS
MBSA workers...............................35.6%
Private-sector job growth 16.7%

BUSINESS
Small business growth 9.2%
Self-employed workers 8.1%

MONEY
Median annual earnings...............$53,492 (★)
Living in poverty...................................4.9% (★)

HOUSING
Home ownership............................. 75.7% (★)
Monthly housing costs.............................35.5%

HEALTH
Health care workers...............................2.4%
Fair or poor health.............................. 10.8% (★)

DIVERSIONS
Stores per 10,000...........................32.1
Restaurants per 10,000...................14.1

INTERNET
Broadband subscriptions .... 77.0% (★)
Smartphone access 81.8%

PROXIMITY
Major hub miles.......................................25 (★)
Major or mid-major miles.........................25 (★)

Discovery Bay, California

Score ....737.9 points
National rank ....161 of 2,084
Percentile..92.32%
West rank..61 of 471
California rank ....10 of 145
Closest major hub ....San Francisco, 34 air miles

TESTS
1. Character................................21.7
2. Stability..................................76.9
3. Growth...................................55.3
4. Education...............................66.8
5. Jobs.......................................60.6
6. Business.................................40.3
7. Money....................................91.5
8. Housing..................................57.2
9. Health....................................53.2
10. Diversions.............................23.4
11. Internet 98.8
12. Proximity...............................92.2

BASIC STATS
Population.............................16,358
Density 4,067.1
Born out of state 31.4%
Homes built since 2000............35.7%
4 or more bedrooms 48.9%

RACE
Whites....................................68.2%
Blacks......................................4.8%
Hispanics...............................18.1%
Asians......................................6.0%
Native Americans 0.2%
Diversity index.......................49.5%

HOUSEHOLD INCOME LADDER
95th percentile ....>$250,000
80th percentile $208,229
60th percentile $146,926
50th percentile $127,917
40th percentile $106,406
20th percentile $60,985

HOME VALUE LADDER
75th percentile $749,000
50th percentile $613,800
25th percentile $477,900

CHARACTER
Resilience................................13.2%
Short commutes 23.8%

STABILITY
Living with two parents 70.7%
Occupied homes.............. 97.7% (★)

GROWTH
Population growth.....................9.3% (★)
Economic growth 11.3%

EDUCATION
High school graduates .....96.5% (★)
College graduates 31.6%

JOBS
MBSA workers..................... 41.1% (★)
Private-sector job growth 9.5%

BUSINESS
Small business growth 8.5%
Self-employed workers 5.1%

MONEY
Median annual earnings ....$81,023 (★)
Living in poverty.......................8.8%

HOUSING
Home ownership .... 82.6% (★)
Monthly housing costs 37.4%

HEALTH
Health care workers....................6.8%
Fair or poor health............. 12.3% (★)

DIVERSIONS
Stores per 10,000............................21.4
Restaurants per 10,000................17.9

INTERNET
Broadband subscriptions .... 91.0% (★)
Smartphone access .... 94.7% (★)

PROXIMITY
Major hub miles ....34 (★)
Major or mid-major miles...........22 (★)

Dorr, Michigan

Score .... *728.5 points*
National rank .... *190 of 2,084*
Percentile *90.93%*
Midwest rank .... *45 of 622*
Michigan rank .... *8 of 67*
Closest major hub .... *Detroit, 128 air miles*

TESTS
1. Character 53.0
2. Stability 74.0
3. Growth 52.1
4. Education 59.2
5. Jobs 43.5
6. Business 43.0
7. Money 69.3
8. Housing 85.5
9. Health 69.4
10. Diversions 29.2
11. Internet 62.1
12. Proximity 88.2

BASIC STATS
Population 5,694
Density 1,037.7
Born out of state 7.7%
Homes built since 2000 .... 17.1%
4 or more bedrooms 28.0%

RACE
Whites 94.2%
Blacks 0.4%
Hispanics 2.5%
Asians 0.2%
Native Americans 0.2%
Diversity index 11.1%

HOUSEHOLD INCOME LADDER
95th percentile $131,301
80th percentile $107,786
60th percentile $74,823
50th percentile $67,404
40th percentile $55,333
20th percentile $41,037

HOME VALUE LADDER
75th percentile $198,400
50th percentile $164,900
25th percentile $124,600

CHARACTER
Resilience .... 35.3% (★)
Short commutes 25.3%

STABILITY
Living with two parents 71.9%
Occupied homes 95.7%

GROWTH
Population growth 6.9%
Economic growth 11.6%

EDUCATION
High school graduates .... 96.7% (★)
College graduates 22.0%

JOBS
MBSA workers 25.5%
Private-sector job growth 9.3%

BUSINESS
Small business growth 9.2%
Self-employed workers 5.8%

MONEY
Median annual earnings $51,907
Living in poverty 8.3%

HOUSING
Home ownership .... 91.6% (★)
Monthly housing costs 23.2%

HEALTH
Health care workers .... 13.9% (★)
Fair or poor health 14.2%

DIVERSIONS
Stores per 10,000 .... 30.4
Restaurants per 10,000 .... 16.9

INTERNET
Broadband subscriptions 63.0%
Smartphone access 82.9%

PROXIMITY
Major hub miles 128
Major or mid-major miles .... 16 (★)

Eagle, Colorado

Score .... *745.4 points*
National rank .... *142 of 2,084*
Percentile *93.23%*
West rank .... *53 of 471*
Colorado rank .... *20 of 47*
Closest major hub .... *Denver, 100 air miles*

TESTS
1. Character 55.3
2. Stability 69.0
3. Growth 54.4
4. Education 65.4
5. Jobs 60.5
6. Business 56.0
7. Money 66.9
8. Housing 29.9
9. Health 44.2
10. Diversions 96.6
11. Internet 68.0
12. Proximity 79.2

BASIC STATS
Population 6,189
Density 2,520.0
Born out of state 52.2%
Homes built since 2000 .... 46.3%
4 or more bedrooms 33.5%

RACE
Whites 69.2%
Blacks 0.1%
Hispanics 30.7%
Asians 0.0%
Native Americans 0.0%
Diversity index 42.7%

HOUSEHOLD INCOME LADDER
95th percentile $214,350
80th percentile $149,783
60th percentile $123,433
50th percentile $93,967
40th percentile $80,320
20th percentile $45,369

HOME VALUE LADDER
75th percentile $637,600
50th percentile $501,000
25th percentile $409,700

CHARACTER
Resilience 31.0%
Short commutes 39.6%

STABILITY
Living with two parents .... 77.0% (★)
Occupied homes 91.2%

GROWTH
Population growth 5.3%
Economic growth 19.0%

EDUCATION
High school graduates 86.2%
College graduates .... 43.4% (★)

JOBS
MBSA workers 37.3%
Private-sector job growth 14.2%

BUSINESS
Small business growth 9.2%
Self-employed workers 10.8%

MONEY
Median annual earnings $50,619
Living in poverty 9.3%

HOUSING
Home ownership 64.8%
Monthly housing costs 53.6%

HEALTH
Health care workers 3.6%
Fair or poor health .... 12.3% (★)

DIVERSIONS
Stores per 10,000 .... 71.2 (★)
Restaurants per 10,000 .... 45.9 (★)

INTERNET
Broadband subscriptions 63.2%
Smartphone access .... 88.4% (★)

PROXIMITY
Major hub miles 100
Major or mid-major miles 100

Eagle Mountain South, Utah

Score .... *799.5 points*
National rank .... *49 of 2,084*
Percentile *97.70%*
West rank .... *24 of 471*
Utah rank .... *4 of 20*
Closest major hub .... *Salt Lake City, 23 air miles*

TESTS
1. Character 30.7
2. Stability 99.0
3. Growth 79.9
4. Education 60.9
5. Jobs 73.5
6. Business 55.8
7. Money 67.9
8. Housing 69.5
9. Health 47.5
10. Diversions 26.3
11. Internet 91.0
12. Proximity 97.5

BASIC STATS
Population 7,727
Density 4,049.8
Born out of state 33.2%
Homes built since 2000 .... 84.3%
4 or more bedrooms 48.8%

RACE
Whites 85.0%
Blacks 0.4%
Hispanics 10.0%
Asians 0.1%
Native Americans 0.0%
Diversity index 26.5%

HOUSEHOLD INCOME LADDER
95th percentile $142,453
80th percentile $104,214
60th percentile $77,461
50th percentile $71,647
40th percentile $64,096
20th percentile $43,613

HOME VALUE LADDER
75th percentile $284,700
50th percentile $240,600
25th percentile $204,200

CHARACTER
Resilience 22.7%
Short commutes 16.7%

STABILITY
Living with two parents .... 91.5% (★)
Occupied homes .... 99.4% (★)

GROWTH
Population growth .... 14.4% (★)
Economic growth .... 39.9% (★)

EDUCATION
High school graduates 95.1%
College graduates 26.2%

JOBS
MBSA workers 35.6%
Private-sector job growth .... 31.8% (★)

BUSINESS
Small business growth .... 24.7% (★)
Self-employed workers 3.0%

MONEY
Median annual earnings $52,462
Living in poverty 10.1%

HOUSING
Home ownership .... 89.6% (★)
Monthly housing costs 31.9%

HEALTH
Health care workers 5.0%
Fair or poor health 12.6%

DIVERSIONS
Stores per 10,000 .... 33.0
Restaurants per 10,000 .... 13.0

INTERNET
Broadband subscriptions .... 82.0% (★)
Smartphone access .... 94.6% (★)

PROXIMITY
Major hub miles .... 23 (★)
Major or mid-major miles .... 15 (★)

East Aurora, New York

Score ....*734.9 points*
National rank ....*173 of 2,084*
Percentile...*91.74%*
East rank.. *25 of 246*
New York rank .... *7 of 65*
Closest major hub .... *Buffalo, 15 air miles*

TESTS

1. Character	37.6
2. Stability	73.3
3. Growth	32.2
4. Education	83.4
5. Jobs	67.6
6. Business	39.3
7. Money	79.9
8. Housing	68.9
9. Health	52.6
10. Diversions	42.2
11. Internet	59.2
12. Proximity	98.7

BASIC STATS

Population	9,244
Density	1,080.7
Born out of state	21.3%
Homes built since 2000	5.8%
4 or more bedrooms	25.6%

RACE

Whites	94.6%
Blacks	1.1%
Hispanics	2.1%
Asians	0.7%
Native Americans	0.2%
Diversity index	10.4%

HOUSEHOLD INCOME LADDER

95th percentile	>$250,000
80th percentile	$145,664
60th percentile	$91,571
50th percentile	$72,795
40th percentile	$61,729
20th percentile	$34,014

HOME VALUE LADDER

75th percentile	$295,300
50th percentile	$223,700
25th percentile	$166,500

CHARACTER

Resilience	18.6%
Short commutes	38.4%

STABILITY

Living with two parents	76.5% (★)
Occupied homes	93.7%

GROWTH

Population growth	-6.2%
Economic growth	8.7%

EDUCATION

High school graduates	95.9% (★)
College graduates	52.7% (★)

JOBS

MBSA workers	52.4% (★)
Private-sector job growth	3.3%

BUSINESS

Small business growth	0.6%
Self-employed workers	8.7%

MONEY

Median annual earnings	$60,298 (★)
Living in poverty	6.2% (★)

HOUSING

Home ownership	74.7% (★)
Monthly housing costs	23.0%

HEALTH

Health care workers	9.2%
Fair or poor health	15.9%

DIVERSIONS

Stores per 10,000	34.8
Restaurants per 10,000	24.2

INTERNET

Broadband subscriptions	70.3%
Smartphone access	75.2%

PROXIMITY

Major hub miles	15 (★)
Major or mid-major miles	15 (★)

Eaton, Colorado

Score .... *750.4 points*
National rank .... *132 of 2,084*
Percentile *93.71%*
West rank .... *52 of 471*
Colorado rank .... *19 of 47*
Closest major hub .... *Denver, 58 air miles*

TESTS
1. Character 42.3
2. Stability 87.4
3. Growth 73.3
4. Education 58.7
5. Jobs 58.0
6. Business 66.3
7. Money 67.4
8. Housing 62.3
9. Health 61.3
10. Diversions 17.7
11. Internet 69.1
12. Proximity 86.6

BASIC STATS
Population 5,098
Density 3,387.4
Born out of state 37.5%
Homes built since 2000 .... 41.6%
4 or more bedrooms 41.6%

RACE
Whites 70.5%
Blacks 0.4%
Hispanics 24.3%
Asians 0.6%
Native Americans 0.0%
Diversity index 44.2%

HOUSEHOLD INCOME LADDER
95th percentile $195,898
80th percentile $115,941
60th percentile $85,846
50th percentile $80,909
40th percentile $70,786
20th percentile $46,152

HOME VALUE LADDER
75th percentile $373,500
50th percentile $281,600
25th percentile $223,900

CHARACTER
Resilience 19.5%
Short commutes 44.5%

STABILITY
Living with two parents .... 90.7% (★)
Occupied homes 95.3%

GROWTH
Population growth .... 9.9% (★)
Economic growth .... 40.1% (★)

EDUCATION
High school graduates 85.8%
College graduates 35.7%

JOBS
MBSA workers 33.2%
Private-sector job growth 16.6%

BUSINESS
Small business growth .... 19.8% (★)
Self-employed workers 9.5%

MONEY
Median annual earnings $48,826
Living in poverty .... 7.2% (★)

HOUSING
Home ownership .... 83.3% (★)
Monthly housing costs 33.7%

HEALTH
Health care workers 10.6%
Fair or poor health 13.6%

DIVERSIONS
Stores per 10,000 .... 20.9
Restaurants per 10,000 .... 13.8

INTERNET
Broadband subscriptions 73.2%
Smartphone access 82.7%

PROXIMITY
Major hub miles 58
Major or mid-major miles 58

Edwards, Colorado

Score ....744.9 points
National rank ....145 of 2,084
Percentile...93.09%
West rank...55 of 471
Colorado rank ....21 of 47
Closest major hub ....Denver, 86 air miles

TESTS
1. Character................67.6
2. Stability....................69.9
3. Growth....................41.7
4. Education................58.7
5. Jobs.........................57.3
6. Business...................52.1
7. Money......................60.9
8. Housing...................35.5
9. Health.....................49.9
10. Diversions..............96.6
11. Internet..................73.1
12. Proximity................81.6

BASIC STATS
Population.................17,044
Density.....................2,005.4
Born out of state...........66.8%
Homes built since 2000............21.8%
4 or more bedrooms................22.7%

RACE
Whites........................52.3%
Blacks..........................2.5%
Hispanics...................40.5%
Asians...........................1.7%
Native Americans 0.4%
Diversity index.............56.1%

HOUSEHOLD INCOME LADDER
95th percentile..................$240,263
80th percentile..................$136,060
60th percentile....................$88,365
50th percentile....................$75,401
40th percentile....................$59,765
20th percentile....................$36,045

HOME VALUE LADDER
75th percentile....................$797,000
50th percentile....................$519,000
25th percentile....................$271,200

CHARACTER
Resilience......................31.0%
Short commutes 60.9%

STABILITY
Living with two parents 74.5%
Occupied homes................92.6%

GROWTH
Population growth...............-3.8%
Economic growth................19.0%

EDUCATION
High school graduates 82.9%
College graduates ....39.5% (★)

JOBS
MBSA workers.....................34.4%
Private-sector job growth 14.2%

BUSINESS
Small business growth 9.2%
Self-employed workers................9.3%

MONEY
Median annual earnings.......$45,705
Living in poverty........................10.4%

HOUSING
Home ownership......................64.5%
Monthly housing costs............43.4%

HEALTH
Health care workers.................5.6%
Fair or poor health.............. 12.3% (★)

DIVERSIONS
Stores per 10,000.....................71.2 (★)
Restaurants per 10,000........... 45.9 (★)

INTERNET
Broadband subscriptions 65.9%
Smartphone access .... 91.5% (★)

PROXIMITY
Major hub miles 86
Major or mid-major miles.............. 86

Ephraim, Utah

Score ....*727.7 points*
National rank ....*194 of 2,084*
Percentile...*90.73%*
West rank..*74 of 471*
Utah rank.. *11 of 20*
Closest major hub ....*Salt Lake City, 91 air miles*

TESTS

1. Character...77.5
2. Stability...81.7
3. Growth..73.1
4. Education...60.4
5. Jobs...65.8
6. Business...63.7
7. Money..39.5
8. Housing...50.6
9. Health..56.3
10. Diversions...17.6
11. Internet 57.5
12. Proximity...84.0

BASIC STATS

Population.. 6,696
Density 3,040.9
Born out of state.....................................25.8%
Homes built since 2000..........................29.4%
4 or more bedrooms 42.6%

RACE

Whites...86.2%
Blacks...0.3%
Hispanics..9.5%
Asians..2.5%
Native Americans 0.2%
Diversity index..24.7%

HOUSEHOLD INCOME LADDER

95th percentile.....................................$129,113
80th percentile.......................................$79,923
60th percentile.......................................$51,696
50th percentile.......................................$41,670
40th percentile.......................................$36,647
20th percentile.......................................$25,267

HOME VALUE LADDER

75th percentile.....................................$301,400
50th percentile.....................................$216,600
25th percentile.....................................$141,700

CHARACTER

Resilience..31.5%
Short commutes 76.7%

STABILITY

Living with two parents ....85.1% (★)
Occupied homes......................................95.1%

GROWTH

Population growth............................14.1% (★)
Economic growth ....29.9% (★)

EDUCATION

High school graduates 92.5%
College graduates 29.0%

JOBS

MBSA workers...38.7%
Private-sector job growth ....18.7% (★)

BUSINESS

Small business growth ....16.2% (★)
Self-employed workers 10.3%

MONEY

Median annual earnings.......................$38,886
Living in poverty.....................................24.1%

HOUSING

Home ownership......................................57.2%
Monthly housing costs...........................26.7%

HEALTH

Health care workers................................10.0%
Fair or poor health..................................15.2%

DIVERSIONS

Stores per 10,000.......................................25.2
Restaurants per 10,000.............................11.1

INTERNET

Broadband subscriptions 63.6%
Smartphone access 78.1%

PROXIMITY

Major hub miles... 91
Major or mid-major miles.............................. 64

Estes Park, Colorado

Score ....781.5 points
National rank ....76 of 2,084
Percentile..96.40%
West rank..33 of 471
Colorado rank .... 15 of 47
Closest major hub ....Denver, 54 air miles

TESTS
1. Character..61.9
2. Stability..78.7
3. Growth..65.0
4. Education..76.4
5. Jobs..66.3
6. Business..69.5
7. Money..63.8
8. Housing...50.5
9. Health..49.7
10. Diversions..41.6
11. Internet..70.8
12. Proximity..87.3

BASIC STATS
Population....................................... 7,978
Density 1,065.2
Born out of state 75.5%
Homes built since 2000........................ 15.2%
4 or more bedrooms 12.9%

RACE
Whites..89.0%
Blacks..0.0%
Hispanics 10.4%
Asians...0.2%
Native Americans 0.0%
Diversity index................................ 19.7%

HOUSEHOLD INCOME LADDER
95th percentile $223,071
80th percentile $122,786
60th percentile $84,425
50th percentile $65,366
40th percentile $47,509
20th percentile $25,916

HOME VALUE LADDER
75th percentile $556,300
50th percentile $423,300
25th percentile $317,900

CHARACTER
Resilience..21.8%
Short commutes 73.0%

STABILITY
Living with two parents 71.6%
Occupied homes............................... 98.3% (★)

GROWTH
Population growth................................9.6% (★)
Economic growth .... 26.9% (★)

EDUCATION
High school graduates 95.0%
College graduates .... 45.3% (★)

JOBS
MBSA workers..40.3%
Private-sector job growth .... 17.3% (★)

BUSINESS
Small business growth .... 14.6% (★)
Self-employed workers .... 13.3% (★)

MONEY
Median annual earnings........................$46,645
Living in poverty..8.5%

HOUSING
Home ownership.....................................59.5%
Monthly housing costs............................28.2%

HEALTH
Health care workers.................................5.1%
Fair or poor health............................ 11.7% (★)

DIVERSIONS
Stores per 10,000.....................................36.0
Restaurants per 10,000.............................23.0

INTERNET
Broadband subscriptions 76.2%
Smartphone access 82.3%

PROXIMITY
Major hub miles.. 54
Major or mid-major miles................................ 54

Eureka, Missouri

Score ....*790.3 points*
National rank ....*67 of 2,084*
Percentile..*96.83%*
Midwest rank...*8 of 622*
Missouri rank.. *1 of 62*
Closest major hub ....*St. Louis, 18 air miles*

TESTS
1. Character..33.0
2. Stability..77.8
3. Growth..51.3
4. Education..89.7
5. Jobs..70.0
6. Business..31.7
7. Money...99.5
8. Housing..66.7
9. Health...48.2
10. Diversions..39.2
11. Internet 85.9
12. Proximity...97.3

BASIC STATS
Population...10,604
Density 1,090.5
Born out of state 29.7%
Homes built since 2000............................41.6%
4 or more bedrooms 43.7%

RACE
Whites...90.4%
Blacks..2.3%
Hispanics...2.7%
Asians...3.1%
Native Americans 0.0%
Diversity index...18.0%

HOUSEHOLD INCOME LADDER
95th percentile ....>$250,000
80th percentile $179,679
60th percentile $128,625
50th percentile $111,904
40th percentile $90,042
20th percentile $51,245

HOME VALUE LADDER
75th percentile $363,700
50th percentile $279,300
25th percentile $201,100

CHARACTER
Resilience..22.4%
Short commutes 21.4%

STABILITY
Living with two parents ....80.1% (★)
Occupied homes.......................................94.8%

GROWTH
Population growth......................................8.7%
Economic growth..6.0%

EDUCATION
High school graduates ....98.3% (★)
College graduates ....55.2% (★)

JOBS
MBSA workers ....52.6% (★)
Private-sector job growth 5.9%

BUSINESS
Small business growth 1.5%
Self-employed workers 5.3%

MONEY
Median annual earnings................$72,765 (★)
Living in poverty.....................................1.2% (★)

HOUSING
Home ownership................................82.4% (★)
Monthly housing costs............................29.6%

HEALTH
Health care workers.....................................8.0%
Fair or poor health....................................16.4%

DIVERSIONS
Stores per 10,000 ....35.7
Restaurants per 10,000..............................21.3

INTERNET
Broadband subscriptions ....86.0% (★)
Smartphone access ....88.3% (★)

PROXIMITY
Major hub miles ....18 (★)
Major or mid-major miles........................18 (★)

Evergreen, Colorado

Score ....875.9 points
National rank ....7 of 2,084
Percentile..99.71%
West rank... 4 of 471
Colorado rank .... 2 of 47
Closest major hub ....Denver, 19 air miles

TESTS
1. Character.......................................34.3
2. Stability..89.2
3. Growth..52.6
4. Education......................................98.4
5. Jobs...81.9
6. Business..73.1
7. Money...96.3
8. Housing...72.7
9. Health...61.7
10. Diversions....................................34.3
11. Internet 85.2
12. Proximity.....................................96.2

BASIC STATS
Population.......................................13,373
Density 981.6
Born out of state 75.3%
Homes built since 2000.....................7.8%
4 or more bedrooms 47.6%

RACE
Whites...91.1%
Blacks..0.4%
Hispanics 6.0%
Asians..1.3%
Native Americans 0.0%
Diversity index.................................16.6%

HOUSEHOLD INCOME LADDER
95th percentile ....>$250,000
80th percentile $232,565
60th percentile $141,905
50th percentile $121,786
40th percentile $99,216
20th percentile $51,245

HOME VALUE LADDER
75th percentile $748,000
50th percentile $554,600
25th percentile $401,500

CHARACTER
Resilience..18.3%
Short commutes 33.5%

STABILITY
Living with two parents ....83.6% (★)
Occupied homes...............................98.5% (★)

GROWTH
Population growth..............................2.8%
Economic growth.............................22.0%

EDUCATION
High school graduates ....99.0% (★)
College graduates ....69.2% (★)

JOBS
MBSA workers................................58.8% (★)
Private-sector job growth 10.6%

BUSINESS
Small business growth 7.4%
Self-employed workers ....18.0% (★)

MONEY
Median annual earnings...............$85,877 (★)
Living in poverty.............................4.9% (★)

HOUSING
Home ownership.............................86.9% (★)
Monthly housing costs.....................27.6%

HEALTH
Health care workers..........................7.6%
Fair or poor health............................9.3% (★)

DIVERSIONS
Stores per 10,000..............................31.4
Restaurants per 10,000......................20.2

INTERNET
Broadband subscriptions ....86.2% (★)
Smartphone access ....87.8% (★)

PROXIMITY
Major hub miles.................................19 (★)
Major or mid-major miles......................19 (★)

Fairview, Tennessee

Score ....765.1 points
National rank .... 106 of 2,084
Percentile...94.96%
South rank .... 32 of 745
Tennessee rank... 2 of 58
Closest major hub .... Nashville, 27 air miles

TESTS

1. Character	58.4
2. Stability	75.6
3. Growth	62.6
4. Education	56.5
5. Jobs	71.4
6. Business	58.8
7. Money	63.9
8. Housing	64.5
9. Health	50.1
10. Diversions	38.5
11. Internet	72.8
12. Proximity	92.0

BASIC STATS

Population	7,127
Density	1,155.5
Born out of state	40.9%
Homes built since 2000	36.5%
4 or more bedrooms	22.6%

RACE

Whites	87.7%
Blacks	5.1%
Hispanics	4.9%
Asians	0.2%
Native Americans	0.9%
Diversity index	22.6%

HOUSEHOLD INCOME LADDER

95th percentile	$175,780
80th percentile	$121,321
60th percentile	$85,091
50th percentile	$70,755
40th percentile	$55,036
20th percentile	$33,164

HOME VALUE LADDER

75th percentile	$297,600
50th percentile	$221,800
25th percentile	$155,200

CHARACTER

Resilience	42.3% (★)
Short commutes	17.9%

STABILITY

Living with two parents	69.8%
Occupied homes	97.3% (★)

GROWTH

Population growth	10.3% (★)
Economic growth	21.2%

EDUCATION

High school graduates	89.5%
College graduates	28.2%

JOBS

MBSA workers	35.1%
Private-sector job growth	30.0% (★)

BUSINESS

Small business growth	16.2% (★)
Self-employed workers	8.4%

MONEY

Median annual earnings	$45,998
Living in poverty	7.8%

HOUSING

Home ownership	77.8% (★)
Monthly housing costs	28.5%

HEALTH

Health care workers	6.7%
Fair or poor health	13.7%

DIVERSIONS

Stores per 10,000	34.9
Restaurants per 10,000	21.3

INTERNET

Broadband subscriptions	77.3% (★)
Smartphone access	83.5%

PROXIMITY

Major hub miles	27 (★)
Major or mid-major miles	27

Fernandina Beach, Florida

Score ....*794.1 points*
National rank ....*61 of 2,084*
Percentile...*97.12%*
South rank ....*21 of 745*
Florida rank .... *3 of 63*
Closest major hub ....*Jacksonville, 28 air miles*

TESTS
1. Character..................................56.7
2. Stability....................................77.3
3. Growth.....................................69.5
4. Education.................................72.3
5. Jobs...72.7
6. Business...................................67.9
7. Money......................................70.4
8. Housing....................................63.4
9. Health......................................54.0
10. Diversions..............................29.9
11. Internet 68.2
12. Proximity................................91.8

BASIC STATS
Population.................................30,399
Density 1,262.0
Born out of state 70.7%
Homes built since 2000...........34.4%
4 or more bedrooms 23.2%

RACE
Whites......................................86.3%
Blacks 7.0%
Hispanics 4.0%
Asians...1.8%
Native Americans 0.0%
Diversity index.........................24.8%

HOUSEHOLD INCOME LADDER
95th percentile .... >$250,000
80th percentile $152,153
60th percentile $95,186
50th percentile $74,908
40th percentile $60,451
20th percentile $34,987

HOME VALUE LADDER
75th percentile $472,300
50th percentile $307,000
25th percentile $216,100

CHARACTER
Resilience...................................29.2%
Short commutes 46.2%

STABILITY
Living with two parents 70.1%
Occupied homes................. 98.1% (★)

GROWTH
Population growth.................... 15.3% (★)
Economic growth 21.1%

EDUCATION
High school graduates 94.9%
College graduates .... 40.4% (★)

JOBS
MBSA workers....................... 42.6% (★)
Private-sector job growth .... 22.0% (★)

BUSINESS
Small business growth .... 14.4% (★)
Self-employed workers .... 12.8% (★)

MONEY
Median annual earnings...............$52,504 (★)
Living in poverty...........................7.8%

HOUSING
Home ownership...................... 78.1% (★)
Monthly housing costs..............29.6%

HEALTH
Health care workers.....................9.2%
Fair or poor health.......................15.2%

DIVERSIONS
Stores per 10,000........................29.9
Restaurants per 10,000................17.7

INTERNET
Broadband subscriptions 71.6%
Smartphone access 82.9%

PROXIMITY
Major hub miles ....28 (★)
Major or mid-major miles.............. 28

Firestone, Colorado

Score ....*773.6 points*
National rank ....*90 of 2,084*
Percentile...*95.73%*
West rank.. *38 of 471*
Colorado rank .... *16 of 47*
Closest major hub ....*Denver, 28 air miles*

TESTS

1. Character..29.7
2. Stability..89.6
3. Growth...85.8
4. Education...64.9
5. Jobs...61.5
6. Business...57.5
7. Money..77.9
8. Housing..60.6
9. Health..50.3
10. Diversions..17.7
11. Internet 86.3
12. Proximity..91.8

BASIC STATS

Population...26,575
Density 2,621.1
Born out of state......................................47.5%
Homes built since 2000...........................66.5%
4 or more bedrooms 37.8%

RACE

Whites...73.0%
Blacks...0.4%
Hispanics...21.3%
Asians...2.4%
Native Americans 0.2%
Diversity index...42.0%

HOUSEHOLD INCOME LADDER

95th percentile $209,157
80th percentile $148,298
60th percentile $107,760
50th percentile $91,171
40th percentile $76,704
20th percentile $48,369

HOME VALUE LADDER

75th percentile $397,000
50th percentile $333,400
25th percentile $251,300

CHARACTER

Resilience... 19.5%
Short commutes 22.6%

STABILITY

Living with two parents .... 83.0% (★)
Occupied homes............................. 98.8% (★)

GROWTH

Population growth............................ 17.6% (★)
Economic growth .... 40.1% (★)

EDUCATION

High school graduates 94.4%
College graduates 32.1%

JOBS

MBSA workers..36.4%
Private-sector job growth 16.6%

BUSINESS

Small business growth .... 19.8% (★)
Self-employed workers 6.1%

MONEY

Median annual earnings.................$55,356 (★)
Living in poverty...................................3.5% (★)

HOUSING

Home ownership .... 85.7% (★)
Monthly housing costs 36.6%

HEALTH

Health care workers..................................6.7%
Fair or poor health...................................13.6%

DIVERSIONS

Stores per 10,000.....................................20.9
Restaurants per 10,000............................13.8

INTERNET

Broadband subscriptions .... 82.0% (★)
Smartphone access .... 91.2% (★)

PROXIMITY

Major hub miles ....28 (★)
Major or mid-major miles................................. 28

Forest Lake, Minnesota

Score ....*738.5 points*
National rank ....*160 of 2,084*
Percentile...*92.37%*
Midwest rank...*34 of 622*
Minnesota rank ....*8 of 53*
Closest major hub ....*Minneapolis, 26 air miles*

TESTS
1. Character..................................63.6
2. Stability....................................72.6
3. Growth.....................................48.9
4. Education.................................63.5
5. Jobs...62.3
6. Business..................................47.3
7. Money......................................72.1
8. Housing...................................54.2
9. Health......................................67.8
10. Diversions..............................25.4
11. Internet 68.6
12. Proximity................................92.2

BASIC STATS
Population...............................22,640
Density 1,265.2
Born out of state.....................21.9%
Homes built since 2000...........31.3%
4 or more bedrooms 30.0%

RACE
Whites.....................................89.2%
Blacks 1.5%
Hispanics 3.9%
Asians.......................................2.8%
Native Americans 0.3%
Diversity index.........................20.1%

HOUSEHOLD INCOME LADDER
95th percentile $230,277
80th percentile $141,100
60th percentile $98,482
50th percentile $79,943
40th percentile $67,209
20th percentile $40,646

HOME VALUE LADDER
75th percentile $347,500
50th percentile $249,200
25th percentile $196,000

CHARACTER
Resilience.............................. 41.3% (★)
Short commutes 29.3%
STABILITY
Living with two parents 69.8%
Occupied homes.......................95.7%
GROWTH
Population growth.....................3.3%
Economic growth 14.5%
EDUCATION
High school graduates 94.9%
College graduates 29.7%
JOBS
MBSA workers.........................37.6%
Private-sector job growth 16.0%
BUSINESS
Small business growth 7.7%
Self-employed workers 8.2%
MONEY
Median annual earnings.......$51,283
Living in poverty.....................5.1% (★)
HOUSING
Home ownership......................73.3%
Monthly housing costs.............33.9%
HEALTH
Health care workers..................9.9%
Fair or poor health..................9.5% (★)
DIVERSIONS
Stores per 10,000.......................28.2
Restaurants per 10,000..............15.3
INTERNET
Broadband subscriptions 72.2%
Smartphone access 82.9%
PROXIMITY
Major hub miles.........................26 (★)
Major or mid-major miles........26 (★)

Forney, Texas

Score ....753.3 points
National rank ....125 of 2,084
Percentile...94.05%
South rank ....38 of 745
Texas rank.. 11 of 173
Closest major hub ....Dallas, 32 air miles

TESTS
1. Character...36.9
2. Stability...81.9
3. Growth...75.1
4. Education...59.4
5. Jobs..64.0
6. Business...57.1
7. Money..75.0
8. Housing..62.4
9. Health..46.0
10. Diversions......................................20.7
11. Internet 83.7
12. Proximity..91.1

BASIC STATS
Population.......................................34,121
Density 1,825.8
Born out of state 30.2%
Homes built since 2000.................. 70.7%
4 or more bedrooms 46.4%

RACE
Whites..63.3%
Blacks...16.1%
Hispanics...16.7%
Asians...2.6%
Native Americans 0.2%
Diversity index.................................54.5%

HOUSEHOLD INCOME LADDER
95th percentile $203,523
80th percentile $146,573
60th percentile $109,004
50th percentile $92,870
40th percentile $73,150
20th percentile $50,313

HOME VALUE LADDER
75th percentile $264,300
50th percentile $205,200
25th percentile $159,100

CHARACTER
Resilience..24.3%
Short commutes 23.7%

STABILITY
Living with two parents ....79.7% (★)
Occupied homes...............................97.1% (★)

GROWTH
Population growth............................19.7% (★)
Economic growth 20.3%

EDUCATION
High school graduates 92.7%
College graduates 27.5%

JOBS
MBSA workers....................................37.5%
Private-sector job growth ....18.2% (★)

BUSINESS
Small business growth ....20.9% (★)
Self-employed workers 5.4%

MONEY
Median annual earnings.................$54,925 (★)
Living in poverty...............................5.7% (★)

HOUSING
Home ownership...............................86.2% (★)
Monthly housing costs 35.5%

HEALTH
Health care workers..........................7.6%
Fair or poor health............................16.9%

DIVERSIONS
Stores per 10,000..............................23.6
Restaurants per 10,000.....................14.5

INTERNET
Broadband subscriptions ....81.1% (★)
Smartphone access ....90.4% (★)

PROXIMITY
Major hub miles................................32 (★)
Major or mid-major miles.................32

Frankenmuth, Michigan

Score ....770.1 points
National rank ....96 of 2,084
Percentile...95.44%
Midwest rank.. 16 of 622
Michigan rank .... 3 of 67
Closest major hub ....Detroit, 64 air miles

TESTS
1. Character...61.7
2. Stability...85.6
3. Growth..45.0
4. Education...87.8
5. Jobs...58.9
6. Business...36.0
7. Money...84.9
8. Housing...69.8
9. Health..58.5
10. Diversions.......................................41.6
11. Internet 54.8
12. Proximity..85.5

BASIC STATS
Population.. 5,294
Density 1,926.5
Born out of state 12.5%
Homes built since 2000.........................6.5%
4 or more bedrooms 23.8%

RACE
Whites...95.5%
Blacks...0.3%
Hispanics 3.7%
Asians...0.3%
Native Americans 0.0%
Diversity index.......................................8.7%

HOUSEHOLD INCOME LADDER
95th percentile $241,446
80th percentile $140,743
60th percentile $90,245
50th percentile $62,209
40th percentile $47,793
20th percentile $28,708

HOME VALUE LADDER
75th percentile $241,000
50th percentile $191,900
25th percentile $152,100

CHARACTER
Resilience...27.2%
Short commutes 59.7%

STABILITY
Living with two parents ....82.3% (★)
Occupied homes...............................97.7% (★)

GROWTH
Population growth...................................4.9%
Economic growth 4.3%

EDUCATION
High school graduates ....97.5% (★)
College graduates ....54.6% (★)

JOBS
MBSA workers.................................. 46.2% (★)
Private-sector job growth 0.9%

BUSINESS
Small business growth ....-4.2%
Self-employed workers 9.8%

MONEY
Median annual earnings ....$63,209 (★)
Living in poverty.................................4.9% (★)

HOUSING
Home ownership.................................69.4%
Monthly housing costs 18.9%

HEALTH
Health care workers...............................12.6%
Fair or poor health.................................17.7%

DIVERSIONS
Stores per 10,000...................................42.0
Restaurants per 10,000..........................19.3

INTERNET
Broadband subscriptions 71.1%
Smartphone access 70.4%

PROXIMITY
Major hub miles 64
Major or mid-major miles..............................64

Frederick, Maryland

Score .... *748.3 points*
National rank .... *137 of 2,084*
Percentile *93.47%*
East rank .... *19 of 246*
Maryland rank .... *4 of 23*
Closest major hub .... *Washington, 38 air miles*

TESTS
1. Character............................48.6
2. Stability...............................74.8
3. Growth................................51.2
4. Education............................76.9
5. Jobs.....................................70.6
6. Business..............................37.5
7. Money.................................82.7
8. Housing...............................50.8
9. Health.................................58.3
10. Diversions.........................29.0
11. Internet.............................77.8
12. Proximity...........................90.1

BASIC STATS
Population............................156,164
Density.................................2,126.7
Born out of state.....................55.1%
Homes built since 2000...........27.9%
4 or more bedrooms................34.4%

RACE
Whites.....................................64.5%
Blacks.....................................13.2%
Hispanics...............................12.8%
Asians......................................6.2%
Native Americans....................0.3%
Diversity index.......................54.5%

HOUSEHOLD INCOME LADDER
95th percentile.................>$250,000
80th percentile..................$165,907
60th percentile..................$113,137
50th percentile....................$93,715
40th percentile....................$74,725
20th percentile....................$42,360

HOME VALUE LADDER
75th percentile...................$429,100
50th percentile...................$315,200
25th percentile...................$236,600

CHARACTER
Resilience................................26.1%
Short commutes.....................39.6%

STABILITY
Living with two parents..........73.4%
Occupied homes.....................95.6%

GROWTH
Population growth....................7.8%
Economic growth......................7.9%

EDUCATION
High school graduates.............93.5%
College graduates............47.9% (★)

JOBS
MBSA workers....................49.0% (★)
Private-sector job growth........11.2%

BUSINESS
Small business growth..............4.4%
Self-employed workers..............6.1%

MONEY
Median annual earnings.............$64,759 (★)
Living in poverty....................7.7% (★)

HOUSING
Home ownership....................68.7%
Monthly housing costs............33.8%

HEALTH
Health care workers..................8.0%
Fair or poor health............11.5% (★)

DIVERSIONS
Stores per 10,000.......................27.8
Restaurants per 10,000..............18.3

INTERNET
Broadband subscriptions.........81.8% (★)
Smartphone access............85.2% (★)

PROXIMITY
Major hub miles.........................38
Major or mid-major miles............38

Fredericksburg, Virginia

Score ....727.0 points
National rank ....198 of 2,084
Percentile...90.54%
South rank .... 49 of 745
Virginia rank... 8 of 41
Closest major hub .... Washington, 46 air miles

TESTS

1. Character.................................55.9
2. Stability...................................72.1
3. Growth....................................47.1
4. Education................................67.6
5. Jobs...63.0
6. Business..................................38.3
7. Money.....................................74.5
8. Housing...................................48.3
9. Health......................................50.8
10. Diversions.............................41.2
11. Internet 79.5
12. Proximity................................88.7

BASIC STATS

Population.................................154,302
Density 1,978.7
Born out of state.........................53.9%
Homes built since 2000...............32.4%
4 or more bedrooms....................36.8%

RACE

Whites...62.5%
Blacks 19.4%
Hispanics 10.6%
Asians..2.7%
Native Americans 0.3%
Diversity index.............................55.8%

HOUSEHOLD INCOME LADDER

95th percentile........................$243,814
80th percentile........................$155,463
60th percentile........................$103,895
50th percentile..........................$85,238
40th percentile..........................$67,534
20th percentile..........................$39,638

HOME VALUE LADDER

75th percentile........................$371,900
50th percentile........................$293,500
25th percentile........................$226,500

CHARACTER

Resilience......................................32.2%
Short commutes 37.7%

STABILITY

Living with two parents 67.9%
Occupied homes.........................96.1%

GROWTH

Population growth........................4.4%
Economic growth..........................8.9%

EDUCATION

High school graduates 92.8%
College graduates 37.4%

JOBS

MBSA workers.................... 43.3% (★)
Private-sector job growth 9.5%

BUSINESS

Small business growth 8.6%
Self-employed workers 4.3%

MONEY

Median annual earnings...............$56,966 (★)
Living in poverty............................8.1%

HOUSING

Home ownership.........................66.2%
Monthly housing costs...............34.2%

HEALTH

Health care workers.......................7.4%
Fair or poor health......................14.3%

DIVERSIONS

Stores per 10,000...........................38.8
Restaurants per 10,000.................21.0

INTERNET

Broadband subscriptions .... 83.4% (★)
Smartphone access .... 85.8% (★)

PROXIMITY

Major hub miles 46
Major or mid-major miles............................. 46

Goodrich, Michigan

Score	*734.5 points*
National rank	*176 of 2,084*
Percentile	*91.60%*
Midwest rank	*38 of 622*
Michigan rank	*6 of 67*
Closest major hub	*Detroit, 30 air miles*

TESTS

1. Character...............43.5
2. Stability................74.7
3. Growth..................33.8
4. Education..............69.4
5. Jobs......................60.3
6. Business................39.3
7. Money...................78.6
8. Housing.................72.1
9. Health...................55.3
10. Diversions............36.8
11. Internet................79.2
12. Proximity..............91.5

BASIC STATS

Population	5,663
Density	864.4
Born out of state	11.8%
Homes built since 2000	14.4%
4 or more bedrooms	26.7%

RACE

Whites	94.9%
Blacks	0.7%
Hispanics	2.8%
Asians	0.4%
Native Americans	0.1%
Diversity index	9.8%

HOUSEHOLD INCOME LADDER

95th percentile	$210,458
80th percentile	$148,579
60th percentile	$104,294
50th percentile	$88,875
40th percentile	$71,286
20th percentile	$44,461

HOME VALUE LADDER

75th percentile	$277,500
50th percentile	$202,500
25th percentile	$155,100

CHARACTER

Resilience	28.3%
Short commutes	25.6%

STABILITY

Living with two parents	70.2%
Occupied homes	96.7% (★)

GROWTH

Population growth	-4.8%
Economic growth	8.2%

EDUCATION

High school graduates	96.0% (★)
College graduates	35.5%

JOBS

MBSA workers	43.7% (★)
Private-sector job growth	5.8%

BUSINESS

Small business growth	0.4%
Self-employed workers	8.8%

MONEY

Median annual earnings	$59,574 (★)
Living in poverty	6.8% (★)

HOUSING

Home ownership	85.9% (★)
Monthly housing costs	27.5%

HEALTH

Health care workers	9.0%
Fair or poor health	14.3%

DIVERSIONS

Stores per 10,000	35.3
Restaurants per 10,000	19.7

INTERNET

Broadband subscriptions	82.2% (★)
Smartphone access	86.3% (★)

PROXIMITY

Major hub miles	30 (★)
Major or mid-major miles	30

Gunnison, Colorado

Score ....*769.6 points*
National rank ....*97 of 2,084*
Percentile...*95.39%*
West rank.. *40 of 471*
Colorado rank .... *17 of 47*
Closest major hub .... *Denver, 133 air miles*

TESTS
1. Character...81.3
2. Stability..67.1
3. Growth..58.6
4. Education...94.0
5. Jobs...53.3
6. Business...44.7
7. Money...33.5
8. Housing..34.4
9. Health...58.9
10. Diversions..98.7
11. Internet...70.0
12. Proximity..75.1

BASIC STATS
Population.. 6,944
Density 2,152.5
Born out of state 56.0%
Homes built since 2000..........................17.3%
4 or more bedrooms 7.8%

RACE
Whites..85.0%
Blacks..0.7%
Hispanics 12.3%
Asians..0.5%
Native Americans 0.2%
Diversity index.................................26.2%

HOUSEHOLD INCOME LADDER
95th percentile $141,453
80th percentile $93,878
60th percentile $52,897
50th percentile $40,990
40th percentile $33,429
20th percentile $20,752

HOME VALUE LADDER
75th percentile $345,100
50th percentile $243,500
25th percentile $155,900

CHARACTER
Resilience..34.2%
Short commutes 76.9%

STABILITY
Living with two parents 51.9%
Occupied homes................................ 99.2% (★)

GROWTH
Population growth............................ 10.7% (★)
Economic growth 13.7%

EDUCATION
High school graduates .... 99.5% (★)
College graduates .... 57.0% (★)

JOBS
MBSA workers...31.7%
Private-sector job growth 12.9%

BUSINESS
Small business growth 10.3%
Self-employed workers 5.9%

MONEY
Median annual earnings.......................$31,034
Living in poverty...22.4%

HOUSING
Home ownership......................................38.7%
Monthly housing costs.............................28.0%

HEALTH
Health care workers...................................9.4%
Fair or poor health 13.1%

DIVERSIONS
Stores per 10,000................................77.5 (★)
Restaurants per 10,000......................54.8 (★)

INTERNET
Broadband subscriptions 74.3%
Smartphone access 82.8%

PROXIMITY
Major hub miles...133
Major or mid-major miles...............................119

Gypsum, Colorado

Score ....750.5 points
National rank ....131 of 2,084
Percentile...93.76%
West rank...51 of 471
Colorado rank ....18 of 47
Closest major hub ....Denver, 106 air miles

TESTS
1. Character..57.5
2. Stability..93.9
3. Growth..64.3
4. Education..49.1
5. Jobs..43.5
6. Business..52.6
7. Money...67.5
8. Housing...43.3
9. Health...46.5
10. Diversions..96.6
11. Internet 57.6
12. Proximity..78.1

BASIC STATS
Population.. 6,881
Density 1,970.5
Born out of state 59.5%
Homes built since 2000...........................27.9%
4 or more bedrooms 21.5%

RACE
Whites..63.6%
Blacks..0.0%
Hispanics 35.4%
Asians..0.0%
Native Americans 0.6%
Diversity index..................................47.0%

HOUSEHOLD INCOME LADDER
95th percentile ....>$250,000
80th percentile $117,115
60th percentile $85,985
50th percentile $78,075
40th percentile $63,386
20th percentile $29,885

HOME VALUE LADDER
75th percentile $462,200
50th percentile $348,800
25th percentile $230,000

CHARACTER
Resilience..31.0%
Short commutes 43.4%

STABILITY
Living with two parents ....93.1% (★)
Occupied homes...............................96.7% (★)

GROWTH
Population growth............................12.5% (★)
Economic growth 19.0%

EDUCATION
High school graduates 80.0%
College graduates 31.6%

JOBS
MBSA workers....................................21.7%
Private-sector job growth 14.2%

BUSINESS
Small business growth 9.2%
Self-employed workers 9.5%

MONEY
Median annual earnings.....................$46,746
Living in poverty....................................5.1% (★)

HOUSING
Home ownership.............................71.4%
Monthly housing costs............................41.5%

HEALTH
Health care workers.............................4.4%
Fair or poor health.............................12.3% (★)

DIVERSIONS
Stores per 10,000..............................71.2 (★)
Restaurants per 10,000.....................45.9 (★)

INTERNET
Broadband subscriptions 46.1%
Smartphone access ....90.0% (★)

PROXIMITY
Major hub miles.................................106
Major or mid-major miles..........................106

Half Moon Bay, California

Score ....*767.7 points*
National rank ....*99 of 2,084*
Percentile...*95.30%*
West rank..*42 of 471*
California rank ....*5 of 145*
Closest major hub ....*San Francisco, 21 air miles*

TESTS
1. Character.......................................16.6
2. Stability..81.9
3. Growth..61.5
4. Education.....................................76.4
5. Jobs..75.7
6. Business.......................................54.5
7. Money..96.0
8. Housing..47.9
9. Health...47.3
10. Diversions..................................37.8
11. Internet 77.9
12. Proximity....................................94.2

BASIC STATS
Population....................................22,114
Density 2,986.8
Born out of state 45.3%
Homes built since 2000............... 17.7%
4 or more bedrooms 28.0%

RACE
Whites...67.1%
Blacks..0.5%
Hispanics 24.5%
Asians..4.1%
Native Americans 0.2%
Diversity index.............................48.7%

HOUSEHOLD INCOME LADDER
95th percentile .... >$250,000
80th percentile .... >$250,000
60th percentile $158,068
50th percentile $122,064
40th percentile $97,350
20th percentile $49,513

HOME VALUE LADDER
75th percentile $1,305,500
50th percentile $978,200
25th percentile $715,000

CHARACTER
Resilience...6.4%
Short commutes 31.2%

STABILITY
Living with two parents ....81.5% (★)
Occupied homes...........................96.5%

GROWTH
Population growth...........................1.4%
Economic growth............. 40.1% (★)

EDUCATION
High school graduates 89.3%
College graduates .... 52.8% (★)

JOBS
MBSA workers...................... 52.2% (★)
Private-sector job growth 12.4%

BUSINESS
Small business growth 5.3%
Self-employed workers .... 12.2% (★)

MONEY
Median annual earnings...............$83,000 (★)
Living in poverty..................4.9% (★)

HOUSING
Home ownership.........................73.9%
Monthly housing costs............................39.4%

HEALTH
Health care workers..........................4.7%
Fair or poor health............................ 12.3% (★)

DIVERSIONS
Stores per 10,000 ....25.3
Restaurants per 10,000........................26.7 (★)

INTERNET
Broadband subscriptions .... 83.5% (★)
Smartphone access 84.2%

PROXIMITY
Major hub miles ....21 (★)
Major or mid-major miles........................21 (★)

Hampstead, North Carolina

Score ....*799.6 points*
National rank ....*48 of 2,084*
Percentile...*97.74%*
South rank ....*16 of 745*
North Carolina rank..*2 of 65*
Closest major hub ....*Raleigh, 111 air miles*

TESTS
1. Character..44.3
2. Stability...78.6
3. Growth...80.5
4. Education..84.0
5. Jobs..75.4
6. Business...75.9
7. Money...73.1
8. Housing..66.2
9. Health...47.9
10. Diversions...24.7
11. Internet...71.8
12. Proximity...77.2

BASIC STATS
Population...13,988
Density 909.6
Born out of state.................................58.8%
Homes built since 2000.........................49.5%
4 or more bedrooms 31.7%

RACE
Whites..94.0%
Blacks...0.8%
Hispanics 1.8%
Asians..0.5%
Native Americans 0.2%
Diversity index....................................11.5%

HOUSEHOLD INCOME LADDER
95th percentile .... >$250,000
80th percentile $142,339
60th percentile $94,104
50th percentile $77,250
40th percentile $63,233
20th percentile $39,120

HOME VALUE LADDER
75th percentile $397,000
50th percentile $279,200
25th percentile $189,000

CHARACTER
Resilience...28.2%
Short commutes 27.1%

STABILITY
Living with two parents ....81.6% (★)
Occupied homes..94.7%

GROWTH
Population growth.............................23.9% (★)
Economic growth 18.6%

EDUCATION
High school graduates ....96.4% (★)
College graduates ....52.8% (★)

JOBS
MBSA workers.......................................41.6% (★)
Private-sector job growth ....25.8% (★)

BUSINESS
Small business growth ....19.4% (★)
Self-employed workers ....12.9% (★)

MONEY
Median annual earnings........................$52,288
Living in poverty......................................5.1% (★)

HOUSING
Home ownership................................85.0% (★)
Monthly housing costs............................31.7%

HEALTH
Health care workers..8.2%
Fair or poor health.......................................16.8%

DIVERSIONS
Stores per 10,000..25.5
Restaurants per 10,000................................16.4

INTERNET
Broadband subscriptions ....78.2% (★)
Smartphone access 81.9%

PROXIMITY
Major hub miles 111
Major or mid-major miles.............................111

Heber, Utah

Score ....870.1 points
National rank .... 8 of 2,084
Percentile..99.66%
West rank.. 5 of 471
Utah rank.. 3 of 20
Closest major hub .... Salt Lake City, 28 air miles

TESTS
1. Character....................70.6
2. Stability......................91.0
3. Growth.......................86.3
4. Education...................70.4
5. Jobs...........................86.9
6. Business.....................87.3
7. Money.......................70.7
8. Housing.....................55.1
9. Health........................55.1
10. Diversions.................27.0
11. Internet 77.3
12. Proximity..................92.4

BASIC STATS
Population.....................21,817
Density 1,699.8
Born out of state.............41.4%
Homes built since 2000............45.7%
4 or more bedrooms 51.8%

RACE
Whites..............................81.9%
Blacks 0.0%
Hispanics 14.6%
Asians.................................1.6%
Native Americans 0.2%
Diversity index................30.7%

HOUSEHOLD INCOME LADDER
95th percentile $235,339
80th percentile $136,381
60th percentile.......................$99,159
50th percentile $81,767
40th percentile $68,921
20th percentile $41,220

HOME VALUE LADDER
75th percentile $493,300
50th percentile $376,200
25th percentile $284,100

CHARACTER
Resilience..............................40.5% (★)
Short commutes 43.3%

STABILITY
Living with two parents ....90.1% (★)
Occupied homes...............................96.8% (★)

GROWTH
Population growth............................16.3% (★)
Economic growth ....43.6% (★)

EDUCATION
High school graduates 93.9%
College graduates ....39.4% (★)

JOBS
MBSA workers.......................................37.6%
Private-sector job growth ....43.2% (★)

BUSINESS
Small business growth ....24.1% (★)
Self-employed workers ....14.1% (★)

MONEY
Median annual earnings.......................$50,720
Living in poverty.................................5.9% (★)

HOUSING
Home ownership...............................74.7% (★)
Monthly housing costs............................34.1%

HEALTH
Health care workers....................................6.8%
Fair or poor health..............................11.4% (★)

DIVERSIONS
Stores per 10,000..29.0
Restaurants per 10,000.................................16.0

INTERNET
Broadband subscriptions 72.2%
Smartphone access ....91.2% (★)

PROXIMITY
Major hub miles...28 (★)
Major or mid-major miles.......................23 (★)

Hilton Head Island, South Carolina

Score ....*748.0 points*
National rank ....*138 of 2,084*
Percentile...*93.42%*
South rank .... *40 of 745*
South Carolina rank.. *4 of 35*
Closest major hub ....*Jacksonville, 147 air miles*

TESTS
1. Character.................................51.5
2. Stability..................................70.4
3. Growth....................................48.4
4. Education................................69.4
5. Jobs...62.8
6. Business..................................68.5
7. Money.....................................61.2
8. Housing...................................51.8
9. Health.....................................53.3
10. Diversions.............................50.9
11. Internet 78.7
12. Proximity...............................81.1

BASIC STATS
Population............................74,486
Density 1,100.9
Born out of state 80.0%
Homes built since 2000............29.7%
4 or more bedrooms 21.4%

RACE
Whites.....................................74.8%
Blacks.......................................5.9%
Hispanics 17.0%
Asians.......................................1.0%
Native Americans 0.1%
Diversity index.......................40.8%

HOUSEHOLD INCOME LADDER
95th percentile ....>$250,000
80th percentile $153,254
60th percentile $96,440
50th percentile $77,631
40th percentile $63,513
20th percentile $34,620

HOME VALUE LADDER
75th percentile $628,200
50th percentile $392,400
25th percentile $236,100

CHARACTER
Resilience.................................23.2%
Short commutes 51.5%

STABILITY
Living with two parents 69.1%
Occupied homes......................94.8%

GROWTH
Population growth.....................3.9%
Economic growth 12.3%

EDUCATION
High school graduates 91.4%
College graduates ....41.5% (★)

JOBS
MBSA workers.........................38.0%
Private-sector job growth 16.1%

BUSINESS
Small business growth ....12.5% (★)
Self-employed workers ....14.0% (★)

MONEY
Median annual earnings.......$44,737
Living in poverty.......................9.2%

HOUSING
Home ownership...............75.2% (★)
Monthly housing costs 37.1%

HEALTH
Health care workers.................6.9%
Fair or poor health.............12.4% (★)

DIVERSIONS
Stores per 10,000....................41.1
Restaurants per 10,000........27.1 (★)

INTERNET
Broadband subscriptions ....79.9% (★)
Smartphone access ....87.4% (★)

PROXIMITY
Major hub miles.......................147
Major or mid-major miles............63

Hood River, Oregon

Score ....802.7 points
National rank ....45 of 2,084
Percentile...97.89%
West rank...22 of 471
Oregon rank ....2 of 45
Closest major hub ....Portland, 56 air miles

TESTS
1. Character...59.4
2. Stability...79.7
3. Growth..60.4
4. Education..68.6
5. Jobs...62.1
6. Business..62.4
7. Money...71.7
8. Housing...58.7
9. Health..57.7
10. Diversions...68.8
11. Internet 66.3
12. Proximity...86.9

BASIC STATS
Population...15,500
Density 1,481.4
Born out of state 68.9%
Homes built since 2000...........................24.3%
4 or more bedrooms 14.9%

RACE
Whites..75.6%
Blacks..0.7%
Hispanics...20.6%
Asians...1.2%
Native Americans 0.1%
Diversity index..38.6%

HOUSEHOLD INCOME LADDER
95th percentile ....>$250,000
80th percentile $126,767
60th percentile $81,394
50th percentile $66,457
40th percentile $53,527
20th percentile $30,069

HOME VALUE LADDER
75th percentile $500,800
50th percentile $379,800
25th percentile $284,500

CHARACTER
Resilience...21.0%
Short commutes 70.5%

STABILITY
Living with two parents ....80.4% (★)
Occupied homes..95.7%

GROWTH
Population growth......................................3.2%
Economic growth ....33.9% (★)

EDUCATION
High school graduates 87.6%
College graduates ....45.5% (★)

JOBS
MBSA workers....................................42.4% (★)
Private-sector job growth 9.6%

BUSINESS
Small business growth 5.0%
Self-employed workers ....15.4% (★)

MONEY
Median annual earnings.......................$51,577
Living in poverty....................................5.7% (★)

HOUSING
Home ownership.......................................63.8%
Monthly housing costs 24.3%

HEALTH
Health care workers................................11.3%
Fair or poor health...................................16.3%

DIVERSIONS
Stores per 10,000....................................55.7 (★)
Restaurants per 10,000........................31.9 (★)

INTERNET
Broadband subscriptions 71.4%
Smartphone access 81.2%

PROXIMITY
Major hub miles..56
Major or mid-major miles...............................56

Hudson, Wisconsin

Score ....789.9 points
National rank ....69 of 2,084
Percentile...96.74%
Midwest rank.. 9 of 622
Wisconsin rank .... 1 of 61
Closest major hub ....Minneapolis, 27 air miles

TESTS
1. Character.......................................72.2
2. Stability...78.0
3. Growth..53.4
4. Education.......................................78.0
5. Jobs..62.6
6. Business...49.6
7. Money...77.6
8. Housing...58.0
9. Health...63.8
10. Diversions....................................31.2
11. Internet 73.5
12. Proximity......................................92.0

BASIC STATS
Population......................................23,454
Density 1,661.4
Born out of state 59.8%
Homes built since 2000...................27.5%
4 or more bedrooms 28.2%

RACE
Whites..92.8%
Blacks..1.3%
Hispanics 3.3%
Asians..1.0%
Native Americans 0.1%
Diversity index................................13.7%

HOUSEHOLD INCOME LADDER
95th percentile $225,462
80th percentile $137,687
60th percentile...........................$99,107
50th percentile...........................$82,049
40th percentile...........................$64,115
20th percentile...........................$38,112

HOME VALUE LADDER
75th percentile $340,800
50th percentile $258,600
25th percentile $199,700

CHARACTER
Resilience...............................43.3% (★)
Short commutes 39.5%

STABILITY
Living with two parents 72.9%
Occupied homes................................ 97.5% (★)

GROWTH
Population growth...................................3.5%
Economic growth 21.6%

EDUCATION
High school graduates .... 97.2% (★)
College graduates .... 44.4% (★)

JOBS
MBSA workers...................................44.1% (★)
Private-sector job growth 8.0%

BUSINESS
Small business growth 7.7%
Self-employed workers 9.1%

MONEY
Median annual earnings................$58,590 (★)
Living in poverty...................................6.8% (★)

HOUSING
Home ownership 70.3%
Monthly housing costs............................29.0%

HEALTH
Health care workers................................8.8%
Fair or poor health................................9.9% (★)

DIVERSIONS
Stores per 10,000................................28.7
Restaurants per 10,000...................19.5

INTERNET
Broadband subscriptions .... 77.0% (★)
Smartphone access 84.3%

PROXIMITY
Major hub miles...27 (★)
Major or mid-major miles................................ 27

Idaho Falls, Idaho

Score ....725.2 points
National rank ....207 of 2,084
Percentile..90.11%
West rank...79 of 471
Idaho rank .... 6 of 21
Closest major hub ....Salt Lake City, 197 air miles

TESTS
1. Character..................66.3
2. Stability.....................76.2
3. Growth......................60.4
4. Education..................60.5
5. Jobs...........................62.2
6. Business....................52.2
7. Money.......................55.9
8. Housing.....................58.4
9. Health.......................55.9
10. Diversions................40.9
11. Internet....................70.2
12. Proximity..................66.1

BASIC STATS
Population..........................98,340
Density 2,206.6
Born out of state................42.5%
Homes built since 2000..........27.6%
4 or more bedrooms 40.7%

RACE
Whites................81.3%
Blacks..................0.5%
Hispanics...........14.3%
Asians...................1.2%
Native Americans 0.4%
Diversity index...................31.8%

HOUSEHOLD INCOME LADDER
95th percentile $193,177
80th percentile $108,606
60th percentile $70,431
50th percentile $57,977
40th percentile $46,092
20th percentile $25,847

HOME VALUE LADDER
75th percentile $236,600
50th percentile $172,200
25th percentile $129,300

CHARACTER
Resilience..........................25.7%
Short commutes 71.3%

STABILITY
Living with two parents ....76.8% (★)
Occupied homes...............95.1%

GROWTH
Population growth...............5.9%
Economic growth ....27.7% (★)

EDUCATION
High school graduates 91.2%
College graduates 30.9%

JOBS
MBSA workers.....................36.2%
Private-sector job growth ....17.7% (★)

BUSINESS
Small business growth ....11.9% (★)
Self-employed workers 8.0%

MONEY
Median annual earnings......................$41,809
Living in poverty..............11.4%

HOUSING
Home ownership................67.3%
Monthly housing costs...........26.8%

HEALTH
Health care workers...............9.5%
Fair or poor health..............14.7%

DIVERSIONS
Stores per 10,000................42.5
Restaurants per 10,000.............18.5

INTERNET
Broadband subscriptions 72.8%
Smartphone access 84.0%

PROXIMITY
Major hub miles...............197
Major or mid-major miles............164

Incline Village, Nevada

Score ....*732.8 points*
National rank ....*181 of 2,084*
Percentile...*91.36%*
West rank...*70 of 471*
Nevada rank ....*2 of 14*
Closest major hub ....*Sacramento, 83 air miles*

TESTS
1. Character...46.0
2. Stability..71.5
3. Growth...46.8
4. Education...67.9
5. Jobs..64.7
6. Business...82.3
7. Money..68.8
8. Housing..37.4
9. Health...39.7
10. Diversions......................................37.7
11. Internet...80.4
12. Proximity..89.6

BASIC STATS
Population.......................................11,853
Density..991.6
Born out of state............................76.1%
Homes built since 2000......................7.3%
4 or more bedrooms.......................23.6%

RACE
Whites..72.5%
Blacks...0.5%
Hispanics...22.8%
Asians...1.6%
Native Americans.............................0.9%
Diversity index...............................42.2%

HOUSEHOLD INCOME LADDER
95th percentile....................... >$250,000
80th percentile......................... $194,031
60th percentile...........................$95,533
50th percentile...........................$75,420
40th percentile...........................$59,257
20th percentile...........................$35,004

HOME VALUE LADDER
75th percentile......................$1,189,000
50th percentile.........................$707,100
25th percentile.........................$446,400

CHARACTER
Resilience...18.2%
Short commutes..............................54.0%

STABILITY
Living with two parents.................75.7%
Occupied homes..............................93.0%

GROWTH
Population growth............................-0.5%
Economic growth.............................20.0%

EDUCATION
High school graduates.....................88.9%
College graduates............................42.9% (★)

JOBS
MBSA workers...................................36.6%
Private-sector job growth...............20.1% (★)

BUSINESS
Small business growth.....................12.4% (★)
Self-employed workers....................20.5% (★)

MONEY
Median annual earnings................$52,953 (★)
Living in poverty................................9.8%

HOUSING
Home ownership.............................67.3%
Monthly housing costs....................43.7%

HEALTH
Health care workers............................3.1%
Fair or poor health..........................13.8%

DIVERSIONS
Stores per 10,000..............................31.6
Restaurants per 10,000.....................22.7

INTERNET
Broadband subscriptions................81.1% (★)
Smartphone access..........................88.2% (★)

PROXIMITY
Major hub miles....................................83
Major or mid-major miles........................22 (★)

Iowa City, Iowa

Score ....*738.8 points*
National rank .... *159 of 2,084*
Percentile...*92.41%*
Midwest rank.. *33 of 622*
Iowa rank... *8 of 55*
Closest major hub ....*Chicago, 189 air miles*

TESTS

1. Character..68.2
2. Stability..73.8
3. Growth..49.8
4. Education..87.9
5. Jobs...60.8
6. Business..37.1
7. Money...53.5
8. Housing...43.0
9. Health...72.3
10. Diversions...42.4
11. Internet 76.7
12. Proximity..73.3

BASIC STATS

Population...121,232
Density 2,684.1
Born out of state 48.3%
Homes built since 2000.............................29.7%
4 or more bedrooms 23.5%

RACE

Whites..75.2%
Blacks...8.6%
Hispanics 6.1%
Asians...7.4%
Native Americans 0.2%
Diversity index...41.7%

HOUSEHOLD INCOME LADDER

95th percentile $225,636
80th percentile $118,256
60th percentile $71,547
50th percentile $56,567
40th percentile $42,637
20th percentile $19,725

HOME VALUE LADDER

75th percentile $302,000
50th percentile $216,000
25th percentile $150,600

CHARACTER

Resilience..31.2%
Short commutes 61.4%

STABILITY

Living with two parents 71.9%
Occupied homes..95.6%

GROWTH

Population growth.....................................8.4%
Economic growth 4.1%

EDUCATION

High school graduates 95.0%
College graduates .... 57.9% (★)

JOBS

MBSA workers..................................... 48.6% (★)
Private-sector job growth 0.1%

BUSINESS

Small business growth 5.1%
Self-employed workers 5.6%

MONEY

Median annual earnings.......................$49,933
Living in poverty.......................................21.3%

HOUSING

Home ownership......................................53.0%
Monthly housing costs 30.1%

HEALTH

Health care workers...........................14.8% (★)
Fair or poor health....................................14.1%

DIVERSIONS

Stores per 10,000......................................32.1
Restaurants per 10,000...................... 26.0 (★)

INTERNET

Broadband subscriptions ....78.3% (★)
Smartphone access ....86.5% (★)

PROXIMITY

Major hub miles 189
Major or mid-major miles............................108

Jackson, Wyoming

Score ....*795.4 points*
National rank ....*57 of 2,084*
Percentile...*97.31%*
West rank...*27 of 471*
Wyoming rank.. *1 of 17*
Closest major hub ....*Salt Lake City, 204 air miles*

TESTS
1. Character................................78.6
2. Stability................................69.6
3. Growth................................50.2
4. Education................................82.4
5. Jobs................................58.6
6. Business................................62.4
7. Money................................68.6
8. Housing................................38.3
9. Health................................51.0
10. Diversions................................98.9
11. Internet................................72.3
12. Proximity................................64.5

BASIC STATS
Population................................12,751
Density................................3,129.1
Born out of state................................75.4%
Homes built since 2000................................23.8%
4 or more bedrooms................................17.9%

RACE
Whites................................75.8%
Blacks................................0.4%
Hispanics................................22.1%
Asians................................0.6%
Native Americans................................0.2%
Diversity index................................37.6%

HOUSEHOLD INCOME LADDER
95th percentile................................>$250,000
80th percentile................................$140,386
60th percentile................................$91,267
50th percentile................................$78,387
40th percentile................................$66,256
20th percentile................................$36,368

HOME VALUE LADDER
75th percentile................................$931,300
50th percentile................................$698,800
25th percentile................................$286,300

CHARACTER
Resilience................................ 34.7% (★)
Short commutes................................ 71.1%

STABILITY
Living with two parents................................ 83.7% (★)
Occupied homes................................89.1%

GROWTH
Population growth................................4.7%
Economic growth................................ 13.5%

EDUCATION
High school graduates................................92.0%
College graduates................................ 56.6% (★)

JOBS
MBSA workers................................35.4%
Private-sector job growth................................14.4%

BUSINESS
Small business growth................................ 11.2% (★)
Self-employed workers................................ 12.3% (★)

MONEY
Median annual earnings................................$48,125
Living in poverty................................5.5% (★)

HOUSING
Home ownership................................47.8%
Monthly housing costs................................30.6%

HEALTH
Health care workers................................5.7%
Fair or poor health................................ 11.9% (★)

DIVERSIONS
Stores per 10,000................................101.9 (★)
Restaurants per 10,000................................42.5 (★)

INTERNET
Broadband subscriptions................................76.3%
Smartphone access................................83.7%

PROXIMITY
Major hub miles................................204
Major or mid-major miles................................174

Jefferson Township North, New Jersey

Score ....*776.1 points*
National rank ....*84 of 2,084*
Percentile..*96.02%*
East rank.. *10 of 246*
New Jersey rank .... *1 of 12*
Closest major hub ....*New York, 36 air miles*

TESTS
1. Character..45.3
2. Stability..76.7
3. Growth..32.2
4. Education.......................................84.3
5. Jobs...66.6
6. Business...40.8
7. Money...96.3
8. Housing..72.7
9. Health...52.8
10. Diversions.....................................42.4
11. Internet 75.6
12. Proximity.......................................90.4

BASIC STATS
Population.......................................13,096
Density 1,076.9
Born out of state 27.7%
Homes built since 2000......................5.4%
4 or more bedrooms 36.2%

RACE
Whites..90.8%
Blacks..0.3%
Hispanics 4.6%
Asians..1.7%
Native Americans 0.0%
Diversity index................................17.2%

HOUSEHOLD INCOME LADDER
95th percentile ....>$250,000
80th percentile.....................$183,156
60th percentile.....................$133,394
50th percentile.....................$112,295
40th percentile.......................$88,133
20th percentile.......................$49,119

HOME VALUE LADDER
75th percentile $433,800
50th percentile $346,600
25th percentile $269,900

CHARACTER
Resilience..32.5%
Short commutes 18.7%

STABILITY
Living with two parents ....79.9% (★)
Occupied homes.............................94.3%

GROWTH
Population growth.............................-3.8%
Economic growth 3.1%

EDUCATION
High school graduates ....97.3% (★)
College graduates ....52.0% (★)

JOBS
MBSA workers...................................50.3% (★)
Private-sector job growth 4.8%

BUSINESS
Small business growth 0.3%
Self-employed workers 9.4%

MONEY
Median annual earnings...............$83,233 (★)
Living in poverty.................................4.7% (★)

HOUSING
Home ownership.............................. 92.7% (★)
Monthly housing costs.....................31.3%

HEALTH
Health care workers.............................7.8%
Fair or poor health............................13.9%

DIVERSIONS
Stores per 10,000...........................34.6
Restaurants per 10,000.................24.5

INTERNET
Broadband subscriptions ....84.5% (★)
Smartphone access 81.3%

PROXIMITY
Major hub miles................................ 36
Major or mid-major miles............................ 36

Johnson Lane, Nevada

Score .... *758.2 points*
National rank .... *114 of 2,084*
Percentile *94.58%*
West rank .... *46 of 471*
Nevada rank .... *1 of 14*
Closest major hub .... *Sacramento, 90 air miles*

TESTS
1. Character................................45.3
2. Stability....................................97.8
3. Growth......................................29.9
4. Education.................................64.8
5. Jobs..70.3
6. Business...................................49.2
7. Money......................................80.5
8. Housing....................................72.4
9. Health.......................................42.5
10. Diversions...............................38.8
11. Internet...................................79.0
12. Proximity................................87.7

BASIC STATS
Population............................... 5,052
Density 1,214.1
Born out of state 88.5%
Homes built since 2000............ 36.9%
4 or more bedrooms 26.8%

RACE
Whites...82.1%
Blacks..1.4%
Hispanics 12.7%
Asians..1.0%
Native Americans 1.0%
Diversity index...........................30.9%

HOUSEHOLD INCOME LADDER
95th percentile $194,771
80th percentile $128,400
60th percentile $95,023
50th percentile $86,101
40th percentile $72,294
20th percentile $38,598

HOME VALUE LADDER
75th percentile $574,700
50th percentile $437,200
25th percentile $326,100

CHARACTER
Resilience....................................23.2%
Short commutes 40.8%

STABILITY
Living with two parents .... 91.1% (★)
Occupied homes................................. 99.0% (★)

GROWTH
Population growth ....-6.3%
Economic growth 5.0%

EDUCATION
High school graduates .... 98.4% (★)
College graduates 26.7%

JOBS
MBSA workers............................. 49.2% (★)
Private-sector job growth 10.6%

BUSINESS
Small business growth 1.4%
Self-employed workers .... 12.1% (★)

MONEY
Median annual earnings...............$59,666 (★)
Living in poverty...................................5.0% (★)

HOUSING
Home ownership............................. 93.1% (★)
Monthly housing costs 31.8%

HEALTH
Health care workers................................5.2%
Fair or poor health................................15.3%

DIVERSIONS
Stores per 10,000................................30.7
Restaurants per 10,000................................24.1

INTERNET
Broadband subscriptions .... 85.4% (★)
Smartphone access 83.9%

PROXIMITY
Major hub miles.. 90
Major or mid-major miles................................. 34

Johnstown, Colorado

Score ....*795.1 points*
National rank ....*58 of 2,084*
Percentile...*97.26%*
West rank...*28 of 471*
Colorado rank .... *12 of 47*
Closest major hub ....*Denver, 43 air miles*

TESTS
1. Character.................................32.1
2. Stability...................................98.6
3. Growth....................................86.2
4. Education................................60.4
5. Jobs...63.4
6. Business..................................67.6
7. Money.....................................77.4
8. Housing...................................62.5
9. Health.....................................52.8
10. Diversions.............................17.7
11. Internet.................................87.2
12. Proximity...............................89.2

BASIC STATS
Population..............................17,525
Density 2,932.6
Born out of state 49.9%
Homes built since 2000............59.0%
4 or more bedrooms 33.1%

RACE
Whites......................................77.1%
Blacks...0.4%
Hispanics 20.6%
Asians...0.4%
Native Americans 0.0%
Diversity index........................36.3%

HOUSEHOLD INCOME LADDER
95th percentile $201,899
80th percentile $132,018
60th percentile $101,247
50th percentile $86,722
40th percentile $77,918
20th percentile $44,798

HOME VALUE LADDER
75th percentile $373,600
50th percentile $294,200
25th percentile $241,800

CHARACTER
Resilience.................................19.5%
Short commutes 26.7%

STABILITY
Living with two parents ....91.9% (★)
Occupied homes..............................99.1% (★)

GROWTH
Population growth............................17.8% (★)
Economic growth ....40.1% (★)

EDUCATION
High school graduates 93.8%
College graduates 27.3%

JOBS
MBSA workers...38.2%
Private-sector job growth 16.6%

BUSINESS
Small business growth ....19.8% (★)
Self-employed workers 10.0%

MONEY
Median annual earnings................$53,242 (★)
Living in poverty.................................2.0% (★)

HOUSING
Home ownership ....85.4% (★)
Monthly housing costs 34.9%

HEALTH
Health care workers................................7.6%
Fair or poor health..................................13.6%

DIVERSIONS
Stores per 10,000 ....20.9
Restaurants per 10,000.............................13.8

INTERNET
Broadband subscriptions ....83.5% (★)
Smartphone access ....90.8% (★)

PROXIMITY
Major hub miles 43
Major or mid-major miles................................43

Jordan, Minnesota

Score .... *728.2 points*
National rank .... *192 of 2,084*
Percentile *90.83%*
Midwest rank .... *46 of 622*
Minnesota rank .... *13 of 53*
Closest major hub .... *Minneapolis, 28 air miles*

TESTS
1. Character..67.0
2. Stability..85.1
3. Growth..62.0
4. Education.......................................54.4
5. Jobs..65.4
6. Business...48.4
7. Money..62.9
8. Housing..50.5
9. Health...53.4
10. Diversions.....................................18.2
11. Internet...69.1
12. Proximity.......................................91.8

BASIC STATS
Population.. 6,057
Density 2,654.3
Born out of state.........................31.0%
Homes built since 2000...................34.4%
4 or more bedrooms........................36.0%

RACE
Whites..78.7%
Blacks..3.1%
Hispanics..15.0%
Asians...1.7%
Native Americans 0.0%
Diversity index..............................35.7%

HOUSEHOLD INCOME LADDER
95th percentile.....................................$195,679
80th percentile.....................................$137,529
60th percentile.......................................$92,147
50th percentile.......................................$76,250
40th percentile.......................................$60,398
20th percentile.......................................$32,754

HOME VALUE LADDER
75th percentile.....................................$316,700
50th percentile.....................................$234,100
25th percentile.....................................$171,300

CHARACTER
Resilience.............................. 42.3% (★)
Short commutes.......................................32.8%

STABILITY
Living with two parents 75.5%
Occupied homes.............................100.0% (★)

GROWTH
Population growth.........................8.7%
Economic growth .... 23.9% (★)

EDUCATION
High school graduates 91.3%
College graduates 23.3%

JOBS
MBSA workers.......................................27.4%
Private-sector job growth .... 32.8% (★)

BUSINESS
Small business growth 6.6%
Self-employed workers 9.2%

MONEY
Median annual earnings.......................$52,391
Living in poverty.......................................14.8%

HOUSING
Home ownership..72.9%
Monthly housing costs...............................36.7%

HEALTH
Health care workers....................................5.6%
Fair or poor health............................ 10.6% (★)

DIVERSIONS
Stores per 10,000...................................21.7
Restaurants per 10,000..............................13.7

INTERNET
Broadband subscriptions 76.2%
Smartphone access 80.7%

PROXIMITY
Major hub miles..28 (★)
Major or mid-major miles.............................. 28

Jupiter Farms, Florida

Score ....808.2 points
National rank ....38 of 2,084
Percentile...98.22%
South rank .... 12 of 745
Florida rank .... 2 of 63
Closest major hub ....Miami, 51 air miles

TESTS
1. Character.......................19.6
2. Stability.........................91.2
3. Growth...........................63.1
4. Education.......................70.8
5. Jobs...............................67.2
6. Business.........................71.5
7. Money............................80.0
8. Housing..........................67.8
9. Health............................54.3
10. Diversions.....................38.6
11. Internet 93.2
12. Proximity.......................90.9

BASIC STATS
Population....................11,678
Density 1,075.9
Born out of state.............57.4%
Homes built since 2000.........19.7%
4 or more bedrooms 39.2%

RACE
Whites...............................87.1%
Blocks 1.5%
Hispanics 9.4%
Asians...............................1.6%
Native Americans 0.0%
Diversity index..................23.2%

HOUSEHOLD INCOME LADDER
95th percentile ....>$250,000
80th percentile $177,519
60th percentile $124,118
50th percentile $109,080
40th percentile $85,983
20th percentile $55,203

HOME VALUE LADDER
75th percentile $480,900
50th percentile $388,200
25th percentile $297,900

CHARACTER
Resilience.............................13.5%
Short commutes 19.5%

STABILITY
Living with two parents ....90.0% (★)
Occupied homes................96.9% (★)

GROWTH
Population growth............10.5% (★)
Economic growth 21.5%

EDUCATION
High school graduates ....96.5% (★)
College graduates 36.5%

JOBS
MBSA workers.......................43.6% (★)
Private-sector job growth 14.1%

BUSINESS
Small business growth ....11.9% (★)
Self-employed workers ....15.3% (★)

MONEY
Median annual earnings...............$57,593 (★)
Living in poverty.....................3.6% (★)

HOUSING
Home ownership...................97.6% (★)
Monthly housing costs............37.9%

HEALTH
Health care workers...................10.9%
Fair or poor health...................17.4%

DIVERSIONS
Stores per 10,000............................37.6
Restaurants per 10,000................19.7

INTERNET
Broadband subscriptions ....88.9% (★)
Smartphone access ....91.3% (★)

PROXIMITY
Major hub miles 51
Major or mid-major miles......................25 (★)

Kasson, Minnesota

Score ....*725.8 points*
National rank ....*206 of 2,084*
Percentile..*90.16%*
Midwest rank.. *49 of 622*
Minnesota rank .... *16 of 53*
Closest major hub ....*Minneapolis, 70 air miles*

TESTS
1. Character.................................66.6
2. Stability...................................69.9
3. Growth....................................41.0
4. Education................................66.5
5. Jobs..52.9
6. Business.................................28.2
7. Money....................................73.0
8. Housing..................................69.6
9. Health.....................................84.5
10. Diversions.............................16.5
11. Internet 72.7
12. Proximity...............................84.4

BASIC STATS
Population...................................... 7,109
Density 1,643.3
Born out of state 23.5%
Homes built since 2000.............................29.7%
4 or more bedrooms 39.2%

RACE
Whites...94.1%
Blacks 0.2%
Hispanics 1.6%
Asians..1.8%
Native Americans 0.4%
Diversity index............................ 11.4%

HOUSEHOLD INCOME LADDER
95th percentile $189,507
80th percentile $126,746
60th percentile $90,650
50th percentile $76,524
40th percentile $66,250
20th percentile $45,152

HOME VALUE LADDER
75th percentile $233,900
50th percentile $179,100
25th percentile $142,800

CHARACTER
Resilience.............................. 39.9% (★)
Short commutes 37.8%

STABILITY
Living with two parents 63.6%
Occupied homes..............................96.5%

GROWTH
Population growth..................................0.1%
Economic growth 8.7%

EDUCATION
High school graduates .... 97.8% (★)
College graduates 29.6%

JOBS
MBSA workers.................................35.1%
Private-sector job growth 8.0%

BUSINESS
Small business growth ....-2.4%
Self-employed workers 5.9%

MONEY
Median annual earnings......................$50,056
Living in poverty...................................3.1% (★)

HOUSING
Home ownership.......................... 86.1% (★)
Monthly housing costs.............................29.6%

HEALTH
Health care workers.......................... 15.3% (★)
Fair or poor health.............................. 10.7% (★)

DIVERSIONS
Stores per 10,000.................................20.7
Restaurants per 10,000...............................13.0

INTERNET
Broadband subscriptions .... 80.3% (★)
Smartphone access 81.3%

PROXIMITY
Major hub miles.................................. 70
Major or mid-major miles............................. 70

Kennebunk, Maine

Score ....805.0 points
National rank ....43 of 2,084
Percentile...97.98%
East rank...5 of 246
Maine rank ....1 of 9
Closest major hub ....Boston, 76 air miles

TESTS
1. Character...61.9
2. Stability..70.1
3. Growth...47.1
4. Education..91.2
5. Jobs..68.1
6. Business...60.9
7. Money...76.3
8. Housing..57.3
9. Health...68.5
10. Diversions....................................51.8
11. Internet..68.4
12. Proximity......................................83.4

BASIC STATS
Population.. 8,889
Density 750.7
Born out of state 62.3%
Homes built since 2000..........................15.8%
4 or more bedrooms 24.7%

RACE
Whites...94.8%
Blacks..0.1%
Hispanics 2.2%
Asians..2.3%
Native Americans 0.2%
Diversity index................................ 10.0%

HOUSEHOLD INCOME LADDER
95th percentile ....>$250,000
80th percentile $136,542
60th percentile $92,984
50th percentile $72,014
40th percentile $55,408
20th percentile $29,833

HOME VALUE LADDER
75th percentile $504,800
50th percentile $362,900
25th percentile $265,400

CHARACTER
Resilience...33.3%
Short commutes 45.4%

STABILITY
Living with two parents 72.3%
Occupied homes.....................................93.5%

GROWTH
Population growth....................................3.4%
Economic growth 11.2%

EDUCATION
High school graduates .... 99.0% (★)
College graduates .... 55.4% (★)

JOBS
MBSA workers.. 47.6% (★)
Private-sector job growth 10.1%

BUSINESS
Small business growth 3.4%
Self-employed workers .... 15.6% (★)

MONEY
Median annual earnings...............$58,426 (★)
Living in poverty...7.8%

HOUSING
Home ownership......................................69.4%
Monthly housing costs 29.0%

HEALTH
Health care workers....................................12.5%
Fair or poor health....................................12.7%

DIVERSIONS
Stores per 10,000....................................40.6
Restaurants per 10,000........................ 28.1 (★)

INTERNET
Broadband subscriptions .... 83.6% (★)
Smartphone access 75.0%

PROXIMITY
Major hub miles.. 76
Major or mid-major miles.................................. 76

Key Largo, Florida

Score .... *740.4 points*
National rank .... *157 of 2,084*
Percentile *92.51%*
South rank .... *45 of 745*
Florida rank .... *8 of 63*
Closest major hub .... *Miami, 83 air miles*

TESTS
1. Character...41.4
2. Stability..68.0
3. Growth...38.3
4. Education...64.9
5. Jobs...53.5
6. Business...72.2
7. Money..57.8
8. Housing...57.3
9. Health..39.4
10. Diversions..98.5
11. Internet...66.9
12. Proximity..82.2

BASIC STATS
Population....................................17,950
Density...1,304.4
Born out of state.........................69.0%
Homes built since 2000.............16.0%
4 or more bedrooms...................11.8%

RACE
Whites..76.7%
Blacks...0.8%
Hispanics......................................20.7%
Asians...1.0%
Native Americans.........................0.1%
Diversity index.............................36.9%

HOUSEHOLD INCOME LADDER
95th percentile....................>$250,000
80th percentile.....................$147,944
60th percentile.......................$85,588
50th percentile.......................$73,197
40th percentile.......................$56,923
20th percentile.......................$28,483

HOME VALUE LADDER
75th percentile.....................$794,300
50th percentile.....................$490,100
25th percentile.....................$307,900

CHARACTER
Resilience......................................15.8%
Short commutes..........................51.7%

STABILITY
Living with two parents...................76.4% (★)
Occupied homes..........................90.9%

GROWTH
Population growth........................-5.0%
Economic growth.........................16.1%

EDUCATION
High school graduates..............92.1%
College graduates.......................35.0%

JOBS
MBSA workers...............................35.6%
Private-sector job growth..........8.1%

BUSINESS
Small business growth................5.8%
Self-employed workers....................20.3% (★)

MONEY
Median annual earnings.......$44,459
Living in poverty..........................12.1%

HOUSING
Home ownership.................75.6% (★)
Monthly housing costs...............32.9%

HEALTH
Health care workers......................4.9%
Fair or poor health.......................16.4%

DIVERSIONS
Stores per 10,000.......................83.5 (★)
Restaurants per 10,000.............50.3 (★)

INTERNET
Broadband subscriptions.........71.6%
Smartphone access.....................81.7%

PROXIMITY
Major hub miles...................................83
Major or mid-major miles.................83

Kill Devil Hills, North Carolina

Score .... 782.8 points
National rank .... 75 of 2,084
Percentile 96.45%
South rank .... 25 of 745
North Carolina rank .... 3 of 65
Closest major hub .... Virginia Beach, 69 air miles

TESTS
1. Character 60.3
2. Stability 48.1
3. Growth 56.7
4. Education 69.7
5. Jobs 50.2
6. Business 70.4
7. Money 61.8
8. Housing 51.3
9. Health 49.6
10. Diversions 99.6
11. Internet 80.5
12. Proximity 84.6

BASIC STATS
Population 20,307
Density 829.2
Born out of state 69.9%
Homes built since 2000 .... 19.7%
4 or more bedrooms 40.9%

RACE
Whites 91.1%
Blacks 0.6%
Hispanics 5.9%
Asians 0.8%
Native Americans 0.1%
Diversity index 16.6%

HOUSEHOLD INCOME LADDER
95th percentile $232,589
80th percentile $124,647
60th percentile $81,152
50th percentile $65,437
40th percentile $53,936
20th percentile $33,067

HOME VALUE LADDER
75th percentile $448,900
50th percentile $306,800
25th percentile $222,600

CHARACTER
Resilience 28.2%
Short commutes 54.8%

STABILITY
Living with two parents 75.8%
Occupied homes 80.5%

GROWTH
Population growth 7.2%
Economic growth 18.6%

EDUCATION
High school graduates 95.3%
College graduates 36.7%

JOBS
MBSA workers 38.2%
Private-sector job growth 0.8%

BUSINESS
Small business growth 3.8%
Self-employed workers .... 22.0% (★)

MONEY
Median annual earnings $43,953
Living in poverty 7.9%

HOUSING
Home ownership .... 77.1% (★)
Monthly housing costs 38.7%

HEALTH
Health care workers 6.9%
Fair or poor health 14.2%

DIVERSIONS
Stores per 10,000 .... 112.5 (★)
Restaurants per 10,000 .... 66.7 (★)

INTERNET
Broadband subscriptions .... 83.3% (★)
Smartphone access .... 86.8% (★)

PROXIMITY
Major hub miles 69
Major or mid-major miles 69

Kuna, Idaho

Score ....*735.7 points*
National rank ....*169 of 2,084*
Percentile...*91.93%*
West rank..*65 of 471*
Idaho rank ....*3 of 21*
Closest major hub ....*Salt Lake City, 303 air miles*

TESTS
1. Character..37.1
2. Stability..81.2
3. Growth..76.2
4. Education..57.7
5. Jobs...68.1
6. Business..43.8
7. Money...57.7
8. Housing...56.5
9. Health...59.7
10. Diversions.......................................36.1
11. Internet 82.6
12. Proximity..79.0

BASIC STATS
Population.......................................18,750
Density 3,537.7
Born out of state 43.7%
Homes built since 2000.....................66.7%
4 or more bedrooms 37.7%

RACE
Whites..84.4%
Blacks..0.0%
Hispanics 10.8%
Asians..0.8%
Native Americans 0.6%
Diversity index.................................27.5%

HOUSEHOLD INCOME LADDER
95th percentile.......................... $163,984
80th percentile.......................... $110,361
60th percentile............................$79,141
50th percentile............................$69,423
40th percentile............................$61,937
20th percentile............................$34,126

HOME VALUE LADDER
75th percentile $275,600
50th percentile $198,200
25th percentile $154,400

CHARACTER
Resilience...26.6%
Short commutes 18.5%

STABILITY
Living with two parents 70.7%
Occupied homes...........................100.0% (★)

GROWTH
Population growth.............................17.9% (★)
Economic growth...............................26.3% (★)

EDUCATION
High school graduates 93.5%
College graduates 24.4%

JOBS
MBSA workers.....................................38.2%
Private-sector job growth ....22.1% (★)

BUSINESS
Small business growth ....16.8% (★)
Self-employed workers 2.3%

MONEY
Median annual earnings.......................$40,387
Living in poverty......................................8.4%

HOUSING
Home ownership..............................77.9% (★)
Monthly housing costs...........................35.0%

HEALTH
Health care workers....................................8.5%
Fair or poor health.............................11.5% (★)

DIVERSIONS
Stores per 10,000.................................32.2
Restaurants per 10,000.................................21.1

INTERNET
Broadband subscriptions ....79.8% (★)
Smartphone access ....90.7% (★)

PROXIMITY
Major hub miles.......................................303
Major or mid-major miles.......................10 (★)

Lafayette, Colorado

Score ....865.1 points
National rank .... 11 of 2,084
Percentile...99.52%
West rank.. 7 of 471
Colorado rank .... 3 of 47
Closest major hub ....Denver, 21 air miles

TESTS
1. Character...33.5
2. Stability..83.7
3. Growth 70.8
4. Education..96.1
5. Jobs 83.8
6. Business 56.5
7. Money 94.5
8. Housing 61.7
9. Health...57.1
10. Diversions.....................................44.0
11. Internet 89.2
12. Proximity.......................................94.2

BASIC STATS
Population.......................................94,416
Density 2,389.1
Born out of state 66.3%
Homes built since 2000.....................34.2%
4 or more bedrooms 38.6%

RACE
Whites 79.6%
Blacks 0.4%
Hispanics 10.5%
Asians...6.6%
Native Americans 0.1%
Diversity index.................................35.0%

HOUSEHOLD INCOME LADDER
95th percentile ....>$250,000
80th percentile $187,305
60th percentile $125,709
50th percentile $103,820
40th percentile $85,211
20th percentile $45,032

HOME VALUE LADDER
75th percentile $676,000
50th percentile $502,100
25th percentile $374,400

CHARACTER
Resilience...16.9%
Short commutes 35.5%

STABILITY
Living with two parents ....80.8% (★)
Occupied homes................................97.7% (★)

GROWTH
Population growth.............................13.4% (★)
Economic growth ....27.7% (★)

EDUCATION
High school graduates ....97.2% (★)
College graduates ....67.0% (★)

JOBS
MBSA workers....................................58.9% (★)
Private-sector job growth 12.4%

BUSINESS
Small business growth ....11.4% (★)
Self-employed workers 9.9%

MONEY
Median annual earnings...............$76,116 (★)
Living in poverty...................................5.7% (★)

HOUSING
Home ownership ....75.1% (★)
Monthly housing costs...........................29.0%

HEALTH
Health care workers...............................7.8%
Fair or poor health.............................11.8% (★)

DIVERSIONS
Stores per 10,000.....................................34.6
Restaurants per 10,000.........................25.7 (★)

INTERNET
Broadband subscriptions ....87.6% (★)
Smartphone access ....89.3% (★)

PROXIMITY
Major hub miles....................................21 (★)
Major or mid-major miles.......................21 (★)

Lago Vista, Texas

Score ....*754.1 points*
National rank ....*122 of 2,084*
Percentile..*94.19%*
South rank ....*37 of 745*
Texas rank..*10 of 173*
Closest major hub ....*Austin, 15 air miles*

TESTS
1. Character................................34.0
2. Stability................................62.4
3. Growth................................62.7
4. Education................................59.1
5. Jobs................................69.9
6. Business................................61.4
7. Money................................87.7
8. Housing................................74.5
9. Health................................39.1
10. Diversions................................39.2
11. Internet................................65.4
12. Proximity................................98.7

BASIC STATS
Population................................5,888
Density................................1,081.4
Born out of state................................48.6%
Homes built since 2000................................32.5%
4 or more bedrooms................................16.2%

RACE
Whites................................77.6%
Blacks................................3.0%
Hispanics................................16.3%
Asians................................0.9%
Native Americans................................0.0%
Diversity index................................37.0%

HOUSEHOLD INCOME LADDER
95th percentile................................$193,671
80th percentile................................$126,893
60th percentile................................$92,565
50th percentile................................$78,000
40th percentile................................$62,077
20th percentile................................$32,393

HOME VALUE LADDER
75th percentile................................$294,900
50th percentile................................$228,800
25th percentile................................$157,800

CHARACTER
Resilience................................18.4%
Short commutes................................32.7%

STABILITY
Living with two parents................................53.0%
Occupied homes................................96.3%

GROWTH
Population growth................................5.1%
Economic growth................................33.4% (★)

EDUCATION
High school graduates................................91.2%
College graduates................................29.2%

JOBS
MBSA workers................................40.0%
Private-sector job growth................................22.0% (★)

BUSINESS
Small business growth................................17.4% (★)
Self-employed workers................................8.8%

MONEY
Median annual earnings................................$63,960 (★)
Living in poverty................................3.9% (★)

HOUSING
Home ownership................................79.0% (★)
Monthly housing costs................................21.2%

HEALTH
Health care workers................................3.7%
Fair or poor health................................14.9%

DIVERSIONS
Stores per 10,000................................30.2
Restaurants per 10,000................................24.7

INTERNET
Broadband subscriptions................................72.7%
Smartphone access................................79.5%

PROXIMITY
Major hub miles................................15 (★)
Major or mid-major miles................................15 (★)

Lake Conroe Eastshore, Texas

Score ....*837.5 points*
National rank ....*22 of 2,084*
Percentile...*98.99%*
South rank ....*9 of 745*
Texas rank...*2 of 173*
Closest major hub ....*Houston, 46 air miles*

TESTS
1. Character...................................48.6
2. Stability......................................76.0
3. Growth.......................................96.0
4. Education...................................65.6
5. Jobs..69.9
6. Business......................................84.1
7. Money...73.6
8. Housing......................................68.6
9. Health...63.5
10. Diversions.................................24.1
11. Internet 78.8
12. Proximity..................................88.7

BASIC STATS
Population...............................11,864
Density 1,639.1
Born out of state.........................41.4%
Homes built since 2000.............53.2%
4 or more bedrooms 21.9%

RACE
Whites...83.9%
Blacks..1.0%
Hispanics 12.3%
Asians..2.2%
Native Americans 0.0%
Diversity index............................28.0%

HOUSEHOLD INCOME LADDER
95th percentile ....>$250,000
80th percentile $154,512
60th percentile $107,478
50th percentile $88,527
40th percentile $59,566
20th percentile $35,439

HOME VALUE LADDER
75th percentile $455,700
50th percentile $292,800
25th percentile $176,500

CHARACTER
Resilience......................................31.6%
Short commutes 26.5%

STABILITY
Living with two parents ....76.8% (★)
Occupied homes...........................95.0%

GROWTH
Population growth............................28.1% (★)
Economic growth ....36.7% (★)

EDUCATION
High school graduates 93.7%
College graduates 33.8%

JOBS
MBSA workers...............................39.6%
Private-sector job growth ....22.5% (★)

BUSINESS
Small business growth ....20.3% (★)
Self-employed workers ....14.9% (★)

MONEY
Median annual earnings...............$52,748 (★)
Living in poverty...................5.0% (★)

HOUSING
Home ownership...........................83.0% (★)
Monthly housing costs 28.5%

HEALTH
Health care workers....................................12.4%
Fair or poor health.............................15.0%

DIVERSIONS
Stores per 10,000.........................25.2
Restaurants per 10,000.................16.1

INTERNET
Broadband subscriptions ....78.0% (★)
Smartphone access ....88.7% (★)

PROXIMITY
Major hub miles...............................46
Major or mid-major miles................46

Lake Conroe Westshore, Texas

Score ....*812.8 points*
National rank ....*35 of 2,084*
Percentile...*98.37%*
South rank ....*11 of 745*
Texas rank...*4 of 173*
Closest major hub ....*Houston, 43 air miles*

TESTS
1. Character..48.3
2. Stability...68.1
3. Growth...68.4
4. Education..66.9
5. Jobs..75.6
6. Business..93.3
7. Money...81.2
8. Housing...73.1
9. Health..49.9
10. Diversions.......................................24.1
11. Internet..74.7
12. Proximity...89.2

BASIC STATS
Population.......................................23,069
Density..1,664.1
Born out of state...............................46.9%
Homes built since 2000..................39.7%
4 or more bedrooms........................22.7%

RACE
Whites...81.7%
Blacks..4.7%
Hispanics...11.2%
Asians...1.6%
Native Americans.............................0.1%
Diversity index.................................31.7%

HOUSEHOLD INCOME LADDER
95th percentile...............................>$250,000
80th percentile.............................$166,107
60th percentile.............................$106,617
50th percentile...............................$77,897
40th percentile...............................$63,694
20th percentile...............................$32,672

HOME VALUE LADDER
75th percentile.............................$334,600
50th percentile.............................$228,700
25th percentile.............................$162,700

CHARACTER
Resilience..31.6%
Short commutes................................25.9%

STABILITY
Living with two parents..................69.5%
Occupied homes................................93.4%

GROWTH
Population growth...............................7.8%
Economic growth...................36.7% (★)

EDUCATION
High school graduates..................93.3%
College graduates.............................35.9%

JOBS
MBSA workers..........................44.3% (★)
Private-sector job growth...............22.5% (★)

BUSINESS
Small business growth....................20.3% (★)
Self-employed workers....................18.4% (★)

MONEY
Median annual earnings...............$62,657 (★)
Living in poverty..................................7.2% (★)

HOUSING
Home ownership..............................80.6% (★)
Monthly housing costs.....................23.3%

HEALTH
Health care workers............................7.6%
Fair or poor health...........................15.0%

DIVERSIONS
Stores per 10,000.............................25.2
Restaurants per 10,000....................16.1

INTERNET
Broadband subscriptions.........................76.2%
Smartphone access..........................86.0% (★)

PROXIMITY
Major hub miles...................................43
Major or mid-major miles..............................43

Lake Mills, Wisconsin

Score ....*737.1 points*
National rank .... *164 of 2,084*
Percentile...*92.17%*
Midwest rank.. *35 of 622*
Wisconsin rank .... *7 of 61*
Closest major hub .... *Milwaukee, 41 air miles*

TESTS
1. Character.................................60.8
2. Stability....................................77.9
3. Growth.....................................47.2
4. Education.................................68.6
5. Jobs..59.6
6. Business...................................37.9
7. Money......................................69.4
8. Housing...................................53.2
9. Health......................................66.6
10. Diversions..............................36.0
11. Internet 68.5
12. Proximity...............................91.4

BASIC STATS
Population.............................. 6,997
Density 1,724.7
Born out of state 27.7%
Homes built since 2000............22.8%
4 or more bedrooms 19.6%

RACE
Whites.....................................85.8%
Blacks.......................................0.2%
Hispanics 11.5%
Asians.......................................0.9%
Native Americans 0.0%
Diversity index.......................25.0%

HOUSEHOLD INCOME LADDER
95th percentile $174,350
80th percentile $122,856
60th percentile $81,303
50th percentile $71,790
40th percentile $60,318
20th percentile $31,609

HOME VALUE LADDER
75th percentile $282,800
50th percentile $204,400
25th percentile $161,200

CHARACTER
Resilience............................ 35.3% (★)
Short commutes 38.8%

STABILITY
Living with two parents .... 77.5% (★)
Occupied homes.............................95.8%

GROWTH
Population growth.........................4.0%
Economic growth 10.0%

EDUCATION
High school graduates 91.9%
College graduates .... 39.8% (★)

JOBS
MBSA workers....................... 46.9% (★)
Private-sector job growth 0.9%

BUSINESS
Small business growth 4.7%
Self-employed workers 6.1%

MONEY
Median annual earnings.......................$50,967
Living in poverty............................7.4% (★)

HOUSING
Home ownership.......................66.6%
Monthly housing costs.............30.5%

HEALTH
Health care workers 11.3%
Fair or poor health.............. 12.0% (★)

DIVERSIONS
Stores per 10,000.......................31.7
Restaurants per 10,000...............21.3

INTERNET
Broadband subscriptions .... 79.1% (★)
Smartphone access 78.1%

PROXIMITY
Major hub miles.................................. 41
Major or mid-major miles.......................26 (★)

Lake Monticello, Virginia

Score .... *767.7 points*
National rank .... *99 of 2,084*
Percentile *95.30%*
South rank .... *30 of 745*
Virginia rank .... *4 of 41*
Closest major hub .... *Richmond, 55 air miles*

TESTS
1. Character...................................44.9
2. Stability....................................78.0
3. Growth.....................................73.5
4. Education.................................76.0
5. Jobs...59.0
6. Business...................................40.9
7. Money......................................78.4
8. Housing....................................73.9
9. Health......................................80.5
10. Diversions................................2.8
11. Internet..................................72.7
12. Proximity................................87.1

BASIC STATS
Population............................. 10,457
Density 1,850.5
Born out of state 49.9%
Homes built since 2000.............33.1%
4 or more bedrooms 29.9%

RACE
Whites...................................80.7%
Blacks 10.5%
Hispanics 3.3%
Asians.....................................1.3%
Native Americans 0.0%
Diversity index........................33.5%

HOUSEHOLD INCOME LADDER
95th percentile $194,565
80th percentile $141,267
60th percentile $93,447
50th percentile $80,113
40th percentile $69,264
20th percentile $45,145

HOME VALUE LADDER
75th percentile $292,700
50th percentile $228,300
25th percentile $180,000

CHARACTER
Resilience................................31.3%
Short commutes 20.8%

STABILITY
Living with two parents 73.9%
Occupied homes................... 97.1% (★)

GROWTH
Population growth.............. 20.0% (★)
Economic growth 16.8%

EDUCATION
High school graduates .... 96.2% (★)
College graduates .... 43.3% (★)

JOBS
MBSA workers............................ 50.8% (★)
Private-sector job growth .... -4.9%

BUSINESS
Small business growth 2.6%
Self-employed workers 8.3%

MONEY
Median annual earnings...............$56,729 (★)
Living in poverty....................................4.3% (★)

HOUSING
Home ownership.............................. 88.8% (★)
Monthly housing costs............................27.9%

HEALTH
Health care workers........................... 16.1% (★)
Fair or poor health...............................13.4%

DIVERSIONS
Stores per 10,000.................................11.9
Restaurants per 10,000.................... 7.8

INTERNET
Broadband subscriptions .... 81.1% (★)
Smartphone access 80.8%

PROXIMITY
Major hub miles................................. 55
Major or mid-major miles............................ 55

Lake Norman of Catawba, North Carolina

Score ....*772.4 points*
National rank ....*93 of 2,084*
Percentile...*95.58%*
South rank ....*28 of 745*
North Carolina rank... *5 of 65*
Closest major hub ....*Charlotte, 24 air miles*

TESTS
1. Character.....................................45.4
2. Stability..81.9
3. Growth...86.5
4. Education......................................62.5
5. Jobs...55.7
6. Business.......................................49.7
7. Money..66.9
8. Housing..67.3
9. Health..55.5
10. Diversions...................................34.4
11. Internet 74.1
12. Proximity.....................................92.5

BASIC STATS
Population.......................................6,638
Density 686.2
Born out of state.............................50.5%
Homes built since 2000.....................37.9%
4 or more bedrooms 24.7%

RACE
Whites...93.3%
Blacks...3.3%
Hispanics..2.9%
Asians...0.2%
Native Americans 0.0%
Diversity index.................................12.8%

HOUSEHOLD INCOME LADDER
95th percentile $228,741
80th percentile $131,296
60th percentile $80,877
50th percentile $63,399
40th percentile $51,418
20th percentile $30,222

HOME VALUE LADDER
75th percentile $442,500
50th percentile $275,100
25th percentile $152,200

CHARACTER
Resilience.......................................29.6%
Short commutes 25.8%

STABILITY
Living with two parents ....77.5% (★)
Occupied homes..............................97.9% (★)

GROWTH
Population growth............................32.7% (★)
Economic growth 21.2%

EDUCATION
High school graduates 94.5%
College graduates 29.0%

JOBS
MBSA workers.................................33.5%
Private-sector job growth 13.4%

BUSINESS
Small business growth 8.4%
Self-employed workers 8.8%

MONEY
Median annual earnings.....................$49,556
Living in poverty..............................8.3%

HOUSING
Home ownership..............................72.4%
Monthly housing costs......................22.8%

HEALTH
Health care workers.........................10.0%
Fair or poor health...........................15.6%

DIVERSIONS
Stores per 10,000...........................35.8
Restaurants per 10,000....................17.6

INTERNET
Broadband subscriptions ....78.2% (★)
Smartphone access 84.1%

PROXIMITY
Major hub miles ....24 (★)
Major or mid-major miles.................24 (★)

Lake of the Pines, California

Score ....*817.0 points*
National rank ....*32 of 2,084*
Percentile...*98.51%*
West rank.. *17 of 471*
California rank .... *1 of 145*
Closest major hub .... *Sacramento, 30 air miles*

TESTS

1. Character................................41.0
2. Stability..................................82.3
3. Growth....................................61.2
4. Education................................74.8
5. Jobs..66.4
6. Business..................................68.0
7. Money....................................96.5
8. Housing..................................65.7
9. Health....................................60.7
10. Diversions...............................40.2
11. Internet.................................68.7
12. Proximity................................91.5

BASIC STATS

Population.. 8,110
Density..1,056.1
Born out of state.............................35.5%
Homes built since 2000.....................8.9%
4 or more bedrooms...............................19.9%

RACE

Whites...86.2%
Blacks..0.4%
Hispanics...8.8%
Asians...1.1%
Native Americans................................0.7%
Diversity index.....................................24.8%

HOUSEHOLD INCOME LADDER

95th percentile.......................... >$250,000
80th percentile.............................$149,333
60th percentile.............................$103,574
50th percentile...............................$88,925
40th percentile...............................$69,324
20th percentile...............................$36,745

HOME VALUE LADDER

75th percentile.....................................$591,600
50th percentile.....................................$442,200
25th percentile.....................................$347,200

CHARACTER

Resilience..24.0%
Short commutes.....................................31.4%

STABILITY

Living with two parents................... 80.1% (★)
Occupied homes.............................. 97.2% (★)

GROWTH

Population growth............................ 10.1% (★)
Economic growth.......................................19.2%

EDUCATION

High school graduates..................... 96.0% (★)
College graduates............................ 42.1% (★)

JOBS

MBSA workers....................................... 41.9% (★)
Private-sector job growth.......................15.3%

BUSINESS

Small business growth...............................8.5%
Self-employed workers.................... 15.8% (★)

MONEY

Median annual earnings...............$75,121 (★)
Living in poverty....................................4.0% (★)

HOUSING

Home ownership.............................. 83.3% (★)
Monthly housing costs............................31.0%

HEALTH

Health care workers.....................................8.7%
Fair or poor health............................. 11.3% (★)

DIVERSIONS

Stores per 10,000...35.1
Restaurants per 10,000..............................22.5

INTERNET

Broadband subscriptions................ 79.9% (★)
Smartphone access......................................77.8%

PROXIMITY

Major hub miles...30 (★)
Major or mid-major miles................................ 30

Lake of the Woods, Virginia

Score ....*746.2 points*
National rank ....*141 of 2,084*
Percentile..*93.28%*
South rank ....*42 of 745*
Virginia rank..*7 of 41*
Closest major hub ....*Washington, 49 air miles*

TESTS
1. Character.......................................45.8
2. Stability...84.9
3. Growth..68.7
4. Education.......................................64.2
5. Jobs..63.4
6. Business..22.6
7. Money...74.7
8. Housing...75.1
9. Health..59.7
10. Diversions....................................27.3
11. Internet 71.7
12. Proximity......................................88.1

BASIC STATS
Population.....................................11,212
Density 1,520.5
Born out of state 65.6%
Homes built since 2000.................47.6%
4 or more bedrooms 37.6%

RACE
Whites...81.6%
Blacks..8.1%
Hispanics 4.4%
Asians...2.7%
Native Americans 0.0%
Diversity index..............................32.4%

HOUSEHOLD INCOME LADDER
95th percentile $199,348
80th percentile $135,454
60th percentile $106,795
50th percentile $87,165
40th percentile $74,582
20th percentile $52,609

HOME VALUE LADDER
75th percentile $347,900
50th percentile $263,800
25th percentile $204,900

CHARACTER
Resilience..32.4%
Short commutes 19.8%

STABILITY
Living with two parents ....79.8% (★)
Occupied homes...............................98.4% (★)

GROWTH
Population growth...........................14.4% (★)
Economic growth 21.8%

EDUCATION
High school graduates 93.9%
College graduates 31.8%

JOBS
MBSA workers.....................................41.4% (★)
Private-sector job growth 12.4%

BUSINESS
Small business growth ....-3.7%
Self-employed workers 4.4%

MONEY
Median annual earnings...............$54,351 (★)
Living in poverty.....................................5.5% (★)

HOUSING
Home ownership.............................95.3% (★)
Monthly housing costs...........................31.0%

HEALTH
Health care workers................................10.4%
Fair or poor health................................14.1%

DIVERSIONS
Stores per 10,000..................................30.6
Restaurants per 10,000................................15.3

INTERNET
Broadband subscriptions ....79.4% (★)
Smartphone access 81.0%

PROXIMITY
Major hub miles...49
Major or mid-major miles...............................49

Lake Pocotopaug, Connecticut

Score ....*784.9 points*
National rank ....*74 of 2,084*
Percentile...*96.50%*
East rank.. *9 of 246*
Connecticut rank... *1 of 8*
Closest major hub ....*Hartford, 14 air miles*

TESTS
1. Character...50.8
2. Stability..72.2
3. Growth...44.7
4. Education...74.7
5. Jobs..59.4
6. Business..42.1
7. Money..86.2
8. Housing...70.1
9. Health..66.5
10. Diversions...47.8
11. Internet..71.3
12. Proximity...99.1

BASIC STATS
Population....................................... 9,590
Density 936.2
Born out of state................................32.1%
Homes built since 2000........................... 16.5%
4 or more bedrooms 21.6%

RACE
Whites...89.7%
Blacks...1.3%
Hispanics 3.4%
Asians...3.3%
Native Americans 0.7%
Diversity index...................................19.3%

HOUSEHOLD INCOME LADDER
95th percentile .... >$250,000
80th percentile $153,170
60th percentile $110,050
50th percentile $92,757
40th percentile $73,821
20th percentile $45,092

HOME VALUE LADDER
75th percentile $353,200
50th percentile $271,300
25th percentile $207,800

CHARACTER
Resilience...34.3%
Short commutes 23.8%

STABILITY
Living with two parents .... 79.8% (★)
Occupied homes................................91.9%

GROWTH
Population growth.............................6.3%
Economic growth 0.5%

EDUCATION
High school graduates 95.3%
College graduates .... 42.8% (★)

JOBS
MBSA workers....................................... 43.9% (★)
Private-sector job growth 4.5%

BUSINESS
Small business growth 1.3%
Self-employed workers 9.4%

MONEY
Median annual earnings................$67,471 (★)
Living in poverty...............................8.1%

HOUSING
Home ownership............................ 85.6% (★)
Monthly housing costs............................28.9%

HEALTH
Health care workers.............................. 10.1%
Fair or poor health............................ 10.4% (★)

DIVERSIONS
Stores per 10,000...............................39.4
Restaurants per 10,000........................25.7 (★)

INTERNET
Broadband subscriptions .... 78.7% (★)
Smartphone access 81.1%

PROXIMITY
Major hub miles...14 (★)
Major or mid-major miles.......................14 (★)

Lebanon, New Hampshire

Score ....*774.7 points*
National rank ....*87 of 2,084*
Percentile...*95.87%*
East rank.. *11 of 246*
New Hampshire rank .... *2 of 10*
Closest major hub ....*Boston, 106 air miles*

TESTS
1. Character.......................77.4
2. Stability............................68.0
3. Growth............................42.6
4. Education........................91.1
5. Jobs................................68.6
6. Business..........................37.9
7. Money.............................67.5
8. Housing...........................34.9
9. Health.............................79.9
10. Diversions......................66.1
11. Internet 60.7
12. Proximity........................80.0

BASIC STATS
Population........................26,047
Density 1,240.1
Born out of state 75.9%
Homes built since 2000 ....14.0%
4 or more bedrooms 17.6%

RACE
Whites................................83.1%
Blacks 2.3%
Hispanics 5.0%
Asians.................................7.2%
Native Americans 0.2%
Diversity index.....................30.1%

HOUSEHOLD INCOME LADDER
95th percentile ....>$250,000
80th percentile $136,647
60th percentile $80,860
50th percentile $64,620
40th percentile $49,917
20th percentile $25,263

HOME VALUE LADDER
75th percentile $386,000
50th percentile $258,800
25th percentile $192,200

CHARACTER
Resilience.............................33.7%
Short commutes 71.3%

STABILITY
Living with two parents 67.7%
Occupied homes.....................94.0%

GROWTH
Population growth.....................1.8%
Economic growth 7.4%

EDUCATION
High school graduates 94.8%
College graduates ....60.9% (★)

JOBS
MBSA workers......................52.9% (★)
Private-sector job growth 3.8%

BUSINESS
Small business growth 0.5%
Self-employed workers 8.2%

MONEY
Median annual earnings ....$53,721 (★)
Living in poverty............................11.6%

HOUSING
Home ownership.....................50.4%
Monthly housing costs...............35.0%

HEALTH
Health care workers..........14.7% (★)
Fair or poor health...........11.7% (★)

DIVERSIONS
Stores per 10,000.................53.5 (★)
Restaurants per 10,000.........31.2 (★)

INTERNET
Broadband subscriptions 75.0%
Smartphone access 73.4%

PROXIMITY
Major hub miles...............................106
Major or mid-major miles................90

Lee's Summit, Missouri

Score .... *775.6 points*
National rank ....*86 of 2,084*
Percentile..*95.92%*
Midwest rank... *14 of 622*
Missouri rank.. *3 of 62*
Closest major hub .... *Kansas City, 15 air miles*

TESTS
1. Character..43.7
2. Stability...76.7
3. Growth..48.4
4. Education...82.8
5. Jobs...69.0
6. Business..41.2
7. Money...83.1
8. Housing...65.6
9. Health..54.4
10. Diversions.......................................33.4
11. Internet...78.6
12. Proximity...98.7

BASIC STATS
Population..91,266
Density...2,205.6
Born out of state..............................42.5%
Homes built since 2000.............................29.3%
4 or more bedrooms.................................35.1%

RACE
Whites...82.1%
Blacks..8.1%
Hispanics...4.4%
Asians..2.2%
Native Americans...0.3%
Diversity index..................................31.6%

HOUSEHOLD INCOME LADDER
95th percentile......................................$238,141
80th percentile......................................$151,704
60th percentile......................................$104,197
50th percentile..$87,602
40th percentile..$72,037
20th percentile..$41,863

HOME VALUE LADDER
75th percentile......................................$300,500
50th percentile......................................$214,700
25th percentile......................................$160,500

CHARACTER
Resilience..24.8%
Short commutes......................................34.2%

STABILITY
Living with two parents...................76.0% (★)
Occupied homes....................................95.7%

GROWTH
Population growth..............................6.0%
Economic growth.................................7.3%

EDUCATION
High school graduates......................97.5% (★)
College graduates...........................49.9% (★)

JOBS
MBSA workers.......................................49.6% (★)
Private-sector job growth..........................8.6%

BUSINESS
Small business growth................................7.0%
Self-employed workers.................................6.2%

MONEY
Median annual earnings...............$62,130 (★)
Living in poverty.......................................5.0% (★)

HOUSING
Home ownership..............................76.1% (★)
Monthly housing costs.............................26.5%

HEALTH
Health care workers...................................10.5%
Fair or poor health.....................................16.8%

DIVERSIONS
Stores per 10,000..30.0
Restaurants per 10,000....................................20.4

INTERNET
Broadband subscriptions................82.3% (★)
Smartphone access...........................85.6% (★)

PROXIMITY
Major hub miles...15 (★)
Major or mid-major miles.........................15 (★)

Leonardtown, Maryland

Score ....*749.5 points*
National rank ....*135 of 2,084*
Percentile...*93.57%*
East rank.. *17 of 246*
Maryland rank .... *3 of 23*
Closest major hub .... *Washington, 51 air miles*

TESTS
1. Character	57.8
2. Stability	67.8
3. Growth	46.5
4. Education	79.7
5. Jobs	78.7
6. Business	40.9
7. Money	96.3
8. Housing	51.5
9. Health	56.0
10. Diversions	25.0
11. Internet	61.5
12. Proximity	87.8

BASIC STATS
Population	5,412
Density	912.0
Born out of state	50.8%
Homes built since 2000	33.2%
4 or more bedrooms	43.6%

RACE
Whites	72.7%
Blacks	14.7%
Hispanics	1.7%
Asians	7.6%
Native Americans	0.1%
Diversity index	44.3%

HOUSEHOLD INCOME LADDER
95th percentile	>$250,000
80th percentile	$207,621
60th percentile	$133,741
50th percentile	$102,955
40th percentile	$78,556
20th percentile	$37,774

HOME VALUE LADDER
75th percentile	$476,300
50th percentile	$398,400
25th percentile	$319,200

CHARACTER
Resilience	35.0% (★)
Short commutes	34.3%

STABILITY
Living with two parents	71.6%
Occupied homes	92.5%

GROWTH
Population growth	3.4%
Economic growth	10.4%

EDUCATION
High school graduates	92.2%
College graduates	53.0% (★)

JOBS
MBSA workers	65.6% (★)
Private-sector job growth	5.8%

BUSINESS
Small business growth	4.4%
Self-employed workers	7.4%

MONEY
Median annual earnings	$86,420 (★)
Living in poverty	5.0% (★)

HOUSING
Home ownership	63.8%
Monthly housing costs	30.1%

HEALTH
Health care workers	8.3%
Fair or poor health	13.0%

DIVERSIONS
Stores per 10,000	27.2
Restaurants per 10,000	15.6

INTERNET
Broadband subscriptions	73.0%
Smartphone access	75.6%

PROXIMITY
Major hub miles	51
Major or mid-major miles	51

Lewes, Delaware

Score ....*807.8 points*
National rank ....*41 of 2,084*
Percentile...*98.08%*
East rank...*4 of 246*
Delaware rank.. *1 of 8*
Closest major hub .... *Philadelphia, 86 air miles*

TESTS

1. Character..54.9
2. Stability..71.2
3. Growth..56.8
4. Education..78.5
5. Jobs..76.4
6. Business...62.4
7. Money...77.9
8. Housing..82.1
9. Health...49.2
10. Diversions...52.7
11. Internet 64.1
12. Proximity...81.6

BASIC STATS

Population...27,227
Density 1,268.1
Born out of state 71.4%
Homes built since 2000............................41.4%
4 or more bedrooms 32.0%

RACE

Whites...91.0%
Blacks..3.3%
Hispanics 1.9%
Asians..1.3%
Native Americans 0.2%
Diversity index.......................................17.0%

HOUSEHOLD INCOME LADDER

95th percentile ....>$250,000
80th percentile $141,548
60th percentile $90,885
50th percentile $73,518
40th percentile $59,751
20th percentile $31,676

HOME VALUE LADDER

75th percentile $560,200
50th percentile $372,500
25th percentile $249,400

CHARACTER

Resilience..24.4%
Short commutes 54.6%

STABILITY

Living with two parents 64.7%
Occupied homes............................. 96.8% (★)

GROWTH

Population growth...............................9.4% (★)
Economic growth 13.5%

EDUCATION

High school graduates 94.7%
College graduates .... 48.3% (★)

JOBS

MBSA workers.. 47.9% (★)
Private-sector job growth .... 18.3% (★)

BUSINESS

Small business growth 5.8%
Self-employed workers .... 15.0% (★)

MONEY

Median annual earnings................$60,041 (★)
Living in poverty..7.9%

HOUSING

Home ownership................................ 84.0% (★)
Monthly housing costs 20.3%

HEALTH

Health care workers..................................9.4%
Fair or poor health...................................17.8%

DIVERSIONS

Stores per 10,000.................................... 47.0 (★)
Restaurants per 10,000............................24.8

INTERNET

Broadband subscriptions 73.9%
Smartphone access 77.4%

PROXIMITY

Major hub miles 86
Major or mid-major miles.............................. 86

Lindstrom, Minnesota

Score ....744.6 points
National rank ....146 of 2,084
Percentile...93.04%
Midwest rank...30 of 622
Minnesota rank ....6 of 53
Closest major hub ....Minneapolis, 34 air miles

TESTS
1. Character.................................66.4
2. Stability.....................................68.3
3. Growth......................................41.2
4. Education.................................65.8
5. Jobs...56.4
6. Business...................................51.7
7. Money.......................................77.9
8. Housing....................................64.8
9. Health.......................................76.8
10. Diversions..............................24.1
11. Internet 60.4
12. Proximity...............................90.8

BASIC STATS
Population..................................8,314
Density 1,649.3
Born out of state 22.4%
Homes built since 2000.............26.0%
4 or more bedrooms 26.6%

RACE
Whites..94.1%
Blacks...0.1%
Hispanics 2.2%
Asians...1.6%
Native Americans 0.2%
Diversity index.........................11.3%

HOUSEHOLD INCOME LADDER
95th percentile $194,141
80th percentile $127,981
60th percentile $97,176
50th percentile $78,260
40th percentile $62,505
20th percentile $34,429

HOME VALUE LADDER
75th percentile $291,100
50th percentile $211,400
25th percentile $160,000

CHARACTER
Resilience............................. 40.1% (★)
Short commutes 37.0%

STABILITY
Living with two parents 65.1%
Occupied homes.......................95.1%

GROWTH
Population growth......................-1.5%
Economic growth 12.7%

EDUCATION
High school graduates ..... 96.6% (★)
College graduates 30.3%

JOBS
MBSA workers.............................35.3%
Private-sector job growth 12.0%

BUSINESS
Small business growth 5.5%
Self-employed workers ..... 11.0% (★)

MONEY
Median annual earnings...............$57,850 (★)
Living in poverty.....................5.8% (★)

HOUSING
Home ownership...................... 76.6% (★)
Monthly housing costs.............27.5%

HEALTH
Health care workers.......................... 13.5% (★)
Fair or poor health.............................. 10.9% (★)

DIVERSIONS
Stores per 10,000.......................30.0
Restaurants per 10,000.............13.2

INTERNET
Broadband subscriptions 66.4%
Smartphone access 79.0%

PROXIMITY
Major hub miles...........................34 (★)
Major or mid-major miles...........................34

Livermore, California

Score ....766.8 points
National rank ....102 of 2,084
Percentile...95.15%
West rank...43 of 471
California rank ....6 of 145
Closest major hub ....San Francisco, 23 air miles

TESTS
1. Character... 16.6
2. Stability..85.3
3. Growth 57.1
4. Education...75.7
5. Jobs..76.1
6. Business 43.4
7. Money 96.8
8. Housing 50.7
9. Health...50.5
10. Diversions.......................................35.1
11. Internet 84.3
12. Proximity...95.2

BASIC STATS
Population.......................................89,014
Density 3,652.6
Born out of state 37.0%
Homes built since 2000............... 16.9%
4 or more bedrooms 33.4%

RACE
Whites...61.8%
Blacks..1.8%
Hispanics 19.9%
Asians...11.7%
Native Americans 0.1%
Diversity index...............................56.2%

HOUSEHOLD INCOME LADDER
95th percentile ....>$250,000
80th percentile $220,202
60th percentile $153,989
50th percentile $125,368
40th percentile $101,861
20th percentile $53,751

HOME VALUE LADDER
75th percentile $947,500
50th percentile $744,100
25th percentile $582,900

CHARACTER
Resilience...3.2%
Short commutes 38.9%

STABILITY
Living with two parents .... 82.3% (★)
Occupied homes.............................. 97.6% (★)

GROWTH
Population growth 5.6%
Economic growth 22.9%

EDUCATION
High school graduates 94.1%
College graduates .... 45.6% (★)

JOBS
MBSA workers...................................... 50.6% (★)
Private-sector job growth 14.6%

BUSINESS
Small business growth 8.9%
Self-employed workers 6.1%

MONEY
Median annual earnings................$86,192 (★)
Living in poverty....................................4.6% (★)

HOUSING
Home ownership.............................. 72.3%
Monthly housing costs.............................36.1%

HEALTH
Health care workers.............................5.9%
Fair or poor health............................ 12.4% (★)

DIVERSIONS
Stores per 10,000......................................25.4
Restaurants per 10,000................................24.5

INTERNET
Broadband subscriptions .... 86.0% (★)
Smartphone access .... 87.4% (★)

PROXIMITY
Major hub miles...................................23 (★)
Major or mid-major miles........................18 (★)

Logan, Utah

Score .... *743.7 points*
National rank .... *148 of 2,084*
Percentile *92.94%*
West rank .... *56 of 471*
Utah rank .... *9 of 20*
Closest major hub .... *Salt Lake City, 75 air miles*

TESTS
1. Character 74.8
2. Stability 80.0
3. Growth 57.9
4. Education 69.4
5. Jobs 62.4
6. Business 59.6
7. Money 49.3
8. Housing 45.8
9. Health 51.8
10. Diversions 30.1
11. Internet 75.0
12. Proximity 87.6

BASIC STATS
Population 103,069
Density 2,349.4
Born out of state 37.0%
Homes built since 2000 .... 28.3%
4 or more bedrooms 41.7%

RACE
Whites 82.0%
Blacks 0.8%
Hispanics 11.6%
Asians 2.8%
Native Americans 0.4%
Diversity index 31.3%

HOUSEHOLD INCOME LADDER
95th percentile $175,423
80th percentile $101,889
60th percentile $69,221
50th percentile $56,373
40th percentile $44,815
20th percentile $26,035

HOME VALUE LADDER
75th percentile $305,600
50th percentile $231,800
25th percentile $170,000

CHARACTER
Resilience 29.5%
Short commutes 76.9%

STABILITY
Living with two parents .... 82.3% (★)
Occupied homes 95.2%

GROWTH
Population growth 5.7%
Economic growth .... 24.0% (★)

EDUCATION
High school graduates 92.8%
College graduates .... 39.7% (★)

JOBS
MBSA workers 38.5%
Private-sector job growth 15.0%

BUSINESS
Small business growth .... 16.8% (★)
Self-employed workers 8.4%

MONEY
Median annual earnings $41,272
Living in poverty 17.1%

HOUSING
Home ownership 58.4%
Monthly housing costs 31.3%

HEALTH
Health care workers 6.3%
Fair or poor health .... 12.3% (★)

DIVERSIONS
Stores per 10,000 .... 37.6
Restaurants per 10,000 .... 13.1

INTERNET
Broadband subscriptions 73.5%
Smartphone access .... 88.1% (★)

PROXIMITY
Major hub miles 75
Major or mid-major miles 42

Longmont, Colorado

Score ....*736.5 points*
National rank ....*165 of 2,084*
Percentile...*92.13%*
West rank...*64 of 471*
Colorado rank ....*22 of 47*
Closest major hub ....*Denver, 33 air miles*

TESTS
1. Character...36.5
2. Stability...72.1
3. Growth...61.0
4. Education..68.9
5. Jobs..64.2
6. Business..50.1
7. Money..68.8
8. Housing...47.2
9. Health..58.4
10. Diversions.....................................46.3
11. Internet 72.0
12. Proximity.......................................91.0

BASIC STATS
Population.......................................98,832
Density 3,763.9
Born out of state 62.7%
Homes built since 2000.................25.5%
4 or more bedrooms 27.6%

RACE
Whites..68.3%
Blacks..1.0%
Hispanics 25.3%
Asians..3.0%
Native Americans 0.5%
Diversity index................................46.8%

HOUSEHOLD INCOME LADDER
95th percentile $225,212
80th percentile $135,854
60th percentile $90,698
50th percentile $74,270
40th percentile $58,267
20th percentile $33,040

HOME VALUE LADDER
75th percentile $462,500
50th percentile $359,100
25th percentile $269,800

CHARACTER
Resilience...16.2%
Short commutes 42.3%

STABILITY
Living with two parents 66.0%
Occupied homes...............................96.8% (★)

GROWTH
Population growth..............................6.5%
Economic growth ....27.3% (★)

EDUCATION
High school graduates 89.7%
College graduates ....43.1% (★)

JOBS
MBSA workers.......................................42.6% (★)
Private-sector job growth 11.8%

BUSINESS
Small business growth 9.9%
Self-employed workers 8.2%

MONEY
Median annual earnings................$52,797 (★)
Living in poverty...............................9.6%

HOUSING
Home ownership.............................61.9%
Monthly housing costs 32.4%

HEALTH
Health care workers...........................8.2%
Fair or poor health.............................11.7% (★)

DIVERSIONS
Stores per 10,000.............................35.7
Restaurants per 10,000.........................26.8 (★)

INTERNET
Broadband subscriptions ....77.4% (★)
Smartphone access 82.6%

PROXIMITY
Major hub miles...33 (★)
Major or mid-major miles..............................33

Los Alamos, New Mexico

Score ....*822.7 points*
National rank ....*28 of 2,084*
Percentile...*98.70%*
West rank... *15 of 471*
New Mexico rank.. *2 of 31*
Closest major hub .... *Denver, 274 air miles*

TESTS
1. Character...96.4
2. Stability..81.8
3. Growth...53.3
4. Education...95.6
5. Jobs...87.8
6. Business...26.9
7. Money...96.4
8. Housing...68.8
9. Health..57.2
10. Diversions..15.9
11. Internet 67.5
12. Proximity..75.1

BASIC STATS
Population......................................11,291
Density 1,396.9
Born out of state 65.5%
Homes built since 2000....................18.3%
4 or more bedrooms 22.6%

RACE
Whites...69.0%
Blacks..0.8%
Hispanics...19.0%
Asians..7.2%
Native Americans 0.7%
Diversity index................................48.1%

HOUSEHOLD INCOME LADDER
95th percentile ....>$250,000
80th percentile $181,983
60th percentile $126,706
50th percentile $109,341
40th percentile $92,000
20th percentile $48,436

HOME VALUE LADDER
75th percentile $410,400
50th percentile $292,400
25th percentile $203,900

CHARACTER
Resilience....................................... 39.5% (★)
Short commutes .... 82.2% (★)

STABILITY
Living with two parents .... 83.2% (★)
Occupied homes...95.8%

GROWTH
Population growth...............................4.3%
Economic growth 19.5%

EDUCATION
High school graduates .... 96.6% (★)
College graduates .... 69.0% (★)

JOBS
MBSA workers....................................... 69.8% (★)
Private-sector job growth 15.0%

BUSINESS
Small business growth ....-3.0%
Self-employed workers 5.7%

MONEY
Median annual earnings...............$93,606 (★)
Living in poverty.................................5.5% (★)

HOUSING
Home ownership...............................64.0%
Monthly housing costs..................... 16.3% (★)

HEALTH
Health care workers.............................6.8%
Fair or poor health............................. 10.4% (★)

DIVERSIONS
Stores per 10,000...............................16.3
Restaurants per 10,000................................15.3

INTERNET
Broadband subscriptions 75.3%
Smartphone access 79.7%

PROXIMITY
Major hub miles................................274
Major or mid-major miles............................. 55

Mandeville, Louisiana

Score ....*791.0 points*
National rank ....*64 of 2,084*
Percentile...*96.98%*
South rank ....*22 of 745*
Louisiana rank ....*1 of 41*
Closest major hub ....*New Orleans, 33 air miles*

TESTS
1. Character................................60.1
2. Stability................................73.0
3. Growth................................63.3
4. Education................................75.3
5. Jobs................................67.4
6. Business................................51.4
7. Money................................73.8
8. Housing................................64.5
9. Health................................54.6
10. Diversions................................39.7
11. Internet................................76.9
12. Proximity................................91.0

BASIC STATS
Population................................100,870
Density................................1,534.2
Born out of state................................30.6%
Homes built since 2000................................38.7%
4 or more bedrooms................................35.7%

RACE
Whites................................83.8%
Blacks................................7.2%
Hispanics................................6.0%
Asians................................1.7%
Native Americans................................0.2%
Diversity index................................28.9%

HOUSEHOLD INCOME LADDER
95th percentile................................>$250,000
80th percentile................................$154,907
60th percentile................................$98,641
50th percentile................................$79,192
40th percentile................................$61,817
20th percentile................................$30,836

HOME VALUE LADDER
75th percentile................................$361,400
50th percentile................................$256,100
25th percentile................................$182,600

CHARACTER
Resilience................................33.3%
Short commutes................................42.3%

STABILITY
Living with two parents................................74.6%
Occupied homes................................94.2%

GROWTH
Population growth................................9.3% (★)
Economic growth................................24.8% (★)

EDUCATION
High school graduates................................93.8%
College graduates................................45.6% (★)

JOBS
MBSA workers................................47.8% (★)
Private-sector job growth................................9.0%

BUSINESS
Small business growth................................6.3%
Self-employed workers................................10.5%

MONEY
Median annual earnings................................$58,034 (★)
Living in poverty................................9.8%

HOUSING
Home ownership................................76.9% (★)
Monthly housing costs................................27.9%

HEALTH
Health care workers................................10.2%
Fair or poor health................................16.3%

DIVERSIONS
Stores per 10,000................................35.1
Restaurants per 10,000................................22.1

INTERNET
Broadband subscriptions................................79.5% (★)
Smartphone access................................85.9% (★)

PROXIMITY
Major hub miles................................33 (★)
Major or mid-major miles................................33

Manor, Texas

Score ....*794.2 points*
National rank ....*60 of 2,084*
Percentile...*97.17%*
South rank ....*20 of 745*
Texas rank..*8 of 173*
Closest major hub ....*Austin, 14 air miles*

TESTS
1. Character.................................29.3
2. Stability..................................75.3
3. Growth...................................94.8
4. Education...............................62.6
5. Jobs......................................72.6
6. Business................................52.1
7. Money...................................64.6
8. Housing.................................63.9
9. Health...................................50.7
10. Diversions............................39.2
11. Internet 90.0
12. Proximity.............................99.1

BASIC STATS
Population....................................7,351
Density 2,030.7
Born out of state 37.5%
Homes built since 2000...................91.1%
4 or more bedrooms 38.4%

RACE
Whites..26.5%
Blacks...25.4%
Hispanics 39.1%
Asians...4.8%
Native Americans 0.0%
Diversity index.............................70.8%

HOUSEHOLD INCOME LADDER
95th percentile........................$244,163
80th percentile........................$127,852
60th percentile..........................$93,567
50th percentile..........................$78,505
40th percentile..........................$65,929
20th percentile..........................$37,741

HOME VALUE LADDER
75th percentile........................$241,500
50th percentile........................$186,100
25th percentile........................$155,800

CHARACTER
Resilience....................................18.4%
Short commutes 24.6%

STABILITY
Living with two parents ....76.6% (★)
Occupied homes............................94.7%

GROWTH
Population growth..........................34.4% (★)
Economic growth ....33.4% (★)

EDUCATION
High school graduates 88.7%
College graduates 36.7%

JOBS
MBSA workers...............................42.5% (★)
Private-sector job growth ....22.0% (★)

BUSINESS
Small business growth ....17.4% (★)
Self-employed workers 5.2%

MONEY
Median annual earnings...................$51,504
Living in poverty............................12.3%

HOUSING
Home ownership............................87.4% (★)
Monthly housing costs 35.0%

HEALTH
Health care workers.........................7.8%
Fair or poor health.........................14.9%

DIVERSIONS
Stores per 10,000...........................30.2
Restaurants per 10,000....................24.7

INTERNET
Broadband subscriptions ....86.2% (★)
Smartphone access ....91.0% (★)

PROXIMITY
Major hub miles.............................14 (★)
Major or mid-major miles..................14 (★)

Manteo, North Carolina

Score ....*779.3 points*
National rank ....*80 of 2,084*
Percentile...*96.21%*
South rank ....*27 of 745*
North Carolina rank.. *4 of 65*
Closest major hub .... *Virginia Beach, 75 air miles*

TESTS
1. Character..69.6
2. Stability..72.9
3. Growth..84.1
4. Education...54.0
5. Jobs..40.6
6. Business...67.7
7. Money...50.2
8. Housing..47.1
9. Health...46.5
10. Diversions.......................................99.8
11. Internet 63.2
12. Proximity...83.6

BASIC STATS
Population...6,956
Density 1,526.4
Born out of state..............................52.4%
Homes built since 2000.....................17.6%
4 or more bedrooms 16.3%

RACE
Whites...73.1%
Blacks...8.8%
Hispanics 14.3%
Asians...1.3%
Native Americans 0.0%
Diversity index..................................43.7%

HOUSEHOLD INCOME LADDER
95th percentile $141,701
80th percentile $84,223
60th percentile $57,289
50th percentile $50,460
40th percentile $41,881
20th percentile $28,372

HOME VALUE LADDER
75th percentile $327,300
50th percentile $238,100
25th percentile $167,500

CHARACTER
Resilience...28.2%
Short commutes 70.9%

STABILITY
Living with two parents 66.9%
Occupied homes...............................96.9% (★)

GROWTH
Population growth...........................28.2% (★)
Economic growth 18.7%

EDUCATION
High school graduates 94.0%
College graduates 19.2%

JOBS
MBSA workers.......................................29.7%
Private-sector job growth 0.5%

BUSINESS
Small business growth 3.7%
Self-employed workers ....19.4% (★)

MONEY
Median annual earnings.......................$34,455
Living in poverty...................................10.0%

HOUSING
Home ownership................................66.2%
Monthly housing costs...........................35.2%

HEALTH
Health care workers...............................5.8%
Fair or poor health..............................14.2%

DIVERSIONS
Stores per 10,000...............................113.9 (★)
Restaurants per 10,000.......................67.5 (★)

INTERNET
Broadband subscriptions 74.1%
Smartphone access 76.4%

PROXIMITY
Major hub miles.......................................75
Major or mid-major miles..............................75

Marysville, Ohio

Score ....755.8 points
National rank ....119 of 2,084
Percentile...94.34%
Midwest rank.. 22 of 622
Ohio rank.. 2 of 88
Closest major hub ....Columbus, 26 air miles

TESTS
1. Character.................................79.1
2. Stability..................................79.2
3. Growth....................................57.4
4. Education................................64.8
5. Jobs..63.5
6. Business..................................32.3
7. Money 78.1
8. Housing...................................55.4
9. Health.....................................60.0
10. Diversions..............................18.2
11. Internet 75.6
12. Proximity...............................92.2

BASIC STATS
Population.............................24,635
Density 2,381.3
Born out of state 24.3%
Homes built since 2000...........34.2%
4 or more bedrooms 26.0%

RACE
Whites...................................88.5%
Blacks 4.2%
Hispanics 2.1%
Asians 2.8%
Native Americans 0.1%
Diversity index.......................21.3%

HOUSEHOLD INCOME LADDER
95th percentile $192,102
80th percentile $132,631
60th percentile $93,606
50th percentile $80,361
40th percentile $63,496
20th percentile $36,659

HOME VALUE LADDER
75th percentile $243,700
50th percentile $191,100
25th percentile $154,700

CHARACTER
Resilience............................ 44.4% (★)
Short commutes 48.8%

STABILITY
Living with two parents 74.4%
Occupied homes.................. 97.6% (★)

GROWTH
Population growth....................7.1%
Economic growth 19.9%

EDUCATION
High school graduates 92.8%
College graduates 34.0%

JOBS
MBSA workers....................... 42.5% (★)
Private-sector job growth 11.2%

BUSINESS
Small business growth 6.0%
Self-employed workers 3.3%

MONEY
Median annual earnings ....$60,417 (★)
Living in poverty......................8.0%

HOUSING
Home ownership......................65.1%
Monthly housing costs 27.8%

HEALTH
Health care workers 10.3%
Fair or poor health..................13.8%

DIVERSIONS
Stores per 10,000 ....21.5
Restaurants per 10,000............13.8

INTERNET
Broadband subscriptions .... 79.8% (★)
Smartphone access 84.5%

PROXIMITY
Major hub miles ....26 (★)
Major or mid-major miles.......................26 (★)

Mauldin, South Carolina

Score ....799.3 points
National rank ....50 of 2,084
Percentile...97.65%
South rank .... 17 of 745
South Carolina rank... 2 of 35
Closest major hub ....Charlotte, 88 air miles

TESTS
1. Character.......................................58.7
2. Stability..78.9
3. Growth...68.1
4. Education.......................................75.6
5. Jobs...68.9
6. Business...47.1
7. Money..73.8
8. Housing..68.7
9. Health..51.2
10. Diversions....................................38.6
11. Internet..79.2
12. Proximity......................................90.5

BASIC STATS
Population...................................144,906
Density..1,733.4
Born out of state.........................54.7%
Homes built since 2000..............42.1%
4 or more bedrooms....................36.8%

RACE
Whites...70.1%
Blacks..16.4%
Hispanics..7.4%
Asians..3.8%
Native Americans...........................0.2%
Diversity index...............................47.4%

HOUSEHOLD INCOME LADDER
95th percentile.........................$244,108
80th percentile.........................$142,549
60th percentile...........................$94,468
50th percentile...........................$79,805
40th percentile...........................$65,464
20th percentile...........................$39,308

HOME VALUE LADDER
75th percentile.........................$287,200
50th percentile.........................$206,700
25th percentile.........................$151,600

CHARACTER
Resilience..32.3%
Short commutes.............................42.3%

STABILITY
Living with two parents..................79.5% (★)
Occupied homes............................95.6%

GROWTH
Population growth...........................14.1% (★)
Economic growth...........................21.5%

EDUCATION
High school graduates...........................94.6%
College graduates............................44.9% (★)

JOBS
MBSA workers.......................................45.8% (★)
Private-sector job growth........................13.3%

BUSINESS
Small business growth............................10.2%
Self-employed workers................................6.9%

MONEY
Median annual earnings...............$53,754 (★)
Living in poverty....................................5.8% (★)

HOUSING
Home ownership.............................78.4% (★)
Monthly housing costs............................25.5%

HEALTH
Health care workers.................................8.4%
Fair or poor health............................15.5%

DIVERSIONS
Stores per 10,000.......................................34.0
Restaurants per 10,000.................................21.9

INTERNET
Broadband subscriptions................83.4% (★)
Smartphone access...........................85.5% (★)

PROXIMITY
Major hub miles.......................................88
Major or mid-major miles........................12 (★)

McPherson, Kansas

Score .... *749.8 points*
National rank .... *133 of 2,084*
Percentile *93.66%*
Midwest rank .... *27 of 622*
Kansas rank .... *1 of 40*
Closest major hub .... *Kansas City, 172 air miles*

TESTS
1. Character..95.2
2. Stability..73.7
3. Growth..66.7
4. Education..60.7
5. Jobs..48.8
6. Business..39.8
7. Money..58.3
8. Housing..55.4
9. Health..59.3
10. Diversions...43.8
11. Internet 66.9
12. Proximity...81.2

BASIC STATS
Population..12,642
Density 1,823.5
Born out of state 32.4%
Homes built since 2000.................14.7%
4 or more bedrooms 23.4%

RACE
Whites..88.8%
Blacks..1.4%
Hispanics 5.8%
Asians..1.1%
Native Americans 0.7%
Diversity index................................20.7%

HOUSEHOLD INCOME LADDER
95th percentile $198,972
80th percentile $107,926
60th percentile $68,940
50th percentile $57,035
40th percentile $44,496
20th percentile $28,785

HOME VALUE LADDER
75th percentile $215,500
50th percentile $142,000
25th percentile $98,700

CHARACTER
Resilience.. 36.0% (★)
Short commutes .... 89.1% (★)

STABILITY
Living with two parents 74.5%
Occupied homes......................................94.6%

GROWTH
Population growth...................................-2.3%
Economic growth .... 57.4% (★)

EDUCATION
High school graduates 93.5%
College graduates 28.1%

JOBS
MBSA workers...32.4%
Private-sector job growth 6.8%

BUSINESS
Small business growth ....-1.0%
Self-employed workers 9.7%

MONEY
Median annual earnings.......................$43,048
Living in poverty.....................................10.3%

HOUSING
Home ownership......................................63.5%
Monthly housing costs...........................26.8%

HEALTH
Health care workers.................................9.6%
Fair or poor health..................................13.2%

DIVERSIONS
Stores per 10,000......................................40.3
Restaurants per 10,000..............................22.1

INTERNET
Broadband subscriptions 71.9%
Smartphone access 81.5%

PROXIMITY
Major hub miles..172
Major or mid-major miles.............................51

Middletown, Delaware

Score ....*758.3 points*
National rank ....*113 of 2,084*
Percentile...*94.62%*
East rank.. *15 of 246*
Delaware rank.. *3 of 8*
Closest major hub .... *Philadelphia, 41 air miles*

TESTS
1. Character................................29.5
2. Stability..................................78.4
3. Growth...................................39.1
4. Education...............................76.8
5. Jobs.......................................70.8
6. Business.................................35.2
7. Money....................................86.5
8. Housing..................................68.1
9. Health....................................53.8
10. Diversions.............................39.0
11. Internet.................................91.6
12. Proximity...............................89.5

BASIC STATS
Population................................32,331
Density.....................................1,838.0
Born out of state.........................56.8%
Homes built since 2000...............64.1%
4 or more bedrooms....................45.9%

RACE
Whites......................................61.8%
Blacks......................................23.4%
Hispanics...................................8.4%
Asians...4.0%
Native Americans.........................0.0%
Diversity index............................55.4%

HOUSEHOLD INCOME LADDER
95th percentile....................... >$250,000
80th percentile.........................$162,490
60th percentile.........................$113,190
50th percentile...........................$97,151
40th percentile...........................$86,131
20th percentile...........................$51,025

HOME VALUE LADDER
75th percentile.........................$384,700
50th percentile.........................$320,800
25th percentile.........................$242,400

CHARACTER
Resilience...................................18.8%
Short commutes..........................24.0%

STABILITY
Living with two parents.................. 76.3% (★)
Occupied homes..........................96.5%

GROWTH
Population growth.........................4.2%
Economic growth.........................-3.9%

EDUCATION
High school graduates .... 96.3% (★)
College graduates .... 44.1% (★)

JOBS
MBSA workers..................................... 53.4% (★)
Private-sector job growth 5.8%

BUSINESS
Small business growth 4.2%
Self-employed workers 5.3%

MONEY
Median annual earnings................$64,832 (★)
Living in poverty...................................5.5% (★)

HOUSING
Home ownership.......................... 85.9% (★)
Monthly housing costs............................30.7%

HEALTH
Health care workers...................................10.3%
Fair or poor health......................................16.8%

DIVERSIONS
Stores per 10,000..............................35.2
Restaurants per 10,000.......................21.5

INTERNET
Broadband subscriptions .... 89.9% (★)
Smartphone access .... 89.6% (★)

PROXIMITY
Major hub miles 41
Major or mid-major miles................................ 41

Midland, Michigan

Score ....*732.1 points*
National rank .... *182 of 2,084*
Percentile..*91.31%*
Midwest rank..*41 of 622*
Michigan rank ....*7 of 67*
Closest major hub ....*Detroit, 92 air miles*

TESTS
1. Character..67.6
2. Stability...77.1
3. Growth..35.5
4. Education..75.6
5. Jobs..59.3
6. Business...38.2
7. Money...70.1
8. Housing..68.2
9. Health...58.3
10. Diversions..31.8
11. Internet 69.1
12. Proximity..81.3

BASIC STATS
Population......................................57,828
Density 1,288.8
Born out of state.............................22.6%
Homes built since 2000.....................11.5%
4 or more bedrooms 25.1%

RACE
Whites...89.8%
Blacks...1.6%
Hispanics 3.1%
Asians...3.2%
Native Americans 0.4%
Diversity index.................................19.1%

HOUSEHOLD INCOME LADDER
95th percentile $241,148
80th percentile $122,856
60th percentile $79,642
50th percentile $65,364
40th percentile $52,447
20th percentile $28,056

HOME VALUE LADDER
75th percentile $214,200
50th percentile $145,400
25th percentile $94,800

CHARACTER
Resilience..30.6%
Short commutes...............................61.7%

STABILITY
Living with two parents 73.5%
Occupied homes...............................96.8% (★)

GROWTH
Population growth.............................-1.8%
Economic growth...............................3.8%

EDUCATION
High school graduates ....96.0% (★)
College graduates ....43.0% (★)

JOBS
MBSA workers.................................45.2% (★)
Private-sector job growth 2.7%

BUSINESS
Small business growth 7.3%
Self-employed workers 4.9%

MONEY
Median annual earnings...............$53,179 (★)
Living in poverty.................................8.8%

HOUSING
Home ownership...............................70.0%
Monthly housing costs.......................20.6%

HEALTH
Health care workers............................9.7%
Fair or poor health............................13.8%

DIVERSIONS
Stores per 10,000..............................32.8
Restaurants per 10,000.......................17.4

INTERNET
Broadband subscriptions 76.5%
Smartphone access 80.5%

PROXIMITY
Major hub miles..................................92
Major or mid-major miles.....................86

Moab, Utah

Score ....*751.3 points*
National rank .... *128 of 2,084*
Percentile..*93.90%*
West rank.. *49 of 471*
Utah rank... *8 of 20*
Closest major hub .... *Salt Lake City, 192 air miles*

TESTS
1. Character...90.0
2. Stability..59.8
3. Growth...52.0
4. Education..59.3
5. Jobs..51.7
6. Business...55.8
7. Money..50.9
8. Housing..56.1
9. Health...43.9
10. Diversions...99.0
11. Internet..66.8
12. Proximity...66.0

BASIC STATS
Population... 7,355
Density 1,726.1
Born out of state 52.9%
Homes built since 2000...........................21.1%
4 or more bedrooms 16.6%

RACE
Whites...79.6%
Blacks..0.4%
Hispanics 11.9%
Asians..2.8%
Native Americans 3.5%
Diversity index...35.0%

HOUSEHOLD INCOME LADDER
95th percentile $127,094
80th percentile $80,750
60th percentile $61,484
50th percentile $51,990
40th percentile $46,125
20th percentile $21,167

HOME VALUE LADDER
75th percentile $323,600
50th percentile $240,000
25th percentile $134,100

CHARACTER
Resilience...32.7%
Short commutes .... 90.3% (★)

STABILITY
Living with two parents 63.0%
Occupied homes...91.3%

GROWTH
Population growth.......................................-0.6%
Economic growth .... 28.8% (★)

EDUCATION
High school graduates 94.6%
College graduates 24.9%

JOBS
MBSA workers...23.0%
Private-sector job growth .... 22.2% (★)

BUSINESS
Small business growth 9.5%
Self-employed workers 10.6%

MONEY
Median annual earnings.......................$36,681
Living in poverty...11.4%

HOUSING
Home ownership...60.1%
Monthly housing costs.............................24.1%

HEALTH
Health care workers....................................4.5%
Fair or poor health......................................13.7%

DIVERSIONS
Stores per 10,000.............................. 81.6 (★)
Restaurants per 10,000........................ 58.8 (★)

INTERNET
Broadband subscriptions .... 77.3% (★)
Smartphone access 77.7%

PROXIMITY
Major hub miles 192
Major or mid-major miles...........................167

Monticello, Illinois

Score ....*743.5 points*
National rank ....*149 of 2,084*
Percentile...*92.89%*
Midwest rank...*31 of 622*
Illinois rank... *1 of 79*
Closest major hub ....*Chicago, 129 air miles*

TESTS
1. Character................................63.8
2. Stability..................................75.9
3. Growth...................................42.4
4. Education...............................77.4
5. Jobs.......................................67.8
6. Business.................................40.8
7. Money....................................67.0
8. Housing..................................69.7
9. Health....................................79.7
10. Diversions............................27.1
11. Internet................................57.8
12. Proximity..............................74.1

BASIC STATS
Population.............................. 5,303
Density 1,538.4
Born out of state 18.0%
Homes built since 2000 ....18.9%
4 or more bedrooms 18.5%

RACE
Whites....................................95.0%
Blacks......................................0.9%
Hispanics 1.1%
Asians......................................1.6%
Native Americans 0.2%
Diversity index..........................9.7%

HOUSEHOLD INCOME LADDER
95th percentile $155,475
80th percentile $109,308
60th percentile $82,599
50th percentile $72,903
40th percentile $58,270
20th percentile $33,500

HOME VALUE LADDER
75th percentile $217,700
50th percentile $159,400
25th percentile $120,800

CHARACTER
Resilience............................ 36.6% (★)
Short commutes 40.8%

STABILITY
Living with two parents .... 76.9% (★)
Occupied homes.......................94.9%

GROWTH
Population growth..........................5.5%
Economic growth ....-1.5%

EDUCATION
High school graduates .... 97.1% (★)
College graduates .... 43.8% (★)

JOBS
MBSA workers............................ 46.4% (★)
Private-sector job growth 11.2%

BUSINESS
Small business growth ....-3.9%
Self-employed workers .... 11.5% (★)

MONEY
Median annual earnings.....................$47,381
Living in poverty.............................6.2% (★)

HOUSING
Home ownership............................. 74.8% (★)
Monthly housing costs.............................22.4%

HEALTH
Health care workers........................... 14.9% (★)
Fair or poor health............................. 12.0% (★)

DIVERSIONS
Stores per 10,000.............................24.4
Restaurants per 10,000.............................18.9

INTERNET
Broadband subscriptions 63.9%
Smartphone access 78.2%

PROXIMITY
Major hub miles.................................129
Major or mid-major miles.............................129

Monticello, Minnesota

Score ....734.2 points
National rank ....178 of 2,084
Percentile...91.50%
Midwest rank..39 of 622
Minnesota rank .... 9 of 53
Closest major hub ....Minneapolis, 35 air miles

TESTS
1. Character...72.0
2. Stability..78.6
3. Growth..39.4
4. Education..58.0
5. Jobs...52.4
6. Business...50.6
7. Money..71.2
8. Housing..60.6
9. Health...63.7
10. Diversions......................................21.4
11. Internet 75.7
12. Proximity..90.6

BASIC STATS
Population.......................................26,544
Density 1,587.3
Born out of state 21.9%
Homes built since 2000...................35.9%
4 or more bedrooms 32.4%

RACE
Whites..86.7%
Blacks...1.6%
Hispanics 7.7%
Asians...0.9%
Native Americans 0.4%
Diversity index..................................24.1%

HOUSEHOLD INCOME LADDER
95th percentile $191,157
80th percentile $131,543
60th percentile $89,961
50th percentile $77,440
40th percentile $63,821
20th percentile $36,187

HOME VALUE LADDER
75th percentile $250,900
50th percentile $198,600
25th percentile $165,800

CHARACTER
Resilience.............................. 43.6% (★)
Short commutes 38.4%

STABILITY
Living with two parents 69.9%
Occupied homes................... 98.9% (★)

GROWTH
Population growth.......................-0.4%
Economic growth..........................7.2%

EDUCATION
High school graduates 92.8%
College graduates 25.7%

JOBS
MBSA workers.............................. 33.0%
Private-sector job growth 10.1%

BUSINESS
Small business growth 10.5%
Self-employed workers 8.1%

MONEY
Median annual earnings.......$51,735
Living in poverty......................6.4% (★)

HOUSING
Home ownership...................... 78.1% (★)
Monthly housing costs.............31.8%

HEALTH
Health care workers.....................9.4%
Fair or poor health.............. 10.8% (★)

DIVERSIONS
Stores per 10,000.........................27.1
Restaurants per 10,000................12.9

INTERNET
Broadband subscriptions .... 79.1% (★)
Smartphone access .... 85.0% (★)

PROXIMITY
Major hub miles.. 35
Major or mid-major miles............................ 35

Morehead City, North Carolina

Score ....**727.7 points**
National rank .... **194 of 2,084**
Percentile **90.73%**
South rank .... **48 of 745**
North Carolina rank .... **8 of 65**
Closest major hub ....**Raleigh, 124 air miles**

TESTS
1. Character 56.5
2. Stability 66.0
3. Growth 47.3
4. Education 63.3
5. Jobs 54.8
6. Business 56.3
7. Money 61.4
8. Housing 62.7
9. Health 52.9
10. Diversions 65.3
11. Internet 66.3
12. Proximity 74.9

BASIC STATS
Population 46,601
Density 978.4
Born out of state 45.4%
Homes built since 2000 ....21.6%
4 or more bedrooms 18.7%

RACE
Whites 85.5%
Blacks 5.5%
Hispanics 4.8%
Asians 1.4%
Native Americans 0.4%
Diversity index 26.3%

HOUSEHOLD INCOME LADDER
95th percentile $200,286
80th percentile $109,575
60th percentile $71,370
50th percentile $57,718
40th percentile $45,824
20th percentile $24,314

HOME VALUE LADDER
75th percentile $363,400
50th percentile $236,200
25th percentile $151,800

CHARACTER
Resilience 24.5%
Short commutes 57.2%

STABILITY
Living with two parents 68.6%
Occupied homes 92.6%

GROWTH
Population growth ....-0.5%
Economic growth 20.7%

EDUCATION
High school graduates 92.7%
College graduates 32.3%

JOBS
MBSA workers 38.6%
Private-sector job growth 5.8%

BUSINESS
Small business growth 5.7%
Self-employed workers ....12.7% (★)

MONEY
Median annual earnings $45,771
Living in poverty 10.0%

HOUSING
Home ownership 70.2%
Monthly housing costs 25.1%

HEALTH
Health care workers 9.3%
Fair or poor health 15.9%

DIVERSIONS
Stores per 10,000 ....54.4 (★)
Restaurants per 10,000 ....30.0 (★)

INTERNET
Broadband subscriptions 74.6%
Smartphone access 79.1%

PROXIMITY
Major hub miles 124
Major or mid-major miles 124

Morro Bay, California

Score .... *734.7 points*
National rank .... *174 of 2,084*
Percentile *91.69%*
West rank .... *67 of 471*
California rank .... *12 of 145*
Closest major hub .... *San Jose, 149 air miles*

TESTS
1. Character 37.8
2. Stability 78.9
3. Growth 54.0
4. Education 68.8
5. Jobs 58.7
6. Business 65.3
7. Money 68.6
8. Housing 49.1
9. Health 58.7
10. Diversions 51.0
11. Internet 67.6
12. Proximity 76.2

BASIC STATS
Population 28,901
Density 2,419.5
Born out of state 35.4%
Homes built since 2000 .... 10.0%
4 or more bedrooms 9.6%

RACE
Whites 77.9%
Blacks 0.6%
Hispanics 14.0%
Asians 3.8%
Native Americans 0.8%
Diversity index 37.1%

HOUSEHOLD INCOME LADDER
95th percentile $231,312
80th percentile $123,594
60th percentile $85,809
50th percentile $72,691
40th percentile $57,511
20th percentile $30,428

HOME VALUE LADDER
75th percentile $738,700
50th percentile $587,200
25th percentile $428,400

CHARACTER
Resilience 16.3%
Short commutes 44.3%

STABILITY
Living with two parents 74.7%
Occupied homes .... 97.3% (★)

GROWTH
Population growth 6.8%
Economic growth 14.9%

EDUCATION
High school graduates 92.4%
College graduates .... 39.4% (★)

JOBS
MBSA workers 40.2%
Private-sector job growth 8.4%

BUSINESS
Small business growth 8.2%
Self-employed workers ..... 14.9% (★)

MONEY
Median annual earnings .... $53,789 (★)
Living in poverty 10.8%

HOUSING
Home ownership 65.1%
Monthly housing costs 32.9%

HEALTH
Health care workers 9.4%
Fair or poor health 13.2%

DIVERSIONS
Stores per 10,000 .... 39.4
Restaurants per 10,000 ...... 28.2 (★)

INTERNET
Broadband subscriptions 75.3%
Smartphone access 79.8%

PROXIMITY
Major hub miles 149
Major or mid-major miles 102

Moscow, Idaho

Score ....*734.7 points*
National rank ....*174 of 2,084*
Percentile...*91.69%*
West rank...*67 of 471*
Idaho rank .... *4 of 21*
Closest major hub ....*Seattle, 253 air miles*

TESTS
1. Character..............................76.5
2. Stability.................................79.7
3. Growth...................................52.0
4. Education.............................89.9
5. Jobs..65.0
6. Business................................50.0
7. Money....................................42.5
8. Housing..................................32.1
9. Health....................................56.2
10. Diversions............................40.4
11. Internet................................75.7
12. Proximity.............................74.7

BASIC STATS
Population.............................25,847
Density 4,405.5
Born out of state......................62.5%
Homes built since 2000.............23.1%
4 or more bedrooms.................16.9%

RACE
Whites......................................87.1%
Blacks..1.5%
Hispanics 4.6%
Asians..3.2%
Native Americans 1.3%
Diversity index........................23.7%

HOUSEHOLD INCOME LADDER
95th percentile.....................$175,946
80th percentile.......................$91,167
60th percentile.......................$51,652
50th percentile.......................$41,842
40th percentile.......................$32,840
20th percentile.......................$17,774

HOME VALUE LADDER
75th percentile.....................$293,500
50th percentile.....................$230,000
25th percentile.....................$175,700

CHARACTER
Resilience.................................32.8%
Short commutes 72.0%

STABILITY
Living with two parents .... 80.9% (★)
Occupied homes.......................95.5%

GROWTH
Population growth......................4.8%
Economic growth 16.2%

EDUCATION
High school graduates .... 97.4% (★)
College graduates .... 56.5% (★)

JOBS
MBSA workers....................... 46.3% (★)
Private-sector job growth 8.0%

BUSINESS
Small business growth 7.6%
Self-employed workers 9.3%

MONEY
Median annual earnings.....................$41,776
Living in poverty............................24.0%

HOUSING
Home ownership.......................41.0%
Monthly housing costs...............31.3%

HEALTH
Health care workers.....................8.8%
Fair or poor health.....................13.6%

DIVERSIONS
Stores per 10,000.......................33.1
Restaurants per 10,000...............23.9

INTERNET
Broadband subscriptions .... 77.3% (★)
Smartphone access .... 86.2% (★)

PROXIMITY
Major hub miles...........................253
Major or mid-major miles............. 68

Mountain House, California

Score ....*774.7 points*
National rank ....*87 of 2,084*
Percentile...*95.87%*
West rank...*36 of 471*
California rank ....*4 of 145*
Closest major hub ....*San Francisco, 35 air miles*

TESTS
1. Character.. 0.0
2. Stability... 80.1
3. Growth.. 75.9
4. Education.. 76.5
5. Jobs... 80.3
6. Business.. 56.2
7. Money... 96.9
8. Housing... 47.3
9. Health... 51.1
10. Diversions.. 19.8
11. Internet 98.9
12. Proximity.. 91.7

BASIC STATS
Population.. 14,152
Density 9,889.6
Born out of state................................ 44.3%
Homes built since 2000...................... 95.6%
4 or more bedrooms 63.3%

RACE
Whites.. 26.4%
Blacks 11.6%
Hispanics 16.1%
Asians.. 37.2%
Native Americans 0.0%
Diversity index................................... 74.5%

HOUSEHOLD INCOME LADDER
95th percentile .... >$250,000
80th percentile $203,908
60th percentile $159,435
50th percentile $134,323
40th percentile $126,376
20th percentile $85,456

HOME VALUE LADDER
75th percentile $682,600
50th percentile $581,400
25th percentile $472,200

CHARACTER
Resilience...4.6%
Short commutes 6.8%

STABILITY
Living with two parents .... 77.4% (★)
Occupied homes................................ 97.0% (★)

GROWTH
Population growth............................. 20.2% (★)
Economic growth 20.4%

EDUCATION
High school graduates 95.2%
College graduates .... 45.2% (★)

JOBS
MBSA workers.................................. 51.0% (★)
Private-sector job growth .... 17.9% (★)

BUSINESS
Small business growth 9.6%
Self-employed workers 10.7%

MONEY
Median annual earnings...............$90,113 (★)
Living in poverty.................................4.8% (★)

HOUSING
Home ownership.................................... 70.4%
Monthly housing costs............................ 37.7%

HEALTH
Health care workers.................................9.7%
Fair or poor health.................................17.3%

DIVERSIONS
Stores per 10,000............................... 21.4
Restaurants per 10,000...................... 15.1

INTERNET
Broadband subscriptions .... 90.9% (★)
Smartphone access .... 94.8% (★)

PROXIMITY
Major hub miles................................. 35
Major or mid-major miles......................26 (★)

Mount Horeb, Wisconsin

Score ....*752.3 points*
National rank ....*127 of 2,084*
Percentile...*93.95%*
Midwest rank...*25 of 622*
Wisconsin rank ....*6 of 61*
Closest major hub ....*Milwaukee, 82 air miles*

TESTS
1. Character.................................43.1
2. Stability..................................79.2
3. Growth....................................52.3
4. Education................................88.6
5. Jobs..68.1
6. Business..................................34.9
7. Money.....................................77.2
8. Housing...................................51.1
9. Health.....................................59.2
10. Diversions..............................37.5
11. Internet 70.8
12. Proximity...............................90.3

BASIC STATS
Population....................................7,291
Density 2,575.4
Born out of state.........................31.2%
Homes built since 2000............24.6%
4 or more bedrooms 25.6%

RACE
Whites...89.2%
Blacks..1.9%
Hispanics 5.1%
Asians...0.7%
Native Americans 0.0%
Diversity index..........................20.0%

HOUSEHOLD INCOME LADDER
95th percentile $186,544
80th percentile $129,970
60th percentile $91,790
50th percentile $79,747
40th percentile $65,559
20th percentile $37,508

HOME VALUE LADDER
75th percentile $340,500
50th percentile $260,400
25th percentile $215,900

CHARACTER
Resilience.......................................27.4%
Short commutes 27.0%

STABILITY
Living with two parents ....76.3% (★)
Occupied homes................................96.9% (★)

GROWTH
Population growth...........................4.0%
Economic growth 18.7%

EDUCATION
High school graduates ....98.7% (★)
College graduates ....53.7% (★)

JOBS
MBSA workers....................................46.6% (★)
Private-sector job growth 11.3%

BUSINESS
Small business growth 6.8%
Self-employed workers 3.9%

MONEY
Median annual earnings...............$55,895 (★)
Living in poverty....................................4.6% (★)

HOUSING
Home ownership.........................67.2%
Monthly housing costs..............32.6%

HEALTH
Health care workers......................8.7%
Fair or poor health............................12.0% (★)

DIVERSIONS
Stores per 10,000.........................30.1
Restaurants per 10,000................23.5

INTERNET
Broadband subscriptions ....79.3% (★)
Smartphone access 80.2%

PROXIMITY
Major hub miles.................................82
Major or mid-major miles........................16 (★)

Mount Vernon, Iowa

Score ....745.2 points
National rank ....143 of 2,084
Percentile...93.18%
Midwest rank...29 of 622
Iowa rank..7 of 55
Closest major hub ....Chicago, 181 air miles

TESTS
1. Character..................................56.7
2. Stability....................................79.7
3. Growth.....................................46.4
4. Education.................................83.3
5. Jobs..56.6
6. Business...................................44.1
7. Money......................................72.1
8. Housing....................................59.5
9. Health.......................................57.7
10. Diversions...............................37.2
11. Internet 79.3
12. Proximity................................72.6

BASIC STATS
Population.................................. 6,624
Density 1,938.0
Born out of state 31.7%
Homes built since 2000.............19.2%
4 or more bedrooms 27.4%

RACE
Whites...92.5%
Blacks 1.6%
Hispanics 2.8%
Asians...0.9%
Native Americans 0.2%
Diversity index..........................14.3%

HOUSEHOLD INCOME LADDER
95th percentile $196,854
80th percentile $120,154
60th percentile $86,303
50th percentile $70,907
40th percentile $57,881
20th percentile $38,912

HOME VALUE LADDER
75th percentile $245,700
50th percentile $180,400
25th percentile $126,800

CHARACTER
Resilience....................................30.4%
Short commutes 43.4%

STABILITY
Living with two parents ....79.3% (★)
Occupied homes........................96.1%

GROWTH
Population growth........................5.0%
Economic growth..........................6.4%

EDUCATION
High school graduates ....97.5% (★)
College graduates ....50.5% (★)

JOBS
MBSA workers.........................42.7% (★)
Private-sector job growth 2.7%

BUSINESS
Small business growth 5.3%
Self-employed workers 8.2%

MONEY
Median annual earnings......................$51,309
Living in poverty....................5.1% (★)

HOUSING
Home ownership.......................72.2%
Monthly housing costs............29.0%

HEALTH
Health care workers.....................8.0%
Fair or poor health.............................11.8% (★)

DIVERSIONS
Stores per 10,000.......................30.7
Restaurants per 10,000................22.9

INTERNET
Broadband subscriptions ....80.5% (★)
Smartphone access ....87.5% (★)

PROXIMITY
Major hub miles..............................181
Major or mid-major miles............118

Mukwonago, Wisconsin

Score ....*776.8 points*
National rank ....*83 of 2,084*
Percentile..*96.06%*
Midwest rank...*13 of 622*
Wisconsin rank ....*2 of 61*
Closest major hub ....*Milwaukee, 18 air miles*

TESTS
1. Character.................................58.9
2. Stability...................................92.2
3. Growth....................................36.8
4. Education................................70.7
5. Jobs...55.3
6. Business..................................36.4
7. Money.....................................82.7
8. Housing...................................66.8
9. Health.....................................66.8
10. Diversions..............................35.7
11. Internet 77.2
12. Proximity...............................97.3

BASIC STATS
Population.............................19,953
Density 914.1
Born out of state 20.3%
Homes built since 2000.............21.1%
4 or more bedrooms 25.2%

RACE
Whites 94.1%
Blacks 0.9%
Hispanics 3.1%
Asians..0.6%
Native Americans 0.2%
Diversity index.........................11.3%

HOUSEHOLD INCOME LADDER
95th percentile $238,146
80th percentile $148,042
60th percentile $107,455
50th percentile $91,178
40th percentile $74,765
20th percentile $45,297

HOME VALUE LADDER
75th percentile $352,200
50th percentile $267,100
25th percentile $208,100

CHARACTER
Resilience.......................... 37.6% (★)
Short commutes 30.0%

STABILITY
Living with two parents .... 87.5% (★)
Occupied homes................................. 98.1% (★)

GROWTH
Population growth.............................-3.0%
Economic growth 8.9%

EDUCATION
High school graduates .... 97.7% (★)
College graduates 34.8%

JOBS
MBSA workers...............................38.0%
Private-sector job growth 7.2%

BUSINESS
Small business growth 1.7%
Self-employed workers 7.0%

MONEY
Median annual earnings ....$60,691 (★)
Living in poverty....................................3.9% (★)

HOUSING
Home ownership............................. 82.7% (★)
Monthly housing costs 29.7%

HEALTH
Health care workers.................................... 10.2%
Fair or poor health............................ 10.4% (★)

DIVERSIONS
Stores per 10,000.............................32.2
Restaurants per 10,000................................20.8

INTERNET
Broadband subscriptions .... 83.6% (★)
Smartphone access 83.4%

PROXIMITY
Major hub miles ....18 (★)
Major or mid-major miles.......................18 (★)

Murfreesboro, Tennessee

Score ....*728.2 points*
National rank ....*192 of 2,084*
Percentile...*90.83%*
South rank ....*47 of 745*
Tennessee rank...*3 of 58*
Closest major hub ....*Nashville, 25 air miles*

TESTS

1. Character.................................58.6
2. Stability...................................72.2
3. Growth....................................69.8
4. Education................................69.2
5. Jobs..65.1
6. Business..................................53.1
7. Money....................................56.1
8. Housing..................................44.1
9. Health....................................46.4
10. Diversions..............................27.1
11. Internet 74.1
12. Proximity...............................92.4

BASIC STATS

Population...............................160,169
Density 2,069.7
Born out of state 46.8%
Homes built since 2000..............39.0%
4 or more bedrooms 23.0%

RACE

Whites......................................69.4%
Blacks 17.0%
Hispanics 6.6%
Asians..3.4%
Native Americans 0.2%
Diversity index..........................48.3%

HOUSEHOLD INCOME LADDER

95th percentile $196,108
80th percentile $115,141
60th percentile $77,276
50th percentile $64,212
40th percentile $52,513
20th percentile $29,965

HOME VALUE LADDER

75th percentile $297,300
50th percentile $228,000
25th percentile $164,100

CHARACTER

Resilience.................................31.7%
Short commutes 43.5%

STABILITY

Living with two parents 68.9%
Occupied homes.......................95.8%

GROWTH

Population growth........... 15.3% (★)
Economic growth 21.6%

EDUCATION

High school graduates 93.4%
College graduates 38.6%

JOBS

MBSA workers...........................36.5%
Private-sector job growth ....20.7% (★)

BUSINESS

Small business growth ....16.0% (★)
Self-employed workers 6.3%

MONEY

Median annual earnings........$43,834
Living in poverty.......................13.1%

HOUSING

Home ownership.......................57.7%
Monthly housing costs..............32.2%

HEALTH

Health care workers....................7.8%
Fair or poor health....................17.0%

DIVERSIONS

Stores per 10,000......................27.5
Restaurants per 10,000..............17.0

INTERNET

Broadband subscriptions 73.7%
Smartphone access ....87.1% (★)

PROXIMITY

Major hub miles.........................25 (★)
Major or mid-major miles.........25 (★)

Nantucket, Massachusetts

Score ....*877.4 points*
National rank ....*6 of 2,084*
Percentile *99.76%*
East rank .... *1 of 246*
Massachusetts rank .... *1 of 12*
Closest major hub ....*Boston, 94 air miles*

TESTS
1. Character..................................96.1
2. Stability...................................66.4
3. Growth....................................59.8
4. Education................................79.7
5. Jobs..57.7
6. Business..................................89.4
7. Money.....................................81.7
8. Housing...................................31.3
9. Health.....................................50.1
10. Diversions............................ 100.0
11. Internet 81.8
12. Proximity...............................83.4

BASIC STATS
Population................................ 8,990
Density 1,118.7
Born out of state........................46.8%
Homes built since 2000.............21.9%
4 or more bedrooms 35.4%

RACE
Whites.......................................85.6%
Blacks...6.8%
Hispanics 3.8%
Asians...0.7%
Native Americans 0.4%
Diversity index..........................26.0%

HOUSEHOLD INCOME LADDER
95th percentile ....>$250,000
80th percentile $184,433
60th percentile $129,820
50th percentile $108,167
40th percentile $79,125
20th percentile $38,686

HOME VALUE LADDER
75th percentile $1,395,200
50th percentile $998,800
25th percentile $706,100

CHARACTER
Resilience............................. 35.2% (★)
Short commutes .... 92.2% (★)

STABILITY
Living with two parents 67.6%
Occupied homes........................93.2%

GROWTH
Population growth.......................7.1%
Economic growth .... 23.8% (★)

EDUCATION
High school graduates 95.1%
College graduates .... 49.2% (★)

JOBS
MBSA workers............................35.5%
Private-sector job growth 13.2%

BUSINESS
Small business growth ..... 17.0% (★)
Self-employed workers .... 22.5% (★)

MONEY
Median annual earnings..............$64,362 (★)
Living in poverty............................8.3%

HOUSING
Home ownership........................66.6%
Monthly housing costs..............48.9%

HEALTH
Health care workers......................5.9%
Fair or poor health.....................12.6%

DIVERSIONS
Stores per 10,000....................139.3 (★)
Restaurants per 10,000.............89.3 (★)

INTERNET
Broadband subscriptions .... 85.6% (★)
Smartphone access ....86.5% (★)

PROXIMITY
Major hub miles 94
Major or mid-major miles 76

Nephi, Utah

Score ....*725.0 points*
National rank ....*208 of 2,084*
Percentile..*90.06%*
West rank...*80 of 471*
Utah rank.. *12 of 20*
Closest major hub .... *Salt Lake City, 64 air miles*

TESTS
1. Character.....................................67.8
2. Stability..78.9
3. Growth...56.2
4. Education.....................................49.6
5. Jobs..52.3
6. Business.......................................63.5
7. Money 58.7
8. Housing..64.4
9. Health..51.1
10. Diversions...................................24.4
11. Internet 69.6
12. Proximity.....................................88.5

BASIC STATS
Population.. 5,743
Density 1,788.5
Born out of state 19.2%
Homes built since 2000............................17.1%
4 or more bedrooms 46.8%

RACE
Whites..89.6%
Blacks 0.5%
Hispanics 6.7%
Asians..0.1%
Native Americans 0.5%
Diversity index...............................19.2%

HOUSEHOLD INCOME LADDER
95th percentile $160,315
80th percentile $106,960
60th percentile $73,428
50th percentile $61,715
40th percentile $45,141
20th percentile $34,600

HOME VALUE LADDER
75th percentile $289,800
50th percentile $212,800
25th percentile $152,300

CHARACTER
Resilience.......................................33.3%
Short commutes 55.6%

STABILITY
Living with two parents .... 76.2% (★)
Occupied homes...............................96.8% (★)

GROWTH
Population growth 7.1%
Economic growth 17.9%

EDUCATION
High school graduates 91.2%
College graduates 17.5%

JOBS
MBSA workers.................................28.1%
Private-sector job growth 16.3%

BUSINESS
Small business growth .... 15.8% (★)
Self-employed workers 10.4%

MONEY
Median annual earnings $45,676
Living in poverty..............................12.4%

HOUSING
Home ownership.............................72.8%
Monthly housing costs....................25.4%

HEALTH
Health care workers.........................6.9%
Fair or poor health...........................13.5%

DIVERSIONS
Stores per 10,000............................22.4
Restaurants per 10,000.....................18.1

INTERNET
Broadband subscriptions 67.7%
Smartphone access .... 86.9% (★)

PROXIMITY
Major hub miles............................... 64
Major or mid-major miles.................... 39

New Bremen, Ohio

Score ....*780.3 points*
National rank ....*77 of 2,084*
Percentile...*96.35%*
Midwest rank.. *10 of 622*
Ohio rank... *1 of 88*
Closest major hub ....*Columbus, 79 air miles*

TESTS

1. Character................................75.6
2. Stability..................................88.6
3. Growth...................................39.3
4. Education...............................76.5
5. Jobs.......................................64.6
6. Business.................................33.1
7. Money 79.2
8. Housing..................................81.0
9. Health....................................50.3
10. Diversions.............................31.0
11. Internet 74.2
12. Proximity...............................86.9

BASIC STATS

Population.. 7,462
Density 1,334.4
Born out of state.................................9.2%
Homes built since 2000.......................16.0%
4 or more bedrooms 20.5%

RACE

Whites...96.7%
Blacks...0.5%
Hispanics 0.6%
Asians...1.6%
Native Americans 0.0%
Diversity index....................................6.5%

HOUSEHOLD INCOME LADDER

95th percentile $207,080
80th percentile $135,620
60th percentile $97,423
50th percentile $78,011
40th percentile $64,488
20th percentile $37,042

HOME VALUE LADDER

75th percentile $252,300
50th percentile $178,800
25th percentile $142,500

CHARACTER

Resilience.............................. 36.4% (★)
Short commutes 61.8%

STABILITY

Living with two parents .... 92.4% (★)
Occupied homes...........................95.1%

GROWTH

Population growth........................ -0.8%
Economic growth...........................8.1%

EDUCATION

High school graduates .... 98.5% (★)
College graduates .... 40.8% (★)

JOBS

MBSA workers...................... 44.8% (★)
Private-sector job growth 9.5%

BUSINESS

Small business growth 1.4%
Self-employed workers 5.9%

MONEY

Median annual earnings...............$55,981 (★)
Living in poverty................................2.8% (★)

HOUSING

Home ownership....................... 82.0% (★)
Monthly housing costs............................ 19.7%

HEALTH

Health care workers............................7.6%
Fair or poor health................................ 14.8%

DIVERSIONS

Stores per 10,000................................31.8
Restaurants per 10,000.....................17.4

INTERNET

Broadband subscriptions .... 82.9% (★)
Smartphone access 81.0%

PROXIMITY

Major hub miles................................. 79
Major or mid-major miles................................ 46

New Prague, Minnesota

Score ....*729.8 points*
National rank ....*185 of 2,084*
Percentile...*91.17%*
Midwest rank... *42 of 622*
Minnesota rank .... *11 of 53*
Closest major hub ....*Minneapolis, 34 air miles*

TESTS
1. Character..62.2
2. Stability..84.1
3. Growth..53.9
4. Education..70.1
5. Jobs..62.2
6. Business..32.2
7. Money...70.5
8. Housing...60.0
9. Health...58.1
10. Diversions...22.1
11. Internet...63.6
12. Proximity...90.8

BASIC STATS
Population.. 8,332
Density 1,895.4
Born out of state 18.6%
Homes built since 2000........................... 37.8%
4 or more bedrooms 35.3%

RACE
Whites..89.7%
Blacks..0.0%
Hispanics 4.0%
Asians..2.6%
Native Americans 1.3%
Diversity index....................................19.2%

HOUSEHOLD INCOME LADDER
95th percentile $217,960
80th percentile $142,147
60th percentile $92,271
50th percentile $80,128
40th percentile $62,569
20th percentile $32,875

HOME VALUE LADDER
75th percentile $322,700
50th percentile $247,700
25th percentile $185,600

CHARACTER
Resilience.. 40.2% (★)
Short commutes 29.5%

STABILITY
Living with two parents .... 85.3% (★)
Occupied homes...96.2%

GROWTH
Population growth...5.0%
Economic growth 18.9%

EDUCATION
High school graduates .... 97.5% (★)
College graduates 34.4%

JOBS
MBSA workers...34.6%
Private-sector job growth .... 19.7% (★)

BUSINESS
Small business growth 4.5%
Self-employed workers 4.0%

MONEY
Median annual earnings.......................$51,033
Living in poverty....................................6.4% (★)

HOUSING
Home ownership............................... 79.2% (★)
Monthly housing costs............................33.0%

HEALTH
Health care workers...................................7.5%
Fair or poor health............................. 10.9% (★)

DIVERSIONS
Stores per 10,000.......................................25.6
Restaurants per 10,000.................................14.3

INTERNET
Broadband subscriptions .... 79.6% (★)
Smartphone access 73.1%

PROXIMITY
Major hub miles...34 (★)
Major or mid-major miles................................ 34

New Ulm, Minnesota

Score ....*726.0 points*
National rank ....*204 of 2,084*
Percentile...*90.25%*
Midwest rank.. *48 of 622*
Minnesota rank .... *15 of 53*
Closest major hub ....*Minneapolis, 74 air miles*

TESTS

1. Character.................................81.7
2. Stability...................................74.2
3. Growth....................................41.3
4. Education................................64.6
5. Jobs..43.2
6. Business..................................40.0
7. Money.....................................62.8
8. Housing...................................71.3
9. Health.....................................58.7
10. Diversions...............................44.1
11. Internet..................................60.4
12. Proximity................................83.7

BASIC STATS

Population.................................12,914
Density.....................................1,826.8
Born out of state.........................25.0%
Homes built since 2000..................9.4%
4 or more bedrooms.....................24.8%

RACE

Whites.......................................91.7%
Blacks..1.2%
Hispanics...................................4.7%
Asians..1.2%
Native Americans........................0.2%
Diversity index............................15.7%

HOUSEHOLD INCOME LADDER

95th percentile.........................$154,144
80th percentile.........................$102,442
60th percentile...........................$75,876
50th percentile...........................$62,396
40th percentile...........................$49,373
20th percentile...........................$29,424

HOME VALUE LADDER

75th percentile.........................$175,000
50th percentile.........................$140,700
25th percentile.........................$103,200

CHARACTER

Resilience...................................33.4%
Short commutes.................... 79.6% (★)

STABILITY

Living with two parents...............75.5%
Occupied homes..........................94.5%

GROWTH

Population growth........................-2.3%
Economic growth.........................14.7%

EDUCATION

High school graduates.......... 95.9% (★)
College graduates.......................29.7%

JOBS

MBSA workers.............................30.0%
Private-sector job growth...............3.2%

BUSINESS

Small business growth....................3.9%
Self-employed workers...................7.3%

MONEY

Median annual earnings.............$43,526
Living in poverty......................6.6% (★)

HOUSING

Home ownership.................... 76.8% (★)
Monthly housing costs...................22.4%

HEALTH

Health care workers.......................8.0%
Fair or poor health................. 11.3% (★)

DIVERSIONS

Stores per 10,000........................41.0
Restaurants per 10,000.................21.9

INTERNET

Broadband subscriptions..............72.1%
Smartphone access......................75.1%

PROXIMITY

Major hub miles.............................. 74
Major or mid-major miles................. 74

Northfield, Minnesota

Score ....*727.0 points*
National rank ....*198 of 2,084*
Percentile..*90.54%*
Midwest rank..*47 of 622*
Minnesota rank ....*14 of 53*
Closest major hub ....*Minneapolis, 37 air miles*

TESTS
1. Character..68.3
2. Stability..73.2
3. Growth..43.8
4. Education..76.5
5. Jobs...63.5
6. Business..34.8
7. Money...69.0
8. Housing...58.5
9. Health...52.4
10. Diversions..27.1
11. Internet 69.7
12. Proximity..90.2

BASIC STATS
Population...21,965
Density 2,391.9
Born out of state 43.6%
Homes built since 2000.............................24.9%
4 or more bedrooms 28.2%

RACE
Whites..82.9%
Blacks...1.9%
Hispanics...8.6%
Asians...3.7%
Native Americans 0.3%
Diversity index...30.3%

HOUSEHOLD INCOME LADDER
95th percentile $220,554
80th percentile $128,100
60th percentile $86,615
50th percentile $71,243
40th percentile $55,730
20th percentile $30,322

HOME VALUE LADDER
75th percentile $297,400
50th percentile $224,900
25th percentile $163,900

CHARACTER
Resilience..32.6%
Short commutes 58.2%

STABILITY
Living with two parents 70.7%
Occupied homes...95.7%

GROWTH
Population growth......................................-0.8%
Economic growth 15.5%

EDUCATION
High school graduates ....96.3% (★)
College graduates ....43.8% (★)

JOBS
MBSA workers.......................................42.0% (★)
Private-sector job growth 11.8%

BUSINESS
Small business growth 2.5%
Self-employed workers 6.0%

MONEY
Median annual earnings................$52,980 (★)
Living in poverty...9.6%

HOUSING
Home ownership...69.5%
Monthly housing costs 28.1%

HEALTH
Health care workers....................................6.5%
Fair or poor health............................12.3% (★)

DIVERSIONS
Stores per 10,000.......................................28.5
Restaurants per 10,000...............................16.4

INTERNET
Broadband subscriptions 76.3%
Smartphone access 81.2%

PROXIMITY
Major hub miles..37
Major or mid-major miles.............................37

Oak Island, North Carolina

Score ....*728.3 points*
National rank ....*191 of 2,084*
Percentile..*90.88%*
South rank ....*46 of 745*
North Carolina rank..*7 of 65*
Closest major hub ....*Raleigh, 132 air miles*

TESTS

1. Character......................................55.1
2. Stability...59.7
3. Growth..69.1
4. Education......................................66.5
5. Jobs...62.5
6. Business..69.1
7. Money...62.2
8. Housing...61.5
9. Health...49.6
10. Diversions...................................34.4
11. Internet 65.1
12. Proximity......................................73.5

BASIC STATS

Population.......................................12,426
Density 1,102.1
Born out of state 57.6%
Homes built since 2000.....................33.7%
4 or more bedrooms 16.1%

RACE

Whites...94.3%
Blacks..2.7%
Hispanics 1.4%
Asians..0.1%
Native Americans 0.5%
Diversity index.................................11.0%

HOUSEHOLD INCOME LADDER

95th percentile $216,414
80th percentile $115,553
60th percentile $74,126
50th percentile $60,648
40th percentile $46,525
20th percentile $25,060

HOME VALUE LADDER

75th percentile $362,900
50th percentile $240,200
25th percentile $167,900

CHARACTER

Resilience..23.7%
Short commutes 56.6%

STABILITY

Living with two parents 56.8%
Occupied homes...............................93.5%

GROWTH

Population growth............................. 16.7% (★)
Economic growth 17.2%

EDUCATION

High school graduates .... 96.0% (★)
College graduates 31.9%

JOBS

MBSA workers..................................39.0%
Private-sector job growth 14.5%

BUSINESS

Small business growth .... 11.1% (★)
Self-employed workers .... 14.9% (★)

MONEY

Median annual earnings.......................$46,292
Living in poverty...............................9.7%

HOUSING

Home ownership...............................77.2% (★)
Monthly housing costs............................30.5%

HEALTH

Health care workers..............................8.5%
Fair or poor health................................16.4%

DIVERSIONS

Stores per 10,000...............................31.2
Restaurants per 10,000................................20.4

INTERNET

Broadband subscriptions 74.3%
Smartphone access 78.1%

PROXIMITY

Major hub miles..................................132
Major or mid-major miles...........................132

Ocean Pines, Maryland

Score ....*788.1 points*
National rank ....*71 of 2,084*
Percentile...*96.64%*
East rank...*8 of 246*
Maryland rank ....*1 of 23*
Closest major hub ....*Baltimore, 101 air miles*

TESTS
1. Character.......................................55.8
2. Stability...77.7
3. Growth...53.4
4. Education......................................67.2
5. Jobs...54.8
6. Business...59.6
7. Money..66.4
8. Housing..61.8
9. Health..51.5
10. Diversions....................................97.2
11. Internet...63.7
12. Proximity......................................79.0

BASIC STATS
Population......................................34,789
Density 1,484.4
Born out of state.............................54.3%
Homes built since 2000...................22.1%
4 or more bedrooms 14.0%

RACE
Whites...87.0%
Blacks...5.3%
Hispanics 3.7%
Asians...1.7%
Native Americans 0.2%
Diversity index................................23.8%

HOUSEHOLD INCOME LADDER
95th percentile $233,420
80th percentile $119,432
60th percentile $79,451
50th percentile $64,271
40th percentile $50,351
20th percentile $28,861

HOME VALUE LADDER
75th percentile $422,200
50th percentile $290,500
25th percentile $216,700

CHARACTER
Resilience...25.4%
Short commutes 53.7%

STABILITY
Living with two parents 74.9%
Occupied homes.............................96.6%

GROWTH
Population growth.............................8.0%
Economic growth 11.1%

EDUCATION
High school graduates 93.8%
College graduates 35.7%

JOBS
MBSA workers.................................36.5%
Private-sector job growth 8.5%

BUSINESS
Small business growth 4.0%
Self-employed workers ....14.8% (★)

MONEY
Median annual earnings.....................$47,546
Living in poverty..............................6.9% (★)

HOUSING
Home ownership ....77.6% (★)
Monthly housing costs............................30.5%

HEALTH
Health care workers.............................7.5%
Fair or poor health.................................14.1%

DIVERSIONS
Stores per 10,000.............................70.4 (★)
Restaurants per 10,000.........................61.4 (★)

INTERNET
Broadband subscriptions 74.8%
Smartphone access 76.4%

PROXIMITY
Major hub miles..101
Major or mid-major miles.............................101

Ocean View, Delaware

Score .... *797.0 points*
National rank .... *53 of 2,084*
Percentile.. *97.50%*
East rank .... *6 of 246*
Delaware rank.. *2 of 8*
Closest major hub .... *Baltimore, 96 air miles*

TESTS
1. Character..................................50.2
2. Stability....................................60.2
3. Growth.....................................75.5
4. Education.................................75.2
5. Jobs...69.6
6. Business...................................61.7
7. Money 74.0
8. Housing 87.5
9. Health......................................44.7
10. Diversions...............................52.7
11. Internet 65.8
12. Proximity.................................79.9

BASIC STATS
Population...............................15,172
Density 738.2
Born out of state 78.8%
Homes built since 2000.............40.3%
4 or more bedrooms 36.0%

RACE
Whites.......................................94.2%
Blacks 1.9%
Hispanics 1.3%
Asians..0.5%
Native Americans 0.1%
Diversity index..........................11.2%

HOUSEHOLD INCOME LADDER
95th percentile $244,653
80th percentile $135,000
60th percentile $90,240
50th percentile $73,438
40th percentile $60,599
20th percentile $37,628

HOME VALUE LADDER
75th percentile $463,800
50th percentile $344,600
25th percentile $258,200

CHARACTER
Resilience...................................24.4%
Short commutes 46.4%

STABILITY
Living with two parents 51.1%
Occupied homes........................95.8%

GROWTH
Population growth............................ 22.9% (★)
Economic growth 13.5%

EDUCATION
High school graduates .... 96.9% (★)
College graduates .... 41.4% (★)

JOBS
MBSA workers.................................. 42.6% (★)
Private-sector job growth .... 18.3% (★)

BUSINESS
Small business growth 5.8%
Self-employed workers .... 14.7% (★)

MONEY
Median annual earnings ....$54,264 (★)
Living in poverty..................................6.1% (★)

HOUSING
Home ownership.............................. 89.7% (★)
Monthly housing costs 20.7%

HEALTH
Health care workers................................7.8%
Fair or poor health.................................17.8%

DIVERSIONS
Stores per 10,000...................... 47.0 (★)
Restaurants per 10,000............................24.8

INTERNET
Broadband subscriptions 75.3%
Smartphone access 78.1%

PROXIMITY
Major hub miles................................. 96
Major or mid-major miles.............................. 96

Olympia, Washington

Score .... *740.4 points*
National rank .... *157 of 2,084*
Percentile *92.51%*
West rank .... *60 of 471*
Washington rank .... *6 of 44*
Closest major hub .... *Seattle, 40 air miles*

TESTS
1. Character 59.1
2. Stability 73.2
3. Growth 58.0
4. Education 70.6
5. Jobs 70.9
6. Business 42.2
7. Money 69.2
8. Housing 46.1
9. Health 59.2
10. Diversions 29.1
11. Internet 73.1
12. Proximity 89.7

BASIC STATS
Population 194,812
Density 1,844.8
Born out of state 56.5%
Homes built since 2000 .... 26.4%
4 or more bedrooms 18.7%

RACE
Whites 72.2%
Blacks 3.8%
Hispanics 9.5%
Asians 7.9%
Native Americans 1.0%
Diversity index 45.9%

HOUSEHOLD INCOME LADDER
95th percentile $205,784
80th percentile $125,375
60th percentile $84,277
50th percentile $69,550
40th percentile $56,112
20th percentile $31,415

HOME VALUE LADDER
75th percentile $378,100
50th percentile $284,100
25th percentile $215,800

CHARACTER
Resilience 29.5%
Short commutes 49.7%

STABILITY
Living with two parents 69.6%
Occupied homes 96.1%

GROWTH
Population growth 7.5%
Economic growth 20.1%

EDUCATION
High school graduates 94.4%
College graduates 39.0%

JOBS
MBSA workers .... 44.2% (★)
Private-sector job growth .... 17.7% (★)

BUSINESS
Small business growth 8.4%
Self-employed workers 5.9%

MONEY
Median annual earnings .... $54,619 (★)
Living in poverty 11.0%

HOUSING
Home ownership 59.0%
Monthly housing costs 31.4%

HEALTH
Health care workers 9.8%
Fair or poor health 13.5%

DIVERSIONS
Stores per 10,000 .... 27.4
Restaurants per 10,000 .... 18.6

INTERNET
Broadband subscriptions .... 78.6% (★)
Smartphone access 82.9%

PROXIMITY
Major hub miles 40
Major or mid-major miles 40

Orange City, Iowa

Score ....780.3 points
National rank ....77 of 2,084
Percentile..96.35%
Midwest rank.. 10 of 622
Iowa rank... 2 of 55
Closest major hub ....Minneapolis, 194 air miles

TESTS

1. Character..93.1
2. Stability..89.8
3. Growth..44.5
4. Education.......................................76.9
5. Jobs..54.4
6. Business...40.1
7. Money..67.2
8. Housing..77.2
9. Health..55.1
10. Diversions....................................42.7
11. Internet 67.9
12. Proximity......................................71.4

BASIC STATS

Population....................................... 6,908
Density 1,906.2
Born out of state.........................36.8%
Homes built since 2000.............. 15.6%
4 or more bedrooms 36.6%

RACE

Whites...91.3%
Blacks...0.4%
Hispanics 5.9%
Asians..1.5%
Native Americans 0.0%
Diversity index.............................. 16.3%

HOUSEHOLD INCOME LADDER

95th percentile $156,665
80th percentile $109,864
60th percentile $82,886
50th percentile $72,904
40th percentile $61,188
20th percentile $32,087

HOME VALUE LADDER

75th percentile $231,300
50th percentile $164,900
25th percentile $114,000

CHARACTER

Resilience............................... 40.8% (★)
Short commutes 74.6%

STABILITY

Living with two parents .... 95.8% (★)
Occupied homes...............................94.3%

GROWTH

Population growth.............................1.8%
Economic growth 10.7%

EDUCATION

High school graduates .... 98.6% (★)
College graduates .... 41.2% (★)

JOBS

MBSA workers.................................38.5%
Private-sector job growth 5.5%

BUSINESS

Small business growth 7.2%
Self-employed workers 5.7%

MONEY

Median annual earnings.....................$47,202
Living in poverty.................................5.8% (★)

HOUSING

Home ownership............................. 79.4% (★)
Monthly housing costs...........................19.7%

HEALTH

Health care workers.....................................7.6%
Fair or poor health............................ 12.5% (★)

DIVERSIONS

Stores per 10,000..............................44.8
Restaurants per 10,000......................18.4

INTERNET

Broadband subscriptions .... 80.2% (★)
Smartphone access 76.8%

PROXIMITY

Major hub miles 194
Major or mid-major miles..............122

Orangetree, Florida

Score ....*779.6 points*
National rank ....*79 of 2,084*
Percentile...*96.26%*
South rank .... *26 of 745*
Florida rank .... *5 of 63*
Closest major hub ....*Miami, 83 air miles*

TESTS
1. Character.................................19.9
2. Stability...................................78.0
3. Growth....................................48.6
4. Education................................65.9
5. Jobs..72.6
6. Business..................................87.7
7. Money.....................................76.5
8. Housing...................................63.0
9. Health.....................................64.7
10. Diversions.............................41.5
11. Internet.................................72.4
12. Proximity..............................88.8

BASIC STATS
Population................................. 9,128
Density 960.9
Born out of state....................57.3%
Homes built since 2000............58.2%
4 or more bedrooms 46.3%

RACE
Whites......................................54.2%
Blacks..3.4%
Hispanics 35.3%
Asians...0.0%
Native Americans 0.0%
Diversity index.........................57.5%

HOUSEHOLD INCOME LADDER
95th percentile $198,474
80th percentile $159,000
60th percentile $117,338
50th percentile $105,806
40th percentile $83,171
20th percentile $27,453

HOME VALUE LADDER
75th percentile $366,100
50th percentile $311,100
25th percentile $265,200

CHARACTER
Resilience.................................17.6%
Short commutes 10.2%

STABILITY
Living with two parents ....80.6% (★)
Occupied homes.......................94.7%

GROWTH
Population growth........................0.1%
Economic growth 21.5%

EDUCATION
High school graduates 94.2%
College graduates 33.5%

JOBS
MBSA workers........................45.3% (★)
Private-sector job growth ....18.4% (★)

BUSINESS
Small business growth ....16.3% (★)
Self-employed workers ....19.2% (★)

MONEY
Median annual earnings.................$54,479 (★)
Living in poverty...........................3.9% (★)

HOUSING
Home ownership.....................94.1% (★)
Monthly housing costs............40.0%

HEALTH
Health care workers...........14.8% (★)
Fair or poor health...................17.7%

DIVERSIONS
Stores per 10,000......................39.1
Restaurants per 10,000................21.0

INTERNET
Broadband subscriptions ....84.6% (★)
Smartphone access 78.2%

PROXIMITY
Major hub miles...........................83
Major or mid-major miles................28

Oregon, Wisconsin

Score ....771.4 points
National rank .... 94 of 2,084
Percentile..95.54%
Midwest rank..15 of 622
Wisconsin rank .... 3 of 61
Closest major hub .... Milwaukee, 65 air miles

TESTS
1. Character....................................46.1
2. Stability......................................80.1
3. Growth.......................................47.7
4. Education...................................83.1
5. Jobs..64.0
6. Business.....................................45.2
7. Money..77.6
8. Housing......................................56.9
9. Health...64.6
10. Diversions................................37.8
11. Internet....................................76.9
12. Proximity..................................91.4

BASIC STATS
Population..............................11,356
Density....................................1,792.0
Born out of state.....................26.5%
Homes built since 2000............25.5%
4 or more bedrooms.................29.4%

RACE
Whites..87.6%
Blacks...7.0%
Hispanics.....................................2.9%
Asians...0.2%
Native Americans 0.5%
Diversity index...........................22.7%

HOUSEHOLD INCOME LADDER
95th percentile.....................$231,719
80th percentile.....................$140,299
60th percentile.....................$101,060
50th percentile.......................$81,164
40th percentile.......................$67,534
20th percentile.......................$40,901

HOME VALUE LADDER
75th percentile.....................$317,200
50th percentile.....................$241,200
25th percentile.....................$200,800

CHARACTER
Resilience....................................27.8%
Short commutes 31.2%

STABILITY
Living with two parents ....76.5% (★)
Occupied homes.................................97.3% (★)

GROWTH
Population growth.............................0.7%
Economic growth 18.5%

EDUCATION
High school graduates ....97.6% (★)
College graduates ....50.1% (★)

JOBS
MBSA workers......................................43.0% (★)
Private-sector job growth 11.1%

BUSINESS
Small business growth 6.9%
Self-employed workers 7.8%

MONEY
Median annual earnings...............$55,603 (★)
Living in poverty....................................4.0% (★)

HOUSING
Home ownership..............................72.9%
Monthly housing costs.....................31.5%

HEALTH
Health care workers................................10.6%
Fair or poor health............................. 12.0% (★)

DIVERSIONS
Stores per 10,000...................................30.4
Restaurants per 10,000...............................23.5

INTERNET
Broadband subscriptions .... 80.9% (★)
Smartphone access .... 85.0% (★)

PROXIMITY
Major hub miles..65
Major or mid-major miles......................15 (★)

Oxford, Mississippi

Score ....758.9 points
National rank ....111 of 2,084
Percentile...94.72%
South rank .... 34 of 745
Mississippi rank.. 1 of 36
Closest major hub .... Memphis, 55 air miles

TESTS
1. Character..75.3
2. Stability..52.7
3. Growth..51.7
4. Education..92.0
5. Jobs..78.8
6. Business..66.6
7. Money...41.0
8. Housing...38.8
9. Health...45.3
10. Diversions..55.9
11. Internet 73.7
12. Proximity..87.1

BASIC STATS
Population...29,075
Density 1,810.3
Born out of state...............................50.2%
Homes built since 2000...................42.1%
4 or more bedrooms 16.1%

RACE
Whites...74.0%
Blacks 19.1%
Hispanics 1.9%
Asians...3.3%
Native Americans 0.5%
Diversity index....................................41.4%

HOUSEHOLD INCOME LADDER
95th percentile $208,322
80th percentile $102,017
60th percentile $58,169
50th percentile $45,528
40th percentile $35,571
20th percentile $15,292

HOME VALUE LADDER
75th percentile $367,600
50th percentile $253,000
25th percentile $176,000

CHARACTER
Resilience..28.0%
Short commutes .... 81.4% (★)

STABILITY
Living with two parents 73.9%
Occupied homes....................................83.6%

GROWTH
Population growth 6.0%
Economic growth 12.9%

EDUCATION
High school graduates .... 96.4% (★)
College graduates .... 59.4% (★)

JOBS
MBSA workers..................................... 45.2% (★)
Private-sector job growth .... 23.9% (★)

BUSINESS
Small business growth .... 20.6% (★)
Self-employed workers 9.2%

MONEY
Median annual earnings......................$44,127
Living in poverty...................................27.7%

HOUSING
Home ownership....................................45.7%
Monthly housing costs...........................28.9%

HEALTH
Health care workers................................9.7%
Fair or poor health................................20.1%

DIVERSIONS
Stores per 10,000.....................................41.3
Restaurants per 10,000.......................30.8 (★)

INTERNET
Broadband subscriptions 69.5%
Smartphone access .... 89.6% (★)

PROXIMITY
Major hub miles....................................... 55
Major or mid-major miles.............................. 55

Paloma Creek South, Texas

Score ....804.6 points
National rank ....44 of 2,084
Percentile...97.94%
South rank .... 14 of 745
Texas rank... 6 of 173
Closest major hub ....Dallas, 28 air miles

TESTS

1. Character.................................21.1
2. Stability....................................77.1
3. Growth.....................................61.5
4. Education.................................74.6
5. Jobs..98.8
6. Business...................................62.7
7. Money......................................81.1
8. Housing....................................59.9
9. Health......................................56.8
10. Diversions...............................22.7
11. Internet 90.4
12. Proximity.................................97.9

BASIC STATS

Population........................... 7,946
Density 6,832.3
Born out of state 51.2%
Homes built since 2000...........93.7%
4 or more bedrooms 39.7%

RACE

Whites...................................61.3%
Blacks 21.8%
Hispanics 8.0%
Asians 1.5%
Native Americans 0.0%
Diversity index......................56.5%

HOUSEHOLD INCOME LADDER

95th percentile $189,191
80th percentile $145,150
60th percentile $110,000
50th percentile $94,063
40th percentile $74,082
20th percentile $48,558

HOME VALUE LADDER

75th percentile $280,700
50th percentile $231,000
25th percentile $187,900

CHARACTER

Resilience...............................18.5%
Short commutes 10.1%

STABILITY

Living with two parents 75.9%
Occupied homes....................95.9%

GROWTH

Population growth....................7.0%
Economic growth .... 27.0% (★)

EDUCATION

High school graduates ....96.2% (★)
College graduates ....41.5% (★)

JOBS

MBSA workers........................58.1% (★)
Private-sector job growth ....28.2% (★)

BUSINESS

Small business growth ....24.2% (★)
Self-employed workers 5.9%

MONEY

Median annual earnings..............$62,500 (★)
Living in poverty.......................7.1% (★)

HOUSING

Home ownership.......................... 79.5% (★)
Monthly housing costs.....................33.3%

HEALTH

Health care workers.......................9.6%
Fair or poor health...........................14.4%

DIVERSIONS

Stores per 10,000.........................20.6
Restaurants per 10,000....................17.9

INTERNET

Broadband subscriptions .... 86.0% (★)
Smartphone access .... 91.4% (★)

PROXIMITY

Major hub miles.........................28 (★)
Major or mid-major miles.......................11 (★)

Park City, Utah

Score ....*935.0 points*
National rank ....*2 of 2,084*
Percentile...*99.95%*
West rank...*2 of 471*
Utah rank..*2 of 20*
Closest major hub ....*Salt Lake City, 22 air miles*

TESTS
1. Character...81.3
2. Stability...70.3
3. Growth..72.7
4. Education...93.2
5. Jobs...77.1
6. Business..82.6
7. Money...81.6
8. Housing...42.2
9. Health...55.2
10. Diversions...97.9
11. Internet..88.0
12. Proximity...92.9

BASIC STATS
Population...................................... 14,573
Density 1,207.2
Born out of state 73.4%
Homes built since 2000............................22.6%
4 or more bedrooms 39.3%

RACE
Whites...80.7%
Blacks...0.5%
Hispanics 13.2%
Asians...3.4%
Native Americans 0.3%
Diversity index.................................33.0%

HOUSEHOLD INCOME LADDER
95th percentile .... >$250,000
80th percentile .... >$250,000
60th percentile $161,261
50th percentile $127,295
40th percentile $98,568
20th percentile $53,388

HOME VALUE LADDER
75th percentile $1,315,000
50th percentile $860,900
25th percentile $585,300

CHARACTER
Resilience................................. 39.2% (★)
Short commutes 65.0%

STABILITY
Living with two parents .... 77.6% (★)
Occupied homes............................91.7%

GROWTH
Population growth........................... 13.7% (★)
Economic growth .... 30.1% (★)

EDUCATION
High school graduates 95.0%
College graduates .... 66.2% (★)

JOBS
MBSA workers............................... 50.3% (★)
Private-sector job growth 15.8%

BUSINESS
Small business growth .... 15.7% (★)
Self-employed workers .... 16.7% (★)

MONEY
Median annual earnings...............$60,208 (★)
Living in poverty.....................................4.5% (★)

HOUSING
Home ownership.............................70.5%
Monthly housing costs............................41.8%

HEALTH
Health care workers..............................6.4%
Fair or poor health........................... 10.8% (★)

DIVERSIONS
Stores per 10,000......................... 79.3 (★)
Restaurants per 10,000...........................43.0 (★)

INTERNET
Broadband subscriptions .... 80.5% (★)
Smartphone access .... 93.3% (★)

PROXIMITY
Major hub miles..22 (★)
Major or mid-major miles.........................22 (★)

Pawleys Island, South Carolina

Score ....*795.6 points*
National rank ....*56 of 2,084*
Percentile...*97.36%*
South rank .... *19 of 745*
South Carolina rank... *3 of 35*
Closest major hub ....*Charlotte, 157 air miles*

TESTS

1. Character.................................51.1
2. Stability...................................82.7
3. Growth....................................59.3
4. Education................................74.5
5. Jobs...65.8
6. Business..................................67.1
7. Money.....................................68.6
8. Housing...................................74.1
9. Health......................................46.1
10. Diversions...............................53.0
11. Internet 72.9
12. Proximity.................................80.4

BASIC STATS

Population.............................12,994
Density 994.5
Born out of state.........................65.4%
Homes built since 2000...........28.4%
4 or more bedrooms 18.2%

RACE

Whites...80.8%
Blacks..10.8%
Hispanics 6.5%
Asians..0.8%
Native Americans 0.1%
Diversity index..........................33.1%

HOUSEHOLD INCOME LADDER

95th percentile ....>$250,000
80th percentile $138,854
60th percentile $88,064
50th percentile $71,823
40th percentile $58,086
20th percentile $29,195

HOME VALUE LADDER

75th percentile $451,700
50th percentile $301,900
25th percentile $199,600

CHARACTER

Resilience.......................................21.5%
Short commutes 55.0%

STABILITY

Living with two parents ....78.5% (★)
Occupied homes................................98.0% (★)

GROWTH

Population growth.............................15.4% (★)
Economic growth...................................3.9%

EDUCATION

High school graduates 93.0%
College graduates ....45.6% (★)

JOBS

MBSA workers.......................................46.5% (★)
Private-sector job growth 8.7%

BUSINESS

Small business growth 3.4%
Self-employed workers ....19.5% (★)

MONEY

Median annual earnings...............$54,279 (★)
Living in poverty...11.2%

HOUSING

Home ownership..............................82.3% (★)
Monthly housing costs...........................23.6%

HEALTH

Health care workers.....................................8.8%
Fair or poor health....................................18.5%

DIVERSIONS

Stores per 10,000..............................47.7 (★)
Restaurants per 10,000............................24.6

INTERNET

Broadband subscriptions ....80.4% (★)
Smartphone access 81.5%

PROXIMITY

Major hub miles...............................157
Major or mid-major miles.............................64

Pecan Plantation, Texas

Score ....*746.7 points*
National rank ....*140 of 2,084*
Percentile..*93.33%*
South rank ....*41 of 745*
Texas rank..*13 of 173*
Closest major hub ....*Dallas, 50 air miles*

TESTS
1. Character..29.0
2. Stability..92.3
3. Growth...53.4
4. Education..63.3
5. Jobs...64.0
6. Business..57.9
7. Money..71.9
8. Housing..83.7
9. Health..46.9
10. Diversions..28.9
11. Internet 67.4
12. Proximity...88.0

BASIC STATS
Population... 7,511
Density 840.3
Born out of state 40.4%
Homes built since 2000...................... 34.5%
4 or more bedrooms 24.4%

RACE
Whites.. 94.6%
Blacks..0.3%
Hispanics 3.2%
Asians...0.8%
Native Americans 0.0%
Diversity index................................. 10.4%

HOUSEHOLD INCOME LADDER
95th percentile $244,545
80th percentile $158,407
60th percentile $100,359
50th percentile $78,008
40th percentile $63,595
20th percentile $42,386

HOME VALUE LADDER
75th percentile $326,400
50th percentile $242,100
25th percentile $179,500

CHARACTER
Resilience... 23.1%
Short commutes 12.8%

STABILITY
Living with two parents .... 92.6% (★)
Occupied homes................................ 96.3%

GROWTH
Population growth............................ 10.1% (★)
Economic growth 6.2%

EDUCATION
High school graduates 90.8%
College graduates 34.8%

JOBS
MBSA workers...................................... 50.0% (★)
Private-sector job growth 2.1%

BUSINESS
Small business growth .... 13.5% (★)
Self-employed workers 9.4%

MONEY
Median annual earnings.......................$52,158
Living in poverty.....................................6.1% (★)

HOUSING
Home ownership............................... 92.0% (★)
Monthly housing costs 24.4%

HEALTH
Health care workers 6.8%
Fair or poor health.................................. 15.4%

DIVERSIONS
Stores per 10,000.................................... 30.8
Restaurants per 10,000 .... 16.4

INTERNET
Broadband subscriptions 69.6%
Smartphone access 83.5%

PROXIMITY
Major hub miles 50
Major or mid-major miles............................. 50

Pella, Iowa

Score ....*763.7 points*
National rank .... *107 of 2,084*
Percentile...*94.91%*
Midwest rank.. *18 of 622*
Iowa rank... *4 of 55*
Closest major hub .... *Kansas City, 186 air miles*

TESTS
1. Character..93.8
2. Stability...83.9
3. Growth...49.1
4. Education..79.3
5. Jobs..56.9
6. Business..41.4
7. Money...73.4
8. Housing...55.5
9. Health..55.1
10. Diversions......................................35.0
11. Internet 58.7
12. Proximity..81.6

BASIC STATS
Population.. 9,607
Density 1,533.7
Born out of state 32.4%
Homes built since 2000.....................11.6%
4 or more bedrooms 23.1%

RACE
Whites...93.1%
Blacks...1.9%
Hispanics 1.4%
Asians...3.0%
Native Americans 0.2%
Diversity index................................13.2%

HOUSEHOLD INCOME LADDER
95th percentile.....................$188,753
80th percentile.....................$108,041
60th percentile.......................$78,397
50th percentile.......................$66,592
40th percentile.......................$54,697
20th percentile.......................$33,903

HOME VALUE LADDER
75th percentile.....................$240,300
50th percentile.....................$183,300
25th percentile.....................$145,900

CHARACTER
Resilience..................................37.6% (★)
Short commutes ....83.1% (★)

STABILITY
Living with two parents ....82.7% (★)
Occupied homes................................97.1% (★)

GROWTH
Population growth.........................-0.4%
Economic growth ....23.5% (★)

EDUCATION
High school graduates ....96.0% (★)
College graduates ....47.5% (★)

JOBS
MBSA workers..................................38.1%
Private-sector job growth 9.0%

BUSINESS
Small business growth 3.8%
Self-employed workers 7.9%

MONEY
Median annual earnings.....................$51,455
Living in poverty.....................................4.0% (★)

HOUSING
Home ownership.............................59.5%
Monthly housing costs.......................24.2%

HEALTH
Health care workers............................7.6%
Fair or poor health.............................. 12.5% (★)

DIVERSIONS
Stores per 10,000..............................35.8
Restaurants per 10,000.......................18.0

INTERNET
Broadband subscriptions 69.3%
Smartphone access 75.4%

PROXIMITY
Major hub miles.................................186
Major or mid-major miles................ 41

Petaluma, California

Score ....*753.8 points*
National rank ....*124 of 2,084*
Percentile...*94.10%*
West rank...*48 of 471*
California rank ....*7 of 145*
Closest major hub ....*San Francisco, 47 air miles*

TESTS
1. Character......................................34.1
2. Stability...82.3
3. Growth...51.7
4. Education......................................67.5
5. Jobs...64.8
6. Business..55.4
7. Money...88.5
8. Housing...46.1
9. Health..55.5
10. Diversions...................................42.2
11. Internet.......................................76.8
12. Proximity.....................................88.9

BASIC STATS
Population....................................67,784
Density 3,181.6
Born out of state..........................37.6%
Homes built since 2000............... 13.9%
4 or more bedrooms 26.8%

RACE
Whites...68.9%
Blacks..1.0%
Hispanics 21.6%
Asians..4.3%
Native Americans 0.1%
Diversity index...............................47.5%

HOUSEHOLD INCOME LADDER
95th percentile ....>$250,000
80th percentile $173,381
60th percentile $113,713
50th percentile $90,830
40th percentile $74,326
20th percentile $39,819

HOME VALUE LADDER
75th percentile $829,900
50th percentile $650,000
25th percentile $507,600

CHARACTER
Resilience...16.1%
Short commutes 38.3%

STABILITY
Living with two parents .... 76.4% (★)
Occupied homes...............................98.5% (★)

GROWTH
Population growth.............................3.9%
Economic growth 17.8%

EDUCATION
High school graduates 90.3%
College graduates ....40.6% (★)

JOBS
MBSA workers.................................. 43.1% (★)
Private-sector job growth 11.9%

BUSINESS
Small business growth 6.8%
Self-employed workers .... 11.8% (★)

MONEY
Median annual earnings...............$67,749 (★)
Living in poverty.................................6.8% (★)

HOUSING
Home ownership.............................66.3%
Monthly housing costs............................36.0%

HEALTH
Health care workers.............................8.9%
Fair or poor health...........................14.1%

DIVERSIONS
Stores per 10,000 ....35.5
Restaurants per 10,000.............................23.8

INTERNET
Broadband subscriptions ....81.6% (★)
Smartphone access 84.4%

PROXIMITY
Major hub miles................................... 47
Major or mid-major miles............................ 44

Petoskey, Michigan

Score ....*735.0 points*
National rank ....*172 of 2,084*
Percentile...*91.79%*
Midwest rank...*37 of 622*
Michigan rank .... *5 of 67*
Closest major hub .... *Detroit, 216 air miles*

TESTS
1. Character......................................74.8
2. Stability......................................67.6
3. Growth...36.1
4. Education....................................69.8
5. Jobs...56.3
6. Business......................................44.9
7. Money...56.0
8. Housing.......................................38.1
9. Health...77.4
10. Diversions.................................91.5
11. Internet 58.3
12. Proximity...................................64.2

BASIC STATS
Population.................................. 8,067
Density 1,351.5
Born out of state 22.0%
Homes built since 2000..............12.3%
4 or more bedrooms 18.1%

RACE
Whites...90.8%
Blacks...0.8%
Hispanics 3.1%
Asians...0.8%
Native Americans 1.6%
Diversity index...........................17.3%

HOUSEHOLD INCOME LADDER
95th percentile $178,317
80th percentile $87,931
60th percentile $61,128
50th percentile $45,666
40th percentile $38,333
20th percentile $25,137

HOME VALUE LADDER
75th percentile $271,700
50th percentile $186,800
25th percentile $139,700

CHARACTER
Resilience....................................30.0%
Short commutes 75.7%

STABILITY
Living with two parents 54.8%
Occupied homes................... 98.4% (★)

GROWTH
Population growth......................-4.5%
Economic growth 11.2%

EDUCATION
High school graduates 94.9%
College graduates 37.4%

JOBS
MBSA workers.............................39.9%
Private-sector job growth 5.9%

BUSINESS
Small business growth 4.9%
Self-employed workers 8.7%

MONEY
Median annual earnings......................$38,909
Living in poverty.........................8.6%

HOUSING
Home ownership.........................46.2%
Monthly housing costs...............29.8%

HEALTH
Health care workers........................ 15.7% (★)
Fair or poor health....................13.8%

DIVERSIONS
Stores per 10,000....................... 81.9 (★)
Restaurants per 10,000........................ 37.6 (★)

INTERNET
Broadband subscriptions 66.3%
Smartphone access 77.0%

PROXIMITY
Major hub miles.............................216
Major or mid-major miles...........................171

Pinehurst, North Carolina

Score ....742.5 points
National rank .... 152 of 2,084
Percentile..92.75%
South rank .... 43 of 745
North Carolina rank.. 6 of 65
Closest major hub ....Raleigh, 59 air miles

TESTS

1. Character..62.7
2. Stability..64.0
3. Growth..44.9
4. Education..80.7
5. Jobs...68.5
6. Business..45.6
7. Money..63.1
8. Housing...57.5
9. Health...64.1
10. Diversions......................................40.0
11. Internet 65.0
12. Proximity..86.4

BASIC STATS

Population.......................................39,890
Density...1,053.6
Born out of state............................61.2%
Homes built since 2000....................29.1%
4 or more bedrooms 20.4%

RACE

Whites...77.1%
Blacks..14.6%
Hispanics 4.6%
Asians..1.5%
Native Americans 0.7%
Diversity index................................38.2%

HOUSEHOLD INCOME LADDER

95th percentile...........................$243,365
80th percentile...........................$123,008
60th percentile.............................$77,795
50th percentile.............................$61,515
40th percentile.............................$50,507
20th percentile.............................$27,144

HOME VALUE LADDER

75th percentile...........................$371,500
50th percentile...........................$260,000
25th percentile...........................$178,100

CHARACTER

Resilience..27.8%
Short commutes 59.9%

STABILITY

Living with two parents 66.0%
Occupied homes................................92.5%

GROWTH

Population growth...............................1.9%
Economic growth 11.1%

EDUCATION

High school graduates ....95.5% (★)
College graduates ....49.9% (★)

JOBS

MBSA workers....................................45.3% (★)
Private-sector job growth 13.5%

BUSINESS

Small business growth 3.4%
Self-employed workers 9.7%

MONEY

Median annual earnings.....................$47,707
Living in poverty...............................10.2%

HOUSING

Home ownership...............................67.6%
Monthly housing costs 27.7%

HEALTH

Health care workers...........................12.7%
Fair or poor health............................15.1%

DIVERSIONS

Stores per 10,000..............................36.9
Restaurants per 10,000......................21.2

INTERNET

Broadband subscriptions 76.6%
Smartphone access 76.5%

PROXIMITY

Major hub miles.................................59
Major or mid-major miles...................59

Platte City, Missouri

Score ....777.1 points
National rank ....82 of 2,084
Percentile...96.11%
Midwest rank.. 12 of 622
Missouri rank.. 2 of 62
Closest major hub .... Kansas City, 23 air miles

TESTS

1. Character....................................66.9
2. Stability......................................67.7
3. Growth.......................................61.6
4. Education...................................78.9
5. Jobs..79.8
6. Business.....................................40.1
7. Money..72.9
8. Housing......................................47.9
9. Health...56.9
10. Diversions................................28.9
11. Internet....................................82.8
12. Proximity..................................92.7

BASIC STATS

Population.................................10,456
Density 1,772.8
Born out of state.........................49.4%
Homes built since 2000.............48.3%
4 or more bedrooms 31.1%

RACE

Whites..90.1%
Blacks...4.2%
Hispanics 3.9%
Asians...0.5%
Native Americans 0.1%
Diversity index...........................18.5%

HOUSEHOLD INCOME LADDER

95th percentile $235,244
80th percentile $136,167
60th percentile $102,694
50th percentile $85,985
40th percentile $65,589
20th percentile $37,869

HOME VALUE LADDER

75th percentile $299,200
50th percentile $224,000
25th percentile $165,000

CHARACTER

Resilience.................................38.9% (★)
Short commutes 40.8%

STABILITY

Living with two parents 59.8%
Occupied homes..................96.7% (★)

GROWTH

Population growth......................7.0%
Economic growth ....27.1% (★)

EDUCATION

High school graduates ......97.7% (★)
College graduates ....44.8% (★)

JOBS

MBSA workers......................49.5% (★)
Private-sector job growth ...19.4% (★)

BUSINESS

Small business growth 7.2%
Self-employed workers 5.7%

MONEY

Median annual earnings...............$52,836 (★)
Living in poverty......................5.8% (★)

HOUSING

Home ownership........................62.2%
Monthly housing costs 32.0%

HEALTH

Health care workers....................9.4%
Fair or poor health......................14.1%

DIVERSIONS

Stores per 10,000.......................29.6
Restaurants per 10,000..............17.1

INTERNET

Broadband subscriptions ......78.9% (★)
Smartphone access ....91.4% (★)

PROXIMITY

Major hub miles............................23 (★)
Major or mid-major miles........23 (★)

Plumas Lake, California

Score ....*729.7 points*
National rank ....*186 of 2,084*
Percentile...*91.12%*
West rank..*72 of 471*
California rank ....*14 of 145*
Closest major hub ....*Sacramento, 28 air miles*

TESTS
1. Character.................................21.5
2. Stability...................................83.6
3. Growth....................................81.7
4. Education................................64.2
5. Jobs...68.7
6. Business..................................33.1
7. Money.....................................84.1
8. Housing...................................61.9
9. Health.....................................45.6
10. Diversions.............................. 8.0
11. Internet 85.5
12. Proximity................................91.8

BASIC STATS
Population... 6,824
Density 3,926.4
Born out of state 32.8%
Homes built since 2000..................... 89.8%
4 or more bedrooms 58.9%

RACE
Whites..57.6%
Blacks..4.1%
Hispanics 20.6%
Asians..8.3%
Native Americans 0.7%
Diversity index...................................61.0%

HOUSEHOLD INCOME LADDER
95th percentile $208,955
80th percentile $152,304
60th percentile $108,784
50th percentile $100,934
40th percentile $86,615
20th percentile $47,439

HOME VALUE LADDER
75th percentile $374,600
50th percentile $320,700
25th percentile $272,400

CHARACTER
Resilience... 16.0%
Short commutes 16.7%

STABILITY
Living with two parents .... 76.1% (★)
Occupied homes................................ 99.3% (★)

GROWTH
Population growth............................. 23.7% (★)
Economic growth 20.8%

EDUCATION
High school graduates .... 98.6% (★)
College graduates 25.7%

JOBS
MBSA workers....................................... 41.4% (★)
Private-sector job growth .... 18.7% (★)

BUSINESS
Small business growth .... -3.0%
Self-employed workers 8.1%

MONEY
Median annual earnings................$62,453 (★)
Living in poverty.....................................4.7% (★)

HOUSING
Home ownership................................ 86.7% (★)
Monthly housing costs...................... 36.2%

HEALTH
Health care workers.............................7.1%
Fair or poor health.................................16.4%

DIVERSIONS
Stores per 10,000 ....14.8
Restaurants per 10,000.......................10.1

INTERNET
Broadband subscriptions .... 79.9% (★)
Smartphone access .... 92.2% (★)

PROXIMITY
Major hub miles ....28 (★)
Major or mid-major miles................................. 28

Portsmouth, New Hampshire

Score ....807.9 points
National rank ....40 of 2,084
Percentile...98.13%
East rank.. 3 of 246
New Hampshire rank .... 1 of 10
Closest major hub ....Boston, 49 air miles

TESTS
1. Character...71.1
2. Stability..78.4
3. Growth..43.8
4. Education...86.1
5. Jobs...67.9
6. Business...47.3
7. Money...82.2
8. Housing..50.3
9. Health...61.6
10. Diversions.......................................57.0
11. Internet 74.1
12. Proximity...88.1

BASIC STATS
Population.......................................89,084
Density 960.5
Born out of state 67.9%
Homes built since 2000...................13.5%
4 or more bedrooms 17.8%

RACE
Whites..91.9%
Blacks..1.1%
Hispanics 2.1%
Asians..3.0%
Native Americans 0.2%
Diversity index................................15.4%

HOUSEHOLD INCOME LADDER
95th percentile ....>$250,000
80th percentile $162,029
60th percentile $103,130
50th percentile $84,255
40th percentile $67,570
20th percentile $37,285

HOME VALUE LADDER
75th percentile $544,300
50th percentile $372,900
25th percentile $259,000

CHARACTER
Resilience.............................. 38.4% (★)
Short commutes 49.2%

STABILITY
Living with two parents .... 77.0% (★)
Occupied homes...96.2%

GROWTH
Population growth...............................-0.6%
Economic growth 15.0%

EDUCATION
High school graduates .... 97.1% (★)
College graduates .... 53.9% (★)

JOBS
MBSA workers...................................... 47.9% (★)
Private-sector job growth 9.4%

BUSINESS
Small business growth 4.5%
Self-employed workers 9.8%

MONEY
Median annual earnings...............$61,663 (★)
Living in poverty.....................................5.3% (★)

HOUSING
Home ownership.....................................66.8%
Monthly housing costs 33.0%

HEALTH
Health care workers......................................8.0%
Fair or poor health.................................9.9% (★)

DIVERSIONS
Stores per 10,000......................... 48.5 (★)
Restaurants per 10,000........................ 27.2 (★)

INTERNET
Broadband subscriptions .... 82.4% (★)
Smartphone access 81.3%

PROXIMITY
Major hub miles... 49
Major or mid-major miles............................. 49

Port Townsend, Washington

Score ....*796.4 points*
National rank ....*55 of 2,084*
Percentile...*97.41%*
West rank..*26 of 471*
Washington rank...*2 of 44*
Closest major hub ....*Seattle, 51 air miles*

TESTS
1. Character..65.8
2. Stability..72.8
3. Growth...54.6
4. Education...82.3
5. Jobs..64.5
6. Business..68.2
7. Money...56.5
8. Housing...53.7
9. Health...86.5
10. Diversions..48.0
11. Internet...55.7
12. Proximity...87.8

BASIC STATS
Population.. 8,821
Density 1,846.2
Born out of state 60.8%
Homes built since 2000.......................23.1%
4 or more bedrooms 9.2%

RACE
Whites..89.8%
Blacks...0.6%
Hispanics 4.8%
Asians...2.3%
Native Americans 0.5%
Diversity index....................................19.0%

HOUSEHOLD INCOME LADDER
95th percentile $224,804
80th percentile $99,563
60th percentile $60,435
50th percentile $50,680
40th percentile $38,887
20th percentile $23,912

HOME VALUE LADDER
75th percentile $475,700
50th percentile $337,500
25th percentile $244,600

CHARACTER
Resilience...19.2%
Short commutes ....85.8% (★)

STABILITY
Living with two parents 64.3%
Occupied homes................................97.8% (★)

GROWTH
Population growth..................................3.3%
Economic growth ....24.1% (★)

EDUCATION
High school graduates 95.3%
College graduates ....52.1% (★)

JOBS
MBSA workers...40.7%
Private-sector job growth 14.7%

BUSINESS
Small business growth 2.0%
Self-employed workers ....23.6% (★)

MONEY
Median annual earnings......................$46,674
Living in poverty...................................15.4%

HOUSING
Home ownership....................................56.8%
Monthly housing costs...........................23.9%

HEALTH
Health care workers..........................17.1% (★)
Fair or poor health............................12.3% (★)

DIVERSIONS
Stores per 10,000...................................41.0
Restaurants per 10,000..........................24.9

INTERNET
Broadband subscriptions 71.5%
Smartphone access 71.0%

PROXIMITY
Major hub miles.......................................51
Major or mid-major miles.............................51

Prairie du Sac, Wisconsin

Score ....*756.1 points*
National rank ....*117 of 2,084*
Percentile..*94.43%*
Midwest rank..*21 of 622*
Wisconsin rank ....*4 of 61*
Closest major hub ....*Milwaukee, 83 air miles*

TESTS
1. Character................................68.2
2. Stability...................................87.2
3. Growth....................................48.5
4. Education................................68.6
5. Jobs..55.7
6. Business..................................36.4
7. Money 72.8
8. Housing...................................51.7
9. Health.....................................57.4
10. Diversions..............................59.2
11. Internet 60.6
12. Proximity................................89.8

BASIC STATS
Population................................ 8,152
Density 2,384.3
Born out of state 21.4%
Homes built since 2000.......................... 23.4%
4 or more bedrooms 19.0%

RACE
Whites.......................................90.5%
Blacks 0.0%
Hispanics 8.7%
Asians...0.0%
Native Americans 0.0%
Diversity index...........................17.3%

HOUSEHOLD INCOME LADDER
95th percentile $176,460
80th percentile $111,038
60th percentile $78,915
50th percentile $62,912
40th percentile $55,343
20th percentile $30,943

HOME VALUE LADDER
75th percentile $289,500
50th percentile $223,800
25th percentile $177,800

CHARACTER
Resilience................................ 36.8% (★)
Short commutes 48.0%

STABILITY
Living with two parents .... 83.3% (★)
Occupied homes.............................. 97.9% (★)

GROWTH
Population growth................................2.9%
Economic growth 14.8%

EDUCATION
High school graduates .... 95.4% (★)
College graduates 35.3%

JOBS
MBSA workers......................................40.7%
Private-sector job growth 4.2%

BUSINESS
Small business growth 2.7%
Self-employed workers 6.5%

MONEY
Median annual earnings ....$52,839 (★)
Living in poverty.....................................5.9% (★)

HOUSING
Home ownership......................................65.2%
Monthly housing costs 30.8%

HEALTH
Health care workers.................................8.8%
Fair or poor health...................................13.0%

DIVERSIONS
Stores per 10,000................................46.4
Restaurants per 10,000....................... 30.2 (★)

INTERNET
Broadband subscriptions 71.2%
Smartphone access 75.9%

PROXIMITY
Major hub miles... 83
Major or mid-major miles.......................20 (★)

Purcellville, Virginia

Score ....*861.5 points*
National rank ....*12 of 2,084*
Percentile...*99.47%*
South rank ....*4 of 745*
Virginia rank...*1 of 41*
Closest major hub ....*Washington, 33 air miles*

TESTS
1. Character...36.5
2. Stability..92.9
3. Growth...71.8
4. Education...89.2
5. Jobs..88.9
6. Business...57.8
7. Money..98.8
8. Housing..64.5
9. Health..60.8
10. Diversions..27.7
11. Internet..81.6
12. Proximity...91.0

BASIC STATS
Population.....................................14,027
Density 2,182.2
Born out of state...........................57.8%
Homes built since 2000................42.8%
4 or more bedrooms 58.9%

RACE
Whites..75.2%
Blacks...4.9%
Hispanics 10.5%
Asians...5.1%
Native Americans 0.3%
Diversity index..............................41.7%

HOUSEHOLD INCOME LADDER
95th percentile ....>$250,000
80th percentile $219,056
60th percentile $161,426
50th percentile $140,049
40th percentile $123,188
20th percentile $73,980

HOME VALUE LADDER
75th percentile $581,300
50th percentile $450,900
25th percentile $357,500

CHARACTER
Resilience..23.9%
Short commutes 23.9%

STABILITY
Living with two parents ....89.6% (★)
Occupied homes.............................97.6% (★)

GROWTH
Population growth...........................13.6% (★)
Economic growth ....29.1% (★)

EDUCATION
High school graduates ....95.7% (★)
College graduates ....58.1% (★)

JOBS
MBSA workers.................................57.4% (★)
Private-sector job growth ....17.7% (★)

BUSINESS
Small business growth ....20.6% (★)
Self-employed workers 5.8%

MONEY
Median annual earnings...............$88,621 (★)
Living in poverty.............................3.1% (★)

HOUSING
Home ownership.............................85.6% (★)
Monthly housing costs....................33.4%

HEALTH
Health care workers.........................8.6%
Fair or poor health..........................11.1% (★)

DIVERSIONS
Stores per 10,000............................25.9
Restaurants per 10,000...................18.5

INTERNET
Broadband subscriptions ....81.8% (★)
Smartphone access ....88.9% (★)

PROXIMITY
Major hub miles..............................33 (★)
Major or mid-major miles................33

Rancho Murieta, California

Score ....*811.6 points*
National rank ....*36 of 2,084*
Percentile...*98.32%*
West rank.. *19 of 471*
California rank .... *2 of 145*
Closest major hub .... *Sacramento, 16 air miles*

TESTS
1. Character... 5.2
2. Stability...97.6
3. Growth..43.4
4. Education...83.5
5. Jobs...86.6
6. Business...56.2
7. Money...97.2
8. Housing..71.7
9. Health...59.3
10. Diversions......................................25.8
11. Internet 87.0
12. Proximity..98.1

BASIC STATS
Population....................................... 5,552
Density 1,336.2
Born out of state 36.1%
Homes built since 2000....................19.6%
4 or more bedrooms 26.9%

RACE
Whites..77.7%
Blacks...6.1%
Hispanics 10.4%
Asians...2.5%
Native Americans 0.8%
Diversity index...............................38.0%

HOUSEHOLD INCOME LADDER
95th percentile .... >$250,000
80th percentile $179,554
60th percentile $128,922
50th percentile $108,525
40th percentile $88,125
20th percentile $48,068

HOME VALUE LADDER
75th percentile $616,700
50th percentile $470,800
25th percentile $364,600

CHARACTER
Resilience..5.7%
Short commutes 13.1%

STABILITY
Living with two parents .... 94.3% (★)
Occupied homes............................... 97.8% (★)

GROWTH
Population growth.............................-1.5%
Economic growth 16.4%

EDUCATION
High school graduates .... 98.1% (★)
College graduates .... 49.9% (★)

JOBS
MBSA workers................................... 57.0% (★)
Private-sector job growth 16.1%

BUSINESS
Small business growth 9.6%
Self-employed workers 10.7%

MONEY
Median annual earnings...............$87,035 (★)
Living in poverty.....................................4.3% (★)

HOUSING
Home ownership...............................90.3% (★)
Monthly housing costs............................30.6%

HEALTH
Health care workers........................ 11.5%
Fair or poor health............................15.8%

DIVERSIONS
Stores per 10,000.............................23.0
Restaurants per 10,000................................18.8

INTERNET
Broadband subscriptions .... 87.7% (★)
Smartphone access .... 87.8% (★)

PROXIMITY
Major hub miles ....16 (★)
Major or mid-major miles.......................16 (★)

Red Hook, New York

Score ....*742.5 points*
National rank ....*152 of 2,084*
Percentile..*92.75%*
East rank..*21 of 246*
New York rank ....*5 of 65*
Closest major hub ....*Bridgeport, 47 air miles*

TESTS
1. Character................................61.2
2. Stability.................................69.3
3. Growth..................................41.2
4. Education..............................84.9
5. Jobs......................................63.7
6. Business...............................39.5
7. Money..................................72.3
8. Housing................................48.6
9. Health..................................50.0
10. Diversions...........................45.3
11. Internet 76.2
12. Proximity............................90.3

BASIC STATS
Population.............................. 6,709
Density 946.0
Born out of state......................43.7%
Homes built since 2000............ 10.2%
4 or more bedrooms 26.1%

RACE
Whites...................................85.2%
Blacks.....................................2.3%
Hispanics 5.6%
Asians.....................................4.9%
Native Americans 0.1%
Diversity index........................26.8%

HOUSEHOLD INCOME LADDER
95th percentile .... >$250,000
80th percentile $148,667
60th percentile $99,100
50th percentile $85,764
40th percentile $70,137
20th percentile $29,244

HOME VALUE LADDER
75th percentile $348,500
50th percentile $273,700
25th percentile $222,500

CHARACTER
Resilience...............................31.4%
Short commutes 48.8%

STABILITY
Living with two parents 73.5%
Occupied homes......................92.6%

GROWTH
Population growth.....................0.8%
Economic growth......................7.3%

EDUCATION
High school graduates 95.3%
College graduates ....55.1% (★)

JOBS
MBSA workers......................47.2% (★)
Private-sector job growth 5.3%

BUSINESS
Small business growth 0.7%
Self-employed workers 8.7%

MONEY
Median annual earnings...............$57,037 (★)
Living in poverty.......................10.3%

HOUSING
Home ownership......................66.6%
Monthly housing costs.............34.2%

HEALTH
Health care workers...................7.4%
Fair or poor health....................14.7%

DIVERSIONS
Stores per 10,000.....................36.3
Restaurants per 10,000...........25.7 (★)

INTERNET
Broadband subscriptions ....85.8% (★)
Smartphone access 81.0%

PROXIMITY
Major hub miles 47
Major or mid-major miles................. 32

Redmond, Oregon

Score ....727.4 points
National rank ....196 of 2,084
Percentile...90.64%
West rank...75 of 471
Oregon rank .... 6 of 45
Closest major hub ....Portland, 112 air miles

TESTS

1. Character...59.6
2. Stability..74.8
3. Growth...72.5
4. Education...42.9
5. Jobs...60.8
6. Business...65.1
7. Money..52.8
8. Housing...40.7
9. Health..54.6
10. Diversions..54.8
11. Internet 71.7
12. Proximity...77.1

BASIC STATS

Population...31,653
Density 2,327.8
Born out of state 51.3%
Homes built since 2000..............................38.0%
4 or more bedrooms 12.2%

RACE

Whites..82.3%
Blacks...1.1%
Hispanics 11.7%
Asians...0.9%
Native Americans 0.9%
Diversity index...30.8%

HOUSEHOLD INCOME LADDER

95th percentile $151,649
80th percentile $102,463
60th percentile $73,224
50th percentile $63,497
40th percentile $48,967
20th percentile $27,153

HOME VALUE LADDER

75th percentile $333,100
50th percentile $254,900
25th percentile $194,100

CHARACTER

Resilience...29.6%
Short commutes 50.3%

STABILITY

Living with two parents 66.2%
Occupied homes..................................98.2% (★)

GROWTH

Population growth............................. 10.0% (★)
Economic growth .... 38.4% (★)

EDUCATION

High school graduates 85.2%
College graduates 17.2%

JOBS

MBSA workers...25.8%
Private-sector job growth .... 29.4% (★)

BUSINESS

Small business growth .... 24.2% (★)
Self-employed workers 6.8%

MONEY

Median annual earnings.......................$39,577
Living in poverty...12.3%

HOUSING

Home ownership......................................60.6%
Monthly housing costs 36.8%

HEALTH

Health care workers....................................7.8%
Fair or poor health....................................13.0%

DIVERSIONS

Stores per 10,000......................................44.7
Restaurants per 10,000.....................27.9 (★)

INTERNET

Broadband subscriptions 75.1%
Smartphone access 83.9%

PROXIMITY

Major hub miles...112
Major or mid-major miles............................112

Rigby, Idaho

Score ....*785.2 points*
National rank ....*73 of 2,084*
Percentile..*96.54%*
West rank...*32 of 471*
Idaho rank ....*1 of 21*
Closest major hub ....*Salt Lake City, 209 air miles*

TESTS
1. Character...60.9
2. Stability..86.1
3. Growth..83.9
4. Education...53.3
5. Jobs...68.4
6. Business..99.6
7. Money...63.1
8. Housing..66.7
9. Health...52.3
10. Diversions......................................10.3
11. Internet 76.6
12. Proximity..64.0

BASIC STATS
Population.. 9,488
Density 1,133.7
Born out of state...........................36.0%
Homes built since 2000...............35.5%
4 or more bedrooms 38.8%

RACE
Whites...81.1%
Blacks..0.0%
Hispanics 14.3%
Asians..0.9%
Native Americans 2.9%
Diversity index................................32.1%

HOUSEHOLD INCOME LADDER
95th percentile $162,571
80th percentile $110,288
60th percentile $65,017
50th percentile $56,566
40th percentile $51,145
20th percentile $35,705

HOME VALUE LADDER
75th percentile $267,500
50th percentile $177,500
25th percentile $120,900

CHARACTER
Resilience..34.2%
Short commutes 41.5%

STABILITY
Living with two parents ....85.1% (★)
Occupied homes...............................96.9% (★)

GROWTH
Population growth............................13.2% (★)
Economic growth.............................48.2% (★)

EDUCATION
High school graduates 89.7%
College graduates 24.0%

JOBS
MBSA workers......................................38.9%
Private-sector job growth ....21.6% (★)

BUSINESS
Small business growth ....24.8% (★)
Self-employed workers ....18.7% (★)

MONEY
Median annual earnings.......................$47,303
Living in poverty................................9.8%

HOUSING
Home ownership................................70.5%
Monthly housing costs...........................22.1%

HEALTH
Health care workers.................................7.2%
Fair or poor health................................13.3%

DIVERSIONS
Stores per 10,000..............................19.7
Restaurants per 10,000.....................8.8

INTERNET
Broadband subscriptions 73.1%
Smartphone access ....89.9% (★)

PROXIMITY
Major hub miles................................209
Major or mid-major miles...........................176

Rochester, Minnesota

Score .... *816.0 points*
National rank .... *33 of 2,084*
Percentile *98.46%*
Midwest rank .... *4 of 622*
Minnesota rank .... *3 of 53*
Closest major hub .... *Minneapolis, 77 air miles*

TESTS
1. Character 81.3
2. Stability 75.7
3. Growth 52.3
4. Education 78.4
5. Jobs 72.0
6. Business 32.5
7. Money 71.8
8. Housing 62.2
9. Health 100.0
10. Diversions 35.7
11. Internet 70.9
12. Proximity 83.2

BASIC STATS
Population 114,709
Density 2,273.5
Born out of state 45.7%
Homes built since 2000 .... 25.8%
4 or more bedrooms 33.1%

RACE
Whites 75.2%
Blacks 7.9%
Hispanics 5.8%
Asians 7.3%
Native Americans 0.3%
Diversity index 41.8%

HOUSEHOLD INCOME LADDER
95th percentile $246,921
80th percentile $136,983
60th percentile $88,626
50th percentile $72,861
40th percentile $58,601
20th percentile $31,636

HOME VALUE LADDER
75th percentile $287,600
50th percentile $198,800
25th percentile $150,700

CHARACTER
Resilience .... 34.9% (★)
Short commutes 75.2%

STABILITY
Living with two parents 73.4%
Occupied homes 96.1%

GROWTH
Population growth 4.3%
Economic growth 18.0%

EDUCATION
High school graduates 94.3%
College graduates .... 48.7% (★)

JOBS
MBSA workers .... 52.0% (★)
Private-sector job growth 9.0%

BUSINESS
Small business growth 2.7%
Self-employed workers 5.0%

MONEY
Median annual earnings .... $56,375 (★)
Living in poverty 10.1%

HOUSING
Home ownership 68.5%
Monthly housing costs 24.5%

HEALTH
Health care workers .... 22.2% (★)
Fair or poor health .... 10.0% (★)

DIVERSIONS
Stores per 10,000 .... 35.8
Restaurants per 10,000 .... 18.6

INTERNET
Broadband subscriptions .... 78.1% (★)
Smartphone access 81.1%

PROXIMITY
Major hub miles 77
Major or mid-major miles 77

Roxborough Park, Colorado

Score ....*882.4 points*
National rank .... *5 of 2,084*
Percentile...*99.81%*
West rank... *3 of 471*
Colorado rank .... *1 of 47*
Closest major hub ....*Denver, 18 air miles*

TESTS
1. Character...40.0
2. Stability..93.6
3. Growth..57.8
4. Education...88.9
5. Jobs..85.8
6. Business...58.0
7. Money..99.5
8. Housing..69.2
9. Health...67.0
10. Diversions.......................................25.3
11. Internet 100.0
12. Proximity.......................................97.3

BASIC STATS
Population....................................... 9,033
Density 3,633.5
Born out of state 57.0%
Homes built since 2000.............47.9%
4 or more bedrooms 47.9%

RACE
Whites...84.8%
Blacks..0.3%
Hispanics 10.5%
Asians..1.5%
Native Americans 0.2%
Diversity index...............................26.9%

HOUSEHOLD INCOME LADDER
95th percentile .... >$250,000
80th percentile $197,000
60th percentile $151,588
50th percentile $134,555
40th percentile $120,000
20th percentile...............................$87,072

HOME VALUE LADDER
75th percentile $572,600
50th percentile $421,500
25th percentile $330,100

CHARACTER
Resilience..28.4%
Short commutes 19.2%

STABILITY
Living with two parents ....88.8% (★)
Occupied homes.............................98.2% (★)

GROWTH
Population growth..............................2.5%
Economic growth ....31.4% (★)

EDUCATION
High school graduates ....99.0% (★)
College graduates ....53.5% (★)

JOBS
MBSA workers.....................................51.5% (★)
Private-sector job growth ....22.4% (★)

BUSINESS
Small business growth ....18.2% (★)
Self-employed workers 7.1%

MONEY
Median annual earnings...............$73,637 (★)
Living in poverty..................................1.4% (★)

HOUSING
Home ownership.............................95.4% (★)
Monthly housing costs...................35.8%

HEALTH
Health care workers...........................8.6%
Fair or poor health............................8.1% (★)

DIVERSIONS
Stores per 10,000.............................26.9
Restaurants per 10,000...................16.0

INTERNET
Broadband subscriptions ....95.1% (★)
Smartphone access ....92.7% (★)

PROXIMITY
Major hub miles...................................18 (★)
Major or mid-major miles......................18 (★)

Ruckersville, Virginia

Score	*790.9 points*
National rank	*65 of 2,084*
Percentile	*96.93%*
South rank	*23 of 745*
Virginia rank	*3 of 41*
Closest major hub	*Richmond, 71 air miles*

TESTS

1. Character	55.5
2. Stability	95.2
3. Growth	80.7
4. Education	75.2
5. Jobs	68.3
6. Business	46.9
7. Money	73.5
8. Housing	57.9
9. Health	59.1
10. Diversions	19.6
11. Internet	74.7
12. Proximity	84.3

BASIC STATS

Population	7,424
Density	1,078.9
Born out of state	52.3%
Homes built since 2000	40.4%
4 or more bedrooms	30.0%

RACE

Whites	75.4%
Blacks	6.2%
Hispanics	10.4%
Asians	2.0%
Native Americans	0.4%
Diversity index	41.3%

HOUSEHOLD INCOME LADDER

95th percentile	$170,762
80th percentile	$124,130
60th percentile	$91,601
50th percentile	$80,081
40th percentile	$66,484
20th percentile	$46,273

HOME VALUE LADDER

75th percentile	$335,600
50th percentile	$261,200
25th percentile	$189,000

CHARACTER

Resilience	31.5%
Short commutes	38.7%

STABILITY

Living with two parents	85.4% (★)
Occupied homes	100.0% (★)

GROWTH

Population growth	29.4% (★)
Economic growth	13.3%

EDUCATION

High school graduates	95.3%
College graduates	43.5% (★)

JOBS

MBSA workers	43.6% (★)
Private-sector job growth	15.4%

BUSINESS

Small business growth	5.6%
Self-employed workers	9.1%

MONEY

Median annual earnings	$51,749
Living in poverty	4.2% (★)

HOUSING

Home ownership	76.1% (★)
Monthly housing costs	32.7%

HEALTH

Health care workers	11.2%
Fair or poor health	15.5%

DIVERSIONS

Stores per 10,000	25.9
Restaurants per 10,000	12.2

INTERNET

Broadband subscriptions	79.1% (★)
Smartphone access	84.1%

PROXIMITY

Major hub miles	71
Major or mid-major miles	71

St. Augustine, Florida

Score ....*770.6 points*
National rank ....*95 of 2,084*
Percentile..*95.49%*
South rank ....*29 of 745*
Florida rank ....*6 of 63*
Closest major hub ....*Jacksonville, 32 air miles*

TESTS
1. Character................................66.6
2. Stability..................................64.5
3. Growth....................................62.0
4. Education................................64.7
5. Jobs...70.0
6. Business..................................76.2
7. Money.....................................53.7
8. Housing...................................61.7
9. Health......................................59.2
10. Diversions.............................39.4
11. Internet 61.5
12. Proximity...............................91.1

BASIC STATS
Population............................78,609
Density 1,826.3
Born out of state....................62.7%
Homes built since 2000............27.8%
4 or more bedrooms 13.3%

RACE
Whites.....................................82.6%
Blacks..7.5%
Hispanics..................................6.6%
Asians..1.2%
Native Americans 0.4%
Diversity index........................30.7%

HOUSEHOLD INCOME LADDER
95th percentile $236,830
80th percentile $118,042
60th percentile $74,042
50th percentile $58,712
40th percentile $46,817
20th percentile $25,610

HOME VALUE LADDER
75th percentile $376,600
50th percentile $255,900
25th percentile $164,200

CHARACTER
Resilience.................................32.0%
Short commutes 56.7%

STABILITY
Living with two parents 66.9%
Occupied homes......................92.4%

GROWTH
Population growth.....................5.2%
Economic growth ....32.0% (★)

EDUCATION
High school graduates 92.9%
College graduates 33.8%

JOBS
MBSA workers...........................36.4%
Private-sector job growth ....26.7% (★)

BUSINESS
Small business growth ......24.1% (★)
Self-employed workers 10.6%

MONEY
Median annual earnings $41,553
Living in poverty.....................13.3%

HOUSING
Home ownership.....................73.1%
Monthly housing costs 27.8%

HEALTH
Health care workers..................9.2%
Fair or poor health..................12.7%

DIVERSIONS
Stores per 10,000.....................35.4
Restaurants per 10,000.............21.7

INTERNET
Broadband subscriptions 68.7%
Smartphone access 78.5%

PROXIMITY
Major hub miles.................32 (★)
Major or mid-major miles................ 32

St. George, Utah

Score ....775.7 points
National rank ....85 of 2,084
Percentile..95.97%
West rank...35 of 471
Utah rank... 7 of 20
Closest major hub ....Las Vegas, 111 air miles

TESTS
1. Character....................69.3
2. Stability......................80.3
3. Growth.......................67.6
4. Education...................58.8
5. Jobs............................69.7
6. Business.....................85.0
7. Money........................55.1
8. Housing......................54.6
9. Health.........................59.0
10. Diversions................35.9
11. Internet....................63.2
12. Proximity.................77.2

BASIC STATS
Population....................110,673
Density 2,461.4
Born out of state 46.5%
Homes built since 2000................42.3%
4 or more bedrooms 30.2%

RACE
Whites.........................81.8%
Blacks...........................0.7%
Hispanics 12.3%
Asians...........................1.8%
Native Americans 1.3%
Diversity index................31.5%

HOUSEHOLD INCOME LADDER
95th percentile....................$208,206
80th percentile....................$109,307
60th percentile......................$71,742
50th percentile......................$59,307
40th percentile......................$48,434
20th percentile......................$27,796

HOME VALUE LADDER
75th percentile....................$378,900
50th percentile....................$274,100
25th percentile....................$203,200

CHARACTER
Resilience....................26.6%
Short commutes 74.2%

STABILITY
Living with two parents ....77.9% (★)
Occupied homes................96.9% (★)

GROWTH
Population growth....................7.0%
Economic growth ....37.2% (★)

EDUCATION
High school graduates 91.9%
College graduates 27.8%

JOBS
MBSA workers....................31.6%
Private-sector job growth ....32.5% (★)

BUSINESS
Small business growth ....28.1% (★)
Self-employed workers ....12.7% (★)

MONEY
Median annual earnings....................$41,807
Living in poverty....................12.2%

HOUSING
Home ownership....................67.0%
Monthly housing costs....................29.6%

HEALTH
Health care workers....................9.5%
Fair or poor health....................13.2%

DIVERSIONS
Stores per 10,000....................38.3
Restaurants per 10,000....................17.2

INTERNET
Broadband subscriptions....................67.6%
Smartphone access 80.8%

PROXIMITY
Major hub miles....................111
Major or mid-major miles....................111

St. Simons, Georgia

Score ....*849.4 points*
National rank ....*16 of 2,084*
Percentile..*99.28%*
South rank ....*6 of 745*
Georgia rank ....*2 of 65*
Closest major hub ....*Jacksonville, 67 air miles*

TESTS
1. Character..54.4
2. Stability..75.2
3. Growth..59.6
4. Education..92.4
5. Jobs...79.3
6. Business..73.1
7. Money...85.6
8. Housing...62.8
9. Health...39.9
10. Diversions.....................................62.5
11. Internet...79.6
12. Proximity.......................................85.0

BASIC STATS
Population....................................13,829
Density 1,544.3
Born out of state............................55.1%
Homes built since 2000..................24.2%
4 or more bedrooms 26.6%

RACE
Whites..92.5%
Blacks...2.7%
Hispanics...2.0%
Asians...1.0%
Native Americans 0.6%
Diversity index...............................14.3%

HOUSEHOLD INCOME LADDER
95th percentile ....>$250,000
80th percentile $175,023
60th percentile $107,027
50th percentile $87,397
40th percentile $71,934
20th percentile $37,373

HOME VALUE LADDER
75th percentile $522,300
50th percentile $362,100
25th percentile $253,700

CHARACTER
Resilience..24.4%
Short commutes 53.8%

STABILITY
Living with two parents ....89.1% (★)
Occupied homes...............................90.2%

GROWTH
Population growth............................10.6% (★)
Economic growth 15.3%

EDUCATION
High school graduates ....97.2% (★)
College graduates ....58.6% (★)

JOBS
MBSA workers....................................50.8% (★)
Private-sector job growth ....17.2% (★)

BUSINESS
Small business growth 6.2%
Self-employed workers ....20.3% (★)

MONEY
Median annual earnings................$62,998 (★)
Living in poverty...............................4.3% (★)

HOUSING
Home ownership...............................74.5%
Monthly housing costs......................27.8%

HEALTH
Health care workers...........................6.3%
Fair or poor health............................18.1%

DIVERSIONS
Stores per 10,000..............................54.1 (★)
Restaurants per 10,000......................28.0 (★)

INTERNET
Broadband subscriptions ....83.0% (★)
Smartphone access ....86.1% (★)

PROXIMITY
Major hub miles.................................67
Major or mid-major miles..................67

Salida, Colorado

Score ....*802.6 points*
National rank ....*46 of 2,084*
Percentile..*97.84%*
West rank..*23 of 471*
Colorado rank ....*11 of 47*
Closest major hub ....*Denver, 99 air miles*

TESTS
1. Character..................................68.7
2. Stability....................................68.0
3. Growth.....................................49.9
4. Education.................................64.1
5. Jobs...63.8
6. Business...................................86.3
7. Money......................................55.6
8. Housing....................................68.1
9. Health......................................51.6
10. Diversions...............................89.7
11. Internet 54.1
12. Proximity.................................82.7

BASIC STATS
Population...................................... 7,121
Density 1,453.6
Born out of state.........................54.6%
Homes built since 2000..........................16.3%
4 or more bedrooms 11.4%

RACE
Whites..76.2%
Blacks...0.1%
Hispanics...................................17.0%
Asians...3.2%
Native Americans 0.0%
Diversity index...........................38.8%

HOUSEHOLD INCOME LADDER
95th percentile $164,140
80th percentile $101,256
60th percentile $62,947
50th percentile $52,083
40th percentile $36,844
20th percentile $19,891

HOME VALUE LADDER
75th percentile $397,700
50th percentile $327,200
25th percentile $234,100

CHARACTER
Resilience....................................26.7%
Short commutes 73.0%

STABILITY
Living with two parents 61.0%
Occupied homes.........................96.4%

GROWTH
Population growth....................................-2.0%
Economic growth ....28.5% (★)

EDUCATION
High school graduates 91.8%
College graduates 34.5%

JOBS
MBSA workers.............................36.4%
Private-sector job growth .... 19.3% (★)

BUSINESS
Small business growth .... 15.3% (★)
Self-employed workers ....19.4% (★)

MONEY
Median annual earnings $42,928
Living in poverty.........................12.8%

HOUSING
Home ownership.......................72.7%
Monthly housing costs...........................22.4%

HEALTH
Health care workers.................................6.6%
Fair or poor health....................12.8%

DIVERSIONS
Stores per 10,000.........................67.9 (★)
Restaurants per 10,000......................39.4 (★)

INTERNET
Broadband subscriptions 70.7%
Smartphone access 70.0%

PROXIMITY
Major hub miles.................................. 99
Major or mid-major miles..............................71

Santa Cruz, California

Score ....*735.5 points*
National rank .... *170 of 2,084*
Percentile...*91.89%*
West rank... *66 of 471*
California rank .... *11 of 145*
Closest major hub .... *San Jose, 19 air miles*

TESTS
1. Character..35.4
2. Stability..74.5
3. Growth..46.1
4. Education..76.9
5. Jobs...67.0
6. Business..52.6
7. Money...80.8
8. Housing...39.1
9. Health..52.9
10. Diversions..37.1
11. Internet..76.9
12. Proximity..96.2

BASIC STATS
Population.......................................170,000
Density 2,915.3
Born out of state 37.4%
Homes built since 2000.......................9.0%
4 or more bedrooms 12.4%

RACE
Whites..69.1%
Blacks..1.2%
Hispanics 19.3%
Asians...5.9%
Native Americans 0.2%
Diversity index................................. 48.0%

HOUSEHOLD INCOME LADDER
95th percentile ....>$250,000
80th percentile $178,338
60th percentile $107,028
50th percentile $85,799
40th percentile $67,680
20th percentile $31,248

HOME VALUE LADDER
75th percentile $994,600
50th percentile $793,800
25th percentile $554,000

CHARACTER
Resilience..12.7%
Short commutes 48.7%

STABILITY
Living with two parents 72.1%
Occupied homes................................95.9%

GROWTH
Population growth.................................1.9%
Economic growth 13.1%

EDUCATION
High school graduates 92.9%
College graduates .... 48.7% (★)

JOBS
MBSA workers...................................... 47.6% (★)
Private-sector job growth 8.7%

BUSINESS
Small business growth 3.8%
Self-employed workers .... 12.2% (★)

MONEY
Median annual earnings...............$68,693 (★)
Living in poverty.................................. 13.2%

HOUSING
Home ownership................................59.5%
Monthly housing costs 37.4%

HEALTH
Health care workers.................................8.8%
Fair or poor health.............................. 15.2%

DIVERSIONS
Stores per 10,000................................32.1
Restaurants per 10,000................................21.9

INTERNET
Broadband subscriptions .... 81.4% (★)
Smartphone access 84.6%

PROXIMITY
Major hub miles.......................................19 (★)
Major or mid-major miles........................19 (★)

Santaquin, Utah

Score ....*777.8 points*
National rank ....*81 of 2,084*
Percentile..*96.16%*
West rank..*34 of 471*
Utah rank..*6 of 20*
Closest major hub ....*Salt Lake City, 47 air miles*

TESTS
1. Character...................................44.5
2. Stability...................................91.7
3. Growth....................................86.0
4. Education................................52.5
5. Jobs.......................................64.1
6. Business..................................70.5
7. Money.....................................64.3
8. Housing...................................60.4
9. Health.....................................49.8
10. Diversions..............................26.2
11. Internet..................................76.3
12. Proximity...............................91.5

BASIC STATS
Population.................................12,667
Density...................................1,459.8
Born out of state.........................22.7%
Homes built since 2000.................52.5%
4 or more bedrooms......................55.0%

RACE
Whites......................................85.0%
Blacks.......................................0.7%
Hispanics..................................12.5%
Asians.......................................0.8%
Native Americans.........................0.3%
Diversity index...........................26.2%

HOUSEHOLD INCOME LADDER
95th percentile.........................$166,868
80th percentile.........................$118,056
60th percentile..........................$84,573
50th percentile..........................$72,016
40th percentile..........................$62,133
20th percentile..........................$37,910

HOME VALUE LADDER
75th percentile.........................$324,500
50th percentile.........................$251,700
25th percentile.........................$199,200

CHARACTER
Resilience...................................23.3%
Short commutes...........................39.2%

STABILITY
Living with two parents...................84.7% (★)
Occupied homes...........................98.9% (★)

GROWTH
Population growth..........................18.3% (★)
Economic growth...........................38.7% (★)

EDUCATION
High school graduates.....................90.6%
College graduates..........................21.9%

JOBS
MBSA workers...............................27.6%
Private-sector job growth................31.0% (★)

BUSINESS
Small business growth.....................24.2% (★)
Self-employed workers.....................8.9%

MONEY
Median annual earnings..................$46,377
Living in poverty............................7.8%

HOUSING
Home ownership...........................83.4% (★)
Monthly housing costs.....................35.3%

HEALTH
Health care workers.........................5.8%
Fair or poor health.........................12.6%

DIVERSIONS
Stores per 10,000..........................32.4
Restaurants per 10,000....................13.3

INTERNET
Broadband subscriptions..................73.3%
Smartphone access........................89.5% (★)

PROXIMITY
Major hub miles.............................47
Major or mid-major miles..................22 (★)

Santa Rosa Beach, Florida

Score ....789.6 points
National rank ....70 of 2,084
Percentile...96.69%
South rank ....24 of 745
Florida rank ....4 of 63
Closest major hub ....New Orleans, 234 air miles

TESTS
1. Character.................................51.7
2. Stability....................................41.1
3. Growth....................................64.0
4. Education...............................72.4
5. Jobs..81.5
6. Business............................... 100.0
7. Money....................................61.4
8. Housing.................................50.1
9. Health....................................50.4
10. Diversions.............................67.0
11. Internet................................92.2
12. Proximity..............................57.8

BASIC STATS
Population................................ 5,150
Density 661.9
Born out of state.........................78.5%
Homes built since 2000..........................58.2%
4 or more bedrooms 30.7%

RACE
Whites......................................90.5%
Blacks..0.7%
Hispanics.................................5.0%
Asians.......................................0.3%
Native Americans 0.0%
Diversity index........................17.7%

HOUSEHOLD INCOME LADDER
95th percentile $225,052
80th percentile $119,609
60th percentile $95,476
50th percentile $88,803
40th percentile $76,500
20th percentile $40,817

HOME VALUE LADDER
75th percentile $465,300
50th percentile $319,300
25th percentile $228,200

CHARACTER
Resilience....................................26.5%
Short commutes 44.0%

STABILITY
Living with two parents ....80.7% (★)
Occupied homes.........................74.4%

GROWTH
Population growth...........................8.1%
Economic growth ....28.7% (★)

EDUCATION
High school graduates ....95.9% (★)
College graduates ....39.2% (★)

JOBS
MBSA workers.......................46.5% (★)
Private-sector job growth ....24.8% (★)

BUSINESS
Small business growth ....29.0% (★)
Self-employed workers ....23.2% (★)

MONEY
Median annual earnings......................$42,284
Living in poverty..............................6.7% (★)

HOUSING
Home ownership...............................82.8% (★)
Monthly housing costs...........................43.2%

HEALTH
Health care workers.......................12.6%
Fair or poor health.............................21.6%

DIVERSIONS
Stores per 10,000................................58.7 (★)
Restaurants per 10,000.......................28.7 (★)

INTERNET
Broadband subscriptions ....87.1% (★)
Smartphone access ....91.9% (★)

PROXIMITY
Major hub miles.................................234
Major or mid-major miles.............................216

Saratoga Springs, New York

Score ....*790.1 points*
National rank ....*68 of 2,084*
Percentile...*96.78%*
East rank.. *7 of 246*
New York rank .... *1 of 65*
Closest major hub ....*Hartford, 108 air miles*

TESTS
1. Character...................................70.4
2. Stability.....................................72.4
3. Growth.......................................49.7
4. Education...................................80.7
5. Jobs..72.1
6. Business....................................45.8
7. Money..82.7
8. Housing.....................................56.0
9. Health..60.8
10. Diversions................................37.0
11. Internet 74.3
12. Proximity.................................88.2

BASIC STATS
Population.................................67,370
Density 1,481.2
Born out of state 32.1%
Homes built since 2000.............26.6%
4 or more bedrooms 22.1%

RACE
Whites..89.9%
Blacks...1.6%
Hispanics 3.7%
Asians...3.3%
Native Americans 0.1%
Diversity index...........................18.9%

HOUSEHOLD INCOME LADDER
95th percentile ....>$250,000
80th percentile $150,448
60th percentile $101,209
50th percentile $83,231
40th percentile $65,709
20th percentile $36,983

HOME VALUE LADDER
75th percentile $391,100
50th percentile $277,700
25th percentile $189,700

CHARACTER
Resilience............................. 39.8% (★)
Short commutes 44.7%

STABILITY
Living with two parents 74.3%
Occupied homes...........................94.0%

GROWTH
Population growth........................3.4%
Economic growth 15.7%

EDUCATION
High school graduates 95.1%
College graduates .... 50.5% (★)

JOBS
MBSA workers...................... 49.6% (★)
Private-sector job growth 12.2%

BUSINESS
Small business growth 5.2%
Self-employed workers 8.9%

MONEY
Median annual earnings...............$62,639 (★)
Living in poverty....................5.7% (★)

HOUSING
Home ownership.........................65.4%
Monthly housing costs 27.5%

HEALTH
Health care workers....................8.6%
Fair or poor health............... 11.1% (★)

DIVERSIONS
Stores per 10,000.......................31.5
Restaurants per 10,000...............22.2

INTERNET
Broadband subscriptions .... 82.2% (★)
Smartphone access 81.6%

PROXIMITY
Major hub miles..........................108
Major or mid-major miles....................22 (★)

Seaside, Oregon

Score ....*737.7 points*
National rank ....*162 of 2,084*
Percentile..*92.27%*
West rank..*62 of 471*
Oregon rank ....*4 of 45*
Closest major hub ....*Portland, 69 air miles*

TESTS
1. Character................................66.1
2. Stability................................62.1
3. Growth................................57.4
4. Education................................55.1
5. Jobs................................55.6
6. Business................................49.7
7. Money................................56.1
8. Housing................................38.8
9. Health................................52.2
10. Diversions................................94.0
11. Internet................................66.0
12. Proximity................................84.6

BASIC STATS
Population................................ 9,075
Density 1,734.8
Born out of state................................55.1%
Homes built since 2000................................ 15.3%
4 or more bedrooms 13.8%

RACE
Whites................................89.5%
Blacks................................1.4%
Hispanics 5.8%
Asians................................1.3%
Native Americans 0.3%
Diversity index................................19.5%

HOUSEHOLD INCOME LADDER
95th percentile $170,375
80th percentile $99,140
60th percentile $64,694
50th percentile $49,648
40th percentile $39,846
20th percentile $23,175

HOME VALUE LADDER
75th percentile $418,700
50th percentile $321,500
25th percentile $234,600

CHARACTER
Resilience................................25.1%
Short commutes 72.3%

STABILITY
Living with two parents 70.4%
Occupied homes................................89.9%

GROWTH
Population growth................................7.8%
Economic growth 18.4%

EDUCATION
High school graduates 92.9%
College graduates 22.0%

JOBS
MBSA workers................................32.2%
Private-sector job growth 15.0%

BUSINESS
Small business growth 5.2%
Self-employed workers 10.4%

MONEY
Median annual earnings................................$40,560
Living in poverty................................10.1%

HOUSING
Home ownership................................49.5%
Monthly housing costs................................31.3%

HEALTH
Health care workers................................8.2%
Fair or poor health................................14.7%

DIVERSIONS
Stores per 10,000................................67.7 (★)
Restaurants per 10,000................................49.9 (★)

INTERNET
Broadband subscriptions 73.9%
Smartphone access 79.3%

PROXIMITY
Major hub miles................................69
Major or mid-major miles................................69

Sedona, Arizona

Score ....*751.1 points*
National rank .... *130 of 2,084*
Percentile...*93.81%*
West rank...*50 of 471*
Arizona rank...*4 of 44*
Closest major hub ....*Phoenix, 95 air miles*

TESTS

1. Character	63.9
2. Stability	61.5
3. Growth	46.5
4. Education	63.1
5. Jobs	65.6
6. Business	77.6
7. Money	67.8
8. Housing	60.4
9. Health	61.0
10. Diversions	41.5
11. Internet	62.2
12. Proximity	80.0

BASIC STATS

Population	6,918
Density	1,480.4
Born out of state	87.3%
Homes built since 2000	11.9%
4 or more bedrooms	7.3%

RACE

Whites	84.8%
Blacks	0.0%
Hispanics	12.5%
Asians	1.4%
Native Americans	0.2%
Diversity index	26.5%

HOUSEHOLD INCOME LADDER

95th percentile	$245,488
80th percentile	$101,208
60th percentile	$68,364
50th percentile	$58,330
40th percentile	$42,236
20th percentile	$21,978

HOME VALUE LADDER

75th percentile	$637,400
50th percentile	$438,000
25th percentile	$259,800

CHARACTER

Resilience	20.8%
Short commutes	78.8%

STABILITY

Living with two parents	60.8%
Occupied homes	93.0%

GROWTH

Population growth	2.4%
Economic growth	12.6%

EDUCATION

High school graduates	90.5%
College graduates	35.0%

JOBS

MBSA workers	42.9% (★)
Private-sector job growth	13.1%

BUSINESS

Small business growth	8.0%
Self-employed workers	26.9% (★)

MONEY

Median annual earnings	$53,866 (★)
Living in poverty	11.5%

HOUSING

Home ownership	75.1% (★)
Monthly housing costs	30.1%

HEALTH

Health care workers	11.9%
Fair or poor health	15.5%

DIVERSIONS

Stores per 10,000	36.0
Restaurants per 10,000	22.9

INTERNET

Broadband subscriptions	72.5%
Smartphone access	76.6%

PROXIMITY

Major hub miles	95
Major or mid-major miles	95

Silverthorne, Colorado

Score ....823.4 points
National rank ....27 of 2,084
Percentile...98.75%
West rank.. 14 of 471
Colorado rank .... 7 of 47
Closest major hub ....Denver, 60 air miles

TESTS

1. Character..67.7
2. Stability..91.4
3. Growth...62.1
4. Education..68.7
5. Jobs...56.3
6. Business...54.9
7. Money..65.1
8. Housing..41.8
9. Health...52.2
10. Diversions...99.5
11. Internet 77.5
12. Proximity...86.2

BASIC STATS

Population...................................... 16,850
Density 1,868.1
Born out of state 70.3%
Homes built since 2000......................9.9%
4 or more bedrooms 16.2%

RACE

Whites.. 76.1%
Blacks..1.6%
Hispanics.. 20.6%
Asians...0.7%
Native Americans 0.0%
Diversity index................................37.8%

HOUSEHOLD INCOME LADDER

95th percentile......................... $236,675
80th percentile......................... $131,206
60th percentile...........................$89,054
50th percentile...........................$77,264
40th percentile...........................$63,984
20th percentile...........................$34,873

HOME VALUE LADDER

75th percentile......................... $735,200
50th percentile......................... $566,200
25th percentile......................... $398,800

CHARACTER

Resilience... 30.2%
Short commutes 62.9%

STABILITY

Living with two parents .... 85.9% (★)
Occupied homes.............................. 98.4% (★)

GROWTH

Population growth..............................5.6%
Economic growth............................ 31.3% (★)

EDUCATION

High school graduates 88.6%
College graduates .... 44.3% (★)

JOBS

MBSA workers................................. 32.1%
Private-sector job growth 16.0%

BUSINESS

Small business growth 5.8%
Self-employed workers .... 12.1% (★)

MONEY

Median annual earnings.......................$46,306
Living in poverty..................................7.0% (★)

HOUSING

Home ownership.............................. 64.4%
Monthly housing costs............................ 38.3%

HEALTH

Health care workers............................5.4%
Fair or poor health.............................. 10.9% (★)

DIVERSIONS

Stores per 10,000....................................99.9 (★)
Restaurants per 10,000........................ 72.0 (★)

INTERNET

Broadband subscriptions 75.0%
Smartphone access .... 89.5% (★)

PROXIMITY

Major hub miles.. 60
Major or mid-major miles................................ 60

Silverton, Oregon

Score ....*725.0 points*
National rank ....*208 of 2,084*
Percentile...*90.06%*
West rank...*80 of 471*
Oregon rank ....*7 of 45*
Closest major hub ....*Portland, 36 air miles*

TESTS
1. Character.................................29.2
2. Stability.....................................79.0
3. Growth.....................................52.1
4. Education.................................60.9
5. Jobs..62.8
6. Business...................................52.4
7. Money......................................64.4
8. Housing...................................52.2
9. Health......................................77.1
10. Diversions.............................36.3
11. Internet 68.2
12. Proximity...............................90.4

BASIC STATS
Population................................10,086
Density......................................2,602.8
Born out of state.......................48.9%
Homes built since 2000.............31.6%
4 or more bedrooms 24.0%

RACE
Whites...85.4%
Blacks 0.5%
Hispanics 10.2%
Asians...0.4%
Native Americans 0.9%
Diversity index...........................26.0%

HOUSEHOLD INCOME LADDER
95th percentile $236,971
80th percentile $120,776
60th percentile $81,450
50th percentile $64,468
40th percentile $49,922
20th percentile $30,618

HOME VALUE LADDER
75th percentile $395,000
50th percentile $288,800
25th percentile $209,800

CHARACTER
Resilience.....................................9.9%
Short commutes 44.7%

STABILITY
Living with two parents 73.0%
Occupied homes.............. 98.0% (★)

GROWTH
Population growth.......................0.1%
Economic growth.............. 27.4% (★)

EDUCATION
High school graduates 92.4%
College graduates 29.8%

JOBS
MBSA workers.............................37.1%
Private-sector job growth ....17.3% (★)

BUSINESS
Small business growth 9.7%
Self-employed workers................9.2%

MONEY
Median annual earnings.......................$47,214
Living in poverty...........................8.5%

HOUSING
Home ownership.......................67.8%
Monthly housing costs.............32.1%

HEALTH
Health care workers.......................18.9% (★)
Fair or poor health.....................18.2%

DIVERSIONS
Stores per 10,000..........................32.6
Restaurants per 10,000................21.0

INTERNET
Broadband subscriptions 76.1%
Smartphone access 79.9%

PROXIMITY
Major hub miles.................................. 36
Major or mid-major miles.................. 36

Sioux Center, Iowa

Score ....*751.2 points*
National rank ....*129 of 2,084*
Percentile..*93.86%*
Midwest rank..*26 of 622*
Iowa rank...*6 of 55*
Closest major hub ....*Minneapolis, 194 air miles*

TESTS
1. Character............................... 100.0
2. Stability...................................92.6
3. Growth....................................40.5
4. Education................................60.6
5. Jobs...59.8
6. Business..................................43.2
7. Money.....................................61.0
8. Housing..................................63.4
9. Health.....................................50.0
10. Diversions............................42.7
11. Internet 66.6
12. Proximity..............................70.8

BASIC STATS
Population.............................. 6,685
Density 1,846.7
Born out of state 36.4%
Homes built since 2000...........................27.5%
4 or more bedrooms 32.4%

RACE
Whites.......................................79.5%
Blacks...0.5%
Hispanics 17.0%
Asians...1.5%
Native Americans 0.1%
Diversity index.............................33.9%

HOUSEHOLD INCOME LADDER
95th percentile.....................$172,990
80th percentile $111,810
60th percentile.......................$80,725
50th percentile.......................$70,074
40th percentile.......................$53,023
20th percentile.......................$29,879

HOME VALUE LADDER
75th percentile $258,500
50th percentile $203,700
25th percentile $145,000

CHARACTER
Resilience................................ 40.8% (★)
Short commutes .... 84.9% (★)

STABILITY
Living with two parents .... 88.1% (★)
Occupied homes............................ 98.0% (★)

GROWTH
Population growth.......................-1.1%
Economic growth....................... 10.7%

EDUCATION
High school graduates 81.4%
College graduates .... 43.8% (★)

JOBS
MBSA workers....................................... 43.5% (★)
Private-sector job growth 5.5%

BUSINESS
Small business growth 7.2%
Self-employed workers 6.9%

MONEY
Median annual earnings.......................$43,563
Living in poverty................................8.3%

HOUSING
Home ownership.....................................70.5%
Monthly housing costs............................24.8%

HEALTH
Health care workers................................5.8%
Fair or poor health............................. 12.5% (★)

DIVERSIONS
Stores per 10,000 ....44.8
Restaurants per 10,000....................... 18.4

INTERNET
Broadband subscriptions 72.7%
Smartphone access 80.6%

PROXIMITY
Major hub miles 194
Major or mid-major miles............................127

Snoqualmie, Washington

Score ....*841.3 points*
National rank ....*18 of 2,084*
Percentile...*99.18%*
West rank...*10 of 471*
Washington rank.......................................*1 of 44*
Closest major hub ....*Seattle, 23 air miles*

TESTS
1. Character.................24.8
2. Stability...................83.0
3. Growth....................70.5
4. Education.................88.1
5. Jobs........................84.4
6. Business..................46.7
7. Money.....................96.6
8. Housing...................60.6
9. Health.....................57.3
10. Diversions...............42.9
11. Internet 93.7
12. Proximity................92.7

BASIC STATS
Population.......................24,383
Density 2,042.1
Born out of state 50.0%
Homes built since 2000............42.0%
4 or more bedrooms 36.7%

RACE
Whites...................................81.2%
Blacks......................................0.9%
Hispanics 6.4%
Asians......................................7.3%
Native Americans 0.2%
Diversity index.........................32.9%

HOUSEHOLD INCOME LADDER
95th percentile ....>$250,000
80th percentile $210,581
60th percentile $150,567
50th percentile $125,686
40th percentile $105,911
20th percentile $66,290

HOME VALUE LADDER
75th percentile $700,900
50th percentile $551,000
25th percentile $403,400

CHARACTER
Resilience.......................................13.5%
Short commutes 28.4%

STABILITY
Living with two parents ....86.4% (★)
Occupied homes...........................95.3%

GROWTH
Population growth...........................10.2% (★)
Economic growth ....34.7% (★)

EDUCATION
High school graduates ....96.6% (★)
College graduates ....55.9% (★)

JOBS
MBSA workers.................................54.7% (★)
Private-sector job growth 17.0%

BUSINESS
Small business growth 9.3%
Self-employed workers 7.2%

MONEY
Median annual earnings...............$89,317 (★)
Living in poverty.....................................5.0% (★)

HOUSING
Home ownership...........................81.9% (★)
Monthly housing costs 34.2%

HEALTH
Health care workers.................................7.2%
Fair or poor health...........................10.9% (★)

DIVERSIONS
Stores per 10,000........................29.2
Restaurants per 10,000.......................28.2 (★)

INTERNET
Broadband subscriptions ....87.7% (★)
Smartphone access ....92.5% (★)

PROXIMITY
Major hub miles...............................23 (★)
Major or mid-major miles.......................23 (★)

Solvang, California

Score .... *727.1 points*
National rank .... *197 of 2,084*
Percentile *90.59%*
West rank .... *76 of 471*
California rank .... *15 of 145*
Closest major hub .... *Los Angeles, 122 air miles*

TESTS
1. Character......................................30.4
2. Stability...73.0
3. Growth..40.8
4. Education.......................................68.6
5. Jobs...62.3
6. Business..62.7
7. Money...91.2
8. Housing...50.4
9. Health...52.7
10. Diversions...................................40.1
11. Internet 74.4
12. Proximity.....................................80.5

BASIC STATS
Population.................................15,140
Density 1,985.3
Born out of state 37.7%
Homes built since 2000...............14.8%
4 or more bedrooms 26.6%

RACE
Whites...68.3%
Blacks..0.7%
Hispanics 22.5%
Asians..2.3%
Native Americans 2.8%
Diversity index...........................48.0%

HOUSEHOLD INCOME LADDER
95th percentile .... >$250,000
80th percentile $169,630
60th percentile $108,088
50th percentile $91,114
40th percentile $68,945
20th percentile $34,697

HOME VALUE LADDER
75th percentile $886,800
50th percentile $689,100
25th percentile $516,300

CHARACTER
Resilience.......................................7.5%
Short commutes 52.4%

STABILITY
Living with two parents 71.2%
Occupied homes..........................95.4%

GROWTH
Population growth........................-3.5%
Economic growth 16.7%

EDUCATION
High school graduates 92.2%
College graduates ....39.5% (★)

JOBS
MBSA workers........................... 43.8% (★)
Private-sector job growth 8.1%

BUSINESS
Small business growth 4.8%
Self-employed workers ....15.6% (★)

MONEY
Median annual earnings...............$70,910 (★)
Living in poverty.......................7.5% (★)

HOUSING
Home ownership........................68.4%
Monthly housing costs..............33.9%

HEALTH
Health care workers 10.1%
Fair or poor health.......................17.1%

DIVERSIONS
Stores per 10,000........................32.3
Restaurants per 10,000..............24.1

INTERNET
Broadband subscriptions ....80.9% (★)
Smartphone access 82.6%

PROXIMITY
Major hub miles...........................122
Major or mid-major miles.............79

South Deerfield, Massachusetts

Score ....*731.6 points*
National rank ....*183 of 2,084*
Percentile...*91.26%*
East rank...*27 of 246*
Massachusetts rank ....*3 of 12*
Closest major hub ....*Hartford, 51 air miles*

TESTS
1. Character..61.0
2. Stability..66.3
3. Growth..44.1
4. Education..80.8
5. Jobs..67.7
6. Business..36.7
7. Money..74.5
8. Housing..50.7
9. Health...50.9
10. Diversions...38.1
11. Internet 69.7
12. Proximity...91.1

BASIC STATS
Population...5,167
Density 784.9
Born out of state 39.8%
Homes built since 2000.......................9.5%
4 or more bedrooms 15.2%

RACE
Whites..86.3%
Blacks..1.1%
Hispanics 4.0%
Asians..4.4%
Native Americans 0.0%
Diversity index...................................25.0%

HOUSEHOLD INCOME LADDER
95th percentile $190,173
80th percentile $104,963
60th percentile $70,583
50th percentile $59,716
40th percentile $50,750
20th percentile $24,161

HOME VALUE LADDER
75th percentile $389,300
50th percentile $310,500
25th percentile $241,800

CHARACTER
Resilience...32.1%
Short commutes 46.7%

STABILITY
Living with two parents 61.0%
Occupied homes................................95.5%

GROWTH
Population growth.................................1.0%
Economic growth 11.9%

EDUCATION
High school graduates ....97.3% (★)
College graduates ....47.7% (★)

JOBS
MBSA workers.................................52.0% (★)
Private-sector job growth 3.9%

BUSINESS
Small business growth ....-0.4%
Self-employed workers 8.2%

MONEY
Median annual earnings...............$58,022 (★)
Living in poverty............................9.1%

HOUSING
Home ownership.................................54.5%
Monthly housing costs............................24.9%

HEALTH
Health care workers.................................6.1%
Fair or poor health............................12.5% (★)

DIVERSIONS
Stores per 10,000 ....35.3
Restaurants per 10,000..................................20.7

INTERNET
Broadband subscriptions 73.8%
Smartphone access 82.9%

PROXIMITY
Major hub miles 51
Major or mid-major miles.........................24 (★)

South Lyon, Michigan

Score ....*793.4 points*
National rank ....*62 of 2,084*
Percentile...*97.07%*
Midwest rank..*6 of 622*
Michigan rank ....*2 of 67*
Closest major hub ....*Detroit, 29 air miles*

TESTS
1. Character..59.5
2. Stability...79.0
3. Growth...52.3
4. Education...75.3
5. Jobs..69.5
6. Business..41.8
7. Money..83.4
8. Housing...71.9
9. Health..64.3
10. Diversions......................................29.0
11. Internet 75.7
12. Proximity..91.7

BASIC STATS
Population..126,935
Density 1,236.3
Born out of state.............................20.5%
Homes built since 2000............................22.9%
4 or more bedrooms 27.0%

RACE
Whites..92.9%
Blacks 1.0%
Hispanics 2.8%
Asians...1.5%
Native Americans 0.1%
Diversity index.................................13.6%

HOUSEHOLD INCOME LADDER
95th percentile ....>$250,000
80th percentile $149,805
60th percentile $98,149
50th percentile $80,234
40th percentile $64,669
20th percentile $36,689

HOME VALUE LADDER
75th percentile $332,500
50th percentile $238,200
25th percentile $165,400

CHARACTER
Resilience................................. 37.3% (★)
Short commutes 31.7%

STABILITY
Living with two parents .... 76.9% (★)
Occupied homes..96.6%

GROWTH
Population growth.............................4.4%
Economic growth 17.7%

EDUCATION
High school graduates .... 96.2% (★)
College graduates .... 42.4% (★)

JOBS
MBSA workers...................................... 44.0% (★)
Private-sector job growth 16.4%

BUSINESS
Small business growth 4.9%
Self-employed workers 7.5%

MONEY
Median annual earnings...............$62,532 (★)
Living in poverty...................................5.2% (★)

HOUSING
Home ownership............................. 81.5% (★)
Monthly housing costs............................24.9%

HEALTH
Health care workers...............................9.7%
Fair or poor health............................ 10.9% (★)

DIVERSIONS
Stores per 10,000...............................31.4
Restaurants per 10,000....................16.1

INTERNET
Broadband subscriptions .... 81.0% (★)
Smartphone access 83.7%

PROXIMITY
Major hub miles...29 (★)
Major or mid-major miles................................ 29

Southold, New York

Score ....*736.1 points*
National rank ....*167 of 2,084*
Percentile..*92.03%*
East rank.. *23 of 246*
New York rank .... *6 of 65*
Closest major hub ....*New York, 86 air miles*

TESTS
1. Character....................55.1
2. Stability.......................64.8
3. Growth........................38.6
4. Education....................60.0
5. Jobs............................52.3
6. Business......................65.5
7. Money.........................67.3
8. Housing.......................60.7
9. Health.........................68.8
10. Diversions..................50.3
11. Internet 60.9
12. Proximity....................91.8

BASIC STATS
Population....................10,303
Density 925.9
Born out of state.............30.6%
Homes built since 2000............13.7%
4 or more bedrooms 24.8%

RACE
Whites............................78.8%
Blacks..............................4.0%
Hispanics 14.5%
Asians...............................1.7%
Native Americans 0.0%
Diversity index.................35.6%

HOUSEHOLD INCOME LADDER
95th percentile .... >$250,000
80th percentile $147,658
60th percentile.........................$81,373
50th percentile.........................$64,596
40th percentile.........................$52,334
20th percentile.........................$29,943

HOME VALUE LADDER
75th percentile $728,400
50th percentile $562,600
25th percentile $418,800

CHARACTER
Resilience.........................23.4%
Short commutes 57.3%

STABILITY
Living with two parents 56.6%
Occupied homes....................96.3%

GROWTH
Population growth...................-0.5%
Economic growth 6.1%

EDUCATION
High school graduates 88.4%
College graduates 33.9%

JOBS
MBSA workers......................37.1%
Private-sector job growth 4.8%

BUSINESS
Small business growth 2.2%
Self-employed workers .... 19.5% (★)

MONEY
Median annual earnings ....$54,350 (★)
Living in poverty............................12.4%

HOUSING
Home ownership..............................76.0% (★)
Monthly housing costs 30.4%

HEALTH
Health care workers................12.9%
Fair or poor health............................13.1%

DIVERSIONS
Stores per 10,000...............................43.1
Restaurants per 10,000........................25.4 (★)

INTERNET
Broadband subscriptions 75.0%
Smartphone access 73.6%

PROXIMITY
Major hub miles 86
Major or mid-major miles.............................. 86

Spirit Lake, Iowa

Score ....*793.4 points*
National rank ....*62 of 2,084*
Percentile...*97.07%*
Midwest rank.. *6 of 622*
Iowa rank.. *1 of 55*
Closest major hub ....*Minneapolis, 142 air miles*

TESTS
1. Character.................................80.9
2. Stability...................................67.4
3. Growth....................................44.7
4. Education................................72.4
5. Jobs...52.8
6. Business..................................64.6
7. Money.....................................61.6
8. Housing...................................67.4
9. Health.....................................63.3
10. Diversions..............................88.4
11. Internet 58.1
12. Proximity................................71.8

BASIC STATS
Population.......................... 11,000
Density 950.9
Born out of state 28.0%
Homes built since 2000............28.4%
4 or more bedrooms 26.9%

RACE
Whites.................................95.2%
Blacks.................................0.5%
Hispanics 2.3%
Asians.................................1.2%
Native Americans 0.2%
Diversity index......................9.3%

HOUSEHOLD INCOME LADDER
95th percentile $189,125
80th percentile $106,667
60th percentile $68,160
50th percentile $55,160
40th percentile $47,256
20th percentile $27,642

HOME VALUE LADDER
75th percentile $289,600
50th percentile $174,800
25th percentile $112,700

CHARACTER
Resilience................................ 35.1% (★)
Short commutes 74.1%

STABILITY
Living with two parents 65.2%
Occupied homes.......................94.6%

GROWTH
Population growth....................3.2%
Economic growth 7.7%

EDUCATION
High school graduates .... 97.7% (★)
College graduates 36.9%

JOBS
MBSA workers 35.9%
Private-sector job growth 6.9%

BUSINESS
Small business growth 3.3%
Self-employed workers .... 17.1% (★)

MONEY
Median annual earnings.......................$45,012
Living in poverty.......................9.1%

HOUSING
Home ownership...................... 75.3% (★)
Monthly housing costs.............24.6%

HEALTH
Health care workers................ 10.2%
Fair or poor health.............. 12.1% (★)

DIVERSIONS
Stores per 10,000...................... 61.9 (★)
Restaurants per 10,000...................... 46.1 (★)

INTERNET
Broadband subscriptions 68.1%
Smartphone access 75.6%

PROXIMITY
Major hub miles..............................142
Major or mid-major miles............................142

Spring Hill, Tennessee

Score ....*850.9 points*
National rank ....*14 of 2,084*
Percentile...*99.38%*
South rank ....*5 of 745*
Tennessee rank..*1 of 58*
Closest major hub ....*Nashville, 30 air miles*

TESTS
1. Character..56.5
2. Stability...82.5
3. Growth..76.4
4. Education.......................................77.7
5. Jobs...86.4
6. Business...58.4
7. Money..81.2
8. Housing..61.3
9. Health..47.9
10. Diversions....................................37.3
11. Internet 93.8
12. Proximity......................................91.5

BASIC STATS
Population....................................40,314
Density 1,855.2
Born out of state 63.3%
Homes built since 2000..............74.1%
4 or more bedrooms 34.8%

RACE
Whites...86.5%
Blacks...4.5%
Hispanics 5.9%
Asians...0.8%
Native Americans 0.0%
Diversity index.............................24.6%

HOUSEHOLD INCOME LADDER
95th percentile $220,357
80th percentile $138,569
60th percentile $104,899
50th percentile $91,326
40th percentile $78,564
20th percentile $44,987

HOME VALUE LADDER
75th percentile $369,500
50th percentile $277,700
25th percentile $218,000

CHARACTER
Resilience.............................. 38.7% (★)
Short commutes 23.2%

STABILITY
Living with two parents ....87.1% (★)
Occupied homes.........................94.8%

GROWTH
Population growth............................ 18.5% (★)
Economic growth .... 25.3% (★)

EDUCATION
High school graduates 94.9%
College graduates .... 47.0% (★)

JOBS
MBSA workers.......................................46.4% (★)
Private-sector job growth ....29.5% (★)

BUSINESS
Small business growth ....14.3% (★)
Self-employed workers 9.2%

MONEY
Median annual earnings..............$57,411 (★)
Living in poverty.......................................2.3% (★)

HOUSING
Home ownership.............................78.7% (★)
Monthly housing costs............................31.6%

HEALTH
Health care workers....................................7.3%
Fair or poor health.................................15.6%

DIVERSIONS
Stores per 10,000..................................34.7
Restaurants per 10,000................................20.5

INTERNET
Broadband subscriptions .... 86.7% (★)
Smartphone access .... 93.2% (★)

PROXIMITY
Major hub miles ....30 (★)
Major or mid-major miles............................. 30

Stansbury Park, Utah

Score .... *790.9 points*
National rank .... *65 of 2,084*
Percentile *96.93%*
West rank .... *30 of 471*
Utah rank .... *5 of 20*
Closest major hub .... *Salt Lake City, 19 air miles*

TESTS
1. Character 54.6
2. Stability 97.3
3. Growth 56.7
4. Education 72.7
5. Jobs 62.8
6. Business 55.5
7. Money 85.4
8. Housing 71.8
9. Health 49.7
10. Diversions 8.3
11. Internet 79.9
12. Proximity 96.2

BASIC STATS
Population 11,085
Density 3,819.8
Born out of state 33.4%
Homes built since 2000 .... 55.8%
4 or more bedrooms 59.9%

RACE
Whites 87.0%
Blacks 0.5%
Hispanics 7.6%
Asians 2.2%
Native Americans 0.0%
Diversity index 23.6%

HOUSEHOLD INCOME LADDER
95th percentile $187,156
80th percentile $128,922
60th percentile $106,639
50th percentile $93,750
40th percentile $85,667
20th percentile $63,041

HOME VALUE LADDER
75th percentile $339,800
50th percentile $265,800
25th percentile $219,600

CHARACTER
Resilience 33.5%
Short commutes 32.4%

STABILITY
Living with two parents .... 89.6% (★)
Occupied homes .... 99.4% (★)

GROWTH
Population growth .... 15.4% (★)
Economic growth .... -0.5%

EDUCATION
High school graduates .... 96.3% (★)
College graduates 39.1%

JOBS
MBSA workers .... 41.4% (★)
Private-sector job growth 11.7%

BUSINESS
Small business growth .... 22.8% (★)
Self-employed workers 3.8%

MONEY
Median annual earnings .... $61,519 (★)
Living in poverty .... 3.0% (★)

HOUSING
Home ownership .... 88.2% (★)
Monthly housing costs 29.2%

HEALTH
Health care workers 6.8%
Fair or poor health 14.0%

DIVERSIONS
Stores per 10,000 .... 15.1
Restaurants per 10,000 .... 10.1

INTERNET
Broadband subscriptions 75.0%
Smartphone access .... 91.8% (★)

PROXIMITY
Major hub miles .... 19 (★)
Major or mid-major miles .... 19 (★)

Star, Idaho

Score .... *766.4 points*
National rank .... *104 of 2,084*
Percentile *95.06%*
West rank .... *45 of 471*
Idaho rank .... *2 of 21*
Closest major hub .... *Salt Lake City, 315 air miles*

TESTS
1. Character 42.9
2. Stability 81.7
3. Growth 90.0
4. Education 69.1
5. Jobs 63.4
6. Business 53.1
7. Money 62.8
8. Housing 61.4
9. Health 59.1
10. Diversions 36.1
11. Internet 68.6
12. Proximity 78.2

BASIC STATS
Population 8,524
Density 2,588.5
Born out of state 52.1%
Homes built since 2000 .... 83.1%
4 or more bedrooms 29.1%

RACE
Whites 88.5%
Blacks 0.4%
Hispanics 7.2%
Asians 0.6%
Native Americans 0.8%
Diversity index 21.1%

HOUSEHOLD INCOME LADDER
95th percentile $204,918
80th percentile $110,867
60th percentile $71,972
50th percentile $60,842
40th percentile $50,228
20th percentile $30,992

HOME VALUE LADDER
75th percentile $369,500
50th percentile $276,900
25th percentile $213,300

CHARACTER
Resilience 26.6%
Short commutes 28.6%

STABILITY
Living with two parents .... 76.9% (★)
Occupied homes .... 98.0% (★)

GROWTH
Population growth .... 33.6% (★)
Economic growth .... 26.3% (★)

EDUCATION
High school graduates .... 96.8% (★)
College graduates 34.0%

JOBS
MBSA workers 33.9%
Private-sector job growth .... 22.1% (★)

BUSINESS
Small business growth .... 16.8% (★)
Self-employed workers 5.9%

MONEY
Median annual earnings $44,091
Living in poverty .... 7.1% (★)

HOUSING
Home ownership .... 80.8% (★)
Monthly housing costs 32.9%

HEALTH
Health care workers 8.3%
Fair or poor health .... 11.5% (★)

DIVERSIONS
Stores per 10,000 .... 32.2
Restaurants per 10,000 .... 21.1

INTERNET
Broadband subscriptions 74.6%
Smartphone access 81.3%

PROXIMITY
Major hub miles 315
Major or mid-major miles .... 11 (★)

State College, Pennsylvania

Score ....*726.0 points*
National rank ....*204 of 2,084*
Percentile...*90.25%*
East rank ....*29 of 246*
Pennsylvania rank .... *1 of 72*
Closest major hub ....*Pittsburgh, 112 air miles*

TESTS
1. Character...73.9
2. Stability...80.1
3. Growth..47.5
4. Education...94.5
5. Jobs..74.0
6. Business...36.1
7. Money..48.0
8. Housing...36.3
9. Health..49.3
10. Diversions......................................28.6
11. Internet 74.9
12. Proximity...82.8

BASIC STATS
Population..93,152
Density 3,235.5
Born out of state 46.0%
Homes built since 2000..........................18.7%
4 or more bedrooms 22.3%

RACE
Whites...77.2%
Blacks...5.6%
Hispanics 4.4%
Asians...10.3%
Native Americans 0.1%
Diversity index...................................38.8%

HOUSEHOLD INCOME LADDER
95th percentile $222,147
80th percentile $120,746
60th percentile $70,906
50th percentile $54,339
40th percentile $40,658
20th percentile $18,222

HOME VALUE LADDER
75th percentile $389,300
50th percentile $280,500
25th percentile $211,200

CHARACTER
Resilience..30.8%
Short commutes 72.2%

STABILITY
Living with two parents ....81.8% (★)
Occupied homes.................................95.4%

GROWTH
Population growth...............................5.2%
Economic growth.................................7.6%

EDUCATION
High school graduates ....96.3% (★)
College graduates ....63.7% (★)

JOBS
MBSA workers.....................................57.6% (★)
Private-sector job growth 4.0%

BUSINESS
Small business growth 3.1%
Self-employed workers 6.2%

MONEY
Median annual earnings.....................$51,197
Living in poverty.................................27.6%

HOUSING
Home ownership.................................46.1%
Monthly housing costs....................31.2%

HEALTH
Health care workers.................................7.6%
Fair or poor health..............................15.3%

DIVERSIONS
Stores per 10,000.......................................27.5
Restaurants per 10,000.................................18.2

INTERNET
Broadband subscriptions 76.7%
Smartphone access ....85.9% (★)

PROXIMITY
Major hub miles...112
Major or mid-major miles...............................65

Steamboat Springs, Colorado

Score ....*814.5 points*
National rank ....*34 of 2,084*
Percentile..*98.42%*
West rank.. *18 of 471*
Colorado rank .... *9 of 47*
Closest major hub .... *Denver, 113 air miles*

TESTS

1. Character...............................72.9
2. Stability................................67.1
3. Growth.................................45.6
4. Education..............................86.4
5. Jobs.....................................57.0
6. Business...............................52.2
7. Money..................................63.3
8. Housing................................45.0
9. Health..................................63.8
10. Diversions...........................98.1
11. Internet 86.2
12. Proximity.............................76.9

BASIC STATS

Population...........................13,856
Density 1,694.3
Born out of state 70.0%
Homes built since 2000............29.4%
4 or more bedrooms 22.3%

RACE

Whites..................................87.0%
Blacks....................................1.4%
Hispanics 8.8%
Asians....................................1.7%
Native Americans 0.1%
Diversity index.......................23.5%

HOUSEHOLD INCOME LADDER

95th percentile ....>$250,000
80th percentile $151,419
60th percentile $103,652
50th percentile $82,486
40th percentile $66,357
20th percentile $37,325

HOME VALUE LADDER

75th percentile $826,700
50th percentile $583,600
25th percentile $373,400

CHARACTER

Resilience..............................29.7%
Short commutes 73.1%

STABILITY

Living with two parents 75.6%
Occupied homes.....................90.7%

GROWTH

Population growth.....................7.4%
Economic growth.....................-0.5%

EDUCATION

High school graduates ....96.5% (★)
College graduates ....54.9% (★)

JOBS

MBSA workers............................39.2%
Private-sector job growth 7.7%

BUSINESS

Small business growth 10.9%
Self-employed workers 8.5%

MONEY

Median annual earnings.........$48,115
Living in poverty.......................10.4%

HOUSING

Home ownership.....................68.9%
Monthly housing costs.............38.6%

HEALTH

Health care workers...................9.6%
Fair or poor health.............. 11.0% (★)

DIVERSIONS

Stores per 10,000.....................76.8 (★)
Restaurants per 10,000.............48.2 (★)

INTERNET

Broadband subscriptions ....84.2% (★)
Smartphone access ....89.7% (★)

PROXIMITY

Major hub miles...............................113
Major or mid-major miles.................113

Sturgeon Bay, Wisconsin

Score ....753.2 points
National rank ....126 of 2,084
Percentile..94.00%
Midwest rank...24 of 622
Wisconsin rank ....5 of 61
Closest major hub ....Milwaukee, 128 air miles

TESTS
1. Character.................................79.1
2. Stability.....................................69.3
3. Growth.......................................37.5
4. Education.................................60.4
5. Jobs..50.4
6. Business...................................32.1
7. Money.......................................69.7
8. Housing....................................63.6
9. Health.......................................66.1
10. Diversions..............................99.1
11. Internet 51.7
12. Proximity................................74.2

BASIC STATS
Population......................................8,144
Density 1,478.0
Born out of state.........................27.5%
Homes built since 2000............15.0%
4 or more bedrooms 14.4%

RACE
Whites...90.2%
Blacks..1.8%
Hispanics..3.9%
Asians...1.2%
Native Americans 0.7%
Diversity index............................18.4%

HOUSEHOLD INCOME LADDER
95th percentile.....................$182,721
80th percentile $108,672
60th percentile.......................$65,003
50th percentile.......................$57,128
40th percentile.......................$44,150
20th percentile.......................$27,019

HOME VALUE LADDER
75th percentile.....................$203,200
50th percentile.....................$148,400
25th percentile.....................$105,700

CHARACTER
Resilience..30.4%
Short commutes ....82.1% (★)

STABILITY
Living with two parents 68.3%
Occupied homes...........................94.5%

GROWTH
Population growth..........................-2.4%
Economic growth............................8.6%

EDUCATION
High school graduates 93.4%
College graduates 27.8%

JOBS
MBSA workers..................................34.3%
Private-sector job growth 6.1%

BUSINESS
Small business growth ....-3.2%
Self-employed workers 7.8%

MONEY
Median annual earnings................$52,955 (★)
Living in poverty............................8.9%

HOUSING
Home ownership...........................64.6%
Monthly housing costs...............20.9%

HEALTH
Health care workers......................11.0%
Fair or poor health.............11.8% (★)

DIVERSIONS
Stores per 10,000.....................88.1 (★)
Restaurants per 10,000.........55.5 (★)

INTERNET
Broadband subscriptions 68.6%
Smartphone access 69.1%

PROXIMITY
Major hub miles................................128
Major or mid-major miles.............128

Summit Park, Utah

Score ....949.7 points
National rank .... 1 of 2,084
Percentile... 100.00%
West rank... 1 of 471
Utah rank.. 1 of 20
Closest major hub .... Salt Lake City, 20 air miles

TESTS
1. Character.......................................61.1
2. Stability...77.4
3. Growth...77.8
4. Education.......................................91.2
5. Jobs...87.4
6. Business...69.6
7. Money..91.9
8. Housing..55.0
9. Health..58.0
10. Diversions....................................97.9
11. Internet..87.6
12. Proximity......................................94.8

BASIC STATS
Population.. 6,645
Density 1,906.7
Born out of state.............................73.3%
Homes built since 2000......................18.4%
4 or more bedrooms...........................60.1%

RACE
Whites...85.4%
Blacks..0.1%
Hispanics 10.4%
Asians..2.5%
Native Americans 0.2%
Diversity index.................................25.9%

HOUSEHOLD INCOME LADDER
95th percentile......................>$250,000
80th percentile......................>$250,000
60th percentile........................$165,250
50th percentile........................$134,375
40th percentile........................$106,203
20th percentile.........................$55,367

HOME VALUE LADDER
75th percentile........................$904,400
50th percentile........................$711,300
25th percentile........................$544,900

CHARACTER
Resilience.............................. 39.2% (★)
Short commutes 30.0%

STABILITY
Living with two parents 73.7%
Occupied homes.................. 96.9% (★)

GROWTH
Population growth................ 17.4% (★)
Economic growth................. 30.1% (★)

EDUCATION
High school graduates 93.0%
College graduates .... 69.6% (★)

JOBS
MBSA workers...................... 57.9% (★)
Private-sector job growth 15.8%

BUSINESS
Small business growth .... 15.7% (★)
Self-employed workers .... 12.8% (★)

MONEY
Median annual earnings...............$71,467 (★)
Living in poverty......................7.3% (★)

HOUSING
Home ownership.................... 84.1% (★)
Monthly housing costs............40.1%

HEALTH
Health care workers.....................7.4%
Fair or poor health.............. 10.8% (★)

DIVERSIONS
Stores per 10,000..................... 79.3 (★)
Restaurants per 10,000........... 43.0 (★)

INTERNET
Broadband subscriptions .... 77.8% (★)
Smartphone access .... 94.9% (★)

PROXIMITY
Major hub miles.........................20 (★)
Major or mid-major miles.........................20 (★)

Sun City Hilton Head, South Carolina

Score ....*801.6 points*
National rank ....*47 of 2,084*
Percentile..*97.79%*
South rank ....*15 of 745*
South Carolina rank..*1 of 35*
Closest major hub ....*Jacksonville, 147 air miles*

TESTS
1. Character................................46.8
2. Stability..................................47.8
3. Growth...................................43.0
4. Education...............................83.3
5. Jobs.......................................69.6
6. Business.................................56.3
7. Money...................................73.9
8. Housing............................. 100.0
9. Health....................................82.2
10. Diversions...........................50.9
11. Internet 67.6
12. Proximity.............................80.2

BASIC STATS
Population............................13,430
Density 1,534.7
Born out of state 93.5%
Homes built since 2000.............62.7%
4 or more bedrooms 4.9%

RACE
Whites......................................93.5%
Blacks..2.4%
Hispanics 1.0%
Asians..1.1%
Native Americans 0.0%
Diversity index........................12.5%

HOUSEHOLD INCOME LADDER
95th percentile $189,005
80th percentile $116,330
60th percentile $78,027
50th percentile $68,723
40th percentile $54,774
20th percentile $35,270

HOME VALUE LADDER
75th percentile $342,900
50th percentile $278,100
25th percentile $234,400

CHARACTER
Resilience.................................23.2%
Short commutes 43.5%

STABILITY
Living with two parents 31.8%
Occupied homes........................96.1%

GROWTH
Population growth......................0.0%
Economic growth......................12.3%

EDUCATION
High school graduates ....100.0% (★)
College graduates ....47.2% (★)

JOBS
MBSA workers................................44.3% (★)
Private-sector job growth 16.1%

BUSINESS
Small business growth ....12.5% (★)
Self-employed workers 9.3%

MONEY
Median annual earnings.......................$51,353
Living in poverty.....................................3.4% (★)

HOUSING
Home ownership...........................93.1% (★)
Monthly housing costs....................13.6% (★)

HEALTH
Health care workers...........................15.9% (★)
Fair or poor health..............................12.4% (★)

DIVERSIONS
Stores per 10,000.......................................41.1
Restaurants per 10,000........................27.1 (★)

INTERNET
Broadband subscriptions ....81.4% (★)
Smartphone access 75.7%

PROXIMITY
Major hub miles...147
Major or mid-major miles................................70

Tea, South Dakota

Score ....842.3 points
National rank .... 17 of 2,084
Percentile...99.23%
Midwest rank... 1 of 622
South Dakota rank... 1 of 17
Closest major hub ....Minneapolis, 205 air miles

TESTS
1. Character...72.5
2. Stability..81.4
3. Growth..90.7
4. Education...70.8
5. Jobs...82.9
6. Business...61.8
7. Money...73.9
8. Housing..50.9
9. Health...80.4
10. Diversions...21.8
11. Internet..88.8
12. Proximity...66.4

BASIC STATS
Population.. 5,129
Density 3,782.4
Born out of state 31.5%
Homes built since 2000......................... 55.0%
4 or more bedrooms 43.1%

RACE
Whites..95.2%
Blacks...0.4%
Hispanics...3.5%
Asians...0.3%
Native Americans 0.2%
Diversity index....................................9.2%

HOUSEHOLD INCOME LADDER
95th percentile $211,688
80th percentile $131,118
60th percentile $96,674
50th percentile $83,676
40th percentile $74,904
20th percentile $53,583

HOME VALUE LADDER
75th percentile $258,000
50th percentile $199,700
25th percentile $161,100

CHARACTER
Resilience.. 37.3% (★)
Short commutes 54.2%

STABILITY
Living with two parents .... 76.8% (★)
Occupied homes............................... 97.9% (★)

GROWTH
Population growth.............................. 23.6% (★)
Economic growth .... 32.6% (★)

EDUCATION
High school graduates .... 96.6% (★)
College graduates 36.4%

JOBS
MBSA workers...................................... 45.4% (★)
Private-sector job growth .... 27.7% (★)

BUSINESS
Small business growth .... 32.2% (★)
Self-employed workers 5.1%

MONEY
Median annual earnings $50,548
Living in poverty...................................2.7% (★)

HOUSING
Home ownership 67.3%
Monthly housing costs 32.8%

HEALTH
Health care workers............................ 13.1%
Fair or poor health................................9.3% (★)

DIVERSIONS
Stores per 10,000 ....28.7
Restaurants per 10,000....................................12.2

INTERNET
Broadband subscriptions .... 85.6% (★)
Smartphone access .... 90.4% (★)

PROXIMITY
Major hub miles...205
Major or mid-major miles............................158

Traverse City, Michigan

Score .... *756.3 points*
National rank .... *116 of 2,084*
Percentile *94.48%*
Midwest rank .... *20 of 622*
Michigan rank .... *4 of 67*
Closest major hub .... *Detroit, 196 air miles*

TESTS
1. Character..................................74.5
2. Stability......................................68.0
3. Growth.......................................49.1
4. Education..................................71.6
5. Jobs..57.2
6. Business....................................48.9
7. Money.......................................56.9
8. Housing....................................56.8
9. Health..71.1
10. Diversions..............................65.1
11. Internet...................................64.5
12. Proximity................................72.6

BASIC STATS
Population................................49,903
Density....................................1,142.4
Born out of state.....................25.4%
Homes built since 2000............21.4%
4 or more bedrooms..................18.8%

RACE
Whites.......................................90.6%
Blacks..0.9%
Hispanics...................................4.0%
Asians..0.8%
Native Americans.....................1.3%
Diversity index........................17.7%

HOUSEHOLD INCOME LADDER
95th percentile......................$230,677
80th percentile......................$111,535
60th percentile........................$70,307
50th percentile........................$56,526
40th percentile........................$45,189
20th percentile........................$25,456

HOME VALUE LADDER
75th percentile......................$333,400
50th percentile......................$214,100
25th percentile......................$144,100

CHARACTER
Resilience..................................32.1%
Short commutes.......................70.1%

STABILITY
Living with two parents...........67.7%
Occupied homes.......................94.0%

GROWTH
Population growth......................3.9%
Economic growth.....................13.4%

EDUCATION
High school graduates.............95.2%
College graduates.............39.2% (★)

JOBS
MBSA workers...........................39.0%
Private-sector job growth..........8.1%

BUSINESS
Small business growth...............4.0%
Self-employed workers............10.7%

MONEY
Median annual earnings......$43,664
Living in poverty.....................12.2%

HOUSING
Home ownership......................66.7%
Monthly housing costs.............27.7%

HEALTH
Health care workers.................12.9%
Fair or poor health.............12.0% (★)

DIVERSIONS
Stores per 10,000....................60.6 (★)
Restaurants per 10,000..........26.0 (★)

INTERNET
Broadband subscriptions........73.7%
Smartphone access..................78.0%

PROXIMITY
Major hub miles............................196
Major or mid-major miles............123

Truckee, California

Score ....*808.0 points*
National rank ....*39 of 2,084*
Percentile..*98.18%*
West rank..*21 of 471*
California rank ....*3 of 145*
Closest major hub ....*Sacramento, 78 air miles*

TESTS
1. Character.....................................56.6
2. Stability......................................80.3
3. Growth..47.1
4. Education....................................76.0
5. Jobs..63.5
6. Business......................................62.7
7. Money...78.8
8. Housing.......................................47.7
9. Health...69.2
10. Diversions..................................41.5
11. Internet 95.0
12. Proximity...................................89.6

BASIC STATS
Population.................................12,493
Density 1,180.0
Born out of state.........................42.1%
Homes built since 2000..............19.4%
4 or more bedrooms 19.1%

RACE
Whites...79.7%
Blacks 0.1%
Hispanics 18.7%
Asians...0.7%
Native Americans 0.0%
Diversity index...........................33.0%

HOUSEHOLD INCOME LADDER
95th percentile ....>$250,000
80th percentile $172,637
60th percentile $113,490
50th percentile $93,500
40th percentile $77,274
20th percentile $44,401

HOME VALUE LADDER
75th percentile $726,900
50th percentile $565,100
25th percentile $405,500

CHARACTER
Resilience....................................25.6%
Short commutes 54.7%

STABILITY
Living with two parents 70.2%
Occupied homes................. 99.7% (★)

GROWTH
Population growth........................1.6%
Economic growth 15.4%

EDUCATION
High school graduates 93.6%
College graduates .... 46.7% (★)

JOBS
MBSA workers...................... 42.5% (★)
Private-sector job growth 11.1%

BUSINESS
Small business growth 5.4%
Self-employed workers ..... 15.3% (★)

MONEY
Median annual earnings...............$62,500 (★)
Living in poverty...........................9.3%

HOUSING
Home ownership............... 75.1% (★)
Monthly housing costs 40.3%

HEALTH
Health care workers....................12.1%
Fair or poor health............. 11.8% (★)

DIVERSIONS
Stores per 10,000.........................37.0
Restaurants per 10,000.................22.3

INTERNET
Broadband subscriptions .... 85.2% (★)
Smartphone access .... 95.3% (★)

PROXIMITY
Major hub miles 78
Major or mid-major miles.......24 (★)

Twin Rivers, New Jersey

Score ....*773.6 points*
National rank ....*90 of 2,084*
Percentile...*95.73%*
East rank...*12 of 246*
New Jersey rank ....*2 of 12*
Closest major hub ....*New York, 44 air miles*

TESTS
1. Character........................37.2
2. Stability..........................77.5
3. Growth............................43.0
4. Education.........................93.5
5. Jobs.................................83.6
6. Business...........................31.0
7. Money.............................96.2
8. Housing...........................50.8
9. Health.............................49.0
10. Diversions......................38.8
11. Internet..........................84.0
12. Proximity........................89.0

BASIC STATS
Population.....................66,253
Density.........................1,877.1
Born out of state...............63.4%
Homes built since 2000.........23.3%
4 or more bedrooms............34.6%

RACE
Whites.............................46.9%
Blacks...............................5.5%
Hispanics.........................13.6%
Asians.............................31.8%
Native Americans................0.3%
Diversity index..................65.7%

HOUSEHOLD INCOME LADDER
95th percentile.............>$250,000
80th percentile.............$238,433
60th percentile.............$152,545
50th percentile.............$116,509
40th percentile..............$92,566
20th percentile..............$50,616

HOME VALUE LADDER
75th percentile.............$658,400
50th percentile.............$445,600
25th percentile.............$295,000

CHARACTER
Resilience.........................21.4%
Short commutes.................31.0%

STABILITY
Living with two parents........78.8% (★)
Occupied homes.................95.1%

GROWTH
Population growth.................0.4%
Economic growth.................11.3%

EDUCATION
High school graduates............95.0%
College graduates.............67.8% (★)

JOBS
MBSA workers..................59.3% (★)
Private-sector job growth.......12.1%

BUSINESS
Small business growth.............0.4%
Self-employed workers............5.6%

MONEY
Median annual earnings........$84,715 (★)
Living in poverty.................4.9% (★)

HOUSING
Home ownership.................68.6%
Monthly housing costs...........33.7%

HEALTH
Health care workers...............7.2%
Fair or poor health..............14.9%

DIVERSIONS
Stores per 10,000.................33.7
Restaurants per 10,000...........22.3

INTERNET
Broadband subscriptions........85.5% (★)
Smartphone access.............87.6% (★)

PROXIMITY
Major hub miles....................44
Major or mid-major miles...........44

Vail, Arizona

Score ....772.6 points
National rank ....92 of 2,084
Percentile...95.63%
West rank...39 of 471
Arizona rank... 2 of 44
Closest major hub ....Phoenix, 123 air miles

TESTS
1. Character.................................22.5
2. Stability...................................96.5
3. Growth...................................82.5
4. Education...............................76.4
5. Jobs.......................................60.2
6. Business.................................27.7
7. Money....................................93.5
8. Housing..................................74.2
9. Health....................................44.8
10. Diversions.............................25.0
11. Internet 81.6
12. Proximity...............................87.7

BASIC STATS
Population..............................11,216
Density 1,593.4
Born out of state 63.3%
Homes built since 2000.............83.8%
4 or more bedrooms 41.2%

RACE
Whites......................................71.3%
Blacks.......................................2.8%
Hispanics 19.1%
Asians.......................................3.3%
Native Americans 0.2%
Diversity index..........................45.2%

HOUSEHOLD INCOME LADDER
95th percentile ....>$250,000
80th percentile $158,667
60th percentile $113,736
50th percentile $95,023
40th percentile $76,929
20th percentile $45,344

HOME VALUE LADDER
75th percentile $335,600
50th percentile $243,800
25th percentile $195,200

CHARACTER
Resilience...................................16.1%
Short commutes 18.3%

STABILITY
Living with two parents ....92.8% (★)
Occupied homes...........................97.9% (★)

GROWTH
Population growth.........................30.1% (★)
Economic growth...........................15.7%

EDUCATION
High school graduates ....96.3% (★)
College graduates ....43.6% (★)

JOBS
MBSA workers...............................41.9% (★)
Private-sector job growth 8.0%

BUSINESS
Small business growth 1.4%
Self-employed workers 3.8%

MONEY
Median annual earnings...............$69,764 (★)
Living in poverty................................4.6% (★)

HOUSING
Home ownership............................86.9% (★)
Monthly housing costs.....................26.4%

HEALTH
Health care workers................................7.4%
Fair or poor health................................17.2%

DIVERSIONS
Stores per 10,000.................................25.5
Restaurants per 10,000..............................16.6

INTERNET
Broadband subscriptions ....78.6% (★)
Smartphone access ....91.0% (★)

PROXIMITY
Major hub miles 123
Major or mid-major miles......................19 (★)

Vail, Colorado

Score .... *818.5 points*
National rank .... *31 of 2,084*
Percentile *98.56%*
West rank .... *16 of 471*
Colorado rank .... *8 of 47*
Closest major hub .... *Denver, 72 air miles*

TESTS
1. Character 75.3
2. Stability 77.4
3. Growth 46.8
4. Education 95.4
5. Jobs 55.6
6. Business 42.2
7. Money 64.4
8. Housing 43.7
9. Health 53.8
10. Diversions 96.6
11. Internet 83.2
12. Proximity 84.1

BASIC STATS
Population 5,898
Density 1,852.4
Born out of state 81.1%
Homes built since 2000 .... 11.3%
4 or more bedrooms 19.0%

RACE
Whites 90.2%
Blacks 0.5%
Hispanics 8.0%
Asians 0.8%
Native Americans 0.0%
Diversity index 18.0%

HOUSEHOLD INCOME LADDER
95th percentile .... >$250,000
80th percentile $162,125
60th percentile $103,319
50th percentile $84,076
40th percentile $70,045
20th percentile $38,768

HOME VALUE LADDER
75th percentile $1,208,800
50th percentile $719,700
25th percentile $413,800

CHARACTER
Resilience 31.0%
Short commutes 74.2%

STABILITY
Living with two parents .... 88.2% (★)
Occupied homes 91.7%

GROWTH
Population growth .... -0.1%
Economic growth 19.0%

EDUCATION
High school graduates .... 99.1% (★)
College graduates .... 59.0% (★)

JOBS
MBSA workers 32.8%
Private-sector job growth 14.2%

BUSINESS
Small business growth 9.2%
Self-employed workers 5.5%

MONEY
Median annual earnings $47,069
Living in poverty 8.4%

HOUSING
Home ownership 68.1%
Monthly housing costs 39.1%

HEALTH
Health care workers 7.0%
Fair or poor health .... 12.3% (★)

DIVERSIONS
Stores per 10,000 .... 71.2 (★)
Restaurants per 10,000 .... 45.9 (★)

INTERNET
Broadband subscriptions .... 81.2% (★)
Smartphone access .... 90.0% (★)

PROXIMITY
Major hub miles 72
Major or mid-major miles 72

Vineyard Haven, Massachusetts

Score .... *836.5 points*
National rank .... *23 of 2,084*
Percentile *98.94%*
East rank .... *2 of 246*
Massachusetts rank .... *2 of 12*
Closest major hub .... *Boston, 71 air miles*

TESTS

1. Character...86.1
2. Stability...76.8
3. Growth..41.1
4. Education..66.4
5. Jobs...58.3
6. Business..78.6
7. Money...73.6
8. Housing...44.5
9. Health...62.8
10. Diversions..99.7
11. Internet..60.5
12. Proximity..88.1

BASIC STATS

Population...10,463
Density 1,067.1
Born out of state................................44.7%
Homes built since 2000.....................12.7%
4 or more bedrooms 24.3%

RACE

Whites...86.0%
Blacks...6.1%
Hispanics...1.0%
Asians...0.3%
Native Americans 0.0%
Diversity index...................................25.2%

HOUSEHOLD INCOME LADDER

95th percentile $228,339
80th percentile $130,446
60th percentile $84,652
50th percentile $64,956
40th percentile $50,801
20th percentile $32,397

HOME VALUE LADDER

75th percentile $829,200
50th percentile $626,000
25th percentile $466,900

CHARACTER

Resilience..32.9%
Short commutes ....85.8% (★)

STABILITY

Living with two parents 68.8%
Occupied homes................................98.3% (★)

GROWTH

Population growth...................................-4.6%
Economic growth 19.7%

EDUCATION

High school graduates 93.1%
College graduates 35.6%

JOBS

MBSA workers...39.7%
Private-sector job growth 8.5%

BUSINESS

Small business growth 8.9%
Self-employed workers ....24.4% (★)

MONEY

Median annual earnings................$56,205 (★)
Living in poverty......................................8.3%

HOUSING

Home ownership.....................................67.0%
Monthly housing costs 37.8%

HEALTH

Health care workers..................................9.3%
Fair or poor health.............................11.1% (★)

DIVERSIONS

Stores per 10,000.............................114.8 (★)
Restaurants per 10,000.......................65.8 (★)

INTERNET

Broadband subscriptions 69.2%
Smartphone access 77.2%

PROXIMITY

Major hub miles..71
Major or mid-major miles.............................49

Vistancia, Arizona

Score ....*866.0 points*
National rank ....*9 of 2,084*
Percentile..*99.62%*
West rank..*6 of 471*
Arizona rank...*1 of 44*
Closest major hub ....*Phoenix, 27 air miles*

TESTS
1. Character..18.1
2. Stability...96.4
3. Growth...84.9
4. Education..87.3
5. Jobs...88.1
6. Business...56.1
7. Money..91.6
8. Housing..73.8
9. Health..53.2
10. Diversions...25.2
11. Internet..99.3
12. Proximity..92.0

BASIC STATS
Population....................................... 8,396
Density 3,393.7
Born out of state 75.3%
Homes built since 2000...........................97.1%
4 or more bedrooms 31.9%

RACE
Whites...83.7%
Blacks..1.4%
Hispanics...8.5%
Asians...1.5%
Native Americans 0.2%
Diversity index....................................28.9%

HOUSEHOLD INCOME LADDER
95th percentile ....>$250,000
80th percentile $182,731
60th percentile $121,569
50th percentile $102,852
40th percentile $86,889
20th percentile $53,500

HOME VALUE LADDER
75th percentile $475,400
50th percentile $374,600
25th percentile $307,500

CHARACTER
Resilience...11.4%
Short commutes 21.9%

STABILITY
Living with two parents ....92.5% (★)
Occupied homes..............................98.0% (★)

GROWTH
Population growth............................27.1% (★)
Economic growth 20.1%

EDUCATION
High school graduates ....98.1% (★)
College graduates ....53.4% (★)

JOBS
MBSA workers.................................55.6% (★)
Private-sector job growth ....19.2% (★)

BUSINESS
Small business growth ....11.3% (★)
Self-employed workers 9.8%

MONEY
Median annual earnings...............$66,774 (★)
Living in poverty...................................3.3% (★)

HOUSING
Home ownership..............................88.4% (★)
Monthly housing costs...........................27.7%

HEALTH
Health care workers................................9.2%
Fair or poor health................................15.6%

DIVERSIONS
Stores per 10,000.................................24.3
Restaurants per 10,000...........................17.5

INTERNET
Broadband subscriptions ....91.6% (★)
Smartphone access ....94.5% (★)

PROXIMITY
Major hub miles.....................................27 (★)
Major or mid-major miles..............................27

Waconia, Minnesota

Score ....*820.5 points*
National rank ....*30 of 2,084*
Percentile...*98.61%*
Midwest rank...*3 of 622*
Minnesota rank ....*2 of 53*
Closest major hub ....*Minneapolis, 27 air miles*

TESTS
1. Character..........................77.8
2. Stability................................91.5
3. Growth.................................45.2
4. Education.............................93.1
5. Jobs.....................................67.1
6. Business...............................36.4
7. Money..................................97.3
8. Housing................................63.1
9. Health...................................63.4
10. Diversions.........................19.8
11. Internet..............................73.8
12. Proximity............................92.0

BASIC STATS
Population.............................11,596
Density................................2,631.9
Born out of state....................27.7%
Homes built since 2000.........42.2%
4 or more bedrooms..............48.3%

RACE
Whites....................................95.3%
Blacks.....................................0.7%
Hispanics................................2.6%
Asians.....................................0.6%
Native Americans...................0.0%
Diversity index........................9.1%

HOUSEHOLD INCOME LADDER
95th percentile......................$247,275
80th percentile......................$176,091
60th percentile......................$115,569
50th percentile........................$98,984
40th percentile........................$82,320
20th percentile........................$48,461

HOME VALUE LADDER
75th percentile......................$380,700
50th percentile......................$299,400
25th percentile......................$232,000

CHARACTER
Resilience............................49.9% (★)
Short commutes......................33.4%

STABILITY
Living with two parents...........83.7% (★)
Occupied homes...................99.2% (★)

GROWTH
Population growth.....................2.8%
Economic growth......................9.6%

EDUCATION
High school graduates..........98.6% (★)
College graduates.................57.3% (★)

JOBS
MBSA workers.......................45.5% (★)
Private-sector job growth........11.6%

BUSINESS
Small business growth..............3.1%
Self-employed workers..............6.3%

MONEY
Median annual earnings...........$70,807 (★)
Living in poverty......................2.6% (★)

HOUSING
Home ownership....................78.7% (★)
Monthly housing costs.............30.2%

HEALTH
Health care workers..................8.2%
Fair or poor health...................9.3% (★)

DIVERSIONS
Stores per 10,000......................20.2
Restaurants per 10,000.............15.9

INTERNET
Broadband subscriptions........77.7% (★)
Smartphone access..................84.2%

PROXIMITY
Major hub miles.........................27 (★)
Major or mid-major miles..............27

Warwick, New York

Score ....*758.8 points*
National rank ....*112 of 2,084*
Percentile..*94.67%*
East rank...*14 of 246*
New York rank ....*3 of 65*
Closest major hub ....*New York, 44 air miles*

TESTS
1. Character.................................47.7
2. Stability..................................80.1
3. Growth...................................45.9
4. Education...............................73.4
5. Jobs.......................................65.1
6. Business.................................50.8
7. Money....................................90.1
8. Housing..................................50.1
9. Health....................................55.2
10. Diversions.............................46.8
11. Internet 62.5
12. Proximity...............................91.1

BASIC STATS
Population.....................................11,884
Density 1,334.8
Born out of state 32.4%
Homes built since 2000.............. 14.3%
4 or more bedrooms 25.9%

RACE
Whites..82.8%
Blacks...1.1%
Hispanics 11.9%
Asians...1.1%
Native Americans 1.5%
Diversity index.................................30.0%

HOUSEHOLD INCOME LADDER
95th percentile $219,964
80th percentile $153,454
60th percentile $104,677
50th percentile $82,763
40th percentile $63,592
20th percentile $34,496

HOME VALUE LADDER
75th percentile $399,000
50th percentile $325,700
25th percentile $251,200

CHARACTER
Resilience..28.4%
Short commutes 32.5%

STABILITY
Living with two parents .... 76.8% (★)
Occupied homes.............................. 97.2% (★)

GROWTH
Population growth.............................0.2%
Economic growth 16.7%

EDUCATION
High school graduates .... 96.6% (★)
College graduates .... 39.5% (★)

JOBS
MBSA workers...................................... 44.2% (★)
Private-sector job growth 10.9%

BUSINESS
Small business growth 5.6%
Self-employed workers 10.6%

MONEY
Median annual earnings................$67,733 (★)
Living in poverty..................................5.5% (★)

HOUSING
Home ownership.............................64.9%
Monthly housing costs 31.9%

HEALTH
Health care workers..........................9.4%
Fair or poor health...........................14.9%

DIVERSIONS
Stores per 10,000.............................41.3
Restaurants per 10,000.....................23.8

INTERNET
Broadband subscriptions 74.6%
Smartphone access 75.4%

PROXIMITY
Major hub miles.............................. 44
Major or mid-major miles................. 27

Weatherford, Texas

Score ....*726.7 points*
National rank ....*201 of 2,084*
Percentile...*90.40%*
South rank ....*50 of 745*
Texas rank...*14 of 173*
Closest major hub ....*Dallas, 44 air miles*

TESTS

1. Character............................58.7
2. Stability...............................72.0
3. Growth.................................50.3
4. Education.............................57.5
5. Jobs....................................56.4
6. Business..............................66.7
7. Money.................................69.7
8. Housing...............................57.8
9. Health.................................57.2
10. Diversions...........................21.8
11. Internet..............................69.6
12. Proximity............................89.0

BASIC STATS

Population................................41,186
Density....................................1,281.4
Born out of state.....................33.1%
Homes built since 2000............32.0%
4 or more bedrooms.................19.7%

RACE

Whites.....................................79.6%
Blacks......................................2.3%
Hispanics................................14.5%
Asians......................................0.5%
Native Americans.....................0.6%
Diversity index........................34.4%

HOUSEHOLD INCOME LADDER

95th percentile.....................$240,860
80th percentile.....................$137,721
60th percentile.....................$87,858
50th percentile.....................$72,525
40th percentile.....................$60,037
20th percentile.....................$31,734

HOME VALUE LADDER

75th percentile.....................$290,800
50th percentile.....................$191,700
25th percentile.....................$122,400

CHARACTER

Resilience................................32.1%
Short commutes.......................42.7%

STABILITY

Living with two parents............71.7%
Occupied homes......................94.7%

GROWTH

Population growth...................10.3% (★)
Economic growth.....................0.5%

EDUCATION

High school graduates.............89.9%
College graduates...................28.9%

JOBS

MBSA workers.........................39.4%
Private-sector job growth.........6.7%

BUSINESS

Small business growth.............22.1% (★)
Self-employed workers.............8.5%

MONEY

Median annual earnings...........$52,648 (★)
Living in poverty......................8.6%

HOUSING

Home ownership......................67.8%
Monthly housing costs..............27.6%

HEALTH

Health care workers.................9.3%
Fair or poor health...................13.8%

DIVERSIONS

Stores per 10,000....................25.9
Restaurants per 10,000............13.9

INTERNET

Broadband subscriptions..........70.4%
Smartphone access..................85.1% (★)

PROXIMITY

Major hub miles.......................44
Major or mid-major miles.........44

Wellington, Colorado

Score ....*826.0 points*
National rank ....*26 of 2,084*
Percentile..*98.80%*
West rank..*13 of 471*
Colorado rank ....*6 of 47*
Closest major hub ....*Denver, 68 air miles*

TESTS
1. Character..35.3
2. Stability...81.1
3. Growth..90.5
4. Education.......................................72.8
5. Jobs..67.4
6. Business...66.6
7. Money...75.3
8. Housing..72.3
9. Health...61.3
10. Diversions......................................41.6
11. Internet 77.0
12. Proximity..84.8

BASIC STATS
Population.. 7,920
Density 2,911.8
Born out of state.............................45.5%
Homes built since 2000...................54.7%
4 or more bedrooms 31.5%

RACE
Whites...86.6%
Blacks 1.2%
Hispanics 9.3%
Asians...0.0%
Native Americans 0.4%
Diversity index.................................24.1%

HOUSEHOLD INCOME LADDER
95th percentile $243,327
80th percentile $140,625
60th percentile $101,449
50th percentile $91,461
40th percentile $82,170
20th percentile $42,394

HOME VALUE LADDER
75th percentile $370,700
50th percentile $316,100
25th percentile $238,100

CHARACTER
Resilience..21.8%
Short commutes 26.9%

STABILITY
Living with two parents 70.5%
Occupied homes.............................100.0% (★)

GROWTH
Population growth............................ 34.3% (★)
Economic growth .... 26.9% (★)

EDUCATION
High school graduates ....96.9% (★)
College graduates 38.4%

JOBS
MBSA workers..................................41.3% (★)
Private-sector job growth .... 17.3% (★)

BUSINESS
Small business growth ....14.6% (★)
Self-employed workers ....12.2% (★)

MONEY
Median annual earnings................$56,545 (★)
Living in poverty..................................7.0% (★)

HOUSING
Home ownership............................. 90.0% (★)
Monthly housing costs......................29.9%

HEALTH
Health care workers...........................9.2%
Fair or poor health........................... 11.7% (★)

DIVERSIONS
Stores per 10,000.............................36.0
Restaurants per 10,000....................23.0

INTERNET
Broadband subscriptions ....80.0% (★)
Smartphone access .... 85.7% (★)

PROXIMITY
Major hub miles.................................. 68
Major or mid-major miles................................ 68

Westminster, Maryland

Score ....*754.8 points*
National rank ....*120 of 2,084*
Percentile *94.29%*
East rank ....*16 of 246*
Maryland rank ....*2 of 23*
Closest major hub ....*Baltimore, 23 air miles*

TESTS
1. Character 61.0
2. Stability 81.5
3. Growth 35.3
4. Education 77.8
5. Jobs 65.6
6. Business 33.9
7. Money 89.2
8. Housing 59.4
9. Health 64.3
10. Diversions 28.0
11. Internet 66.1
12. Proximity 92.7

BASIC STATS
Population 71,361
Density 1,236.9
Born out of state 35.1%
Homes built since 2000 .... 16.5%
4 or more bedrooms 36.8%

RACE
Whites 85.4%
Blacks 5.4%
Hispanics 3.9%
Asians 2.8%
Native Americans 0.2%
Diversity index 26.5%

HOUSEHOLD INCOME LADDER
95th percentile .... >$250,000
80th percentile $167,818
60th percentile $114,582
50th percentile $97,720
40th percentile $79,539
20th percentile $40,653

HOME VALUE LADDER
75th percentile $439,200
50th percentile $345,500
25th percentile $260,900

CHARACTER
Resilience .... 38.4% (★)
Short commutes 31.7%

STABILITY
Living with two parents .... 81.1% (★)
Occupied homes 96.4%

GROWTH
Population growth .... -4.2%
Economic growth 9.2%

EDUCATION
High school graduates 94.7%
College graduates .... 47.4% (★)

JOBS
MBSA workers .... 49.4% (★)
Private-sector job growth 4.8%

BUSINESS
Small business growth .... -1.0%
Self-employed workers 7.4%

MONEY
Median annual earnings .... $66,472 (★)
Living in poverty .... 5.0% (★)

HOUSING
Home ownership .... 77.3% (★)
Monthly housing costs 32.3%

HEALTH
Health care workers 9.4%
Fair or poor health .... 10.5% (★)

DIVERSIONS
Stores per 10,000 .... 29.6
Restaurants per 10,000 .... 16.4

INTERNET
Broadband subscriptions 71.6%
Smartphone access 80.9%

PROXIMITY
Major hub miles .... 23 (★)
Major or mid-major miles .... 23 (★)

West Point, New York

Score .... *759.4 points*
National rank .... *109 of 2,084*
Percentile *94.82%*
East rank .... *13 of 246*
New York rank .... *2 of 65*
Closest major hub .... *Bridgeport, 39 air miles*

TESTS

1. Character	70.7
2. Stability	71.0
3. Growth	43.5
4. Education	85.7
5. Jobs	64.6
6. Business	40.4
7. Money	81.9
8. Housing	28.0
9. Health	51.8
10. Diversions	46.8
11. Internet	79.9
12. Proximity	95.1

BASIC STATS

Population	11,912
Density	2,889.9
Born out of state	63.6%
Homes built since 2000	14.7%
4 or more bedrooms	22.0%

RACE

Whites	64.6%
Blacks	10.2%
Hispanics	11.9%
Asians	6.5%
Native Americans	0.3%
Diversity index	55.0%

HOUSEHOLD INCOME LADDER

95th percentile	$244,839
80th percentile	$165,016
60th percentile	$116,000
50th percentile	$98,904
40th percentile	$81,160
20th percentile	$48,663

HOME VALUE LADDER

75th percentile	$311,700
50th percentile	$235,900
25th percentile	$159,600

CHARACTER

Resilience	28.4%
Short commutes	72.4%

STABILITY

Living with two parents	84.5% (★)
Occupied homes	89.6%

GROWTH

Population growth	-1.5%
Economic growth	16.7%

EDUCATION

High school graduates	95.2%
College graduates	56.1% (★)

JOBS

MBSA workers	43.7% (★)
Private-sector job growth	10.9%

BUSINESS

Small business growth	5.6%
Self-employed workers	6.6%

MONEY

Median annual earnings	$59,174 (★)
Living in poverty	3.3% (★)

HOUSING

Home ownership	43.7%
Monthly housing costs	36.3%

HEALTH

Health care workers	8.2%
Fair or poor health	14.9%

DIVERSIONS

Stores per 10,000	41.3
Restaurants per 10,000	23.8

INTERNET

Broadband subscriptions	84.6% (★)
Smartphone access	85.3% (★)

PROXIMITY

Major hub miles	39
Major or mid-major miles	11 (★)

Whitefish, Montana

Score ....*796.6 points*
National rank ....*54 of 2,084*
Percentile..*97.46%*
West rank...*25 of 471*
Montana rank .... *1 of 19*
Closest major hub ....*Seattle, 373 air miles*

TESTS
1. Character.............................61.4
2. Stability................................82.7
3. Growth.................................75.3
4. Education.............................91.8
5. Jobs.....................................71.1
6. Business...............................58.2
7. Money..................................62.7
8. Housing................................46.0
9. Health..................................62.1
10. Diversions...........................57.4
11. Internet...............................69.5
12. Proximity.............................58.4

BASIC STATS
Population.......................... 7,657
Density............................. 1,683.6
Born out of state.................63.5%
Homes built since 2000............33.2%
4 or more bedrooms 18.3%

RACE
Whites..................................96.6%
Blacks....................................0.0%
Hispanics...............................2.2%
Asians....................................0.3%
Native Americans 0.6%
Diversity index.......................6.6%

HOUSEHOLD INCOME LADDER
95th percentile $242,590
80th percentile $119,353
60th percentile $65,890
50th percentile $51,468
40th percentile $46,223
20th percentile $24,250

HOME VALUE LADDER
75th percentile $550,500
50th percentile $360,300
25th percentile $270,700

CHARACTER
Resilience..............................26.4%
Short commutes.....................61.1%

STABILITY
Living with two parents ....87.1% (★)
Occupied homes.....................94.9%

GROWTH
Population growth...........................22.3% (★)
Economic growth....................14.6%

EDUCATION
High school graduates ....97.6% (★)
College graduates ....57.7% (★)

JOBS
MBSA workers.......................47.3% (★)
Private-sector job growth 14.0%

BUSINESS
Small business growth 9.7%
Self-employed workers ....11.4% (★)

MONEY
Median annual earnings.......................$45,483
Living in poverty............................8.5%

HOUSING
Home ownership.....................58.5%
Monthly housing costs...........31.2%

HEALTH
Health care workers................10.8%
Fair or poor health.................13.5%

DIVERSIONS
Stores per 10,000....................46.4
Restaurants per 10,000..................28.8 (★)

INTERNET
Broadband subscriptions 74.0%
Smartphone access 82.5%

PROXIMITY
Major hub miles.......................373
Major or mid-major miles............148

White Rock, New Mexico

Score ....*837.6 points*
National rank ....*21 of 2,084*
Percentile...*99.04%*
West rank.. *11 of 471*
New Mexico rank... *1 of 31*
Closest major hub .... *Denver, 277 air miles*

TESTS
1. Character...73.9
2. Stability..96.2
3. Growth..48.6
4. Education...99.7
5. Jobs...88.0
6. Business...20.4
7. Money..99.7
8. Housing..95.7
9. Health..50.4
10. Diversions..15.9
11. Internet 73.8
12. Proximity..75.3

BASIC STATS
Population... 5,274
Density 2,770.0
Born out of state 61.1%
Homes built since 2000.....................6.5%
4 or more bedrooms 36.5%

RACE
Whites...76.5%
Blacks...0.4%
Hispanics 15.4%
Asians...1.8%
Native Americans 1.6%
Diversity index...................................38.9%

HOUSEHOLD INCOME LADDER
95th percentile ....>$250,000
80th percentile $206,375
60th percentile $162,469
50th percentile $133,125
40th percentile $120,178
20th percentile $76,692

HOME VALUE LADDER
75th percentile $391,100
50th percentile $294,200
25th percentile $230,400

CHARACTER
Resilience................................ 39.5% (★)
Short commutes 51.5%

STABILITY
Living with two parents .... 90.0% (★)
Occupied homes............................. 98.8% (★)

GROWTH
Population growth.......................................0.9%
Economic growth 19.5%

EDUCATION
High school graduates ....100.0% (★)
College graduates .... 70.2% (★)

JOBS
MBSA workers.. 75.1% (★)
Private-sector job growth 15.0%

BUSINESS
Small business growth ....-3.0%
Self-employed workers 3.2%

MONEY
Median annual earnings............. $102,451 (★)
Living in poverty.....................................2.4% (★)

HOUSING
Home ownership................................ 91.6% (★)
Monthly housing costs..................... 16.0% (★)

HEALTH
Health care workers......................................4.4%
Fair or poor health............................... 10.4% (★)

DIVERSIONS
Stores per 10,000 .... 16.3
Restaurants per 10,000...........................15.3

INTERNET
Broadband subscriptions .... 83.9% (★)
Smartphone access 80.0%

PROXIMITY
Major hub miles...277
Major or mid-major miles................................ 52

Williamsburg, Virginia

Score	*767.6 points*
National rank	*101 of 2,084*
Percentile	*95.20%*
South rank	*31 of 745*
Virginia rank	*5 of 41*
Closest major hub	*Virginia Beach, 35 air miles*

TESTS

1. Character	60.2
2. Stability	66.8
3. Growth	51.8
4. Education	82.0
5. Jobs	68.3
6. Business	39.1
7. Money	70.7
8. Housing	57.2
9. Health	54.4
10. Diversions	53.2
11. Internet	73.3
12. Proximity	90.6

BASIC STATS

Population	81,242
Density	1,452.5
Born out of state	61.3%
Homes built since 2000	34.3%
4 or more bedrooms	29.7%

RACE

Whites	74.2%
Blacks	13.1%
Hispanics	5.8%
Asians	3.5%
Native Americans	0.2%
Diversity index	42.7%

HOUSEHOLD INCOME LADDER

95th percentile	>$250,000
80th percentile	$149,895
60th percentile	$102,636
50th percentile	$85,468
40th percentile	$68,521
20th percentile	$37,744

HOME VALUE LADDER

75th percentile	$453,600
50th percentile	$328,400
25th percentile	$239,200

CHARACTER

Resilience	28.3%
Short commutes	54.5%

STABILITY

Living with two parents	71.2%
Occupied homes	92.1%

GROWTH

Population growth	3.9%
Economic growth	18.1%

EDUCATION

High school graduates	96.0% (★)
College graduates	50.8% (★)

JOBS

MBSA workers	49.2% (★)
Private-sector job growth	8.3%

BUSINESS

Small business growth	3.6%
Self-employed workers	7.1%

MONEY

Median annual earnings	$53,403 (★)
Living in poverty	8.4%

HOUSING

Home ownership	72.3%
Monthly housing costs	30.9%

HEALTH

Health care workers	8.3%
Fair or poor health	13.8%

DIVERSIONS

Stores per 10,000	43.0
Restaurants per 10,000	27.7 (★)

INTERNET

Broadband subscriptions	80.0% (★)
Smartphone access	82.1%

PROXIMITY

Major hub miles	35
Major or mid-major miles	35

Woodcreek, Texas

Score ....*797.8 points*
National rank ....*51 of 2,084*
Percentile...*97.60%*
South rank .... *18 of 745*
Texas rank... *7 of 173*
Closest major hub ....*Austin, 32 air miles*

TESTS
1. Character.......................................51.9
2. Stability...74.2
3. Growth...71.7
4. Education.......................................70.5
5. Jobs..80.4
6. Business...90.5
7. Money..64.4
8. Housing..60.1
9. Health...44.9
10. Diversions....................................32.4
11. Internet 65.7
12. Proximity......................................91.1

BASIC STATS
Population.. 5,311
Density 1,086.1
Born out of state 29.2%
Homes built since 2000............................41.7%
4 or more bedrooms 14.8%

RACE
Whites..88.8%
Blacks..0.0%
Hispanics 10.0%
Asians..0.0%
Native Americans 0.0%
Diversity index................................20.1%

HOUSEHOLD INCOME LADDER
95th percentile $164,154
80th percentile $110,609
60th percentile $81,339
50th percentile $67,016
40th percentile $58,778
20th percentile $32,821

HOME VALUE LADDER
75th percentile $286,200
50th percentile $217,700
25th percentile $162,500

CHARACTER
Resilience...25.7%
Short commutes 46.2%

STABILITY
Living with two parents .... 78.6% (★)
Occupied homes..............................93.4%

GROWTH
Population growth............................ 14.5% (★)
Economic growth .... 26.8% (★)

EDUCATION
High school graduates 94.2%
College graduates ....39.2% (★)

JOBS
MBSA workers.......................................42.1% (★)
Private-sector job growth .... 29.4% (★)

BUSINESS
Small business growth ....25.3% (★)
Self-employed workers ....14.7% (★)

MONEY
Median annual earnings.......................$44,500
Living in poverty...............................6.0% (★)

HOUSING
Home ownership............................. 80.6% (★)
Monthly housing costs...........................33.8%

HEALTH
Health care workers...............................8.0%
Fair or poor health...............................18.0%

DIVERSIONS
Stores per 10,000...................................31.1
Restaurants per 10,000..................................18.9

INTERNET
Broadband subscriptions 62.3%
Smartphone access ....86.8% (★)

PROXIMITY
Major hub miles...32 (★)
Major or mid-major miles...............................32

Woodland Park, Colorado

Score ....*794.7 points*
National rank ....*59 of 2,084*
Percentile..*97.22%*
West rank..*29 of 471*
Colorado rank .... *13 of 47*
Closest major hub ....*Denver, 50 air miles*

TESTS
1. Character....................................52.0
2. Stability......................................82.1
3. Growth.......................................44.5
4. Education....................................78.7
5. Jobs...70.9
6. Business.....................................62.7
7. Money 71.6
8. Housing......................................61.7
9. Health..71.1
10. Diversions..................................30.1
11. Internet 77.5
12. Proximity....................................91.8

BASIC STATS
Population..................................10,839
Density 1,275.3
Born out of state..........................73.2%
Homes built since 2000................24.0%
4 or more bedrooms 30.0%

RACE
Whites...89.6%
Blacks...0.8%
Hispanics 4.9%
Asians...1.1%
Native Americans 0.6%
Diversity index.............................19.4%

HOUSEHOLD INCOME LADDER
95th percentile $214,350
80th percentile $128,596
60th percentile $88,080
50th percentile $69,653
40th percentile $57,799
20th percentile $36,580

HOME VALUE LADDER
75th percentile $396,100
50th percentile $321,700
25th percentile $240,200

CHARACTER
Resilience......................................29.5%
Short commutes 37.3%

STABILITY
Living with two parents .... 76.7% (★)
Occupied homes.............................. 98.3% (★)

GROWTH
Population growth..........................-1.3%
Economic growth 17.8%

EDUCATION
High school graduates .... 98.5% (★)
College graduates .... 43.5% (★)

JOBS
MBSA workers................................ 48.4% (★)
Private-sector job growth 12.3%

BUSINESS
Small business growth 10.2%
Self-employed workers .... 12.9% (★)

MONEY
Median annual earnings...............$53,329 (★)
Living in poverty.................................7.5% (★)

HOUSING
Home ownership .... 79.6% (★)
Monthly housing costs...........................31.9%

HEALTH
Health care workers................................12.1%
Fair or poor health.......................... 10.9% (★)

DIVERSIONS
Stores per 10,000.................................29.4
Restaurants per 10,000...........................18.2

INTERNET
Broadband subscriptions .... 78.1% (★)
Smartphone access .... 87.4% (★)

PROXIMITY
Major hub miles.................................... 50
Major or mid-major miles.......................18 (★)

World Golf Village, Florida

Score .... *904.1 points*
National rank .... *4 of 2,084*
Percentile *99.86%*
South rank .... *2 of 745*
Florida rank .... *1 of 63*
Closest major hub .... *Jacksonville, 21 air miles*

TESTS
1. Character..41.0
2. Stability..73.0
3. Growth..94.5
4. Education..86.7
5. Jobs..97.4
6. Business..74.2
7. Money...84.3
8. Housing...67.5
9. Health...60.0
10. Diversions..39.4
11. Internet..91.9
12. Proximity..94.2

BASIC STATS
Population...11,225
Density..1,739.8
Born out of state...................................67.2%
Homes built since 2000.........................93.5%
4 or more bedrooms..............................60.9%

RACE
Whites..76.0%
Blacks...6.2%
Hispanics...12.5%
Asians...2.9%
Native Americans....................................0.0%
Diversity index......................................40.2%

HOUSEHOLD INCOME LADDER
95th percentile..................................$237,070
80th percentile..................................$158,694
60th percentile..................................$116,756
50th percentile..................................$101,243
40th percentile....................................$90,684
20th percentile....................................$72,261

HOME VALUE LADDER
75th percentile..................................$300,100
50th percentile..................................$267,800
25th percentile..................................$230,600

CHARACTER
Resilience...32.0%
Short commutes.....................................12.4%

STABILITY
Living with two parents.........................62.4%
Occupied homes...............................98.6% (★)

GROWTH
Population growth.............................60.2% (★)
Economic growth...............................32.0% (★)

EDUCATION
High school graduates......................97.8% (★)
College graduates.............................53.3% (★)

JOBS
MBSA workers....................................58.6% (★)
Private-sector job growth................26.7% (★)

BUSINESS
Small business growth......................24.1% (★)
Self-employed workers...........................10.0%

MONEY
Median annual earnings...............$64,254 (★)
Living in poverty.................................6.3% (★)

HOUSING
Home ownership...............................89.1% (★)
Monthly housing costs............................33.2%

HEALTH
Health care workers..................................9.5%
Fair or poor health................................12.7%

DIVERSIONS
Stores per 10,000......................................35.4
Restaurants per 10,000.............................21.7

INTERNET
Broadband subscriptions................84.0% (★)
Smartphone access............................93.8% (★)

PROXIMITY
Major hub miles.......................................21 (★)
Major or mid-major miles.......................21 (★)

Zimmerman, Minnesota

Score ....*728.9 points*
National rank ....*189 of 2,084*
Percentile...*90.97%*
Midwest rank...*44 of 622*
Minnesota rank ....*12 of 53*
Closest major hub ....*Minneapolis, 37 air miles*

TESTS
1. Character..............................62.8
2. Stability.................................93.8
3. Growth.................................35.0
4. Education.............................56.0
5. Jobs.......................................44.5
6. Business................................50.4
7. Money...................................72.6
8. Housing................................68.9
9. Health...................................60.9
10. Diversions...........................14.4
11. Internet 79.4
12. Proximity............................90.2

BASIC STATS
Population............................. 8,081
Density 855.8
Born out of state 17.5%
Homes built since 2000............42.1%
4 or more bedrooms 43.0%

RACE
Whites....................................91.3%
Blacks......................................0.4%
Hispanics 2.8%
Asians......................................1.3%
Native Americans 0.0%
Diversity index........................16.4%

HOUSEHOLD INCOME LADDER
95th percentile $217,076
80th percentile $137,463
60th percentile $96,393
50th percentile $83,131
40th percentile $73,013
20th percentile $45,458

HOME VALUE LADDER
75th percentile $256,600
50th percentile $202,700
25th percentile $156,000

CHARACTER
Resilience...........................44.9% (★)
Short commutes 19.4%

STABILITY
Living with two parents ....86.1% (★)
Occupied homes................................99.2% (★)

GROWTH
Population growth............................-0.8%
Economic growth 0.7%

EDUCATION
High school graduates ....97.6% (★)
College graduates 17.0%

JOBS
MBSA workers.............................32.3%
Private-sector job growth 1.8%

BUSINESS
Small business growth ....12.1% (★)
Self-employed workers 7.2%

MONEY
Median annual earnings...............$52,753 (★)
Living in poverty....................................6.0% (★)

HOUSING
Home ownership.............................87.5% (★)
Monthly housing costs............................31.1%

HEALTH
Health care workers............................8.4%
Fair or poor health..............................10.8% (★)

DIVERSIONS
Stores per 10,000............................20.8
Restaurants per 10,000......................11.3

INTERNET
Broadband subscriptions ....79.4% (★)
Smartphone access ....88.4% (★)

PROXIMITY
Major hub miles 37
Major or mid-major miles...............37

Chapter 5

MADE TO ORDER

That should be enough information, don't you think?

The previous three chapters submerged you in results for 24 parts of 12 tests, lists of 209 Dreamtowns and 313 Honorable Mentions, and detailed scorecards with 62 statistics for each Dreamtown. What more could you possibly need?

A little assistance, perhaps.

This chapter is designed to help you cut through the statistical thicket. It offers dozens of quality-of-life standings that have been filtered for specific characteristics. If you know precisely what attributes you're seeking, these lists are made to order for you.

But be careful. It's important that you understand the concept of filtering. The standings in this chapter do not necessarily pinpoint a town's greatest strengths or most glaring weaknesses. That's what the 12 test scores are supposed to do.

The filtering process begins with the final quality-of-life standings that you saw in Chapter 3 — and then winnows out any communities that fail to meet a specific standard. The result is a new set of rankings — still based on the results of all 12 tests, yet excluding any town that lacks a certain characteristic.

The filtered rankings for a given state, say Alabama, are naturally limited to towns within its boundaries. The same principle holds true for the other lists in this chapter, such as places that have populations between 100,000 and 199,999, or are located north of the 40th parallel, or contain more than 50 stores per 100,000 residents. All communities that fail to reach a threshold are removed, while those that qualify are ranked by their overall quality-of-life scores.

You'll notice that each town's name is preceded by one number and followed by a second. The former is its rank in the filtered standings. The latter, which is in parentheses, is its position in the master rankings for quality of life. Two examples: Daphne is the No. 1 small town in Alabama, while its national rank is 110th. And Vineyard Haven, Massachusetts, is second in the East and 23rd nationally.

You'll also see a numeral in brackets at the end of each list's subhead. It shows the number of small towns that qualify for that particular set of standings — not just Dreamtowns, but all towns that meet the standard. Alabama, for instance, has 37 small towns, while there are 246 in the East and 121 in the 100,000-199,999 population range.

The following state-by-state rankings include all Dreamtowns and Honorable Mentions within each state, no matter how many. The subsequent two sections — the standings for regions and population groups — encompass all Dreamtowns. The remainder of the chapter is confined to lists of the 25 highest-rated towns under each subhead, excluding any additional Dreamtowns that also meet the standard (yet are lower in the overall rankings).

States

Five states contain more than 70 small towns, offering an exceptionally wide range of options. All five, as you would expect, are among the nation's most populous states. They include the two biggest, California and Texas, as well as three others in the top seven: Pennsylvania, Illinois, and Ohio.

That's where the similarities end. An impressive number of small towns in California (16) and Texas (14) have achieved the status of Dreamtowns. But the other three states have enjoyed very little success, gathering only five elite designations between them — two Dreamtowns each in Illinois and Ohio, just one in Pennsylvania.

You'll find similar patterns across the country. Some states are blessed with unexpectedly high concentrations of top-flight communities, while others have virtually nothing to show.

The most prosperous are Colorado (22 Dreamtowns out of 47 small towns), Minnesota (16 of 53), and Utah (12 of 20). They're the only three states to meet a stringent pair of statistical standards: a minimum of 10 Dreamtowns and a conversion rate of 30% or better. The rate for the entire nation, of course, is 10% — 209 Dreamtowns out of 2,084 small towns.

At the opposite end of the scale are 10 states that contain a grand total of 273 small towns, yet don't have a Dreamtown among them: Alaska, Arkansas, Hawaii, Indiana, Kentucky, Nebraska, North Dakota,

Oklahoma, Rhode Island, and West Virginia. One member of this unfortunate group, Rhode Island, is unique in its complete lack of small towns. Rhode Island's only urbanized area, Providence, is a major hub, while its only urban cluster, Charlestown, has just 2,724 residents, short of the threshold for inclusion in this book.

Each state is listed below with its Dreamtowns and Honorable Mentions, the only time in this chapter that the latter are included.

Alabama [37]

DREAMTOWNS
1. Daphne (110)

HONORABLE MENTIONS
2. Auburn (427)

Alaska [9]

[none]

Arizona [44]

DREAMTOWNS
1. Vistancia (9)
2. Vail (92)
3. Corona de Tucson (98)
4. Sedona (130)

HONORABLE MENTIONS
5. Estrella (211)
6. Marana West (247)
7. Sahuarita (260)
8. Prescott Valley (277)
9. Village of Oak Creek (Big Park) (370)
10. Flagstaff (378)

Arkansas [39]

[none]

California [145]

DREAMTOWNS
1. Lake of the Pines (32)
2. Rancho Murieta (36)
3. Truckee (39)
4. Mountain House (87)
5. Half Moon Bay (99)

6. Livermore (102)
7. Petaluma (124)
8. Davis (154)
9. Auburn (155)
10. Discovery Bay (161)
11. Santa Cruz (170)
12. Morro Bay (174)
13. Bishop (177)
14. Plumas Lake (186)
15. Solvang (197)
16. Cambria (198)

HONORABLE MENTIONS
17. St. Helena (211)
18. Camarillo (218)
19. Placerville (220)
20. Rio Vista (228)
21. Gilroy (234)
22. Mammoth Lakes (242)
23. Lake Wildwood (259)
24. Arroyo Grande (264)
25. Forestville (273)
26. Paso Robles (283)
27. Grass Valley (288)
28. Sonora (315)
29. Sonoma (325)
30. Silver Lakes (336)
31. San Luis Obispo (342)
32. Jackson (353)
33. Simi Valley (376)
34. Rancho Calaveras (404)
35. South Lake Tahoe (425)
36. Bonadelle Ranchos (434)
37. Chico (440)
38. Escalon (474)
39. Cloverdale (506)
40. Redding (515)
40. Vacaville (515)

Colorado [47]

DREAMTOWNS
1. Roxborough Park (5)
2. Evergreen (7)
3. Lafayette (11)

4. Aspen (13)
5. Breckenridge (25)
6. Wellington (26)
7. Silverthorne (27)
8. Vail (31)
9. Steamboat Springs (34)
10. Boulder (37)
11. Salida (46)
12. Johnstown (58)
13. Woodland Park (59)
14. Basalt (72)
15. Estes Park (76)
16. Firestone (90)
17. Gunnison (97)
18. Gypsum (131)
19. Eaton (132)
20. Eagle (142)
21. Edwards (145)
22. Longmont (165)

HONORABLE MENTIONS

23. Durango (210)
24. Leadville (283)
25. New Castle (304)
26. Carbondale (321)
27. Pagosa Springs (335)
28. Canon City (457)
29. Montrose (492)
30. Greeley (495)

Connecticut [8]

DREAMTOWNS

1. Lake Pocotopaug (74)
2. Colchester (166)

HONORABLE MENTIONS

3. Danbury (215)

Delaware [8]

DREAMTOWNS

1. Lewes (41)
2. Ocean View (53)
3. Middletown (113)

HONORABLE MENTIONS

4. Long Neck (326)

Florida [63]

DREAMTOWNS
1. World Golf Village (4)
2. Jupiter Farms (38)
3. Fernandina Beach (61)
4. Santa Rosa Beach (70)
5. Orangetree (79)
6. St. Augustine (95)
7. Big Pine Key (156)
8. Key Largo (157)

HONORABLE MENTIONS
9. Sugarmill Woods (222)
10. Wedgefield (230)
11. Sebastian (307)
12. Yulee (312)
13. North Port (355)
14. Alachua (361)
15. Spring Hill (397)
16. Marathon (400)
17. Leesburg (424)
18. Lady Lake (442)
19. Titusville (447)
20. Crawfordville (498)
21. Keystone Heights (501)

Georgia [65]

DREAMTOWNS
1. Buckhead (Bryan County) (10)
2. St. Simons (16)

HONORABLE MENTIONS
3. Jefferson (235)
4. Rincon (391)
5. Athens (469)
6. Winder (478)
7. Warner Robins (487)

Hawaii [15]

[none]

Idaho [21]

DREAMTOWNS
1. Rigby (73)

2. Star (104)
3. Kuna (169)
4. Moscow (174)
5. Coeur d'Alene (183)
6. Idaho Falls (207)

HONORABLE MENTIONS
7. Hailey (302)
8. Pocatello (334)
9. Sandpoint (343)
10. Rathdrum (374)
11. Twin Falls (427)

Illinois [79]

DREAMTOWNS
1. Monticello (149)
2. Breese (168)

HONORABLE MENTIONS
3. Waterloo (217)
4. Mahomet (257)
5. Effingham (273)
6. St. Joseph (294)
7. Byron (341)
8. Bloomington (370)
9. Highland (377)
10. Morris (414)
11. Jerseyville (420)
12. Springfield (436)
13. Mascoutah (447)
14. Braidwood (490)
15. Lake Holiday (501)

Indiana [68]

HONORABLE MENTIONS
1. Jasper (295)
2. Columbus (319)
3. Lebanon (365)
4. Bloomington (380)
5. Lafayette (441)
6. Columbia City (445)
7. Batesville (467)
8. Angola (495)
9. Warsaw (511)

Iowa [55]

DREAMTOWNS
1. Spirit Lake (62)
2. Orange City (77)
3. Decorah (105)
4. Pella (107)
5. Carroll (108)
6. Sioux Center (129)
7. Mount Vernon (143)
8. Iowa City (159)

HONORABLE MENTIONS
9. Clear Lake (213)
10. Indianola (244)
11. Winterset (246)
12. Ames (250)
13. Le Mars (279)
14. Cedar Rapids (286)
15. Waverly (309)
16. Dubuque (387)
17. Grinnell (411)
18. Fairfield (416)
19. Algona (419)
20. Nevada (456)
21. Independence (457)
22. Spencer (460)
23. Mason City (477)

Kansas [40]

DREAMTOWNS
1. McPherson (133)
2. Colby (187)

HONORABLE MENTIONS
3. Spring Hill (254)
4. Eudora (263)
5. Lawrence (308)
6. Wamego (354)
7. Pratt (373)
8. Tonganoxie (382)
9. El Dorado (409)

Kentucky [48]

HONORABLE MENTIONS
   1. Versailles (394)
   2. Georgetown (518)

Louisiana [41]

DREAMTOWNS
   1. Mandeville (64)

HONORABLE MENTIONS
   2. Slidell (289)

Maine [9]

DREAMTOWNS
   1. Kennebunk (43)
   2. Brunswick (179)

Maryland [23]

DREAMTOWNS
   1. Ocean Pines (71)
   2. Westminster (120)
   3. Leonardtown (135)
   4. Frederick (137)
   5. Chesapeake Beach (147)
   6. Brunswick (203)

HONORABLE MENTIONS
   7. Easton (218)
   8. Shady Side (262)
   9. Manchester (300)
   10. Emmitsburg (320)
   11. Lexington Park (336)
   12. Thurmont (360)
   13. Long Beach (363)
   14. Waldorf (437)

Massachusetts [12]

DREAMTOWNS
   1. Nantucket (6)
   2. Vineyard Haven (23)
   3. South Deerfield (183)

HONORABLE MENTIONS
4. Lee (280)
5. North Brookfield (411)
6. Pittsfield (500)

Michigan [67]

DREAMTOWNS
1. Chelsea (52)
2. South Lyon (62)
3. Frankenmuth (96)
4. Traverse City (116)
5. Petoskey (172)
6. Goodrich (176)
7. Midland (182)
8. Dorr (190)

HONORABLE MENTIONS
9. Williamston (224)
10. Holland (231)
11. Milan (256)
12. Lowell (282)
13. South Haven (426)
14. Holly (442)
15. Hastings (466)
16. Richmond (520)

Minnesota [53]

DREAMTOWNS
1. Byron (24)
2. Waconia (30)
3. Rochester (33)
4. Delano (122)
5. Buffalo (139)
6. Lindstrom (146)
7. Alexandria (150)
8. Forest Lake (160)
9. Monticello (178)
10. Belle Plaine (179)
11. New Prague (185)
12. Zimmerman (189)
13. Jordan (192)
14. Northfield (198)
15. New Ulm (204)
16. Kasson (206)

Mississippi [36]

Missouri [62]

Montana [19]

HONORABLE MENTIONS
  4. Livingston (225)
  5. Kalispell (245)
  6. Missoula (343)
  7. Helena (357)
  8. Columbia Falls (382)

Nebraska [23]

HONORABLE MENTIONS
  1. Wayne (248)
  2. Seward (329)
  3. Holdrege (332)
  4. York (362)
  5. Kearney (366)
  6. Blair (479)
  7. Columbus (510)

Nevada [14]

DREAMTOWNS
  1. Johnson Lane (114)
  2. Incline Village (181)

HONORABLE MENTIONS
  3. Moapa Valley (327)
  4. Boulder City (509)

New Hampshire [10]

DREAMTOWNS
  1. Portsmouth (40)
  2. Lebanon (87)

HONORABLE MENTIONS
  3. Laconia (278)
  4. Concord (298)
  5. Manchester (397)
  6. Keene (421)
  7. Dover (452)

New Jersey [12]

DREAMTOWNS
  1. Jefferson Township North (84)
  2. Twin Rivers (90)

HONORABLE MENTIONS
   3. Villas (229)
   4. Franklin (395)
   5. Mystic Island (431)
   6. Washington (464)

New Mexico [31]

DREAMTOWNS
   1. White Rock (21)
   2. Los Alamos (28)

HONORABLE MENTIONS
   3. Carlsbad (498)
   4. Santa Fe (513)

New York [65]

DREAMTOWNS
   1. Saratoga Springs (68)
   2. West Point (109)
   3. Warwick (112)
   4. Chester (136)
   5. Red Hook (152)
   6. Southold (167)
   7. East Aurora (173)

HONORABLE MENTIONS
   8. Springs (240)
   9. Ithaca (266)
   10. Honeoye Falls (311)
   11. Canton (343)
   12. Glens Falls (358)
   13. Walden (422)
   14. Geneva (445)
   15. Newfane (450)
   16. Corning (459)
   17. Kingston (481)
   18. Clifton Springs (488)

North Carolina [65]

DREAMTOWNS
   1. Archer Lodge (19)
   2. Hampstead (48)
   3. Kill Devil Hills (75)
   4. Manteo (80)

5. Lake Norman of Catawba (93)
6. Pinehurst (152)
7. Oak Island (191)
8. Morehead City (194)

HONORABLE MENTIONS
9. Wendell (265)
10. Brevard (347)
11. Franklin (463)
12. Spout Springs (486)
13. Butner (519)

North Dakota [9]

[none]

Ohio [88]

DREAMTOWNS
1. New Bremen (77)
2. Marysville (119)

HONORABLE MENTIONS
3. Port Clinton (286)
4. Seville (303)
5. Chardon (306)
6. Ottawa (384)
7. Celina (385)
8. Oxford (400)
9. Findlay (402)
10. Newark (470)
10. Wauseon (470)
12. Orrville (474)
13. Wooster (482)
14. St. Marys (497)
15. Johnstown (506)

Oklahoma [44]

HONORABLE MENTIONS
1. Norman (431)

Oregon [45]

DREAMTOWNS
1. Bend (15)
2. Hood River (45)
3. Astoria (144)

4. Seaside (162)
5. Corvallis (188)
6. Redmond (196)
7. Silverton (208)

HONORABLE MENTIONS

8. Sandy (240)
9. Canby (252)
10. Albany (339)
11. Baker City (348)
12. Dallas (405)
13. Newberg (415)
14. Newport (431)
15. St. Helens (467)
16. Medford (504)
17. Lincoln City (505)

Pennsylvania [72]

DREAMTOWNS

1. State College (204)

HONORABLE MENTIONS

2. Pocono Woodland Lakes (214)
3. New Freedom (225)
4. Pottstown (313)
5. Orwigsburg (374)
6. Butler (386)
7. Grove City (403)
8. St. Marys (454)
9. Saw Creek (482)

Rhode Island [0]

[none]

South Carolina [35]

DREAMTOWNS

1. Sun City Hilton Head (47)
2. Mauldin (50)
3. Pawleys Island (56)
4. Hilton Head Island (138)

HONORABLE MENTIONS

5. Rock Hill (291)
6. Beaufort (300)

7. Spartanburg (489)
8. Anderson (501)

South Dakota [17]

DREAMTOWNS
1. Tea (17)

HONORABLE MENTIONS
2. Brandon (222)
3. Yankton (261)
4. Spearfish (298)
5. Brookings (321)
6. Sioux Falls (340)
7. Watertown (409)
8. Madison (438)
9. Vermillion (453)
10. Pierre (521)

Tennessee [58]

DREAMTOWNS
1. Spring Hill (14)
2. Fairview (106)
3. Murfreesboro (192)

HONORABLE MENTIONS
4. Arlington (227)
5. Lebanon (290)
6. Oakland (323)
7. Dandridge (330)
8. Columbia (484)

Texas [173]

DREAMTOWNS
1. Belterra (3)
2. Lake Conroe Eastshore (22)
3. Boerne (29)
4. Lake Conroe Westshore (35)
5. Aledo (42)
6. Paloma Creek South (44)
7. Woodcreek (51)
8. Manor (60)
9. Anna (115)
10. Lago Vista (122)
11. Forney (125)

12. Canyon Lake (133)
13. Pecan Plantation (140)
14. Weatherford (201)

HONORABLE MENTIONS
15. Fredericksburg (238)
16. Marble Falls (250)
17. Granite Shoals (255)
18. Midland (356)
19. Bastrop (390)
20. Sanger (391)
21. Granbury (411)
22. Lindale (462)

Utah [20]

DREAMTOWNS
1. Summit Park (1)
2. Park City (2)
3. Heber (8)
4. Eagle Mountain South (49)
5. Stansbury Park (65)
6. Santaquin (81)
7. St. George (85)
8. Moab (128)
9. Logan (148)
10. Cedar City (163)
11. Ephraim (194)
12. Nephi (208)

HONORABLE MENTIONS
13. Hurricane (315)
14. Tremonton (378)
15. Grantsville (416)
16. Richfield (423)
17. Tooele (427)

Vermont [9]

DREAMTOWNS
1. Burlington (171)

HONORABLE MENTIONS
2. Milton (271)
3. Middlebury (359)
4. Barre (511)

Virginia [41]

DREAMTOWNS
1. Purcellville (12)
2. Crozet (20)
3. Ruckersville (65)
4. Lake Monticello (99)
5. Williamsburg (101)
6. Charlottesville (117)
7. Lake of the Woods (141)
8. Fredericksburg (198)

HONORABLE MENTIONS
9. Winchester (285)
10. Smithfield (369)
11. Lexington (447)
12. Blacksburg (517)
13. Lynchburg (521)

Washington [44]

DREAMTOWNS
1. Snoqualmie (18)
2. Port Townsend (55)
3. Anacortes (102)
4. Birch Bay (121)
5. Bellingham (151)
6. Olympia (157)

HONORABLE MENTIONS
7. Lynden (231)
8. Indianola (239)
9. Sequim (248)
10. Ellensburg (267)
11. Stanwood (271)
12. Camano (280)
13. Colville (292)
14. Marysville (293)
15. Oak Harbor (399)
16. Everson (450)
17. Pullman (464)
18. Mount Vernon (479)
19. Yelm (485)
20. Granite Falls (490)

West Virginia [18]

HONORABLE MENTIONS
1. Morgantown (268)
2. Charles Town (389)

Wisconsin [61]

DREAMTOWNS
1. Hudson (69)
2. Mukwonago (83)
3. Oregon (94)
4. Prairie du Sac (117)
5. Sturgeon Bay (126)
6. Mount Horeb (127)
7. Lake Mills (164)

HONORABLE MENTIONS
8. Columbus (220)
9. West Bend (235)
10. Lake Geneva (237)
11. Marshfield (242)
12. Stevens Point (253)
13. New Richmond (270)
14. Baldwin (275)
15. Edgerton (314)
16. Monroe (317)
17. Eau Claire (327)
18. Evansville (330)
19. River Falls (333)
20. Plymouth (346)
21. Baraboo (348)
21. La Crosse (348)
23. Wausau (352)
24. Elkhorn (370)
25. Lake Delton (387)
26. Reedsburg (416)
27. Janesville (427)
28. Rice Lake (444)
29. Sheboygan (455)
30. Burlington (460)
31. Fort Atkinson (472)
32. Rhinelander (508)

Wyoming [17]

DREAMTOWNS
  1. Jackson (57)

HONORABLE MENTIONS
  2. Cody (309)
  3. Sheridan (396)
  4. Cheyenne (407)
  5. Lander (408)
  6. Evanston (434)
  7. Laramie (492)

Regions

Perhaps you'd prefer to remain in the same part of the country, yet you consider the state-by-state listings to be too restrictive. You're not bothered by the thought of crossing a state line or two to find the ideal place to live. Your interests can be addressed by grouping the 50 states into four regions.

East: Connecticut, Delaware, Maine, Maryland, Massachusetts, New Hampshire, New Jersey, New York, Pennsylvania, Rhode Island, Vermont, and West Virginia.

Midwest: Illinois, Indiana, Iowa, Kansas, Michigan, Minnesota, Missouri, Nebraska, North Dakota, Ohio, South Dakota, and Wisconsin.

South: Alabama, Arkansas, Florida, Georgia, Kentucky, Louisiana, Mississippi, North Carolina, Oklahoma, South Carolina, Tennessee, Texas, and Virginia.

West: Alaska, Arizona, California, Colorado, Hawaii, Idaho, Montana, Nevada, New Mexico, Oregon, Utah, Washington, and Wyoming.

The South encompasses 745 small towns, accounting for more than a third of the national total of 2,084. It's followed by the Midwest (622), West (471), and East (246).

Yet it might reasonably be said that the two smallest regions are the most successful. The West contains 81 Dreamtowns — 31 more than any other region — and it also boasts the nation's highest conversion rate. Roughly one-sixth of the West's small communities (81 of 471, 17.2%) have attained Dreamtown status. The East is the runner-up with a conversion rate of 11.8% (29 of 246), followed by the Midwest at 7.9% (49 of 622) and the South at 6.7% (50 of 745).

Each region's full complement of Dreamtowns is shown below.

East [246]

1. Nantucket, MA (6)
2. Vineyard Haven, MA (23)
3. Portsmouth, NH (40)
4. Lewes, DE (41)
5. Kennebunk, ME (43)
6. Ocean View, DE (53)
7. Saratoga Springs, NY (68)
8. Ocean Pines, MD (71)
9. Lake Pocotopaug, CT (74)
10. Jefferson Township North, NJ (84)
11. Lebanon, NH (87)
12. Twin Rivers, NJ (90)
13. West Point, NY (109)
14. Warwick, NY (112)
15. Middletown, DE (113)
16. Westminster, MD (120)
17. Leonardtown, MD (135)
18. Chester, NY (136)
19. Frederick, MD (137)
20. Chesapeake Beach, MD (147)
21. Red Hook, NY (152)
22. Colchester, CT (166)
23. Southold, NY (167)
24. Burlington, VT (171)
25. East Aurora, NY (173)
26. Brunswick, ME (179)
27. South Deerfield, MA (183)
28. Brunswick, MD (203)
29. State College, PA (204)

Midwest [622]

1. Tea, SD (17)
2. Byron, MN (24)
3. Waconia, MN (30)
4. Rochester, MN (33)
5. Chelsea, MI (52)
6. South Lyon, MI (62)
6. Spirit Lake, IA (62)
8. Eureka, MO (67)
9. Hudson, WI (69)
10. New Bremen, OH (77)

10. Orange City, IA (77)
12. Platte City, MO (82)
13. Mukwonago, WI (83)
14. Lee's Summit, MO (86)
15. Oregon, WI (94)
16. Frankenmuth, MI (96)
17. Decorah, IA (105)
18. Pella, IA (107)
19. Carroll, IA (108)
20. Traverse City, MI (116)
21. Prairie du Sac, WI (117)
22. Marysville, OH (119)
23. Delano, MN (122)
24. Sturgeon Bay, WI (126)
25. Mount Horeb, WI (127)
26. Sioux Center, IA (129)
27. McPherson, KS (133)
28. Buffalo, MN (139)
29. Mount Vernon, IA (143)
30. Lindstrom, MN (146)
31. Monticello, IL (149)
32. Alexandria, MN (150)
33. Iowa City, IA (159)
34. Forest Lake, MN (160)
35. Lake Mills, WI (164)
36. Breese, IL (168)
37. Petoskey, MI (172)
38. Goodrich, MI (176)
39. Monticello, MN (178)
40. Belle Plaine, MN (179)
41. Midland, MI (182)
42. New Prague, MN (185)
43. Colby, KS (187)
44. Zimmerman, MN (189)
45. Dorr, MI (190)
46. Jordan, MN (192)
47. Northfield, MN (198)
48. New Ulm, MN (204)
49. Kasson, MN (206)

South [745]

1. Belterra, TX (3)
2. World Golf Village, FL (4)
3. Buckhead (Bryan County), GA (10)

4. Purcellville, VA (12)
5. Spring Hill, TN (14)
6. St. Simons, GA (16)
7. Archer Lodge, NC (19)
8. Crozet, VA (20)
9. Lake Conroe Eastshore, TX (22)
10. Boerne, TX (29)
11. Lake Conroe Westshore, TX (35)
12. Jupiter Farms, FL (38)
13. Aledo, TX (42)
14. Paloma Creek South, TX (44)
15. Sun City Hilton Head, SC (47)
16. Hampstead, NC (48)
17. Mauldin, SC (50)
18. Woodcreek, TX (51)
19. Pawleys Island, SC (56)
20. Manor, TX (60)
21. Fernandina Beach, FL (61)
22. Mandeville, LA (64)
23. Ruckersville, VA (65)
24. Santa Rosa Beach, FL (70)
25. Kill Devil Hills, NC (75)
26. Orangetree, FL (79)
27. Manteo, NC (80)
28. Lake Norman of Catawba, NC (93)
29. St. Augustine, FL (95)
30. Lake Monticello, VA (99)
31. Williamsburg, VA (101)
32. Fairview, TN (106)
33. Daphne, AL (110)
34. Oxford, MS (111)
35. Anna, TX (115)
36. Charlottesville, VA (117)
37. Lago Vista, TX (122)
38. Forney, TX (125)
39. Canyon Lake, TX (133)
40. Hilton Head Island, SC (138)
41. Pecan Plantation, TX (140)
42. Lake of the Woods, VA (141)
43. Pinehurst, NC (152)
44. Big Pine Key, FL (156)
45. Key Largo, FL (157)
46. Oak Island, NC (191)
47. Murfreesboro, TN (192)

48. Morehead City, NC (194)
49. Fredericksburg, VA (198)
50. Weatherford, TX (201)

West [471]

1. Summit Park, UT (1)
2. Park City, UT (2)
3. Roxborough Park, CO (5)
4. Evergreen, CO (7)
5. Heber, UT (8)
6. Vistancia, AZ (9)
7. Lafayette, CO (11)
8. Aspen, CO (13)
9. Bend, OR (15)
10. Snoqualmie, WA (18)
11. White Rock, NM (21)
12. Breckenridge, CO (25)
13. Wellington, CO (26)
14. Silverthorne, CO (27)
15. Los Alamos, NM (28)
16. Vail, CO (31)
17. Lake of the Pines, CA (32)
18. Steamboat Springs, CO (34)
19. Rancho Murieta, CA (36)
20. Boulder, CO (37)
21. Truckee, CA (39)
22. Hood River, OR (45)
23. Salida, CO (46)
24. Eagle Mountain South, UT (49)
25. Whitefish, MT (54)
26. Port Townsend, WA (55)
27. Jackson, WY (57)
28. Johnstown, CO (58)
29. Woodland Park, CO (59)
30. Stansbury Park, UT (65)
31. Basalt, CO (72)
32. Rigby, ID (73)
33. Estes Park, CO (76)
34. Santaquin, UT (81)
35. St. George, UT (85)
36. Mountain House, CA (87)
37. Bozeman, MT (89)
38. Firestone, CO (90)
39. Vail, AZ (92)

40. Gunnison, CO (97)
41. Corona de Tucson, AZ (98)
42. Half Moon Bay, CA (99)
43. Anacortes, WA (102)
43. Livermore, CA (102)
45. Star, ID (104)
46. Johnson Lane, NV (114)
47. Birch Bay, WA (121)
48. Petaluma, CA (124)
49. Moab, UT (128)
50. Sedona, AZ (130)
51. Gypsum, CO (131)
52. Eaton, CO (132)
53. Eagle, CO (142)
54. Astoria, OR (144)
55. Edwards, CO (145)
56. Logan, UT (148)
57. Bellingham, WA (151)
58. Davis, CA (154)
59. Auburn, CA (155)
60. Olympia, WA (157)
61. Discovery Bay, CA (161)
62. Seaside, OR (162)
63. Cedar City, UT (163)
64. Longmont, CO (165)
65. Kuna, ID (169)
66. Santa Cruz, CA (170)
67. Morro Bay, CA (174)
67. Moscow, ID (174)
69. Bishop, CA (177)
70. Incline Village, NV (181)
71. Coeur d'Alene, ID (183)
72. Plumas Lake, CA (186)
73. Corvallis, OR (188)
74. Ephraim, UT (194)
75. Redmond, OR (196)
76. Solvang, CA (197)
77. Cambria, CA (198)
78. Belgrade, MT (202)
79. Idaho Falls, ID (207)
80. Nephi, UT (208)
80. Silverton, OR (208)

Population

"Small town" is a relative term, as I acknowledged in Chapter 1. Somebody from New York or Chicago or Los Angeles might deem any community to be small if it contains fewer than a quarter-million people. The rest of us would probably drop the ceiling lower — some of us, much lower.

I tried to keep these differing perceptions in mind when I established the population extremes for this book. That's why small towns can be as large as Deltona, Florida, at 199,388, and as tiny as Grangerland, Texas, and Kaplan, Louisiana, both at 5,003. It's admittedly a broad range.

The following five lists divide the 209 Dreamtowns by size. You'll notice that the pools grow larger as the populations decline. Only 121 small towns have 100,000 to 199,999 residents, but the count explodes to 870 by the time we reach the smallest range, 5,000 to 9,999.

The same inverse relationship exists between population and Dreamtowns. The two lists encompassing the largest communities — the groups above 50,000 — include 18 Dreamtowns apiece. The number of elite towns increases to 31 as the range drops to 20,000 to 49,999, then to 56 (10,000 to 19,999), and finally to 86 (5,000 to 9,999).

100,000 to 199,999 Residents [121]

1. Bend, OR (15)
2. Rochester, MN (33)
3. Boulder, CO (37)
4. Mauldin, SC (50)
5. South Lyon, MI (62)
6. Mandeville, LA (64)
7. St. George, UT (85)
8. Charlottesville, VA (117)
9. Frederick, MD (137)
10. Logan, UT (148)
11. Bellingham, WA (151)
12. Olympia, WA (157)
13. Iowa City, IA (159)
14. Santa Cruz, CA (170)
15. Burlington, VT (171)
16. Coeur d'Alene, ID (183)
17. Murfreesboro, TN (192)
18. Fredericksburg, VA (198)

50,000 to 99,999 Residents [182]

1. Lafayette, CO (11)
2. Portsmouth, NH (40)
3. Saratoga Springs, NY (68)
4. Lee's Summit, MO (86)
5. Twin Rivers, NJ (90)
6. St. Augustine, FL (95)
7. Williamsburg, VA (101)
8. Livermore, CA (102)
9. Daphne, AL (110)
10. Westminster, MD (120)
11. Petaluma, CA (124)
12. Hilton Head Island, SC (138)
13. Davis, CA (154)
14. Longmont, CO (165)
15. Midland, MI (182)
16. Corvallis, OR (188)
17. State College, PA (204)
18. Idaho Falls, ID (207)

20,000 to 49,999 Residents [372]

1. Heber, UT (8)
2. Spring Hill, TN (14)
3. Snoqualmie, WA (18)
4. Lake Conroe Westshore, TX (35)
5. Lewes, DE (41)
6. Fernandina Beach, FL (61)
7. Hudson, WI (69)
8. Ocean Pines, MD (71)
9. Kill Devil Hills, NC (75)
10. Lebanon, NH (87)
11. Bozeman, MT (89)
12. Firestone, CO (90)
13. Half Moon Bay, CA (99)
14. Oxford, MS (111)
15. Middletown, DE (113)
16. Traverse City, MI (116)
17. Marysville, OH (119)
18. Forney, TX (125)
19. Chesapeake Beach, MD (147)
20. Pinehurst, NC (152)
21. Auburn, CA (155)
22. Forest Lake, MN (160)

23. Cedar City, UT (163)
24. Morro Bay, CA (174)
24. Moscow, ID (174)
26. Monticello, MN (178)
27. Brunswick, ME (179)
28. Morehead City, NC (194)
29. Redmond, OR (196)
30. Northfield, MN (198)
31. Weatherford, TX (201)

10,000 to 19,999 Residents [539]

1. Park City, UT (2)
2. World Golf Village, FL (4)
3. Evergreen, CO (7)
4. Purcellville, VA (12)
5. St. Simons, GA (16)
6. Archer Lodge, NC (19)
7. Lake Conroe Eastshore, TX (22)
8. Vineyard Haven, MA (23)
9. Silverthorne, CO (27)
10. Los Alamos, NM (28)
11. Boerne, TX (29)
12. Waconia, MN (30)
13. Steamboat Springs, CO (34)
14. Jupiter Farms, FL (38)
15. Truckee, CA (39)
16. Hood River, OR (45)
17. Sun City Hilton Head, SC (47)
18. Hampstead, NC (48)
19. Ocean View, DE (53)
20. Pawleys Island, SC (56)
21. Jackson, WY (57)
22. Johnstown, CO (58)
23. Woodland Park, CO (59)
24. Spirit Lake, IA (62)
25. Stansbury Park, UT (65)
26. Eureka, MO (67)
27. Basalt, CO (72)
28. Santaquin, UT (81)
29. Platte City, MO (82)
30. Mukwonago, WI (83)
31. Jefferson Township North, NJ (84)
32. Mountain House, CA (87)
33. Vail, AZ (92)

34. Oregon, WI (94)
35. Lake Monticello, VA (99)
36. Anacortes, WA (102)
37. West Point, NY (109)
38. Warwick, NY (112)
39. Anna, TX (115)
40. Birch Bay, WA (121)
41. McPherson, KS (133)
42. Buffalo, MN (139)
43. Lake of the Woods, VA (141)
44. Astoria, OR (144)
45. Edwards, CO (145)
46. Alexandria, MN (150)
47. Key Largo, FL (157)
48. Discovery Bay, CA (161)
49. Southold, NY (167)
50. Kuna, ID (169)
51. Incline Village, NV (181)
52. Oak Island, NC (191)
53. Solvang, CA (197)
54. Belgrade, MT (202)
55. New Ulm, MN (204)
56. Silverton, OR (208)

5,000 to 9,999 Residents [870]

1. Summit Park, UT (1)
2. Belterra, TX (3)
3. Roxborough Park, CO (5)
4. Nantucket, MA (6)
5. Vistancia, AZ (9)
6. Buckhead (Bryan County), GA (10)
7. Aspen, CO (13)
8. Tea, SD (17)
9. Crozet, VA (20)
10. White Rock, NM (21)
11. Byron, MN (24)
12. Breckenridge, CO (25)
13. Wellington, CO (26)
14. Vail, CO (31)
15. Lake of the Pines, CA (32)
16. Rancho Murieta, CA (36)
17. Aledo, TX (42)
18. Kennebunk, ME (43)
19. Paloma Creek South, TX (44)

20. Salida, CO (46)
21. Eagle Mountain South, UT (49)
22. Woodcreek, TX (51)
23. Chelsea, MI (52)
24. Whitefish, MT (54)
25. Port Townsend, WA (55)
26. Manor, TX (60)
27. Ruckersville, VA (65)
28. Santa Rosa Beach, FL (70)
29. Rigby, ID (73)
30. Lake Pocotopaug, CT (74)
31. Estes Park, CO (76)
32. New Bremen, OH (77)
32. Orange City, IA (77)
34. Orangetree, FL (79)
35. Manteo, NC (80)
36. Lake Norman of Catawba, NC (93)
37. Frankenmuth, MI (96)
38. Gunnison, CO (97)
39. Corona de Tucson, AZ (98)
40. Star, ID (104)
41. Decorah, IA (105)
42. Fairview, TN (106)
43. Pella, IA (107)
44. Carroll, IA (108)
45. Johnson Lane, NV (114)
46. Prairie du Sac, WI (117)
47. Delano, MN (122)
47. Lago Vista, TX (122)
49. Sturgeon Bay, WI (126)
50. Mount Horeb, WI (127)
51. Moab, UT (128)
52. Sioux Center, IA (129)
53. Sedona, AZ (130)
54. Gypsum, CO (131)
55. Eaton, CO (132)
56. Canyon Lake, TX (133)
57. Leonardtown, MD (135)
58. Chester, NY (136)
59. Pecan Plantation, TX (140)
60. Eagle, CO (142)
61. Mount Vernon, IA (143)
62. Lindstrom, MN (146)
63. Monticello, IL (149)

64. Red Hook, NY (152)
65. Big Pine Key, FL (156)
66. Seaside, OR (162)
67. Lake Mills, WI (164)
68. Colchester, CT (166)
69. Breese, IL (168)
70. Petoskey, MI (172)
71. East Aurora, NY (173)
72. Goodrich, MI (176)
73. Bishop, CA (177)
74. Belle Plaine, MN (179)
75. South Deerfield, MA (183)
76. New Prague, MN (185)
77. Plumas Lake, CA (186)
78. Colby, KS (187)
79. Zimmerman, MN (189)
80. Dorr, MI (190)
81. Jordan, MN (192)
82. Ephraim, UT (194)
83. Cambria, CA (198)
84. Brunswick, MD (203)
85. Kasson, MN (206)
86. Nephi, UT (208)

Population Density

The typical Dreamtown has a population density of 1,784 persons per square mile. You might look with horror at that number, convinced that it's much too large, too tightly packed. You'd be wrong.

Just compare it to the average density of the 50 major urban hubs — 3,336 people in a given square mile — or to the really scary figures for some of America's biggest cities. Nine hubs have densities above 4,000 per square mile, including such centers of gridlock as Los Angeles (7,224), San Francisco (6,748), and New York (5,435).

Below are lists of the 25 highest-rated Dreamtowns in three density ranges. (I'll follow the same format for the rest of this chapter, confining each list to the top 25. Refer back to Chapter 4 if you'd like to study density — or any other stat — in greater detail.)

The largest number of Dreamtowns, as you might expect, are in the middle range. Sixty-six elite communities contain at least 2,000 residents per square mile, while 93 Dreamtowns are arrayed between 1,200 and 1,999, and the remaining 50 towns have fewer than 1,200 persons per square mile.

2,000 or More Per Square Mile [570]

1. Roxborough Park, CO (5)
2. Vistancia, AZ (9)
3. Lafayette, CO (11)
4. Purcellville, VA (12)
5. Bend, OR (15)
6. Tea, SD (17)
7. Snoqualmie, WA (18)
8. White Rock, NM (21)
9. Byron, MN (24)
10. Wellington, CO (26)
11. Boerne, TX (29)
12. Waconia, MN (30)
13. Rochester, MN (33)
14. Boulder, CO (37)
15. Paloma Creek South, TX (44)
16. Eagle Mountain South, UT (49)
17. Jackson, WY (57)
18. Johnstown, CO (58)
19. Manor, TX (60)
20. Stansbury Park, UT (65)
21. Basalt, CO (72)
22. St. George, UT (85)
23. Lee's Summit, MO (86)
24. Mountain House, CA (87)
25. Bozeman, MT (89)

1,200 to 1,999 Per Square Mile [1,085]

1. Summit Park, UT (1)
2. Park City, UT (2)
3. Belterra, TX (3)
4. World Golf Village, FL (4)
5. Heber, UT (8)
6. Aspen, CO (13)
7. Spring Hill, TN (14)
8. St. Simons, GA (16)
9. Crozet, VA (20)
10. Lake Conroe Eastshore, TX (22)
11. Breckenridge, CO (25)
12. Silverthorne, CO (27)
13. Los Alamos, NM (28)
14. Vail, CO (31)
15. Steamboat Springs, CO (34)

16. Lake Conroe Westshore, TX (35)
17. Rancho Murieta, CA (36)
18. Lewes, DE (41)
19. Aledo, TX (42)
20. Hood River, OR (45)
21. Salida, CO (46)
22. Sun City Hilton Head, SC (47)
23. Mauldin, SC (50)
24. Chelsea, MI (52)
25. Whitefish, MT (54)

Less Than 1,200 Per Square Mile [429]

1. Nantucket, MA (6)
2. Evergreen, CO (7)
3. Buckhead (Bryan County), GA (10)
4. Archer Lodge, NC (19)
5. Vineyard Haven, MA (23)
6. Lake of the Pines, CA (32)
7. Jupiter Farms, FL (38)
8. Truckee, CA (39)
9. Portsmouth, NH (40)
10. Kennebunk, ME (43)
11. Hampstead, NC (48)
12. Woodcreek, TX (51)
13. Ocean View, DE (53)
14. Pawleys Island, SC (56)
15. Spirit Lake, IA (62)
16. Ruckersville, VA (65)
17. Eureka, MO (67)
18. Santa Rosa Beach, FL (70)
19. Rigby, ID (73)
20. Lake Pocotopaug, CT (74)
21. Kill Devil Hills, NC (75)
22. Estes Park, CO (76)
23. Orangetree, FL (79)
24. Mukwonago, WI (83)
25. Jefferson Township North, NJ (84)

Latitude

Nearly 30 million Americans changed addresses between 2019 and 2020, according to Census Bureau estimates. That's a vast number of movers — an average of 570,000 per week — and you might assume that they had a similarly broad array of reasons for hitting the road.

Yet that wasn't the case at all. The bureau surveyed a cross section of these movers and inquired about their motivations. Most cited one of these three:

- Housing-related reasons, 40.1%
- Family-related reasons, 25.5%
- Employment-related reasons, 19.8%

A better house, a better place for their family, a better job. Those were the reasons why 85.4% of Americans filed change-of-address forms. Very, very few of them said anything about climate. Only 0.4% of movers cited better weather as their prime motivation.

That's one reason why I didn't include climate as a factor in the quality-of-life rankings. Another is the matter of personal taste. We might all agree about the desirability of education, money, and health, but we'll never reach a consensus on weather. Some people love the snow; some prefer desert heat. Never the twain shall meet.

My one concession to the climate issue is to present the two latitude lists below. The first encompasses Dreamtowns north of the 40th parallel, which runs from southern Pennsylvania to central Illinois to northern California. The second includes towns south of the 37th parallel, which passes just north of the border between Virginia and North Carolina, skirts the northern tip of Texas, and slides into southern California.

These are imperfect demarcations of climate, to be sure. But they offer a decent selection of Dreamtowns that experience all four seasons (above the 40th) or primarily enjoy warm weather (below the 37th).

Above 40th Parallel [799]

1. Summit Park, UT (1)
2. Park City, UT (2)
3. Nantucket, MA (6)
4. Heber, UT (8)
5. Bend, OR (15)
6. Tea, SD (17)
7. Snoqualmie, WA (18)
8. Vineyard Haven, MA (23)
9. Byron, MN (24)
10. Wellington, CO (26)
11. Waconia, MN (30)
12. Rochester, MN (33)
13. Steamboat Springs, CO (34)
14. Boulder, CO (37)

15. Portsmouth, NH (40)
16. Kennebunk, ME (43)
17. Hood River, OR (45)
18. Eagle Mountain South, UT (49)
19. Chelsea, MI (52)
20. Whitefish, MT (54)
21. Port Townsend, WA (55)
22. Jackson, WY (57)
23. Johnstown, CO (58)
24. South Lyon, MI (62)
24. Spirit Lake, IA (62)

Below 37th Parallel [856]

1. Belterra, TX (3)
2. World Golf Village, FL (4)
3. Vistancia, AZ (9)
4. Buckhead (Bryan County), GA (10)
5. Spring Hill, TN (14)
6. St. Simons, GA (16)
7. Archer Lodge, NC (19)
8. White Rock, NM (21)
9. Lake Conroe Eastshore, TX (22)
10. Los Alamos, NM (28)
11. Boerne, TX (29)
12. Lake Conroe Westshore, TX (35)
13. Jupiter Farms, FL (38)
14. Aledo, TX (42)
15. Paloma Creek South, TX (44)
16. Sun City Hilton Head, SC (47)
17. Hampstead, NC (48)
18. Mauldin, SC (50)
19. Woodcreek, TX (51)
20. Pawleys Island, SC (56)
21. Manor, TX (60)
22. Fernandina Beach, FL (61)
23. Mandeville, LA (64)
24. Santa Rosa Beach, FL (70)
25. Kill Devil Hills, NC (75)

Closest Major Hub

You're probably of two minds on this issue. You hope to escape the big city's grime and congestion, yet you wouldn't mind being close enough to pay an occasional visit.

Well, you're in luck. Almost half of America's Dreamtowns — 93 of 209 — are less than 50 air miles from the closest major hub. Another 53 are a bit farther removed, situated in a 50-to-99-mile radius. That means 70% of all Dreamtowns are located within a two-hour drive of one of the nation's 50 biggest cities.

The remaining 63 Dreamtowns are at least 100 air miles distant from any hub, a group that includes nine towns that are more than 250 miles away. (Whitefish, Montana, is the most isolated Dreamtown, 373 air miles from Seattle.)

The following lists show the 25 highest-rated small towns for each radius.

Less Than 50 Miles [471]

1. Summit Park, UT (1)
2. Park City, UT (2)
3. Belterra, TX (3)
4. World Golf Village, FL (4)
5. Roxborough Park, CO (5)
6. Evergreen, CO (7)
7. Heber, UT (8)
8. Vistancia, AZ (9)
9. Lafayette, CO (11)
10. Purcellville, VA (12)
11. Spring Hill, TN (14)
12. Snoqualmie, WA (18)
13. Archer Lodge, NC (19)
14. Lake Conroe Eastshore, TX (22)
15. Boerne, TX (29)
16. Waconia, MN (30)
17. Lake of the Pines, CA (32)
18. Lake Conroe Westshore, TX (35)
19. Rancho Murieta, CA (36)
20. Boulder, CO (37)
21. Portsmouth, NH (40)
22. Aledo, TX (42)
23. Paloma Creek South, TX (44)
24. Eagle Mountain South, UT (49)
25. Woodcreek, TX (51)

50 to 99 Miles [706]

1. Nantucket, MA (6)
2. St. Simons, GA (16)

3. Crozet, VA (20)
4. Vineyard Haven, MA (23)
5. Byron, MN (24)
6. Breckenridge, CO (25)
7. Wellington, CO (26)
8. Silverthorne, CO (27)
9. Vail, CO (31)
10. Rochester, MN (33)
11. Jupiter Farms, FL (38)
12. Truckee, CA (39)
13. Lewes, DE (41)
14. Kennebunk, ME (43)
15. Hood River, OR (45)
16. Salida, CO (46)
17. Mauldin, SC (50)
18. Ocean View, DE (53)
19. Port Townsend, WA (55)
20. Woodland Park, CO (59)
21. Ruckersville, VA (65)
22. Kill Devil Hills, NC (75)
23. Estes Park, CO (76)
24. New Bremen, OH (77)
25. Orangetree, FL (79)

100 or More Miles [907]

1. Buckhead (Bryan County), GA (10)
2. Aspen, CO (13)
3. Bend, OR (15)
4. Tea, SD (17)
5. White Rock, NM (21)
6. Los Alamos, NM (28)
7. Steamboat Springs, CO (34)
8. Sun City Hilton Head, SC (47)
9. Hampstead, NC (48)
10. Whitefish, MT (54)
11. Pawleys Island, SC (56)
12. Jackson, WY (57)
13. Spirit Lake, IA (62)
14. Saratoga Springs, NY (68)
15. Santa Rosa Beach, FL (70)
16. Ocean Pines, MD (71)
17. Basalt, CO (72)
18. Rigby, ID (73)
19. Orange City, IA (77)

20. St. George, UT (85)
21. Lebanon, NH (87)
22. Bozeman, MT (89)
23. Vail, AZ (92)
24. Gunnison, CO (97)
25. Corona de Tucson, AZ (98)

Diversions

Test No. 10, as you may recall, was designed to pinpoint the small towns that are blessed with the most vibrant mixes of stores and restaurants. The test's two parts were ratios per 10,000 residents, showing the local concentrations of retail establishments and eating places.

Nantucket achieved the highest scores on both parts — and hence on the Diversions test as a whole. It has 139.3 stores for every 10,000 people, roughly four times the median of 33.3 for all small towns. Its second ratio is even more impressive, 89.3 restaurants per 10,000, representing a fivefold increase over the small-town median of 17.9.

If you prefer to check out the 20 towns that earned the best marks on the Diversions exam, flip back to Chapter 2. The two lists below are something different. They show the 25 highest-rated Dreamtowns — the ones with the best overall quality-of-life scores — that surpass each of two separate thresholds. Both filters are expressed per 10,000 residents — first, more than 50 stores; second, more than 30 restaurants.

More Than 50 Stores Per 10,000 [142]

1. Summit Park, UT (1)
2. Park City, UT (2)
3. Nantucket, MA (6)
4. Aspen, CO (13)
5. St. Simons, GA (16)
6. Vineyard Haven, MA (23)
7. Breckenridge, CO (25)
8. Silverthorne, CO (27)
9. Vail, CO (31)
10. Steamboat Springs, CO (34)
11. Hood River, OR (45)
12. Salida, CO (46)
13. Jackson, WY (57)
14. Spirit Lake, IA (62)
15. Santa Rosa Beach, FL (70)
16. Ocean Pines, MD (71)

17. Basalt, CO (72)
18. Kill Devil Hills, NC (75)
19. Manteo, NC (80)
20. Lebanon, NH (87)
21. Bozeman, MT (89)
22. Gunnison, CO (97)
23. Decorah, IA (105)
24. Carroll, IA (108)
25. Traverse City, MI (116)

More Than 30 Restaurants Per 10,000 [98]

1. Summit Park, UT (1)
2. Park City, UT (2)
3. Nantucket, MA (6)
4. Aspen, CO (13)
5. Vineyard Haven, MA (23)
6. Breckenridge, CO (25)
7. Silverthorne, CO (27)
8. Vail, CO (31)
9. Steamboat Springs, CO (34)
10. Hood River, OR (45)
11. Salida, CO (46)
12. Jackson, WY (57)
13. Spirit Lake, IA (62)
14. Ocean Pines, MD (71)
15. Basalt, CO (72)
16. Kill Devil Hills, NC (75)
17. Manteo, NC (80)
18. Lebanon, NH (87)
19. Bozeman, MT (89)
20. Gunnison, CO (97)
21. Oxford, MS (111)
22. Charlottesville, VA (117)
22. Prairie du Sac, WI (117)
24. Sturgeon Bay, WI (126)
25. Moab, UT (128)

Commuting

This book, as you know, has made a big issue of commuting speed.

Nearly three-fifths of the employees in America's 2,084 small towns (58.3%) are able to travel from home to worksite in less than 20 minutes, based on Census Bureau figures for 2019, the year prior to the Covid-19 outbreak. Commutes of such rapidity are less common when the focus is narrowed to the 209 Dreamtowns (50.4%), yet even that figure is a drastic improvement over the 50 major hubs, where only 32.8% of workers make their trips in 19 minutes or less.

Nobody really knows what the nation's commuting patterns will be like in the future — what with the greater popularity of working from home — yet it seems likely that urban congestion will remain a nagging concern. Traffic jams will always be part of big-city life.

The following list offers 25 Dreamtowns as calming alternatives. These places have the highest quality-of-life scores among the 582 small towns where more than 70% of all commuters — yes, *70%* — get from their homes to their workplaces in less than 20 minutes.

More Than 70% Commute Less Than 20 Minutes [582]

1. Nantucket, MA (6)
2. Aspen, CO (13)
3. Bend, OR (15)
4. Vineyard Haven, MA (23)
5. Breckenridge, CO (25)
6. Los Alamos, NM (28)
7. Vail, CO (31)
8. Rochester, MN (33)
9. Steamboat Springs, CO (34)
10. Hood River, OR (45)
11. Salida, CO (46)
12. Port Townsend, WA (55)
13. Jackson, WY (57)
14. Spirit Lake, IA (62)
15. Estes Park, CO (76)
16. Orange City, IA (77)
17. Manteo, NC (80)
18. St. George, UT (85)
19. Lebanon, NH (87)
20. Bozeman, MT (89)
21. Gunnison, CO (97)
22. Decorah, IA (105)
23. Pella, IA (107)
24. Carroll, IA (108)
25. West Point, NY (109)

Population Growth

Population growth? What population growth? Nearly half of America's small towns (955 of 2,084) actually had fewer residents in 2019 than in 2014, according to the latest estimates by the Census Bureau. The number of towns experiencing solid growth — at least 10% over five years — was nearly six times smaller, just 169.

Unbridled population increases can be dangerous, of course, but sustainable gains are much to be desired. Steady growth allows a community to expand and diversify its economy, widen its base of skilled employees, and improve its infrastructure and services.

The list below is confined to the top-rated Dreamtowns that experienced population growth of at least 10% during the 2014-2019 span.

Growth of 10% or More in Five Years [169]

1. Summit Park, UT (1)
2. Park City, UT (2)
3. Belterra, TX (3)
4. World Golf Village, FL (4)
5. Heber, UT (8)
6. Vistancia, AZ (9)
7. Lafayette, CO (11)
8. Purcellville, VA (12)
9. Spring Hill, TN (14)
10. Bend, OR (15)
11. St. Simons, GA (16)
12. Tea, SD (17)
13. Snoqualmie, WA (18)
14. Archer Lodge, NC (19)
15. Lake Conroe Eastshore, TX (22)
16. Wellington, CO (26)
17. Boerne, TX (29)
18. Lake of the Pines, CA (32)
19. Jupiter Farms, FL (38)
20. Hampstead, NC (48)
21. Eagle Mountain South, UT (49)
22. Mauldin, SC (50)
23. Woodcreek, TX (51)
24. Ocean View, DE (53)
25. Whitefish, MT (54)

Education

Brainpower is more heavily concentrated in elite small towns than in big cities. That's based on the relative percentages of working-age adults (25 to 64) who hold bachelor's degrees: 44.6% in the 209 Dreamtowns, 40.1% in the 50 major urban hubs.

College graduates actually constitute a majority of the adults in 74 small towns, 54 of which have been classified as Dreamtowns. That means slightly more than a quarter of all Dreamtowns have college-graduation rates of 50% or higher. Compare that to the nation's big cities. Only one-tenth of those hubs — five of 50 — reach the 50% threshold for bachelor's degrees.

The following list includes the 25 highest-rated Dreamtowns where at least half of all persons in the 25-64 age range have four-year college degrees.

50% or More With Bachelor's Degrees [74]

1. Summit Park, UT (1)
2. Park City, UT (2)
3. Belterra, TX (3)
4. World Golf Village, FL (4)
5. Roxborough Park, CO (5)
6. Evergreen, CO (7)
7. Vistancia, AZ (9)
8. Buckhead (Bryan County), GA (10)
9. Lafayette, CO (11)
10. Purcellville, VA (12)
11. Aspen, CO (13)
12. St. Simons, GA (16)
13. Snoqualmie, WA (18)
14. Crozet, VA (20)
15. White Rock, NM (21)
16. Breckenridge, CO (25)
17. Los Alamos, NM (28)
18. Waconia, MN (30)
19. Vail, CO (31)
20. Steamboat Springs, CO (34)
21. Boulder, CO (37)
22. Portsmouth, NH (40)
23. Aledo, TX (42)
24. Kennebunk, ME (43)
25. Hampstead, NC (48)

Money

The cost of living varies from place to place, but an annual salary of $60,000 would be considered substantial in almost all of them. The typical fulltime employee doesn't earn that much in big cities such as New York (median earnings of $59,968), Chicago ($54,665), or Los Angeles ($47,675). If you lined up the salaries for all 109 million fulltime workers across the country, you'd find that the median for annual earnings — the national midpoint — is $49,041.

About 15% of America's small towns (326 of 2,084) exceed the U.S. median, and 83 do better than $60,000. A pair even boast six-figure medians, with typical fulltime workers being paid $116,476 per year in Belterra, Texas, and $102,451 in White Rock, New Mexico.

You know the way this chapter works by now. The following list doesn't rank earnings. (If that's your primary interest, look back to the Money test in Chapter 2.) What you see below is a filtered version of the overall quality-of-life standings, confined to Dreamtowns with median annual earnings of at least $60,000.

Median Annual Earnings of $60,000 or More [83]

1. Summit Park, UT (1)
2. Park City, UT (2)
3. Belterra, TX (3)
4. World Golf Village, FL (4)
5. Roxborough Park, CO (5)
6. Nantucket, MA (6)
7. Evergreen, CO (7)
8. Vistancia, AZ (9)
9. Buckhead (Bryan County), GA (10)
10. Lafayette, CO (11)
11. Purcellville, VA (12)
12. St. Simons, GA (16)
13. Snoqualmie, WA (18)
14. Archer Lodge, NC (19)
15. Crozet, VA (20)
16. White Rock, NM (21)
17. Los Alamos, NM (28)
18. Waconia, MN (30)
19. Lake of the Pines, CA (32)
20. Lake Conroe Westshore, TX (35)
21. Rancho Murieta, CA (36)

22. Boulder, CO (37)
23. Truckee, CA (39)
24. Portsmouth, NH (40)
25. Lewes, DE (41)

Age

This section is concerned with the two extremes of adulthood — young adults (ages 25 to 39) and senior citizens (65 or older).

The typical small town has more of the former. Roughly one-fifth of the residents of all 2,084 towns (19.8%) are classified as young adults, while one-sixth (16.3%) are seniors. The difference between those groups, as you can see, is three and a half percentage points.

But the balance can vary widely. Young adults outnumber senior citizens by at least 10 points in 306 small towns, including such well-regarded Dreamtowns as Roxborough Park, Colorado, and Nantucket, Massachusetts. The elderly hold a lead of 10 percentage points or more in 98 towns, with high-rated Dreamtowns such as Vistancia, Arizona, and St. Simons, Georgia, among them.

The pair of rankings below are limited to places where the specified group accounts for a minimum of 20% of all residents. Young adults cross that threshold in 867 towns, while seniors do the same in 446.

20% or More Are Young Adults [867]

1. Roxborough Park, CO (5)
2. Nantucket, MA (6)
3. Heber, UT (8)
4. Aspen, CO (13)
5. Spring Hill, TN (14)
6. Bend, OR (15)
7. Tea, SD (17)
8. Snoqualmie, WA (18)
9. Byron, MN (24)
10. Breckenridge, CO (25)
11. Wellington, CO (26)
12. Silverthorne, CO (27)
13. Los Alamos, NM (28)
14. Vail, CO (31)
15. Rochester, MN (33)
16. Steamboat Springs, CO (34)
17. Boulder, CO (37)
18. Truckee, CA (39)

19. Paloma Creek South, TX (44)
20. Eagle Mountain South, UT (49)
21. Whitefish, MT (54)
22. Jackson, WY (57)
23. Johnstown, CO (58)
24. Manor, TX (60)
25. Ruckersville, VA (65)
25. Stansbury Park, UT (65)

20% or More Are Seniors [446]

1. Vistancia, AZ (9)
2. St. Simons, GA (16)
3. Lake Conroe Eastshore, TX (22)
4. Lake of the Pines, CA (32)
5. Rancho Murieta, CA (36)
6. Lewes, DE (41)
7. Kennebunk, ME (43)
8. Sun City Hilton Head, SC (47)
9. Ocean View, DE (53)
10. Port Townsend, WA (55)
11. Pawleys Island, SC (56)
12. Fernandina Beach, FL (61)
13. Ocean Pines, MD (71)
14. Estes Park, CO (76)
15. Frankenmuth, MI (96)
16. Anacortes, WA (102)
17. Johnson Lane, NV (114)
18. Sedona, AZ (130)
19. Hilton Head Island, SC (138)
20. Pecan Plantation, TX (140)
21. Pinehurst, NC (152)
22. Big Pine Key, FL (156)
23. Key Largo, FL (157)
24. Southold, NY (167)
25. Morro Bay, CA (174)

Diversity

Diversity has more than one aspect. We commonly think in racial terms — and this section will certainly focus on that angle — but geography also plays a role that shouldn't be overlooked.

The relevance of diversity was dramatized during the Covid summer, when the Black Lives Matter movement swept the nation. But its importance extends beyond a basic question of fairness. Diversity is also an essential ingredient in the generation of local prosperity, the maintenance of a strong educational system, and the facilitation of a broad exchange of ideas.

Let's start with the matter of race. An especially good indicator is the Gini-Simpson racial diversity index, which determines the likelihood that two randomly selected persons would come from different races. Slightly more than two-fifths of the nation's small towns (889 of 2,084) have indexes greater than 40%, suggesting that their odds of drawing such a racial mix are better than four in 10.

Geographic diversity is determined by the percentage of local residents who were born in a different state or country, a surprisingly rare trait. Five-sixths of America's small towns (1,739 of 2,084) contain majorities who were born in the same state where they currently live. That leaves only 345 communities where out-of-staters have the statistical advantage, including 170 places where more than 60% of present-day residents trace their roots beyond the state line.

The following lists show the 25 top-rated Dreamtowns that exceed the respective thresholds for racial and geographic diversity.

Racial Diversity Index of 40% or More [889]

1. Belterra, TX (3)
2. World Golf Village, FL (4)
3. Purcellville, VA (12)
4. Los Alamos, NM (28)
5. Boerne, TX (29)
6. Rochester, MN (33)
7. Paloma Creek South, TX (44)
8. Mauldin, SC (50)
9. Manor, TX (60)
10. Ruckersville, VA (65)
11. Basalt, CO (72)
12. Orangetree, FL (79)
13. Manteo, NC (80)
14. Mountain House, CA (87)
15. Firestone, CO (90)
15. Twin Rivers, NJ (90)
17. Vail, AZ (92)
18. Corona de Tucson, AZ (98)
19. Half Moon Bay, CA (99)
20. Williamsburg, VA (101)

21. Livermore, CA (102)
22. West Point, NY (109)
23. Oxford, MS (111)
24. Middletown, DE (113)
25. Anna, TX (115)

More Than 60% Born Outside of State [170]

1. Summit Park, UT (1)
2. Park City, UT (2)
3. World Golf Village, FL (4)
4. Evergreen, CO (7)
5. Vistancia, AZ (9)
6. Buckhead (Bryan County), GA (10)
7. Lafayette, CO (11)
8. Aspen, CO (13)
9. Spring Hill, TN (14)
10. Bend, OR (15)
11. White Rock, NM (21)
12. Breckenridge, CO (25)
13. Silverthorne, CO (27)
14. Los Alamos, NM (28)
15. Vail, CO (31)
16. Steamboat Springs, CO (34)
17. Boulder, CO (37)
18. Portsmouth, NH (40)
19. Lewes, DE (41)
20. Kennebunk, ME (43)
21. Hood River, OR (45)
22. Sun City Hilton Head, SC (47)
23. Ocean View, DE (53)
24. Whitefish, MT (54)
25. Port Townsend, WA (55)

Housing

The pursuit of a better home is the most powerful motivation for moving, bar none.

A Census Bureau survey found that 40.1% of all U.S. moves between 2019 and 2020 were inspired by housing factors, such as the desire to own (rather than rent), the wish for a larger and/or newer home, and the dream of relocating to a nicer neighborhood. Family-related reasons came second on the motivation list at 25.5%, nearly 15 points behind housing.

Three important housing concerns are addressed by the final lists in this chapter. They show the 25 best Dreamtowns after the quality-of-life rankings have been filtered for the cost, age, or size of local homes.

Affordability is calculated by the percentage of a typical worker's monthly earnings that would be needed to pay the median costs of home ownership (mortgage, taxes, insurance, and utilities). The average for all 2,084 small towns is 27.2%. Expenses are a bit steeper (30.7% of monthly earnings) when we look solely at the 209 Dreamtowns, though they remain a bargain in comparison to the nation's 50 major hubs (34.8%). The list below contains the top-rated communities whose housing costs fall below 25%.

The year 2000 is our starting point for determining if a town possesses a sizable supply of new homes. More than a quarter of all housing units in Dreamtowns (28.0%) have been constructed since the turn of the century, putting them far ahead of big cities (17.1%). The following list sets the bar extremely high, including only those towns where more than 40% of all homes are considered to be new.

Our size threshold is the number of bedrooms, specifically four. Dreamtowns again have the edge over major hubs. The percentage of homes containing at least four bedrooms is 26.1% in Dreamtowns, 22.2% in big cities. Inclusion on the list below is restricted to highly rated towns where more than 40% of all housing units are defined as large.

Less Than 25% of Earnings Needed for Housing [1,085]

1. Crozet, VA (20)
2. White Rock, NM (21)
3. Los Alamos, NM (28)
4. Rochester, MN (33)
5. Lake Conroe Westshore, TX (35)
6. Lewes, DE (41)
7. Hood River, OR (45)
8. Salida, CO (46)
9. Sun City Hilton Head, SC (47)
10. Ocean View, DE (53)
11. Port Townsend, WA (55)
12. Pawleys Island, SC (56)
13. South Lyon, MI (62)
13. Spirit Lake, IA (62)
15. Rigby, ID (73)
16. New Bremen, OH (77)
16. Orange City, IA (77)

18. Lake Norman of Catawba, NC (93)
19. Frankenmuth, MI (96)
20. Pella, IA (107)
21. Carroll, IA (108)
22. Lago Vista, TX (122)
23. Sturgeon Bay, WI (126)
24. Moab, UT (128)
25. Sioux Center, IA (129)

More Than 40% Built Since 2000 [111]

1. Belterra, TX (3)
2. World Golf Village, FL (4)
3. Roxborough Park, CO (5)
4. Heber, UT (8)
5. Vistancia, AZ (9)
6. Buckhead (Bryan County), GA (10)
7. Purcellville, VA (12)
8. Spring Hill, TN (14)
9. Tea, SD (17)
10. Snoqualmie, WA (18)
11. Archer Lodge, NC (19)
12. Crozet, VA (20)
13. Lake Conroe Eastshore, TX (22)
14. Byron, MN (24)
15. Wellington, CO (26)
16. Boerne, TX (29)
17. Waconia, MN (30)
18. Lewes, DE (41)
19. Aledo, TX (42)
20. Paloma Creek South, TX (44)
21. Sun City Hilton Head, SC (47)
22. Hampstead, NC (48)
23. Eagle Mountain South, UT (49)
24. Mauldin, SC (50)
25. Woodcreek, TX (51)

More Than 40% With 4 or More Bedrooms [49]

1. Summit Park, UT (1)
2. Belterra, TX (3)
3. World Golf Village, FL (4)
4. Roxborough Park, CO (5)
5. Evergreen, CO (7)
6. Heber, UT (8)
7. Buckhead (Bryan County), GA (10)

8. Purcellville, VA (12)
9. Tea, SD (17)
10. Byron, MN (24)
11. Waconia, MN (30)
12. Aledo, TX (42)
13. Eagle Mountain South, UT (49)
14. Stansbury Park, UT (65)
15. Eureka, MO (67)
16. Kill Devil Hills, NC (75)
17. Orangetree, FL (79)
18. Santaquin, UT (81)
19. Mountain House, CA (87)
20. Vail, AZ (92)
21. Corona de Tucson, AZ (98)
22. Middletown, DE (113)
23. Delano, MN (122)
24. Forney, TX (125)
25. Eaton, CO (132)

Chapter 6
ESCAPE ROUTES

Glenn Kelman could see it coming. "We're preparing for a seismic demographic shift toward smaller cities," the CEO of Redfin, an online real-estate brokerage, predicted in May 2020.

Kelman spoke two months after America entered the Covid-19 shutdown, yet his forecast wasn't inspired solely by the pandemic. He cited the lack of affordable housing in major metropolitan areas as the primary reason for the anticipated exodus. The Covid crisis simply proved that millions of employees could productively work from home, freeing them to seek cheaper addresses.

"More people will leave San Francisco, New York, and even Seattle," said Kelman, "some for nearby towns like Sacramento and Tacoma that are close enough to support a weekly office visit, others for a completely remote life in Charleston, Boise, Bozeman, or Madison."

Many of these refugees escaped to communities even smaller than those named by Kelman. The Census Bureau estimated that 861,000 people moved from metros to nonmetropolitan parts of America between 2019 and 2020, a span that included the initial Covid outbreak. These big-city refugees — an average of 16,500 per week — relocated to the small towns that dot the nation's micropolitan areas and rural counties.

They generally didn't move far. A majority still wanted access to the urban hubs where their employers are based, just as Kelman had suggested they would. A separate Census Bureau study found that nearly three-quarters of the 29.8 million Americans who moved during the 2019-2020 span (73.7%) traveled less than 50 miles from their old addresses to their new homes. Another 9.7% fell in the range of 50 to 199 miles, which means that just one-sixth of all moves (16.6%) involved distances of 200 miles or more.

This chapter is designed to help you plot an escape route away from your big city. It's based on the assumption — amply documented in the previous paragraph — that you would prefer to remain in reasonable proximity.

That doesn't mean you're bound by geographic limits, not at all. If you live in Miami and determine that Snoqualmie, Washington, is truly the town of your dreams, go ahead and plot your course. Try not to be intimidated by the extreme length of the route — 2,682 miles by air, 3,332 miles by highway.

But a majority of prospective movers will focus on nearby options, not distant fantasies. Snoqualmie is more likely to pique your interest if you live in Seattle or Portland, which lie 23 and 143 air miles away, respectively. A Miami resident will probably concentrate on the three Dreamtowns within a 100-mile radius of that city, close enough to allow quick return visits for office meetings or football games or shopping weekends.

This chapter splits the nation into 50 exclusive territories, each centered on a major urban hub. (Refer to Chapter 1 for a complete list.) The 209 Dreamtowns and 313 Honorable Mentions have been distributed among these territories, linking each town to the hub that is the shortest air mileage away. It should be noted that adjustments were required for a few towns on Long Island and in Michigan, since their closest hubs sit on the opposite shores of unbridged waterways. These communities have been reattached to the big cities most easily reached by land.

Think of these territories as enormous polygons that subdivide the map of the United States. They function almost as alternate versions of states, with their major cities serving as their capitals. The boundaries for each territory encompass every small town that is closer to its hub than to any other.

Minneapolis boasts the broadest roster of satellites. Its territory includes 113 small towns in Minnesota, Iowa, Michigan, Montana, North Dakota, South Dakota, and Wisconsin. Five other hubs are surrounded by more than 70 towns: Kansas City (96), Denver (84), Memphis (80), Atlanta (73), and Oklahoma City (71). At the opposite end of the list are three territories that contain fewer than 10 small communities apiece: San Diego (eight), Virginia Beach (seven), and Providence (three).

Those totals, of course, encompass every small town, regardless of their quality-of-life scores. The count changes considerably when the conversation is restricted to Dreamtowns. Denver moves into first place, offering the widest selection of elite options in any territory. It's blessed with 25 Dreamtowns. The runners-up are Minneapolis with 22, Salt Lake City with 17, and Sacramento and Seattle with nine apiece.

Quality of life, unfortunately, is not distributed evenly from coast to coast. Eleven territories have a combined total of 327 small towns, yet contain no Dreamtowns whatsoever: Atlanta, Cincinnati, Cleveland, Indianapolis, Louisville, Oklahoma City, Orlando, Providence, Riverside, San Diego, and Tampa. But don't despair. Ten of these hubs — all but San Diego — offer options that are almost as good, since they have Honorable Mentions within their territory boundaries.

This chapter provides breakdowns for all 50 hubs, arrayed in alphabetical order. Each entry starts with the territory's totals of small towns, Dreamtowns, and Honorable Mentions, and then enumerates the latter two groups. Each community is preceded by its rank within the territory. It's followed by its national quality-of-life rank (in parentheses) and its air mileage from the hub.

The final three lines of each breakdown can help expand your search beyond a specific hub. These respective numbers indicate how many Dreamtowns can be found within 50, 100, and 200 air miles of a given big city, regardless of territorial boundaries.

Belterra, Texas, for example, is the top-rated small town in Austin's territory, sitting just 19 air miles west of that hub. But it's also 54 miles by air from San Antonio, 158 from Houston, and 191 from Dallas. Belterra appears by name only in the standings for Austin, though it's also included in the Dreamtown totals for San Antonio at the 100- and 200-mile levels, as well as the counts for Dallas and Houston at the longer radius.

Atlanta

TOTALS FOR TERRITORY
  All small towns: 73
  Dreamtowns: 0
  Honorable Mentions: 7

HONORABLE MENTIONS (TERRITORY)
  1. Jefferson, GA (235), 47 air miles
  2. Auburn, AL (427), 105 air miles
  3. Franklin, NC (463), 108 air miles
  4. Athens, GA (469), 54 air miles
  5. Winder, GA (478), 37 air miles
  6. Warner Robins, GA (487), 94 air miles
  7. Anderson, SC (501), 107 air miles

DREAMTOWNS (ALL TERRITORIES)
  50-mile radius: 0
  100-mile radius: 0
  200-mile radius: 3

Austin

TOTALS FOR TERRITORY
  All small towns: 27
  Dreamtowns: 4
  Honorable Mentions: 3

DREAMTOWNS (TERRITORY)
  1. Belterra, TX (3), 19 air miles
  2. Woodcreek, TX (51), 32 air miles
  3. Manor, TX (60), 14 air miles
  4. Lago Vista, TX (122), 15 air miles

HONORABLE MENTIONS (TERRITORY)
  5. Marble Falls, TX (250), 34 air miles
  6. Granite Shoals, TX (255), 39 air miles
  7. Bastrop, TX (390), 30 air miles

DREAMTOWNS (ALL TERRITORIES)
  50-mile radius: 5
  100-mile radius: 6
  200-mile radius: 12

Baltimore

TOTALS FOR TERRITORY
  All small towns: 25
  Dreamtowns: 3
  Honorable Mentions: 7

DREAMTOWNS (TERRITORY)
  1. Ocean View, DE (53), 96 air miles
  2. Ocean Pines, MD (71), 101 air miles
  3. Westminster, MD (120), 23 air miles

HONORABLE MENTIONS (TERRITORY)
  4. Easton, MD (218), 45 air miles
  5. New Freedom, PA (225), 37 air miles
  6. Shady Side, MD (262), 29 air miles
  7. Manchester, MD (300), 32 air miles
  8. Emmitsburg, MD (320), 51 air miles
  9. Long Neck, DE (326), 90 air miles
  10. Thurmont, MD (360), 49 air miles

DREAMTOWNS (ALL TERRITORIES)
50-mile radius: 3
100-mile radius: 11
200-mile radius: 22

Boston

TOTALS FOR TERRITORY
All small towns: 31
Dreamtowns: 7
Honorable Mentions: 8

DREAMTOWNS (TERRITORY)
1. Nantucket, MA (6), 94 air miles
2. Vineyard Haven, MA (23), 71 air miles
3. Portsmouth, NH (40), 49 air miles
4. Kennebunk, ME (43), 76 air miles
5. Lebanon, NH (87), 106 air miles
6. Burlington, VT (171), 177 air miles
7. Brunswick, ME (179), 123 air miles

HONORABLE MENTIONS (TERRITORY)
8. Milton, VT (271), 186 air miles
9. Laconia, NH (278), 82 air miles
10. Concord, NH (298), 63 air miles
11. Middlebury, VT (359), 152 air miles
12. Manchester, NH (397), 46 air miles
13. Keene, NH (421), 70 air miles
14. Dover, NH (452), 60 air miles
15. Barre, VT (511), 144 air miles

DREAMTOWNS (ALL TERRITORIES)
50-mile radius: 1
100-mile radius: 7
200-mile radius: 17

Bridgeport

TOTALS FOR TERRITORY
All small towns: 21
Dreamtowns: 2
Honorable Mentions: 3

DREAMTOWNS (TERRITORY)
1. West Point, NY (109), 39 air miles
2. Red Hook, NY (152), 47 air miles

HONORABLE MENTIONS (TERRITORY)
3. Danbury, CT (215), 12 air miles

4. Walden, NY (422), 51 air miles
5. Kingston, NY (481), 52 air miles

DREAMTOWNS (ALL TERRITORIES)
50-mile radius: 4
100-mile radius: 9
200-mile radius: 17

Buffalo

TOTALS FOR TERRITORY
All small towns: 40
Dreamtowns: 1
Honorable Mentions: 7

DREAMTOWNS (TERRITORY)
1. East Aurora, NY (173), 15 air miles

HONORABLE MENTIONS (TERRITORY)
2. Ithaca, NY (266), 123 air miles
3. Honeoye Falls, NY (311), 62 air miles
4. Canton, NY (343), 216 air miles
5. Geneva, NY (445), 104 air miles
6. Newfane, NY (450), 27 air miles
7. Corning, NY (459), 105 air miles
8. Clifton Springs, NY (488), 85 air miles

DREAMTOWNS (ALL TERRITORIES)
50-mile radius: 1
100-mile radius: 1
200-mile radius: 2

Charlotte

TOTALS FOR TERRITORY
All small towns: 67
Dreamtowns: 3
Honorable Mentions: 5

DREAMTOWNS (TERRITORY)
1. Mauldin, SC (50), 88 air miles
2. Pawleys Island, SC (56), 157 air miles
3. Lake Norman of Catawba, NC (93), 24 air miles

HONORABLE MENTIONS (TERRITORY)
4. Rock Hill, SC (291), 23 air miles
5. Dandridge, TN (330), 156 air miles
6. Brevard, NC (347), 108 air miles
7. Spartanburg, SC (489), 69 air miles
8. Blacksburg, VA (517), 138 air miles

DREAMTOWNS (ALL TERRITORIES)
　50-mile radius: 1
　100-mile radius: 3
　200-mile radius: 7

Chicago

TOTALS FOR TERRITORY
　All small towns: 51
　Dreamtowns: 3
　Honorable Mentions: 9

DREAMTOWNS (TERRITORY)
　1. Mount Vernon, IA (143), 181 air miles
　2. Monticello, IL (149), 129 air miles
　3. Iowa City, IA (159), 189 air miles

HONORABLE MENTIONS (TERRITORY)
　4. Holland, MI (231), 114 air miles
　5. Mahomet, IL (257), 115 air miles
　6. Cedar Rapids, IA (286), 194 air miles
　7. Byron, IL (341), 74 air miles
　8. Bloomington, IL (370), 108 air miles
　9. Morris, IL (414), 42 air miles
　10. South Haven, MI (426), 92 air miles
　11. Braidwood, IL (490), 42 air miles
　12. Lake Holiday, IL (501), 42 air miles

DREAMTOWNS (ALL TERRITORIES)
　50-mile radius: 0
　100-mile radius: 1
　200-mile radius: 9

Cincinnati

TOTALS FOR TERRITORY
　All small towns: 23
　Dreamtowns: 0
　Honorable Mentions: 2

HONORABLE MENTIONS (TERRITORY)
　1. Oxford, OH (400), 27 air miles
　2. Batesville, IN (467), 40 air miles

DREAMTOWNS (ALL TERRITORIES)
　50-mile radius: 0
　100-mile radius: 2
　200-mile radius: 2

Cleveland

TOTALS FOR TERRITORY
All small towns: 24
Dreamtowns: 0
Honorable Mentions: 5

HONORABLE MENTIONS (TERRITORY)
1. Port Clinton, OH (286), 65 air miles
2. Seville, OH (303), 33 air miles
3. Chardon, OH (306), 22 air miles
4. Orrville, OH (474), 42 air miles
5. Wooster, OH (482), 46 air miles

DREAMTOWNS (ALL TERRITORIES)
50-mile radius: 0
100-mile radius: 0
200-mile radius: 7

Columbus

TOTALS FOR TERRITORY
All small towns: 55
Dreamtowns: 2
Honorable Mentions: 6

DREAMTOWNS (TERRITORY)
1. New Bremen, OH (77), 79 air miles
2. Marysville, OH (119), 26 air miles

HONORABLE MENTIONS (TERRITORY)
3. Ottawa, OH (384), 89 air miles
4. Celina, OH (385), 92 air miles
5. Findlay, OH (402), 79 air miles
6. Newark, OH (470), 27 air miles
7. St. Marys, OH (497), 84 air miles
8. Johnstown, OH (506), 17 air miles

DREAMTOWNS (ALL TERRITORIES)
50-mile radius: 1
100-mile radius: 2
200-mile radius: 4

Dallas

TOTALS FOR TERRITORY
All small towns: 67
Dreamtowns: 6
Honorable Mentions: 3

DREAMTOWNS (TERRITORY)
1. Aledo, TX (42), 40 air miles
2. Paloma Creek South, TX (44), 28 air miles
3. Anna, TX (115), 46 air miles
4. Forney, TX (125), 32 air miles
5. Pecan Plantation, TX (140), 50 air miles
6. Weatherford, TX (201), 44 air miles

HONORABLE MENTIONS (TERRITORY)
7. Sanger, TX (391), 39 air miles
8. Granbury, TX (411), 52 air miles
9. Lindale, TX (462), 93 air miles

DREAMTOWNS (ALL TERRITORIES)
50-mile radius: 6
100-mile radius: 6
200-mile radius: 11

Denver

TOTALS FOR TERRITORY
All small towns: 84
Dreamtowns: 25
Honorable Mentions: 13

DREAMTOWNS (TERRITORY)
1. Roxborough Park, CO (5), 18 air miles
2. Evergreen, CO (7), 19 air miles
3. Lafayette, CO (11), 21 air miles
4. Aspen, CO (13), 107 air miles
5. White Rock, NM (21), 277 air miles
6. Breckenridge, CO (25), 60 air miles
7. Wellington, CO (26), 68 air miles
8. Silverthorne, CO (27), 60 air miles
9. Los Alamos, NM (28), 274 air miles
10. Vail, CO (31), 72 air miles
11. Steamboat Springs, CO (34), 113 air miles
12. Boulder, CO (37), 27 air miles
13. Salida, CO (46), 99 air miles
14. Johnstown, CO (58), 43 air miles
15. Woodland Park, CO (59), 50 air miles
16. Basalt, CO (72), 116 air miles
17. Estes Park, CO (76), 54 air miles
18. Firestone, CO (90), 28 air miles
19. Gunnison, CO (97), 133 air miles
20. Gypsum, CO (131), 106 air miles
21. Eaton, CO (132), 58 air miles

22. Eagle, CO (142), 100 air miles
23. Edwards, CO (145), 86 air miles
24. Longmont, CO (165), 33 air miles
25. Colby, KS (187), 209 air miles

HONORABLE MENTIONS (TERRITORY)

26. Durango, CO (210), 230 air miles
27. Leadville, CO (283), 78 air miles
28. Spearfish, SD (298), 335 air miles
29. New Castle, CO (304), 137 air miles
30. Carbondale, CO (321), 122 air miles
31. Pagosa Springs, CO (335), 204 air miles
32. Sheridan, WY (396), 365 air miles
33. Cheyenne, WY (407), 99 air miles
34. Canon City, CO (457), 89 air miles
35. Laramie, WY (492), 116 air miles
35. Montrose, CO (492), 178 air miles
37. Greeley, CO (495), 49 air miles
38. Santa Fe, NM (513), 287 air miles

DREAMTOWNS (ALL TERRITORIES)

50-mile radius: 8
100-mile radius: 17
200-mile radius: 22

Detroit

TOTALS FOR TERRITORY

All small towns: 51
Dreamtowns: 8
Honorable Mentions: 8

DREAMTOWNS (TERRITORY)

1. Chelsea, MI (52), 42 air miles
2. South Lyon, MI (62), 29 air miles
3. Frankenmuth, MI (96), 64 air miles
4. Traverse City, MI (116), 196 air miles
5. Petoskey, MI (172), 216 air miles
6. Goodrich, MI (176), 30 air miles
7. Midland, MI (182), 92 air miles
8. Dorr, MI (190), 128 air miles

HONORABLE MENTIONS (TERRITORY)

9. Williamston, MI (224), 54 air miles
10. Milan, MI (256), 36 air miles
11. Lowell, MI (282), 114 air miles
12. Holly, MI (442), 29 air miles
13. Hastings, MI (466), 106 air miles

14. Wauseon, OH (470), 80 air miles
15. Angola, IN (495), 108 air miles
16. Richmond, MI (520), 33 air miles

DREAMTOWNS (ALL TERRITORIES)
50-mile radius: 3
100-mile radius: 5
200-mile radius: 9

Hartford

TOTALS FOR TERRITORY
All small towns: 16
Dreamtowns: 4
Honorable Mentions: 3

DREAMTOWNS (TERRITORY)
1. Saratoga Springs, NY (68), 108 air miles
2. Lake Pocotopaug, CT (74), 14 air miles
3. Colchester, CT (166), 22 air miles
4. South Deerfield, MA (183), 51 air miles

HONORABLE MENTIONS (TERRITORY)
5. Lee, MA (280), 49 air miles
6. Glens Falls, NY (358), 120 air miles
7. Pittsfield, MA (500), 58 air miles

DREAMTOWNS (ALL TERRITORIES)
50-mile radius: 3
100-mile radius: 8
200-mile radius: 17

Houston

TOTALS FOR TERRITORY
All small towns: 37
Dreamtowns: 2
Honorable Mentions: 0

DREAMTOWNS (TERRITORY)
1. Lake Conroe Eastshore, TX (22), 46 air miles
2. Lake Conroe Westshore, TX (35), 43 air miles

DREAMTOWNS (ALL TERRITORIES)
50-mile radius: 2
100-mile radius: 2
200-mile radius: 7

Indianapolis

TOTALS FOR TERRITORY
All small towns: 47
Dreamtowns: 0
Honorable Mentions: 7

HONORABLE MENTIONS (TERRITORY)
1. St. Joseph, IL (294), 102 air miles
2. Columbus, IN (319), 42 air miles
3. Lebanon, IN (365), 24 air miles
4. Bloomington, IN (380), 50 air miles
5. Lafayette, IN (441), 58 air miles
6. Columbia City, IN (445), 99 air miles
7. Warsaw, IN (511), 101 air miles

DREAMTOWNS (ALL TERRITORIES)
50-mile radius: 0
100-mile radius: 0
200-mile radius: 3

Jacksonville

TOTALS FOR TERRITORY
All small towns: 48
Dreamtowns: 7
Honorable Mentions: 6

DREAMTOWNS (TERRITORY)
1. World Golf Village, FL (4), 21 air miles
2. Buckhead (Bryan County), GA (10), 114 air miles
3. St. Simons, GA (16), 67 air miles
4. Sun City Hilton Head, SC (47), 147 air miles
5. Fernandina Beach, FL (61), 28 air miles
6. St. Augustine, FL (95), 32 air miles
7. Hilton Head Island, SC (138), 147 air miles

HONORABLE MENTIONS (TERRITORY)
8. Beaufort, SC (300), 160 air miles
9. Yulee, FL (312), 26 air miles
10. Alachua, FL (361), 60 air miles
11. Rincon, GA (391), 143 air miles
12. Crawfordville, FL (498), 161 air miles
13. Keystone Heights, FL (501), 38 air miles

DREAMTOWNS (ALL TERRITORIES)
50-mile radius: 3
100-mile radius: 4
200-mile radius: 7

Kansas City

TOTALS FOR TERRITORY
All small towns: 96
Dreamtowns: 5
Honorable Mentions: 19

DREAMTOWNS (TERRITORY)
1. Platte City, MO (82), 23 air miles
2. Lee's Summit, MO (86), 15 air miles
3. Pella, IA (107), 186 air miles
4. Carroll, IA (108), 210 air miles
5. McPherson, KS (133), 172 air miles

HONORABLE MENTIONS (TERRITORY)
6. Indianola, IA (244), 169 air miles
7. Winterset, IA (246), 161 air miles
8. Wayne, NE (248), 254 air miles
9. Spring Hill, KS (254), 24 air miles
10. Eudora, KS (263), 28 air miles
11. Kearney, MO (276), 26 air miles
12. Lawrence, KS (308), 36 air miles
13. Willard, MO (318), 136 air miles
14. Seward, NE (329), 185 air miles
15. Holdrege, NE (332), 272 air miles
16. Pleasant Hill, MO (351), 25 air miles
17. Wamego, KS (354), 93 air miles
18. York, NE (362), 203 air miles
19. Kearney, NE (366), 264 air miles
20. Tonganoxie, KS (382), 26 air miles
21. El Dorado, KS (409), 148 air miles
22. Grinnell, IA (411), 211 air miles
23. Blair, NE (479), 191 air miles
24. Columbus, NE (510), 220 air miles

DREAMTOWNS (ALL TERRITORIES)
50-mile radius: 2
100-mile radius: 2
200-mile radius: 4

Las Vegas

TOTALS FOR TERRITORY
All small towns: 14
Dreamtowns: 2
Honorable Mentions: 3

DREAMTOWNS (TERRITORY)
1. St. George, UT (85), 111 air miles
2. Cedar City, UT (163), 159 air miles

HONORABLE MENTIONS (TERRITORY)
3. Hurricane, UT (315), 124 air miles
4. Moapa Valley, NV (327), 50 air miles
5. Boulder City, NV (509), 21 air miles

DREAMTOWNS (ALL TERRITORIES)
50-mile radius: 0
100-mile radius: 0
200-mile radius: 3

Los Angeles

TOTALS FOR TERRITORY
All small towns: 23
Dreamtowns: 1
Honorable Mentions: 3

DREAMTOWNS (TERRITORY)
1. Solvang, CA (197), 122 air miles

HONORABLE MENTIONS (TERRITORY)
2. Camarillo, CA (218), 56 air miles
3. Arroyo Grande, CA (264), 163 air miles
4. Simi Valley, CA (376), 42 air miles

DREAMTOWNS (ALL TERRITORIES)
50-mile radius: 0
100-mile radius: 0
200-mile radius: 2

Louisville

TOTALS FOR TERRITORY
All small towns: 43
Dreamtowns: 0
Honorable Mentions: 3

HONORABLE MENTIONS (TERRITORY)
1. Jasper, IN (295), 70 air miles
2. Versailles, KY (394), 54 air miles
3. Georgetown, KY (518), 60 air miles

DREAMTOWNS (ALL TERRITORIES)
50-mile radius: 0
100-mile radius: 0
200-mile radius: 6

Memphis

TOTALS FOR TERRITORY
All small towns: 80
Dreamtowns: 1
Honorable Mentions: 2

DREAMTOWNS (TERRITORY)
1. Oxford, MS (111), 55 air miles

HONORABLE MENTIONS (TERRITORY)
2. Arlington, TN (227), 19 air miles
3. Oakland, TN (323), 25 air miles

DREAMTOWNS (ALL TERRITORIES)
50-mile radius: 0
100-mile radius: 1
200-mile radius: 3

Miami

TOTALS FOR TERRITORY
All small towns: 13
Dreamtowns: 4
Honorable Mentions: 1

DREAMTOWNS (TERRITORY)
1. Jupiter Farms, FL (38), 51 air miles
2. Orangetree, FL (79), 83 air miles
3. Big Pine Key, FL (156), 126 air miles
4. Key Largo, FL (157), 83 air miles

HONORABLE MENTIONS (TERRITORY)
5. Marathon, FL (400), 111 air miles

DREAMTOWNS (ALL TERRITORIES)
50-mile radius: 0
100-mile radius: 3
200-mile radius: 4

Milwaukee

TOTALS FOR TERRITORY
All small towns: 64
Dreamtowns: 6
Honorable Mentions: 20

DREAMTOWNS (TERRITORY)
1. Mukwonago, WI (83), 18 air miles
2. Oregon, WI (94), 65 air miles
3. Prairie du Sac, WI (117), 83 air miles

4. Sturgeon Bay, WI (126), 128 air miles
5. Mount Horeb, WI (127), 82 air miles
6. Lake Mills, WI (164), 41 air miles

HONORABLE MENTIONS (TERRITORY)

7. Columbus, WI (220), 50 air miles
8. West Bend, WI (235), 23 air miles
9. Lake Geneva, WI (237), 37 air miles
10. Marshfield, WI (242), 151 air miles
11. Stevens Point, WI (253), 124 air miles
12. Edgerton, WI (314), 51 air miles
13. Monroe, WI (317), 84 air miles
14. Evansville, WI (330), 63 air miles
15. Plymouth, WI (346), 49 air miles
16. Baraboo, WI (348), 88 air miles
17. Wausau, WI (352), 149 air miles
18. Elkhorn, WI (370), 33 air miles
19. Dubuque, IA (387), 137 air miles
19. Lake Delton, WI (387), 93 air miles
21. Reedsburg, WI (416), 101 air miles
22. Janesville, WI (427), 52 air miles
23. Sheboygan, WI (455), 51 air miles
24. Burlington, WI (460), 25 air miles
25. Fort Atkinson, WI (472), 37 air miles
26. Rhinelander, WI (508), 191 air miles

DREAMTOWNS (ALL TERRITORIES)

50-mile radius: 2
100-mile radius: 5
200-mile radius: 11

Minneapolis

TOTALS FOR TERRITORY

All small towns: 113
Dreamtowns: 22
Honorable Mentions: 39

DREAMTOWNS (TERRITORY)

1. Tea, SD (17), 205 air miles
2. Byron, MN (24), 72 air miles
3. Waconia, MN (30), 27 air miles
4. Rochester, MN (33), 77 air miles
5. Spirit Lake, IA (62), 142 air miles
6. Hudson, WI (69), 27 air miles
7. Orange City, IA (77), 194 air miles
8. Decorah, IA (105), 137 air miles

9. Delano, MN (122), 25 air miles
10. Sioux Center, IA (129), 194 air miles
11. Buffalo, MN (139), 32 air miles
12. Lindstrom, MN (146), 34 air miles
13. Alexandria, MN (150), 120 air miles
14. Forest Lake, MN (160), 26 air miles
15. Monticello, MN (178), 35 air miles
16. Belle Plaine, MN (179), 34 air miles
17. New Prague, MN (185), 34 air miles
18. Zimmerman, MN (189), 37 air miles
19. Jordan, MN (192), 28 air miles
20. Northfield, MN (198), 37 air miles
21. New Ulm, MN (204), 74 air miles
22. Kasson, MN (206), 70 air miles

HONORABLE MENTIONS (TERRITORY)
23. Clear Lake, IA (213), 127 air miles
24. Brandon, SD (222), 189 air miles
25. Owatonna, MN (231), 61 air miles
26. Ames, IA (250), 204 air miles
27. Stewartville, MN (258), 86 air miles
28. Yankton, SD (261), 250 air miles
29. Hastings, MN (268), 26 air miles
30. New Richmond, WI (270), 37 air miles
31. Baldwin, WI (275), 42 air miles
32. Le Mars, IA (279), 209 air miles
33. North Branch, MN (295), 39 air miles
34. Lake City, MN (305), 62 air miles
35. Waverly, IA (309), 160 air miles
36. Brookings, SD (321), 178 air miles
37. Eau Claire, WI (327), 90 air miles
38. River Falls, WI (333), 34 air miles
39. Mankato, MN (338), 66 air miles
40. Sioux Falls, SD (340), 198 air miles
41. La Crosse, WI (348), 127 air miles
42. St. Francis, MN (363), 27 air miles
43. Hutchinson, MN (367), 54 air miles
44. St. Peter, MN (368), 56 air miles
45. St. Cloud, MN (380), 60 air miles
46. Fergus Falls, MN (391), 162 air miles
47. Fairmont, MN (405), 109 air miles
48. Watertown, SD (409), 188 air miles
49. Algona, IA (419), 140 air miles
50. Madison, SD (438), 201 air miles
51. Cambridge, MN (439), 38 air miles

52. Rice Lake, WI (444), 83 air miles
53. Vermillion, SD (453), 236 air miles
54. Nevada, IA (456), 205 air miles
55. Independence, IA (457), 186 air miles
56. Spencer, IA (460), 157 air miles
57. Litchfield, MN (473), 61 air miles
58. Duluth, MN (476), 135 air miles
59. Mason City, IA (477), 126 air miles
60. Brainerd, MN (494), 106 air miles
61. Pierre, SD (521), 348 air miles

DREAMTOWNS (ALL TERRITORIES)
50-mile radius: 12
100-mile radius: 16
200-mile radius: 21

Nashville

TOTALS FOR TERRITORY
All small towns: 48
Dreamtowns: 3
Honorable Mentions: 2

DREAMTOWNS (TERRITORY)
1. Spring Hill, TN (14), 30 air miles
2. Fairview, TN (106), 27 air miles
3. Murfreesboro, TN (192), 25 air miles

HONORABLE MENTIONS (TERRITORY)
4. Lebanon, TN (290), 21 air miles
5. Columbia, TN (484), 41 air miles

DREAMTOWNS (ALL TERRITORIES)
50-mile radius: 3
100-mile radius: 3
200-mile radius: 3

New Orleans

TOTALS FOR TERRITORY
All small towns: 52
Dreamtowns: 3
Honorable Mentions: 2

DREAMTOWNS (TERRITORY)
1. Mandeville, LA (64), 33 air miles
2. Santa Rosa Beach, FL (70), 234 air miles
3. Daphne, AL (110), 145 air miles

    4. Diamondhead, MS (216), 55 air miles
    5. Slidell, LA (289), 32 air miles

DREAMTOWNS (ALL TERRITORIES)
    50-mile radius: 1
    100-mile radius: 1
    200-mile radius: 2

New York

TOTALS FOR TERRITORY
    All small towns: 18
    Dreamtowns: 5
    Honorable Mentions: 5

DREAMTOWNS (TERRITORY)
    1. Jefferson Township North, NJ (84), 36 air miles
    2. Twin Rivers, NJ (90), 44 air miles
    3. Warwick, NY (112), 44 air miles
    4. Chester, NY (136), 47 air miles
    5. Southold, NY (167), 86 air miles

HONORABLE MENTIONS (TERRITORY)
    6. Pocono Woodland Lakes, PA (214), 66 air miles
    7. Springs, NY (240), 95 air miles
    8. Franklin, NJ (395), 43 air miles
    9. Washington, NJ (464), 54 air miles
    10. Saw Creek, PA (482), 62 air miles

DREAMTOWNS (ALL TERRITORIES)
    50-mile radius: 5
    100-mile radius: 8
    200-mile radius: 18

Oklahoma City

TOTALS FOR TERRITORY
    All small towns: 71
    Dreamtowns: 0
    Honorable Mentions: 2

HONORABLE MENTIONS (TERRITORY)
    1. Pratt, KS (373), 162 air miles
    2. Norman, OK (431), 21 air miles

DREAMTOWNS (ALL TERRITORIES)
    50-mile radius: 0
    100-mile radius: 0
    200-mile radius: 5

Orlando

TOTALS FOR TERRITORY
All small towns: 15
Dreamtowns: 0
Honorable Mentions: 5

HONORABLE MENTIONS (TERRITORY)
1. Wedgefield, FL (230), 21 air miles
2. Sebastian, FL (307), 88 air miles
3. Leesburg, FL (424), 27 air miles
4. Lady Lake, FL (442), 44 air miles
5. Titusville, FL (447), 35 air miles

DREAMTOWNS (ALL TERRITORIES)
50-mile radius: 0
100-mile radius: 2
200-mile radius: 6

Philadelphia

TOTALS FOR TERRITORY
All small towns: 29
Dreamtowns: 2
Honorable Mentions: 4

DREAMTOWNS (TERRITORY)
1. Lewes, DE (41), 86 air miles
2. Middletown, DE (113), 41 air miles

HONORABLE MENTIONS (TERRITORY)
3. Villas, NJ (229), 70 air miles
4. Pottstown, PA (313), 28 air miles
5. Orwigsburg, PA (374), 64 air miles
6. Mystic Island, NJ (431), 57 air miles

DREAMTOWNS (ALL TERRITORIES)
50-mile radius: 2
100-mile radius: 6
200-mile radius: 22

Phoenix

TOTALS FOR TERRITORY
All small towns: 50
Dreamtowns: 4
Honorable Mentions: 6

DREAMTOWNS (TERRITORY)
1. Vistancia, AZ (9), 27 air miles

2. Vail, AZ (92), 123 air miles
3. Corona de Tucson, AZ (98), 127 air miles
4. Sedona, AZ (130), 95 air miles

HONORABLE MENTIONS (TERRITORY)

5. Estrella, AZ (211), 30 air miles
6. Marana West, AZ (247), 85 air miles
7. Sahuarita, AZ (260), 124 air miles
8. Prescott Valley, AZ (277), 79 air miles
9. Village of Oak Creek (Big Park), AZ (370), 90 air miles
10. Flagstaff, AZ (378), 119 air miles

DREAMTOWNS (ALL TERRITORIES)

50-mile radius: 1
100-mile radius: 2
200-mile radius: 4

Pittsburgh

TOTALS FOR TERRITORY

All small towns: 46
Dreamtowns: 1
Honorable Mentions: 4

DREAMTOWNS (TERRITORY)

1. State College, PA (204), 112 air miles

HONORABLE MENTIONS (TERRITORY)

2. Morgantown, WV (268), 56 air miles
3. Butler, PA (386), 28 air miles
4. Grove City, PA (403), 49 air miles
5. St. Marys, PA (454), 99 air miles

DREAMTOWNS (ALL TERRITORIES)

50-mile radius: 0
100-mile radius: 0
200-mile radius: 13

Portland

TOTALS FOR TERRITORY

All small towns: 49
Dreamtowns: 7
Honorable Mentions: 10

DREAMTOWNS (TERRITORY)

1. Bend, OR (15), 121 air miles
2. Hood River, OR (45), 56 air miles
3. Astoria, OR (144), 74 air miles
4. Seaside, OR (162), 69 air miles

  5. Corvallis, OR (188), 72 air miles

  6. Redmond, OR (196), 112 air miles

  7. Silverton, OR (208), 36 air miles

HONORABLE MENTIONS (TERRITORY)

  8. Sandy, OR (240), 20 air miles

  9. Canby, OR (252), 18 air miles

  10. Albany, OR (339), 65 air miles

  11. Baker City, OR (348), 240 air miles

  12. Dallas, OR (405), 52 air miles

  13. Newberg, OR (415), 22 air miles

  14. Newport, OR (431), 92 air miles

  15. St. Helens, OR (467), 23 air miles

  16. Medford, OR (504), 220 air miles

  17. Lincoln City, OR (505), 77 air miles

DREAMTOWNS (ALL TERRITORIES)

  50-mile radius: 1

  100-mile radius: 5

  200-mile radius: 10

Providence

TOTALS FOR TERRITORY

  All small towns: 3

  Dreamtowns: 0

  Honorable Mentions: 1

HONORABLE MENTIONS (TERRITORY)

  1. North Brookfield, MA (411), 46 air miles

DREAMTOWNS (ALL TERRITORIES)

  50-mile radius: 1

  100-mile radius: 7

  200-mile radius: 17

Raleigh

TOTALS FOR TERRITORY

  All small towns: 43

  Dreamtowns: 5

  Honorable Mentions: 3

DREAMTOWNS (TERRITORY)

  1. Archer Lodge, NC (19), 18 air miles

  2. Hampstead, NC (48), 111 air miles

  3. Pinehurst, NC (152), 59 air miles

4. Oak Island, NC (191), 132 air miles
5. Morehead City, NC (194), 124 air miles

HONORABLE MENTIONS (TERRITORY)

6. Wendell, NC (265), 19 air miles
7. Spout Springs, NC (486), 40 air miles
8. Butner, NC (519), 26 air miles

DREAMTOWNS (ALL TERRITORIES)

50-mile radius: 1
100-mile radius: 2
200-mile radius: 16

Richmond

TOTALS FOR TERRITORY

All small towns: 17
Dreamtowns: 4
Honorable Mentions: 2

DREAMTOWNS (TERRITORY)

1. Crozet, VA (20), 77 air miles
2. Ruckersville, VA (65), 71 air miles
3. Lake Monticello, VA (99), 55 air miles
4. Charlottesville, VA (117), 67 air miles

HONORABLE MENTIONS (TERRITORY)

5. Lexington, VA (447), 108 air miles
6. Lynchburg, VA (521), 94 air miles

DREAMTOWNS (ALL TERRITORIES)

50-mile radius: 1
100-mile radius: 9
200-mile radius: 22

Riverside

TOTALS FOR TERRITORY

All small towns: 10
Dreamtowns: 0
Honorable Mentions: 1

HONORABLE MENTIONS (TERRITORY)

1. Silver Lakes, CA (336), 53 air miles

DREAMTOWNS (ALL TERRITORIES)

50-mile radius: 0
100-mile radius: 0
200-mile radius: 1

Sacramento

TOTALS FOR TERRITORY
All small towns: 57
Dreamtowns: 9
Honorable Mentions: 13

DREAMTOWNS (TERRITORY)
1. Lake of the Pines, CA (32), 30 air miles
2. Rancho Murieta, CA (36), 16 air miles
3. Truckee, CA (39), 78 air miles
4. Johnson Lane, NV (114), 90 air miles
5. Davis, CA (154), 23 air miles
6. Auburn, CA (155), 24 air miles
7. Bishop, CA (177), 181 air miles
8. Incline Village, NV (181), 83 air miles
9. Plumas Lake, CA (186), 28 air miles

HONORABLE MENTIONS (TERRITORY)
10. Placerville, CA (220), 30 air miles
11. Rio Vista, CA (228), 38 air miles
12. Mammoth Lakes, CA (242), 145 air miles
13. Lake Wildwood, CA (259), 41 air miles
14. Grass Valley, CA (288), 42 air miles
15. Sonora, CA (315), 70 air miles
16. Jackson, CA (353), 36 air miles
17. Rancho Calaveras, CA (404), 43 air miles
18. South Lake Tahoe, CA (425), 75 air miles
19. Chico, CA (440), 82 air miles
20. Escalon, CA (474), 61 air miles
21. Redding, CA (515), 145 air miles
21. Vacaville, CA (515), 40 air miles

DREAMTOWNS (ALL TERRITORIES)
50-mile radius: 5
100-mile radius: 13
200-mile radius: 15

St. Louis

TOTALS FOR TERRITORY
All small towns: 68
Dreamtowns: 2
Honorable Mentions: 10

DREAMTOWNS (TERRITORY)
1. Eureka, MO (67), 18 air miles
2. Breese, IL (168), 44 air miles

HONORABLE MENTIONS (TERRITORY)

3. Waterloo, IL (217), 23 air miles
4. Effingham, IL (273), 103 air miles
5. Columbia, MO (295), 109 air miles
6. Washington, MO (323), 37 air miles
7. Highland, IL (377), 37 air miles
8. Fairfield, IA (416), 185 air miles
9. Jerseyville, IL (420), 34 air miles
10. Springfield, IL (436), 88 air miles
11. Mascoutah, IL (447), 30 air miles
12. Cape Girardeau, MO (514), 99 air miles

DREAMTOWNS (ALL TERRITORIES)

50-mile radius: 2
100-mile radius: 2
200-mile radius: 3

Salt Lake City

TOTALS FOR TERRITORY

All small towns: 52
Dreamtowns: 17
Honorable Mentions: 12

DREAMTOWNS (TERRITORY)

1. Summit Park, UT (1), 20 air miles
2. Park City, UT (2), 22 air miles
3. Heber, UT (8), 28 air miles
4. Eagle Mountain South, UT (49), 23 air miles
5. Jackson, WY (57), 204 air miles
6. Stansbury Park, UT (65), 19 air miles
7. Rigby, ID (73), 209 air miles
8. Santaquin, UT (81), 47 air miles
9. Bozeman, MT (89), 351 air miles
10. Star, ID (104), 315 air miles
11. Moab, UT (128), 192 air miles
12. Logan, UT (148), 75 air miles
13. Kuna, ID (169), 303 air miles
14. Ephraim, UT (194), 91 air miles
15. Belgrade, MT (202), 357 air miles
16. Idaho Falls, ID (207), 197 air miles
17. Nephi, UT (208), 64 air miles

HONORABLE MENTIONS (TERRITORY)
   18. Livingston, MT (225), 353 air miles
   19. Hailey, ID (302), 232 air miles
   20. Cody, WY (309), 305 air miles
   21. Pocatello, ID (334), 157 air miles
   22. Helena, MT (357), 412 air miles
   23. Tremonton, UT (378), 76 air miles
   24. Lander, WY (408), 224 air miles
   25. Grantsville, UT (416), 28 air miles
   26. Richfield, UT (423), 130 air miles
   27. Tooele, UT (427), 21 air miles
   27. Twin Falls, ID (427), 186 air miles
   29. Evanston, WY (434), 66 air miles

DREAMTOWNS (ALL TERRITORIES)
   50-mile radius: 6
   100-mile radius: 9
   200-mile radius: 11

San Antonio

TOTALS FOR TERRITORY
   All small towns: 45
   Dreamtowns: 2
   Honorable Mentions: 3

DREAMTOWNS (TERRITORY)
   1. Boerne, TX (29), 24 air miles
   2. Canyon Lake, TX (133), 27 air miles

HONORABLE MENTIONS (TERRITORY)
   3. Fredericksburg, TX (238), 57 air miles
   4. Midland, TX (356), 275 air miles
   5. Carlsbad, NM (498), 395 air miles

DREAMTOWNS (ALL TERRITORIES)
   50-mile radius: 3
   100-mile radius: 6
   200-mile radius: 8

San Diego

TOTALS FOR TERRITORY
   All small towns: 8
   Dreamtowns: 0
   Honorable Mentions: 0

DREAMTOWNS (ALL TERRITORIES)
50-mile radius: 0
100-mile radius: 0
200-mile radius: 0

San Francisco

TOTALS FOR TERRITORY
All small towns: 28
Dreamtowns: 5
Honorable Mentions: 4

DREAMTOWNS (TERRITORY)
1. Mountain House, CA (87), 35 air miles
2. Half Moon Bay, CA (99), 21 air miles
3. Livermore, CA (102), 23 air miles
4. Petaluma, CA (124), 47 air miles
5. Discovery Bay, CA (161), 34 air miles

HONORABLE MENTIONS (TERRITORY)
6. St. Helena, CA (211), 59 air miles
7. Forestville, CA (273), 67 air miles
8. Sonoma, CA (325), 46 air miles
9. Cloverdale, CA (506), 90 air miles

DREAMTOWNS (ALL TERRITORIES)
50-mile radius: 6
100-mile radius: 9
200-mile radius: 16

San Jose

TOTALS FOR TERRITORY
All small towns: 43
Dreamtowns: 3
Honorable Mentions: 4

DREAMTOWNS (TERRITORY)
1. Santa Cruz, CA (170), 19 air miles
2. Morro Bay, CA (174), 149 air miles
3. Cambria, CA (198), 131 air miles

HONORABLE MENTIONS (TERRITORY)
4. Gilroy, CA (234), 25 air miles
5. Paso Robles, CA (283), 138 air miles
6. San Luis Obispo, CA (342), 158 air miles
7. Bonadelle Ranchos, CA (434), 116 air miles

DREAMTOWNS (ALL TERRITORIES)
50-mile radius: 5
100-mile radius: 8
200-mile radius: 17

Seattle

TOTALS FOR TERRITORY
All small towns: 61
Dreamtowns: 9
Honorable Mentions: 19

DREAMTOWNS (TERRITORY)
1. Snoqualmie, WA (18), 23 air miles
2. Whitefish, MT (54), 373 air miles
3. Port Townsend, WA (55), 51 air miles
4. Anacortes, WA (102), 72 air miles
5. Birch Bay, WA (121), 105 air miles
6. Bellingham, WA (151), 91 air miles
7. Olympia, WA (157), 40 air miles
8. Moscow, ID (174), 253 air miles
9. Coeur d'Alene, ID (183), 257 air miles

HONORABLE MENTIONS (TERRITORY)
10. Lynden, WA (231), 101 air miles
11. Indianola, WA (239), 22 air miles
12. Kalispell, MT (245), 373 air miles
13. Sequim, WA (248), 59 air miles
14. Ellensburg, WA (267), 88 air miles
15. Stanwood, WA (271), 54 air miles
16. Camano, WA (280), 49 air miles
17. Colville, WA (292), 215 air miles
18. Marysville, WA (293), 41 air miles
19. Missoula, MT (343), 389 air miles
19. Sandpoint, ID (343), 271 air miles
21. Rathdrum, ID (374), 252 air miles
22. Columbia Falls, MT (382), 379 air miles
23. Oak Harbor, WA (399), 61 air miles
24. Everson, WA (450), 99 air miles
25. Pullman, WA (464), 245 air miles
26. Mount Vernon, WA (479), 68 air miles
27. Yelm, WA (485), 38 air miles
28. Granite Falls, WA (490), 46 air miles

DREAMTOWNS (ALL TERRITORIES)
  50-mile radius: 2
  100-mile radius: 5
  200-mile radius: 10

Tampa

TOTALS FOR TERRITORY
  All small towns: 10
  Dreamtowns: 0
  Honorable Mentions: 3

HONORABLE MENTIONS (TERRITORY)
  1. Sugarmill Woods, FL (222), 50 air miles
  2. North Port, FL (355), 73 air miles
  3. Spring Hill, FL (397), 33 air miles

DREAMTOWNS (ALL TERRITORIES)
  50-mile radius: 0
  100-mile radius: 0
  200-mile radius: 5

Virginia Beach

TOTALS FOR TERRITORY
  All small towns: 7
  Dreamtowns: 3
  Honorable Mentions: 1

DREAMTOWNS (TERRITORY)
  1. Kill Devil Hills, NC (75), 69 air miles
  2. Manteo, NC (80), 75 air miles
  3. Williamsburg, VA (101), 35 air miles

HONORABLE MENTIONS (TERRITORY)
  4. Smithfield, VA (369), 16 air miles

DREAMTOWNS (ALL TERRITORIES)
  50-mile radius: 1
  100-mile radius: 4
  200-mile radius: 22

Washington

TOTALS FOR TERRITORY
  All small towns: 21
  Dreamtowns: 7
  Honorable Mentions: 5

DREAMTOWNS (TERRITORY)

1. Purcellville, VA (12), 33 air miles
2. Leonardtown, MD (135), 51 air miles
3. Frederick, MD (137), 38 air miles
4. Lake of the Woods, VA (141), 49 air miles
5. Chesapeake Beach, MD (147), 34 air miles
6. Fredericksburg, VA (198), 46 air miles
7. Brunswick, MD (203), 37 air miles

HONORABLE MENTIONS (TERRITORY)

8. Winchester, VA (285), 55 air miles
9. Lexington Park, MD (336), 56 air miles
10. Long Beach, MD (363), 48 air miles
11. Charles Town, WV (389), 45 air miles
12. Waldorf, MD (437), 23 air miles

DREAMTOWNS (ALL TERRITORIES)

50-mile radius: 7
100-mile radius: 13
200-mile radius: 19

Chapter 7
FULL STANDINGS

This final chapter, to be honest, is really an appendix. It features the complete quality-of-life standings for all 2,084 small towns across America. The rankings are presented in two ways — first in numerical order, then in alphabetical order by state.

If you desire a detailed map of any of the towns below, do a web search for "census urban area reference maps." You'll be directed to a Census Bureau site offering downloadable PDF maps for all urbanized areas and urban clusters. The boundaries were drawn back in 2010, but they remain in force today.

Top to Bottom

Each town is linked with its point total, which you'll see in parentheses. The rankings have been divided into three groups. The first two — the 209 Dreamtowns and 313 Honorable Mentions — were previously revealed in Chapter 3. They're followed here by the other 1,562 towns.

Dreamtowns

1. Summit Park, UT (949.7)
2. Park City, UT (935.0)
3. Belterra, TX (926.4)
4. World Golf Village, FL (904.1)
5. Roxborough Park, CO (882.4)
6. Nantucket, MA (877.4)
7. Evergreen, CO (875.9)
8. Heber, UT (870.1)
9. Vistancia, AZ (866.0)
10. Buckhead (Bryan County), GA (865.2)
11. Lafayette, CO (865.1)
12. Purcellville, VA (861.5)
13. Aspen, CO (857.0)
14. Spring Hill, TN (850.9)
15. Bend, OR (850.8)
16. St. Simons, GA (849.4)
17. Tea, SD (842.3)
18. Snoqualmie, WA (841.3)
19. Archer Lodge, NC (840.9)
20. Crozet, VA (839.9)
21. White Rock, NM (837.6)
22. Lake Conroe Eastshore, TX (837.5)

23. Vineyard Haven, MA (836.5)
24. Byron, MN (832.8)
25. Breckenridge, CO (828.6)
26. Wellington, CO (826.0)
27. Silverthorne, CO (823.4)
28. Los Alamos, NM (822.7)
29. Boerne, TX (822.1)
30. Waconia, MN (820.5)
31. Vail, CO (818.5)
32. Lake of the Pines, CA (817.0)
33. Rochester, MN (816.0)
34. Steamboat Springs, CO (814.5)
35. Lake Conroe Westshore, TX (812.8)
36. Rancho Murieta, CA (811.6)
37. Boulder, CO (809.1)
38. Jupiter Farms, FL (808.2)
39. Truckee, CA (808.0)
40. Portsmouth, NH (807.9)
41. Lewes, DE (807.8)
42. Aledo, TX (806.7)
43. Kennebunk, ME (805.0)
44. Paloma Creek South, TX (804.6)
45. Hood River, OR (802.7)
46. Salida, CO (802.6)
47. Sun City Hilton Head, SC (801.6)
48. Hampstead, NC (799.6)
49. Eagle Mountain South, UT (799.5)
50. Mauldin, SC (799.3)
51. Woodcreek, TX (797.8)
52. Chelsea, MI (797.6)
53. Ocean View, DE (797.0)
54. Whitefish, MT (796.6)
55. Port Townsend, WA (796.4)
56. Pawleys Island, SC (795.6)
57. Jackson, WY (795.4)
58. Johnstown, CO (795.1)
59. Woodland Park, CO (794.7)
60. Manor, TX (794.2)
61. Fernandina Beach, FL (794.1)
62. South Lyon, MI (793.4)
62. Spirit Lake, IA (793.4)
64. Mandeville, LA (791.0)
65. Ruckersville, VA (790.9)
65. Stansbury Park, UT (790.9)
67. Eureka, MO (790.3)
68. Saratoga Springs, NY (790.1)
69. Hudson, WI (789.9)
70. Santa Rosa Beach, FL (789.6)
71. Ocean Pines, MD (788.1)
72. Basalt, CO (787.0)
73. Rigby, ID (785.2)
74. Lake Pocotopaug, CT (784.9)
75. Kill Devil Hills, NC (782.8)
76. Estes Park, CO (781.5)
77. New Bremen, OH (780.3)
77. Orange City, IA (780.3)
79. Orangetree, FL (779.6)
80. Manteo, NC (779.3)
81. Santaquin, UT (777.8)
82. Platte City, MO (777.1)
83. Mukwonago, WI (776.8)
84. Jefferson Township North, NJ (776.1)
85. St. George, UT (775.7)
86. Lee's Summit, MO (775.6)
87. Lebanon, NH (774.7)
87. Mountain House, CA (774.7)
89. Bozeman, MT (774.5)
90. Firestone, CO (773.6)
90. Twin Rivers, NJ (773.6)
92. Vail, AZ (772.6)
93. Lake Norman of Catawba, NC (772.4)
94. Oregon, WI (771.4)
95. St. Augustine, FL (770.6)
96. Frankenmuth, MI (770.1)
97. Gunnison, CO (769.6)
98. Corona de Tucson, AZ (768.2)
99. Half Moon Bay, CA (767.7)
99. Lake Monticello, VA (767.7)
101. Williamsburg, VA (767.6)
102. Anacortes, WA (766.8)
102. Livermore, CA (766.8)

104. Star, ID (766.4)
105. Decorah, IA (765.3)
106. Fairview, TN (765.1)
107. Pella, IA (763.7)
108. Carroll, IA (760.8)
109. West Point, NY (759.4)
110. Daphne, AL (759.1)
111. Oxford, MS (758.9)
112. Warwick, NY (758.8)
113. Middletown, DE (758.3)
114. Johnson Lane, NV (758.2)
115. Anna, TX (757.2)
116. Traverse City, MI (756.3)
117. Charlottesville, VA (756.1)
117. Prairie du Sac, WI (756.1)
119. Marysville, OH (755.8)
120. Westminster, MD (754.8)
121. Birch Bay, WA (754.4)
122. Delano, MN (754.1)
122. Lago Vista, TX (754.1)
124. Petaluma, CA (753.8)
125. Forney, TX (753.3)
126. Sturgeon Bay, WI (753.2)
127. Mount Horeb, WI (752.3)
128. Moab, UT (751.3)
129. Sioux Center, IA (751.2)
130. Sedona, AZ (751.1)
131. Gypsum, CO (750.5)
132. Eaton, CO (750.4)
133. Canyon Lake, TX (749.8)
133. McPherson, KS (749.8)
135. Leonardtown, MD (749.5)
136. Chester, NY (748.8)
137. Frederick, MD (748.3)
138. Hilton Head Island, SC (748.0)
139. Buffalo, MN (746.9)
140. Pecan Plantation, TX (746.7)
141. Lake of the Woods, VA (746.2)
142. Eagle, CO (745.4)
143. Mount Vernon, IA (745.2)
144. Astoria, OR (745.0)
145. Edwards, CO (744.9)
146. Lindstrom, MN (744.6)
147. Chesapeake Beach, MD (744.5)
148. Logan, UT (743.7)
149. Monticello, IL (743.5)
150. Alexandria, MN (743.4)
151. Bellingham, WA (743.1)
152. Pinehurst, NC (742.5)
152. Red Hook, NY (742.5)
154. Davis, CA (742.0)
155. Auburn, CA (741.7)
156. Big Pine Key, FL (741.0)
157. Key Largo, FL (740.4)
157. Olympia, WA (740.4)
159. Iowa City, IA (738.8)
160. Forest Lake, MN (738.5)
161. Discovery Bay, CA (737.9)
162. Seaside, OR (737.7)
163. Cedar City, UT (737.6)
164. Lake Mills, WI (737.1)
165. Longmont, CO (736.5)
166. Colchester, CT (736.2)
167. Southold, NY (736.1)
168. Breese, IL (735.9)
169. Kuna, ID (735.7)
170. Santa Cruz, CA (735.5)
171. Burlington, VT (735.3)
172. Petoskey, MI (735.0)
173. East Aurora, NY (734.9)
174. Morro Bay, CA (734.7)
174. Moscow, ID (734.7)
176. Goodrich, MI (734.5)
177. Bishop, CA (734.4)
178. Monticello, MN (734.2)
179. Belle Plaine, MN (733.9)
179. Brunswick, ME (733.9)
181. Incline Village, NV (732.8)
182. Midland, MI (732.1)
183. Coeur d'Alene, ID (731.6)
183. South Deerfield, MA (731.6)
185. New Prague, MN (729.8)
186. Plumas Lake, CA (729.7)
187. Colby, KS (729.2)
188. Corvallis, OR (729.1)

189. Zimmerman, MN (728.9)
190. Dorr, MI (728.5)
191. Oak Island, NC (728.3)
192. Jordan, MN (728.2)
192. Murfreesboro, TN (728.2)
194. Ephraim, UT (727.7)
194. Morehead City, NC (727.7)
196. Redmond, OR (727.4)
197. Solvang, CA (727.1)
198. Cambria, CA (727.0)
198. Fredericksburg, VA (727.0)
198. Northfield, MN (727.0)
201. Weatherford, TX (726.7)
202. Belgrade, MT (726.4)
203. Brunswick, MD (726.3)
204. New Ulm, MN (726.0)
204. State College, PA (726.0)
206. Kasson, MN (725.8)
207. Idaho Falls, ID (725.2)
208. Nephi, UT (725.0)
208. Silverton, OR (725.0)

Honorable Mentions

210. Durango, CO (724.3)
211. Estrella, AZ (724.2)
211. St. Helena, CA (724.2)
213. Clear Lake, IA (723.9)
214. Pocono Woodland Lakes, PA
     (723.8)
215. Danbury, CT (723.7)
216. Diamondhead, MS (723.5)
217. Waterloo, IL (723.3)
218. Camarillo, CA (723.1)
218. Easton, MD (723.1)
220. Columbus, WI (722.9)
220. Placerville, CA (722.9)
222. Brandon, SD (722.5)
222. Sugarmill Woods, FL (722.5)
224. Williamston, MI (722.3)
225. Livingston, MT (722.0)
225. New Freedom, PA (722.0)
227. Arlington, TN (721.9)
228. Rio Vista, CA (721.7)
229. Villas, NJ (721.6)

230. Wedgefield, FL (721.4)
231. Holland, MI (720.6)
231. Lynden, WA (720.6)
231. Owatonna, MN (720.6)
234. Gilroy, CA (720.5)
235. Jefferson, GA (720.3)
235. West Bend, WI (720.3)
237. Lake Geneva, WI (720.1)
238. Fredericksburg, TX (719.7)
239. Indianola, WA (719.1)
240. Sandy, OR (718.9)
240. Springs, NY (718.9)
242. Mammoth Lakes, CA (718.8)
242. Marshfield, WI (718.8)
244. Indianola, IA (718.7)
245. Kalispell, MT (718.4)
246. Winterset, IA (718.2)
247. Marana West, AZ (717.9)
248. Sequim, WA (717.3)
248. Wayne, NE (717.3)
250. Ames, IA (717.2)
250. Marble Falls, TX (717.2)
252. Canby, OR (716.7)
253. Stevens Point, WI (716.3)
254. Spring Hill, KS (716.2)
255. Granite Shoals, TX (715.6)
256. Milan, MI (715.5)
257. Mahomet, IL (715.4)
258. Stewartville, MN (715.1)
259. Lake Wildwood, CA (714.3)
260. Sahuarita, AZ (713.6)
261. Yankton, SD (713.5)
262. Shady Side, MD (713.2)
263. Eudora, KS (713.1)
264. Arroyo Grande, CA (712.8)
265. Wendell, NC (712.7)
266. Ithaca, NY (712.6)
267. Ellensburg, WA (712.5)
268. Hastings, MN (712.4)
268. Morgantown, WV (712.4)
270. New Richmond, WI (712.3)
271. Milton, VT (712.1)
271. Stanwood, WA (712.1)
273. Effingham, IL (712.0)

273. Forestville, CA (712.0)
275. Baldwin, WI (711.5)
276. Kearney, MO (710.4)
277. Prescott Valley, AZ (710.1)
278. Laconia, NH (710.0)
279. Le Mars, IA (709.2)
280. Camano, WA (709.0)
280. Lee, MA (709.0)
282. Lowell, MI (708.9)
283. Leadville, CO (708.2)
283. Paso Robles, CA (708.2)
285. Winchester, VA (708.1)
286. Cedar Rapids, IA (707.4)
286. Port Clinton, OH (707.4)
288. Grass Valley, CA (707.2)
289. Slidell, LA (707.1)
290. Lebanon, TN (706.9)
291. Rock Hill, SC (706.3)
292. Colville, WA (706.1)
293. Marysville, WA (705.8)
294. St. Joseph, IL (705.7)
295. Columbia, MO (705.3)
295. Jasper, IN (705.3)
295. North Branch, MN (705.3)
298. Concord, NH (705.0)
298. Spearfish, SD (705.0)
300. Beaufort, SC (704.5)
300. Manchester, MD (704.5)
302. Hailey, ID (704.3)
303. Seville, OH (703.5)
304. New Castle, CO (703.4)
305. Lake City, MN (702.9)
306. Chardon, OH (702.8)
307. Sebastian, FL (702.7)
308. Lawrence, KS (702.2)
309. Cody, WY (702.0)
309. Waverly, IA (702.0)
311. Honeoye Falls, NY (701.9)
312. Yulee, FL (701.8)
313. Pottstown, PA (701.2)
314. Edgerton, WI (700.7)
315. Hurricane, UT (700.6)
315. Sonora, CA (700.6)
317. Monroe, WI (700.5)

318. Willard, MO (700.0)
319. Columbus, IN (699.7)
320. Emmitsburg, MD (699.5)
321. Brookings, SD (699.4)
321. Carbondale, CO (699.4)
323. Oakland, TN (699.3)
323. Washington, MO (699.3)
325. Sonoma, CA (699.0)
326. Long Neck, DE (698.9)
327. Eau Claire, WI (698.8)
327. Moapa Valley, NV (698.8)
329. Seward, NE (698.5)
330. Dandridge, TN (698.4)
330. Evansville, WI (698.4)
332. Holdrege, NE (698.3)
333. River Falls, WI (697.8)
334. Pocatello, ID (697.3)
335. Pagosa Springs, CO (697.1)
336. Lexington Park, MD (696.9)
336. Silver Lakes, CA (696.9)
338. Mankato, MN (696.7)
339. Albany, OR (696.5)
340. Sioux Falls, SD (696.2)
341. Byron, IL (695.9)
342. San Luis Obispo, CA (695.8)
343. Canton, NY (695.6)
343. Missoula, MT (695.6)
343. Sandpoint, ID (695.6)
346. Plymouth, WI (695.2)
347. Brevard, NC (695.1)
348. Baker City, OR (695.0)
348. Baraboo, WI (695.0)
348. La Crosse, WI (695.0)
351. Pleasant Hill, MO (694.9)
352. Wausau, WI (694.4)
353. Jackson, CA (694.2)
354. Wamego, KS (693.8)
355. North Port, FL (693.7)
356. Midland, TX (693.6)
357. Helena, MT (693.5)
358. Glens Falls, NY (693.4)
359. Middlebury, VT (693.3)
360. Thurmont, MD (693.0)
361. Alachua, FL (692.6)

362. York, NE (692.1)
363. Long Beach, MD (691.7)
363. St. Francis, MN (691.7)
365. Lebanon, IN (690.9)
366. Kearney, NE (690.8)
367. Hutchinson, MN (690.6)
368. St. Peter, MN (690.4)
369. Smithfield, VA (690.0)
370. Bloomington, IL (689.9)
370. Elkhorn, WI (689.9)
370. Village of Oak Creek (Big Park), AZ (689.9)
373. Pratt, KS (689.8)
374. Orwigsburg, PA (689.7)
374. Rathdrum, ID (689.7)
376. Simi Valley, CA (689.5)
377. Highland, IL (689.4)
378. Flagstaff, AZ (689.0)
378. Tremonton, UT (689.0)
380. Bloomington, IN (688.9)
380. St. Cloud, MN (688.9)
382. Columbia Falls, MT (688.8)
382. Tonganoxie, KS (688.8)
384. Ottawa, OH (688.7)
385. Celina, OH (688.5)
386. Butler, PA (688.3)
387. Dubuque, IA (688.2)
387. Lake Delton, WI (688.2)
389. Charles Town, WV (688.1)
390. Bastrop, TX (688.0)
391. Fergus Falls, MN (687.6)
391. Rincon, GA (687.6)
391. Sanger, TX (687.6)
394. Versailles, KY (687.5)
395. Franklin, NJ (687.2)
396. Sheridan, WY (686.8)
397. Manchester, NH (686.4)
397. Spring Hill, FL (686.4)
399. Oak Harbor, WA (686.1)
400. Marathon, FL (686.0)
400. Oxford, OH (686.0)
402. Findlay, OH (685.6)
403. Grove City, PA (685.5)
404. Rancho Calaveras, CA (685.3)

405. Dallas, OR (685.1)
405. Fairmont, MN (685.1)
407. Cheyenne, WY (685.0)
408. Lander, WY (684.5)
409. El Dorado, KS (683.9)
409. Watertown, SD (683.9)
411. Granbury, TX (683.3)
411. Grinnell, IA (683.3)
411. North Brookfield, MA (683.3)
414. Morris, IL (683.1)
415. Newberg, OR (683.0)
416. Fairfield, IA (682.7)
416. Grantsville, UT (682.7)
416. Reedsburg, WI (682.7)
419. Algona, IA (682.5)
420. Jerseyville, IL (682.4)
421. Keene, NH (682.2)
422. Walden, NY (682.0)
423. Richfield, UT (681.5)
424. Leesburg, FL (681.1)
425. South Lake Tahoe, CA (681.0)
426. South Haven, MI (680.9)
427. Auburn, AL (680.8)
427. Janesville, WI (680.8)
427. Tooele, UT (680.8)
427. Twin Falls, ID (680.8)
431. Mystic Island, NJ (680.7)
431. Newport, OR (680.7)
431. Norman, OK (680.7)
434. Bonadelle Ranchos, CA (680.6)
434. Evanston, WY (680.6)
436. Springfield, IL (680.2)
437. Waldorf, MD (680.1)
438. Madison, SD (679.8)
439. Cambridge, MN (679.7)
440. Chico, CA (679.3)
441. Lafayette, IN (679.2)
442. Holly, MI (679.1)
442. Lady Lake, FL (679.1)
444. Rice Lake, WI (678.9)
445. Columbia City, IN (678.6)
445. Geneva, NY (678.6)
447. Lexington, VA (678.5)

447. Mascoutah, IL (678.5)
447. Titusville, FL (678.5)
450. Everson, WA (678.4)
450. Newfane, NY (678.4)
452. Dover, NH (678.2)
453. Vermillion, SD (678.1)
454. St. Marys, PA (677.9)
455. Sheboygan, WI (677.7)
456. Nevada, IA (677.6)
457. Canon City, CO (677.4)
457. Independence, IA (677.4)
459. Corning, NY (677.0)
460. Burlington, WI (676.8)
460. Spencer, IA (676.8)
462. Lindale, TX (676.7)
463. Franklin, NC (676.6)
464. Pullman, WA (676.0)
464. Washington, NJ (676.0)
466. Hastings, MI (675.9)
467. Batesville, IN (675.1)
467. St. Helens, OR (675.1)
469. Athens, GA (675.0)
470. Newark, OH (674.8)
470. Wauseon, OH (674.8)
472. Fort Atkinson, WI (674.5)
473. Litchfield, MN (674.3)
474. Escalon, CA (674.2)
474. Orrville, OH (674.2)
476. Duluth, MN (674.0)
477. Mason City, IA (673.9)
478. Winder, GA (673.8)
479. Blair, NE (673.7)
479. Mount Vernon, WA (673.7)
481. Kingston, NY (673.5)
482. Saw Creek, PA (673.4)
482. Wooster, OH (673.4)
484. Columbia, TN (673.2)
485. Yelm, WA (673.1)
486. Spout Springs, NC (672.9)
487. Warner Robins, GA (672.6)
488. Clifton Springs, NY (672.5)
489. Spartanburg, SC (672.4)
490. Braidwood, IL (672.3)
490. Granite Falls, WA (672.3)

492. Laramie, WY (672.1)
492. Montrose, CO (672.1)
494. Brainerd, MN (672.0)
495. Angola, IN (671.8)
495. Greeley, CO (671.8)
497. St. Marys, OH (671.4)
498. Carlsbad, NM (670.9)
498. Crawfordville, FL (670.9)
500. Pittsfield, MA (670.8)
501. Anderson, SC (670.7)
501. Keystone Heights, FL (670.7)
501. Lake Holiday, IL (670.7)
504. Medford, OR (670.5)
505. Lincoln City, OR (670.4)
506. Cloverdale, CA (670.1)
506. Johnstown, OH (670.1)
508. Rhinelander, WI (669.9)
509. Boulder City, NV (669.7)
510. Columbus, NE (669.6)
511. Barre, VT (669.4)
511. Warsaw, IN (669.4)
513. Santa Fe, NM (669.3)
514. Cape Girardeau, MO (669.2)
515. Redding, CA (668.8)
515. Vacaville, CA (668.8)
517. Blacksburg, VA (668.6)
518. Georgetown, KY (668.5)
519. Butner, NC (668.4)
520. Richmond, MI (668.0)
521. Lynchburg, VA (667.9)
521. Pierre, SD (667.9)

Rest of the Pack

523. Rutland, VT (667.8)
524. Dover, DE (667.7)
524. Platteville, WI (667.7)
526. Hays, KS (667.6)
527. McMinnville, OR (667.4)
528. Sultan, WA (667.3)
529. Newton, KS (667.1)
530. Gaylord, MI (667.0)
531. Napa, CA (666.8)
532. McCook, NE (666.4)
533. Cottonwood, AZ (666.2)

533. Key West, FL (666.2)
533. Lowell, IN (666.2)
533. Sidney, NE (666.2)
537. Maricopa, AZ (666.1)
537. Nipomo, CA (666.1)
539. Augusta, KS (666.0)
540. Greenfield, MA (665.6)
540. Molalla, OR (665.6)
542. Shelbyville, KY (665.5)
543. Artesia, NM (665.4)
544. Lebanon, OR (665.1)
545. Mitchell, SD (664.8)
545. Rockland, ME (664.8)
547. Beatrice, NE (664.7)
547. Kenosha, WI (664.7)
549. Alpena, MI (664.5)
550. Marshall, MN (664.4)
551. Harrison, OH (664.2)
551. Kapaa, HI (664.2)
553. Powell, WY (664.0)
554. Benton Harbor, MI (663.9)
555. Kiel, WI (663.8)
555. North Adams, MA (663.8)
557. Benton, LA (663.7)
558. Grand Junction, CO (663.4)
559. Lewiston, ID (663.3)
560. Lake Arrowhead, CA (663.2)
561. Valley City, ND (663.0)
562. Boone, NC (662.8)
562. Red Wing, MN (662.8)
562. Seaside, CA (662.8)
565. Bismarck, ND (662.6)
565. Deltona, FL (662.6)
567. Champaign, IL (662.5)
568. Jefferson City, MO (662.4)
568. Oneonta, NY (662.4)
570. Rifle, CO (662.3)
571. Wenatchee, WA (662.2)
572. Battlement Mesa, CO (661.9)
572. Cartersville, GA (661.9)
574. Otsego, MI (661.8)
575. Calistoga, CA (661.7)
575. Ramona, CA (661.7)
577. Bennington, VT (661.6)

578. Bremen, GA (661.3)
578. Stuarts Draft, VA (661.3)
580. Winona, MN (661.2)
581. Merrill, WI (661.0)
582. Wapakoneta, OH (660.9)
583. Mocksville, NC (660.8)
584. Ludington, MI (660.7)
585. Leominster, MA (660.5)
585. Sierra View, PA (660.5)
587. Paola, KS (660.3)
587. Willmar, MN (660.3)
589. Nampa, ID (660.2)
590. Hot Springs Village, AR (659.9)
591. Canyon, TX (659.7)
591. Roseburg, OR (659.7)
593. Clarksburg, WV (659.5)
593. Dixon, IL (659.5)
595. Ione, CA (659.1)
595. Lake Charles, LA (659.1)
595. Woodstock, IL (659.1)
598. Fairfield Glade, TN (658.9)
598. Veneta, OR (658.9)
600. East Stroudsburg, PA (658.7)
601. Aberdeen, SD (658.6)
601. Rensselaer, IN (658.6)
603. Milford, DE (658.2)
603. Newton, NJ (658.2)
605. Temple, TX (657.9)
605. Wisconsin Rapids, WI (657.9)
607. Humboldt, IA (657.7)
608. Oshkosh, WI (657.5)
608. Rainbow Lakes Estates, FL (657.5)
610. Gardnerville Ranchos, NV (657.3)
610. Marshall, MI (657.3)
612. Charlotte, MI (657.2)
613. Tipton, IN (657.0)
614. Littlestown, PA (656.9)
615. Millsboro, DE (656.7)
616. Mountain Home, AR (656.6)
617. Alliance, NE (656.5)
617. Dayton, NV (656.5)

617. Glenwood Springs, CO (656.5)
617. Middletown, NY (656.5)
617. Richlands South, NC (656.5)
622. Detroit Lakes, MN (656.1)
623. Glenwood, IA (656.0)
624. Walla Walla, WA (655.9)
625. Jonesboro, AR (655.8)
625. Taneytown, MD (655.8)
625. Wilmore, KY (655.8)
628. Milton, PA (655.7)
629. Bellefonte, PA (655.5)
630. Chestertown, MD (655.4)
631. Kerrville, TX (655.2)
631. Tomah, WI (655.2)
633. Monahans, TX (655.0)
634. Cookeville, TN (654.7)
634. Tillamook, OR (654.7)
636. Centralia, WA (654.6)
637. College Station, TX (654.5)
638. Bonham, TX (654.4)
639. Clover, SC (654.3)
640. Marengo, IL (653.7)
641. Sterling, CO (653.6)
642. Clarksville, TN (653.4)
642. Whiteman AFB, MO (653.4)
644. Lake Jackson, TX (653.3)
645. Delavan, WI (653.2)
645. La Grande, OR (653.2)
647. Eureka, IL (653.0)
647. Geneseo, IL (653.0)
649. Paducah, KY (652.9)
650. Boiling Spring Lakes, NC (652.7)
650. Chambersburg, PA (652.7)
650. Glencoe, MN (652.7)
650. Leavenworth, KS (652.7)
650. Wahpeton, ND (652.7)
655. Paradise, CA (652.5)
655. Rolla, MO (652.5)
657. West Columbia, TX (652.3)
658. Devils Lake, ND (652.2)
658. Norfolk, NE (652.2)
658. The Dalles, OR (652.2)

661. Iron Mountain, MI (652.1)
662. Arab, AL (651.9)
662. Brookings, OR (651.9)
664. Boone, IA (651.6)
664. Brush, CO (651.6)
664. Staunton, IL (651.6)
667. Portage, WI (651.4)
668. Lakeport, CA (651.3)
669. Bowling Green, KY (651.2)
670. Billings, MT (651.1)
670. Brattleboro, VT (651.1)
670. Burlington, NC (651.1)
673. Crestview, FL (651.0)
673. Plattsmouth, NE (651.0)
675. Big Bear City, CA (650.5)
675. Denver City, TX (650.5)
677. Liberty, TX (650.3)
678. Brockport, NY (650.2)
678. Port Jervis, NY (650.2)
678. Watertown, WI (650.2)
681. Greensburg, IN (650.1)
681. Hanover, PA (650.1)
681. Thief River Falls, MN (650.1)
684. Fairfield, CA (649.7)
685. Bryan, OH (649.6)
686. St. Albans, VT (649.5)
687. Vallejo, CA (649.4)
688. Jewett City, CT (649.2)
688. Torrington, CT (649.2)
690. Potsdam, NY (649.1)
691. Soldotna, AK (648.9)
692. Staunton, VA (648.7)
693. Lake Havasu City, AZ (648.6)
693. Pecos, TX (648.6)
695. Browns Mills, NJ (648.5)
695. St. Johns, MI (648.5)
697. Pukalani, HI (648.2)
697. Rapid City, SD (648.2)
699. Tracy, CA (648.0)
699. Waupaca, WI (648.0)
701. Berrien Springs, MI (647.9)
701. Foley, AL (647.9)
703. Muskegon, MI (647.8)
704. Edinboro, PA (647.6)

705. Menomonie, WI (647.3)
706. Florence, OR (647.2)
706. Johnson City, TN (647.2)
708. Quincy, IL (647.1)
709. Waupun, WI (647.0)
710. Berne, IN (646.8)
710. Columbiana, OH (646.8)
712. Juneau, AK (646.7)
713. Atoka, TN (646.6)
714. Houghton, MI (646.5)
715. Knoxville, IA (646.2)
716. Fond du Lac, WI (646.0)
717. Harrisonburg, VA (645.7)
718. Mount Pocono, PA (645.6)
718. Sparta, WI (645.6)
720. Camden, SC (645.2)
720. Fort Lupton, CO (645.2)
722. Kalaheo, HI (645.0)
723. Coos Bay, OR (644.9)
724. Bardstown, KY (644.8)
725. Bellows Falls, VT (644.7)
726. Lake Land'Or, VA (644.6)
726. Nassau Village, FL (644.6)
728. Bealeton, VA (644.4)
729. Clarinda, IA (644.3)
730. Floresville, TX (644.2)
731. Grants Pass, OR (644.1)
732. Kailua (Honolulu County), HI (644.0)
732. Port Angeles, WA (644.0)
734. Woodland, CA (643.9)
735. York, SC (643.8)
736. Altoona, PA (643.7)
736. Milan, TN (643.7)
738. Conway, AR (643.5)
738. Iowa Park, TX (643.5)
740. Chino Valley, AZ (643.3)
740. Oneida, NY (643.3)
742. Cloquet, MN (643.1)
743. Clare, MI (643.0)
744. Hibbing, MN (642.9)
745. Grand Rapids, MN (642.8)
746. Bangor, ME (642.7)
746. Ottawa, IL (642.7)

748. Hamilton, MT (642.4)
749. International Falls, MN (642.3)
749. Manitowoc, WI (642.3)
749. Montevideo, MN (642.3)
752. Eaton Rapids, MI (642.2)
752. Four Corners, FL (642.2)
752. Meadville, PA (642.2)
755. Warren, PA (642.1)
756. Cadillac, MI (642.0)
756. Medina, NY (642.0)
756. Weatherford, OK (642.0)
759. Manhattan, KS (641.9)
760. Chadron, NE (641.8)
760. Greencastle, IN (641.8)
760. Marquette, MI (641.8)
760. Portland, MI (641.8)
764. Faribault, MN (641.7)
764. Lapeer, MI (641.7)
764. Monmouth, OR (641.7)
764. Robertsdale, AL (641.7)
768. Muscatine, IA (641.6)
768. San Marcos, TX (641.6)
770. Arcata, CA (641.4)
771. De Soto, KS (641.3)
771. Stephenville, TX (641.3)
771. Woodland, WA (641.3)
774. Marion Oaks, FL (641.2)
775. Peru, IL (641.1)
775. Sutherlin, OR (641.1)
777. Excelsior Springs, MO (641.0)
777. Kutztown, PA (641.0)
779. Marietta, OH (640.4)
779. New Philadelphia, OH (640.4)
781. Kermit, TX (640.3)
781. Taylor, TX (640.3)
783. Branson, MO (640.1)
784. Allegan, MI (640.0)
785. Warrensburg, MO (639.9)
786. Washington Court House, OH (639.8)
787. Oskaloosa, IA (639.7)
788. Cheney, WA (639.6)

788. Rock Springs, WY (639.6)
790. Mount Vernon, IN (639.5)
791. Joplin, MO (639.2)
792. Upper Sandusky, OH (639.0)
793. Binghamton, NY (638.9)
793. Whitehall, MI (638.9)
795. Waterbury, CT (638.8)
796. Van Wert, OH (638.7)
797. Maquoketa, IA (638.5)
797. Portland, TN (638.5)
799. Douglas, WY (638.4)
800. Uniontown, PA (638.3)
801. Bellevue, OH (638.0)
802. Siloam Springs, AR (637.9)
803. Concordia, KS (637.8)
804. Payson, AZ (637.7)
804. Stillwater, OK (637.7)
806. Rexburg, ID (637.5)
807. Au Sable, MI (637.3)
808. Carlinville, IL (637.2)
808. Port Huron, MI (637.2)
808. Sunbury, PA (637.2)
811. Ashland, OH (637.0)
812. Nebraska City, NE (636.9)
813. Blackfoot, ID (636.8)
813. Delphos, OH (636.8)
813. Utica, NY (636.8)
816. Commerce, GA (636.6)
817. Beaver Dam, WI (636.5)
818. Ellwood City, PA (636.4)
819. Union, MO (636.3)
820. DeKalb, IL (636.2)
820. Ellenville, NY (636.2)
822. Atlantic, IA (636.0)
822. Lihue, HI (636.0)
824. Pacific, MO (635.9)
825. Homosassa Springs, FL (635.7)
825. Ocala, FL (635.7)
827. Emporia, KS (635.6)
828. Gastonia, NC (635.3)
828. St. Marys, GA (635.3)
830. Galt, CA (635.2)
830. Hammonton, NJ (635.2)
830. Jamestown, ND (635.2)
830. Kingsport, TN (635.2)
830. Seminole, TX (635.2)
830. Yreka, CA (635.2)
836. Caldwell, OH (635.1)
837. Grand Forks, ND (635.0)
838. Bloomsburg, PA (634.6)
838. Carrollton, GA (634.6)
838. Eaton, OH (634.6)
841. Bemidji, MN (634.4)
841. Prince Frederick, MD (634.4)
843. Manistee, MI (634.3)
844. Sevierville, TN (634.2)
845. Wheeling, WV (633.8)
846. Athol, MA (633.7)
846. Waterville, ME (633.7)
848. Adrian, MI (633.5)
848. Waterloo, IA (633.5)
850. Starkville, MS (633.4)
851. Berlin, NH (633.2)
851. Greenwood, AR (633.2)
853. Burley, ID (633.1)
854. High Point, NC (633.0)
854. Rochester, IN (633.0)
856. Hastings, NE (632.9)
856. Winters, CA (632.9)
858. New Bedford, MA (632.7)
859. Creswell, OR (632.6)
859. Topeka, KS (632.6)
861. Perryville, MO (632.5)
862. Lakes, AK (632.4)
863. Kekaha, HI (632.2)
864. Anchorage Northeast, AK (632.1)
864. Augusta, ME (632.1)
866. Lewistown, MT (631.9)
866. Middletown, OH (631.9)
868. North East, PA (631.8)
869. Bolivar, MO (631.7)
869. Texas City, TX (631.7)
871. Casper, WY (631.6)
871. Covington, VA (631.6)
873. Savannah, MO (631.5)

874. Lake of the Woods, AZ (631.4)
875. Hilmar, CA (631.3)
876. Cullman, AL (631.2)
876. Shippensburg, PA (631.2)
878. Bartlesville, OK (631.1)
878. Little Falls, MN (631.1)
878. Mount Vernon, OH (631.1)
881. Alpine, TX (631.0)
881. Moses Lake, WA (631.0)
883. Eureka, CA (630.9)
883. Sitka, AK (630.9)
885. Junction City, OR (630.6)
885. Plattsburgh, NY (630.6)
885. Seymour, IN (630.6)
888. Pittsburg, KS (630.4)
889. Ridgecrest, CA (630.2)
889. Yucca Valley, CA (630.2)
891. Front Royal, VA (629.9)
891. Jim Thorpe, PA (629.9)
893. Slippery Rock, PA (629.7)
894. Mesquite, NV (629.6)
894. Prairie du Chien, WI (629.6)
894. Princeton, IL (629.6)
897. Bowling Green, OH (629.5)
897. Fremont, NE (629.5)
897. Oil City, PA (629.5)
897. Smithfield, NC (629.5)
901. Culpeper, VA (629.3)
902. Alton, IL (629.2)
903. Ashville, OH (629.1)
904. Ennis, TX (629.0)
905. Salisbury, MD (628.9)
906. Paragould, AR (628.8)
906. Washington, IA (628.8)
906. Winchester, TN (628.8)
909. Bristol, TN (628.7)
909. Escanaba, MI (628.7)
911. Kankakee, IL (628.6)
912. Greenville, NC (628.5)
913. New Castle, PA (628.4)
914. Fort Bragg, CA (628.2)
914. Phelan, CA (628.2)
916. Athens, AL (628.0)

917. Saranac Lake, NY (627.8)
918. Florence, SC (627.7)
918. Monessen, PA (627.7)
918. Tuscaloosa, AL (627.7)
921. Greenville, PA (627.5)
921. Vandalia, IL (627.5)
923. Roosevelt, UT (627.4)
923. Waseca, MN (627.4)
925. Ripon, WI (627.3)
926. Manteca, CA (627.2)
927. Elmira, NY (627.1)
927. Hagerstown, MD (627.1)
929. Monticello, IN (627.0)
930. Perry, IA (626.7)
931. Berea, KY (626.6)
932. North Platte, NE (626.5)
932. Panama City, FL (626.5)
934. Rawlins, WY (626.3)
935. Graham, TX (626.2)
936. Dixon, CA (625.9)
937. Abilene, KS (625.8)
937. Hutchinson, KS (625.8)
939. Oberlin, OH (625.7)
940. Hartsville, SC (625.6)
940. Salina, KS (625.6)
940. Zephyrhills, FL (625.6)
943. Gainesville, GA (625.4)
944. Fallon, NV (625.3)
945. Antigo, WI (625.2)
945. Boonville, IN (625.2)
947. Hammond, LA (625.1)
947. Hillsdale, MI (625.1)
947. Lancaster, OH (625.1)
947. Owensboro, KY (625.1)
951. Batavia, NY (624.6)
951. Sandusky, OH (624.6)
953. Wytheville, VA (624.5)
954. Lawrenceburg, KY (624.3)
954. Lewiston, ME (624.3)
954. Red Oak, IA (624.3)
957. Dunkirk, NY (624.2)
958. Olean, NY (624.1)
959. Glendive, MT (623.9)
960. Mount Vernon, IL (623.8)

960. Stayton, OR (623.8)
962. Chillicothe, OH (623.6)
962. Darbydale, OH (623.6)
964. Creston, IA (623.5)
964. Swansboro, NC (623.5)
966. Abilene, TX (623.4)
966. Ottawa, KS (623.4)
968. Elko, NV (623.3)
969. Hannibal, MO (623.1)
969. Sealy, TX (623.1)
971. Genoa, IL (623.0)
972. Carson City, NV (622.8)
972. Frankfort, KY (622.8)
972. Green River, WY (622.8)
972. Lewisburg, WV (622.8)
976. Jasper, GA (622.6)
976. Monroe, MI (622.6)
978. Mount Carmel, IL (622.5)
979. Jacksonville, IL (622.4)
979. Syracuse, IN (622.4)
981. Sturgis, SD (622.3)
982. Dickson, TN (622.1)
982. Ravena, NY (622.1)
984. Cullowhee, NC (622.0)
984. Paw Paw, MI (622.0)
986. Sheridan, OR (621.8)
987. Ruidoso, NM (621.7)
988. Butte, MT (621.5)
989. Cherryville, NC (621.3)
989. Defiance, OH (621.3)
991. Clarion, PA (621.2)
992. La Grange, TX (621.0)
993. Lancaster, SC (620.9)
993. Portage, PA (620.9)
993. Tupelo, MS (620.9)
996. Gillette, WY (620.8)
997. Elgin, TX (620.7)
998. Gowanda, NY (620.5)
999. Bay City, MI (620.4)
1,000. Franklin (Venango County), PA (620.3)
1,000. Parkersburg, WV (620.3)
1,002. Sayre, PA (620.2)
1,003. Erie, PA (620.1)

1,004. Lincolnton, NC (620.0)
1,004. Union Grove, WI (620.0)
1,006. DuBois, PA (619.6)
1,007. Tyler, TX (619.5)
1,008. Hot Springs, AR (619.4)
1,008. Paris, IL (619.4)
1,010. Dalhart, TX (619.3)
1,010. Newark, NY (619.3)
1,012. Beloit, WI (619.2)
1,013. Enterprise, AL (618.6)
1,014. Bay Minette, AL (618.2)
1,015. Jackson, TN (618.1)
1,016. Kokomo, IN (618.0)
1,017. Albert Lea, MN (617.9)
1,018. Alva, OK (617.8)
1,018. Ishpeming, MI (617.8)
1,020. Cresson, PA (617.7)
1,020. Mount Pleasant, IA (617.7)
1,022. Kahului, HI (617.5)
1,022. Mountain Home, ID (617.5)
1,024. Galveston, TX (617.4)
1,024. Longview, WA (617.4)
1,024. Sherman, TX (617.4)
1,027. Bedford, IN (617.3)
1,027. Coldwater, MI (617.3)
1,027. Lockport, NY (617.3)
1,030. Fortuna, CA (617.2)
1,031. Emmett, ID (617.1)
1,031. Terrell, TX (617.1)
1,033. Thomasville, GA (616.8)
1,034. Salem, OH (616.7)
1,035. Athens, OH (616.6)
1,035. Pahrump, NV (616.6)
1,035. Taylorville, IL (616.6)
1,038. Racine, WI (616.4)
1,038. Rome, NY (616.4)
1,038. Safford, AZ (616.4)
1,041. Lock Haven, PA (616.2)
1,041. Prineville, OR (616.2)
1,043. Atchison, KS (616.1)
1,043. Attica, NY (616.1)
1,045. Cortland, NY (616.0)
1,045. Nicholasville, KY (616.0)
1,047. Fort Dodge, IA (615.9)

1,047. Harrisonville, MO (615.9)
1,047. Muncy, PA (615.9)
1,050. Carbondale, IL (615.6)
1,051. Massena, NY (615.5)
1,051. Penn Yan, NY (615.5)
1,053. Batesville, AR (615.4)
1,053. Cortez, CO (615.4)
1,055. Anamosa, IA (615.3)
1,056. Klamath Falls, OR (615.2)
1,057. Bedford, VA (615.1)
1,057. Broadway, VA (615.1)
1,059. Galax, VA (614.9)
1,060. Ashland, WI (614.8)
1,061. Laurel, MT (614.7)
1,061. Scottsbluff, NE (614.7)
1,063. Danville, KY (614.6)
1,063. New Bern, NC (614.6)
1,065. North Manchester, IN (614.4)
1,066. Shawano, WI (614.2)
1,067. New London, WI (614.0)
1,068. Kingman, AZ (613.9)
1,068. Sierra Vista, AZ (613.9)
1,070. Lebanon, PA (613.8)
1,071. Stafford Springs, CT (613.6)
1,072. Bradford, PA (613.4)
1,072. Monmouth, IL (613.4)
1,074. Ketchikan, AK (613.2)
1,075. Lake City, FL (613.1)
1,075. Napoleon, OH (613.1)
1,075. Winchester, KY (613.1)
1,078. Auburn, IN (613.0)
1,078. Clinton, IL (613.0)
1,078. Price, UT (613.0)
1,081. Pueblo, CO (612.9)
1,081. Tullahoma, TN (612.9)
1,083. Dayton, TX (612.8)
1,083. Torrington, WY (612.8)
1,085. London, OH (612.4)
1,085. Maryville, MO (612.4)
1,085. Ware, MA (612.4)
1,088. Gramercy, LA (612.3)
1,089. Montesano, WA (611.7)
1,090. Bluffton, IN (611.4)

1,090. De Funiak Springs, FL (611.4)
1,092. Auburn, NY (611.3)
1,093. Clearfield, PA (610.9)
1,093. Jackson, MI (610.9)
1,095. Havre, MT (610.8)
1,095. Williamsport, PA (610.8)
1,097. Marinette, WI (610.7)
1,098. Alamosa, CO (610.5)
1,099. Forsyth, MO (610.3)
1,100. Quarryville, PA (610.2)
1,100. Somerset, KY (610.2)
1,102. Lampasas, TX (610.1)
1,103. Kihei, HI (609.9)
1,104. Grove, OK (609.8)
1,105. Owosso, MI (609.6)
1,105. Poinciana, FL (609.6)
1,107. Tehachapi, CA (609.5)
1,108. Hattiesburg, MS (608.9)
1,108. Sanford, ME (608.9)
1,108. Willows, CA (608.9)
1,111. Richmond, KY (608.7)
1,111. Searcy, AR (608.7)
1,113. Lincoln, IL (608.6)
1,114. Charlestown, IN (608.5)
1,114. Fort Meade, FL (608.5)
1,116. Logan, OH (608.3)
1,116. Muncie, IN (608.3)
1,118. Sioux City, IA (608.2)
1,119. Aberdeen, WA (608.1)
1,119. Brenham, TX (608.1)
1,119. Indiana, PA (608.1)
1,119. Webster City, IA (608.1)
1,123. Robinson, IL (608.0)
1,124. San Angelo, TX (607.9)
1,125. Charles City, IA (607.7)
1,126. Alma, MI (607.5)
1,126. Box Elder, SD (607.5)
1,126. Whitewater, WI (607.5)
1,129. Franklin, NH (607.4)
1,130. Pottsville, PA (607.3)
1,131. Lewistown, PA (607.0)
1,132. Charleston, IL (606.9)
1,132. Cottage Grove, OR (606.9)

1,132. Tyrone, PA (606.9)
1,135. Elkhart, IN (606.8)
1,135. Lodi, CA (606.8)
1,135. Okeechobee, FL (606.8)
1,135. Spruce Pine, NC (606.8)
1,135. Strasburg, VA (606.8)
1,140. Huntington, WV (606.7)
1,140. Oswego, NY (606.7)
1,142. Cleveland, TN (606.6)
1,142. Lawrenceburg, TN (606.6)
1,144. Ada, OH (606.5)
1,144. Brunswick, GA (606.5)
1,144. Somerset, PA (606.5)
1,147. Clyde, OH (606.4)
1,148. Fort Madison, IA (606.1)
1,148. Page, AZ (606.1)
1,150. Litchfield, IL (605.9)
1,150. Waynesboro, PA (605.9)
1,152. Oroville, CA (605.8)
1,153. Heber Springs, AR (605.7)
1,153. Shelbyville, IN (605.7)
1,155. Russells Point, OH (605.4)
1,156. Hemet, CA (605.3)
1,157. Florence, AL (604.9)
1,158. Ada, OK (604.7)
1,158. Kittanning, PA (604.7)
1,158. Wilmington, OH (604.7)
1,161. Kingsland, TX (604.5)
1,161. Seneca, SC (604.5)
1,163. Farmington, MO (604.4)
1,164. Dahlonega, GA (604.3)
1,164. Mount Shasta, CA (604.3)
1,166. Havelock, NC (604.2)
1,167. Charleston, WV (603.9)
1,168. Wellington, KS (603.8)
1,169. Pell City, AL (603.7)
1,169. Sidney, MT (603.7)
1,171. Big Rapids, MI (603.6)
1,171. Madison, IN (603.6)
1,173. Brownwood, TX (603.5)
1,173. Cumberland, MD (603.5)
1,175. Beebe, AR (603.3)
1,175. Haleiwa, HI (603.3)
1,177. Oelwein, IA (603.1)

1,177. Purcell, OK (603.1)
1,177. Winnemucca, NV (603.1)
1,180. Pleasanton, TX (602.9)
1,180. Poinciana Southwest, FL (602.9)
1,182. Crawfordsville, IN (602.7)
1,182. Snowflake, AZ (602.7)
1,184. Ukiah, CA (602.6)
1,185. Fairmont, WV (602.5)
1,185. Piqua, OH (602.5)
1,187. Clinton, OK (602.4)
1,187. West Plains, MO (602.4)
1,189. Ilion, NY (602.3)
1,189. Omak, WA (602.3)
1,191. Crossville, TN (602.0)
1,191. Tiffin, OH (602.0)
1,193. Ionia, MI (601.9)
1,194. Circleville, OH (601.6)
1,194. Cobleskill, NY (601.6)
1,194. Waimea (Hawaii County), HI (601.6)
1,197. Troy, MO (601.5)
1,198. Hillsboro, IL (601.4)
1,198. Keokuk, IA (601.4)
1,198. Lima, OH (601.4)
1,201. Watertown, NY (601.3)
1,202. Streator, IL (601.2)
1,203. Canton, IL (601.0)
1,203. Johnstown, PA (601.0)
1,205. Athens, TX (600.8)
1,205. Claremore, OK (600.8)
1,207. Clinton, MO (600.6)
1,208. Enid, OK (600.5)
1,208. Sebring, FL (600.5)
1,208. Willits, CA (600.5)
1,211. Kirksville, MO (600.4)
1,212. Decatur, IN (600.3)
1,213. Bellefontaine, OH (600.2)
1,214. Rome, GA (600.1)
1,214. Virginia, MN (600.1)
1,216. Attica, IN (600.0)
1,216. Carmi, IL (600.0)
1,218. Great Falls, MT (599.9)
1,218. Nappanee, IN (599.9)

1,218. Wichita Falls, TX (599.9)
1,221. Dothan, AL (599.8)
1,221. Ogdensburg, NY (599.8)
1,221. Panama City Northeast, FL (599.8)
1,224. Washington, IN (599.7)
1,225. Kailua (Hawaii County), HI (599.6)
1,226. Turlock, CA (599.3)
1,227. Macclenny, FL (599.2)
1,228. Hudson, NY (599.0)
1,229. Grand Island, NE (598.9)
1,230. Camp Verde, AZ (598.8)
1,231. Albemarle, NC (598.6)
1,232. El Reno, OK (598.5)
1,232. Pocahontas, AR (598.5)
1,234. Odessa, MO (598.4)
1,234. Saginaw, MI (598.4)
1,236. Pendleton, OR (598.3)
1,237. Rochelle, IL (598.2)
1,237. Waco, TX (598.2)
1,239. Coxsackie, NY (598.1)
1,240. Black River Falls, WI (598.0)
1,241. Florence, CO (597.9)
1,242. Buies Creek, NC (597.7)
1,242. Three Rivers, MI (597.7)
1,244. Madisonville, TN (597.6)
1,245. Lebanon, MO (597.5)
1,245. Sidney, NY (597.5)
1,247. Elizabethtown, KY (597.4)
1,247. Murray, KY (597.4)
1,249. Winfield, KS (597.2)
1,250. Belle Fourche, SD (597.1)
1,250. Norton, VA (597.1)
1,252. Burlington, IA (597.0)
1,252. Huntingburg, IN (597.0)
1,254. Miles City, MT (596.9)
1,254. Murphysboro, IL (596.9)
1,256. Batesburg, SC (596.8)
1,257. Battle Creek, MI (596.7)
1,257. Houghton Lake, MI (596.7)
1,259. Harrison, AR (596.5)
1,259. Hilo, HI (596.5)
1,261. Weirton, WV (596.4)

1,262. Decatur, AL (596.3)
1,262. Morristown, TN (596.3)
1,264. Salem, IL (596.1)
1,265. Silsbee, TX (596.0)
1,266. Cameron, MO (595.9)
1,266. Estherville, IA (595.9)
1,268. Olney, IL (595.8)
1,269. Chickasha, OK (595.7)
1,269. Hollister, CA (595.7)
1,271. Craig, CO (595.0)
1,271. Fort Morgan, CO (595.0)
1,271. Sidney, OH (595.0)
1,274. Buckeye, AZ (594.9)
1,274. Claremont, NH (594.9)
1,274. Woodburn, OR (594.9)
1,277. Huntington, IN (594.7)
1,278. Morehead, KY (594.6)
1,278. North Wilkesboro, NC (594.6)
1,280. Sanford, NC (594.5)
1,281. Decatur, IL (594.3)
1,282. Danville, VA (594.2)
1,282. Greenville, MI (594.2)
1,282. Monticello, AR (594.2)
1,282. Waynesburg, PA (594.2)
1,286. Minot, ND (594.0)
1,286. Ottumwa, IA (594.0)
1,288. Chillicothe, MO (593.9)
1,288. Salem, IN (593.9)
1,290. Austin, MN (593.6)
1,291. Yuba City, CA (593.5)
1,292. Princeton, KY (593.4)
1,293. Laie, HI (593.3)
1,294. Albertville, AL (593.1)
1,295. Hornell, NY (593.0)
1,296. Athens, TN (592.7)
1,296. Greeneville, TN (592.7)
1,296. Jacksonville, NC (592.7)
1,296. Williston, ND (592.7)
1,300. Big Spring, TX (592.2)
1,301. Mattoon, IL (591.9)
1,301. Paris, KY (591.9)
1,303. Crookston, MN (591.8)
1,304. Newton, IA (591.5)

1,304. Sedalia, MO (591.5)
1,306. Gloversville, NY (591.1)
1,307. Conneaut, OH (590.7)
1,307. Garrettsville, OH (590.7)
1,307. Huntingdon, PA (590.7)
1,307. Paw Paw Lake, MI (590.7)
1,311. Greenville, IL (590.6)
1,312. Port Lavaca, TX (590.4)
1,313. Kenedy, TX (590.3)
1,313. Sterling, IL (590.3)
1,313. Wetumpka, AL (590.3)
1,316. Jasper, AL (590.1)
1,317. Breaux Bridge, LA (589.9)
1,317. Fremont, OH (589.9)
1,317. Willimantic, CT (589.9)
1,320. Geneseo, NY (589.8)
1,321. Grangerland, TX (589.7)
1,322. Ontario, OR (589.6)
1,322. Tell City, IN (589.6)
1,324. Wabash, IN (589.4)
1,324. Wellsville, NY (589.4)
1,326. Longview, TX (589.2)
1,327. Corry, PA (589.0)
1,327. Emporia, VA (589.0)
1,327. Mendota, IL (589.0)
1,330. Bucyrus, OH (588.8)
1,330. Gun Barrel City, TX (588.8)
1,330. Woodward, OK (588.8)
1,333. Anna, IL (588.7)
1,334. Princeton, IN (588.6)
1,335. Buckhannon, WV (588.3)
1,335. Mansfield, OH (588.3)
1,335. Ulysses, KS (588.3)
1,338. Statesboro, GA (588.2)
1,339. Franklin, KY (588.1)
1,340. Guthrie, OK (588.0)
1,341. Crete, NE (587.9)
1,341. Twentynine Palms, CA (587.9)
1,343. Jamestown, NY (587.8)
1,343. Waverly City, OH (587.8)
1,345. Sumter, SC (587.6)
1,346. Macomb, IL (587.2)
1,347. Needles, CA (587.1)

1,348. Greenwood, SC (586.9)
1,348. Northern Cambria, PA (586.9)
1,350. Durant, OK (586.7)
1,350. Hartford City, IN (586.7)
1,350. Taos, NM (586.7)
1,353. Gridley, CA (586.6)
1,353. Lawrenceburg, IN (586.6)
1,353. Madras, OR (586.6)
1,356. Mount Airy, NC (586.4)
1,357. Devine, TX (586.2)
1,358. Harriman, TN (586.1)
1,358. Marion, NC (586.1)
1,360. Andrews, TX (585.8)
1,361. Clinton, IA (585.6)
1,361. Rushville, IN (585.6)
1,361. Yakima, WA (585.6)
1,364. Dyersburg, TN (585.2)
1,364. Rocky Mount, VA (585.2)
1,366. Beaumont, TX (585.1)
1,367. Chanute, KS (585.0)
1,367. Shelton, WA (585.0)
1,369. Lewisburg, TN (584.9)
1,369. Lorain, OH (584.9)
1,371. Iola, KS (584.8)
1,372. Ephrata, WA (584.6)
1,372. Greenville, OH (584.6)
1,374. Anderson, IN (584.5)
1,375. Norwalk, OH (584.4)
1,375. Pecan Acres, TX (584.4)
1,377. Arkansas City, KS (584.2)
1,377. Sulphur Springs, TX (584.2)
1,379. Great Bend, KS (584.1)
1,380. Los Lunas, NM (584.0)
1,381. Norwich, NY (583.9)
1,381. Wellington, OH (583.9)
1,383. Franklin, VA (583.8)
1,383. Marshfield, MO (583.8)
1,385. Casa Grande, AZ (583.6)
1,385. Galion, OH (583.6)
1,385. Houma, LA (583.6)
1,385. Michigan City, IN (583.6)
1,389. Ocean Shores, WA (583.5)
1,389. Victoria, TX (583.5)

1,391. Fulton, MO (583.3)
1,391. Richmond, MO (583.3)
1,393. Laurium, MI (583.2)
1,393. Vineland, NJ (583.2)
1,393. Warrenton, MO (583.2)
1,396. St. Joseph, MO (583.0)
1,397. Lamar, CO (582.8)
1,398. Pulaski, VA (582.6)
1,399. Titusville, PA (582.5)
1,400. Manchester, TN (582.3)
1,401. Honesdale, PA (582.1)
1,402. Oxford, NC (582.0)
1,403. Dickinson, ND (581.8)
1,404. Sikeston, MO (581.7)
1,405. Show Low, AZ (581.6)
1,406. Albion, NY (581.2)
1,407. Belton, SC (581.0)
1,407. Coolidge, AZ (581.0)
1,409. Bullhead City, AZ (580.8)
1,410. Wagoner, OK (580.7)
1,411. Fort Scott, KS (580.4)
1,412. Harrisburg, IL (580.3)
1,413. Anaconda, MT (580.1)
1,413. Port Arthur, TX (580.1)
1,415. Bath, NY (580.0)
1,416. Belding, MI (579.9)
1,416. Ironwood, MI (579.9)
1,418. Elkins, WV (579.8)
1,418. Hobbs, NM (579.8)
1,420. Catskill, NY (579.6)
1,420. Greenville, TX (579.6)
1,420. Shawnee, OK (579.6)
1,420. Vernal, UT (579.6)
1,424. Worland, WY (579.5)
1,425. Campbellsville, KY (579.3)
1,426. La Junta, CO (578.9)
1,427. Parsons, KS (578.8)
1,428. Huron, SD (578.6)
1,429. Washington, NC (578.5)
1,430. Hempstead, TX (578.4)
1,430. Jackson, OH (578.4)
1,432. Texarkana, TX (578.3)
1,433. Colusa, CA (578.1)
1,434. Terre Haute, IN (577.9)

1,435. Henderson, TN (577.8)
1,435. Punxsutawney, PA (577.8)
1,437. Paris, TX (577.7)
1,438. Lawrenceville, IL (577.6)
1,439. Kennett, MO (577.5)
1,440. Tuba City, AZ (577.1)
1,441. Cleburne, TX (577.0)
1,442. Centralia, IL (576.8)
1,443. Beckley, WV (576.7)
1,444. New Castle, IN (576.5)
1,445. Martin, TN (576.4)
1,446. Newman, CA (576.3)
1,447. Seguin, TX (576.1)
1,447. Toccoa, GA (576.1)
1,449. Kilgore, TX (575.9)
1,450. Corinth, MS (575.7)
1,450. Garden City, KS (575.7)
1,452. Amsterdam, NY (575.3)
1,452. Savannah, TN (575.3)
1,454. Alexandria, LA (575.0)
1,454. Ardmore, OK (575.0)
1,454. Sweetwater, TN (575.0)
1,457. Shelby, OH (574.9)
1,457. Vincennes, IN (574.9)
1,459. Ashtabula, OH (574.8)
1,459. Breckenridge, TX (574.8)
1,461. Springfield, TN (574.7)
1,461. Tri-City, OR (574.7)
1,463. Connell, WA (574.5)
1,464. Lisbon, OH (574.4)
1,465. Sweet Home, OR (574.3)
1,466. Aurora, MO (574.1)
1,466. Bisbee, AZ (574.1)
1,466. Lompoc, CA (574.1)
1,469. Arkadelphia, AR (573.9)
1,470. Fairbanks, AK (573.8)
1,471. Jackson, GA (573.6)
1,471. Trinidad, CO (573.6)
1,471. Woodstock, VA (573.6)
1,474. Alliance, OH (573.4)
1,475. Dexter, MO (573.3)
1,476. New Lexington, OH (573.2)
1,477. Martinsville, IN (573.1)
1,477. Scott City, MO (573.1)

1,479. Independence, KS (573.0)
1,480. Roaring Spring, PA (572.9)
1,480. Tamaqua, PA (572.9)
1,482. Fernley, NV (572.8)
1,482. Gadsden, AL (572.8)
1,484. Richmond, IN (572.7)
1,485. Hanford, CA (572.6)
1,485. London, KY (572.6)
1,487. Walnut Ridge, AR (572.5)
1,488. Marshalltown, IA (572.2)
1,489. Fort Smith, AR (572.1)
1,489. Gillespie, IL (572.1)
1,489. Kaufman, TX (572.1)
1,489. New Albany, MS (572.1)
1,493. De Soto, MO (571.9)
1,494. Corydon, IN (571.7)
1,494. Riverton, WY (571.7)
1,496. Ponca City, OK (571.3)
1,497. Batesville, MS (571.2)
1,497. Philipsburg, PA (571.2)
1,499. Commerce, TX (571.1)
1,499. Las Cruces, NM (571.1)
1,501. Elwood, IN (571.0)
1,502. Mount Pleasant, MI (570.8)
1,503. Fillmore, CA (570.6)
1,503. Marshall, MO (570.6)
1,505. Elizabeth City, NC (570.5)
1,506. Bluefield, WV (570.4)
1,507. Macon, GA (570.2)
1,508. Geneva, OH (569.9)
1,509. Hondo, TX (569.7)
1,510. Benton, IL (569.6)
1,510. Boonville, MO (569.6)
1,510. Clinton, IN (569.6)
1,513. Kendallville, IN (569.3)
1,514. Lake Placid, FL (569.2)
1,515. New Martinsville, WV (569.1)
1,516. Lufkin, TX (569.0)
1,516. Red Bluff, CA (569.0)
1,518. Fort Leonard Wood, MO (568.8)
1,518. Linton, IN (568.8)
1,518. Malvern, AR (568.8)

1,521. Freeport, IL (568.4)
1,522. Edna, TX (568.3)
1,523. Bridgeport, TX (568.0)
1,523. Sault Ste. Marie, MI (568.0)
1,525. Parker, AZ (567.9)
1,526. Pana, IL (567.8)
1,527. McAlester, OK (567.4)
1,527. Pontiac, IL (567.4)
1,527. Zanesville, OH (567.4)
1,530. Altus, OK (566.7)
1,530. Dunn, NC (566.7)
1,530. Port Isabel, TX (566.7)
1,533. Giddings, TX (566.6)
1,534. Paintsville, KY (566.5)
1,535. Senatobia, MS (566.3)
1,536. Arizona City, AZ (566.1)
1,537. Galliano, LA (565.7)
1,537. Westville, IN (565.7)
1,539. Wilson, NC (565.4)
1,540. Galesburg, IL (565.3)
1,540. Glasgow, KY (565.3)
1,540. Marion, OH (565.3)
1,540. Orland, CA (565.3)
1,544. Stuttgart, AR (565.2)
1,545. Moberly, MO (565.1)
1,545. Neosho, MO (565.1)
1,545. Plymouth, IN (565.1)
1,548. Coshocton, OH (565.0)
1,549. Urbana, OH (564.9)
1,550. Waynesboro, GA (564.6)
1,551. Cambridge, OH (564.5)
1,551. Hillsboro, OH (564.5)
1,553. Lawton, OK (564.3)
1,554. Fostoria, OH (564.1)
1,555. Coalinga, CA (563.8)
1,556. Lockhart, TX (563.7)
1,557. Russellville, AR (563.5)
1,558. Anniston, AL (563.3)
1,558. Cuero, TX (563.3)
1,560. Duncan, OK (563.0)
1,561. Maysville, KY (562.9)
1,562. Beaver Dam, KY (562.4)
1,562. Crescent City, CA (562.4)
1,564. Fort Polk, LA (562.2)

1,565. Presque Isle, ME (562.1)

1,566. Dodge City, KS (562.0)

1,566. Grenada, MS (562.0)

1,566. Hazleton, PA (562.0)

1,569. Junction City, KS (561.9)

1,570. Jersey Shore, PA (561.4)

1,571. Lahaina, HI (561.3)

1,572. Blountstown, FL (561.1)

1,572. Delta, CO (561.1)

1,574. Centerville, IA (560.8)

1,575. Goldsboro, NC (560.7)

1,576. Hermiston, OR (560.4)

1,577. Waycross, GA (560.2)

1,578. Elk City, OK (560.1)

1,578. Westernport, MD (560.1)

1,580. Georgetown, SC (560.0)

1,580. Jesup, GA (560.0)

1,580. Kenton, OH (560.0)

1,583. Springfield, OH (559.9)

1,584. Sullivan, MO (559.5)

1,585. Live Oak, FL (559.4)

1,586. Williamsburg, KY (559.3)

1,586. Yuma, AZ (559.3)

1,588. Ruston, LA (559.2)

1,589. Willard, OH (559.1)

1,590. Paris, TN (559.0)

1,591. Valdosta, GA (558.9)

1,592. Corsicana, TX (558.6)

1,592. Gatesville, TX (558.6)

1,592. Pryor Creek, OK (558.6)

1,595. Fairfield, IL (558.5)

1,596. Alamogordo, NM (558.4)

1,597. Blairsville, PA (558.0)

1,597. Farmville, VA (558.0)

1,599. Hawaiian Paradise Park, HI (557.7)

1,600. Brookhaven, MS (557.4)

1,601. Lake Los Angeles, CA (557.3)

1,601. Shelby, NC (557.3)

1,603. Calhoun, GA (556.9)

1,604. Asheboro, NC (556.7)

1,605. East Liverpool, OH (556.3)

1,605. Lebanon, KY (556.3)

1,607. Sturgis, MI (556.0)

1,608. Odessa, TX (555.9)

1,608. Patterson, CA (555.9)

1,610. Hinesville, GA (555.7)

1,610. Worthington, MN (555.7)

1,612. Pikeville, KY (555.6)

1,613. El Campo, TX (555.3)

1,614. Madisonville, KY (555.2)

1,614. Waterford, CA (555.2)

1,616. Pontotoc, MS (554.7)

1,617. Forest City, NC (554.5)

1,618. Portsmouth, OH (554.4)

1,619. Central City, KY (554.2)

1,619. West Frankfort, IL (554.2)

1,621. North Vernon, IN (554.1)

1,622. Bowling Green, MO (554.0)

1,622. Eagar, AZ (554.0)

1,622. Trumann, AR (554.0)

1,625. Burkburnett, TX (553.9)

1,626. Erwin, TN (553.6)

1,627. Storm Lake, IA (553.4)

1,628. Scottsboro, AL (552.9)

1,629. Keyser, WV (552.7)

1,630. Donaldsonville, LA (552.6)

1,630. Santa Maria, CA (552.6)

1,632. Hazard, KY (552.5)

1,633. West Tawakoni, TX (552.4)

1,634. Rockport, TX (552.0)

1,634. St. Clair, MO (552.0)

1,636. Selma, CA (551.8)

1,637. Dumas, TX (551.7)

1,638. South Pittsburg, TN (551.5)

1,639. Connersville, IN (551.4)

1,640. Harrodsburg, KY (551.3)

1,640. Susanville, CA (551.3)

1,642. Fellsmere, FL (551.2)

1,643. Martinsville, VA (551.1)

1,644. Kewanee, IL (550.9)

1,645. Cushing, OK (550.7)

1,646. Fort Stockton, TX (550.6)

1,647. Skiatook, OK (550.4)

1,648. Lexington, TN (550.2)

1,649. Danville, IL (550.1)

1,650. Decatur, TX (550.0)

1,651. Nevada, MO (549.7)
1,652. Dublin, GA (549.3)
1,653. Monroe, LA (548.7)
1,654. Mexico, MO (548.1)
1,655. Muskogee, OK (547.8)
1,656. Scottsburg, IN (547.7)
1,657. Lovington, NM (547.5)
1,658. Grafton, WV (547.4)
1,659. McGregor, TX (547.2)
1,659. Portland, IN (547.2)
1,661. Ashland, PA (546.7)
1,662. Gilmer, TX (546.5)
1,663. Live Oak (Sutter County), CA (546.4)
1,664. Monroe, GA (546.2)
1,665. La Follette, TN (546.1)
1,665. Sweetwater, TX (546.1)
1,667. Livingston, TX (545.8)
1,668. Desert Hot Springs, CA (545.7)
1,669. Blythe, CA (545.6)
1,670. Pulaski, TN (545.2)
1,671. Pascagoula, MS (545.1)
1,672. Rosamond, CA (545.0)
1,672. Tahlequah, OK (545.0)
1,674. Clinton, NC (544.9)
1,675. Lake City, SC (544.6)
1,675. Monticello, NY (544.6)
1,677. Orangeburg, SC (544.5)
1,678. Grandview, WA (544.4)
1,679. Logansport, IN (544.3)
1,680. Du Quoin, IL (544.0)
1,681. Gallup, NM (543.9)
1,682. Socorro, NM (543.6)
1,683. Huntsville, TX (543.2)
1,684. Raton, NM (543.1)
1,685. Elkin, NC (542.7)
1,685. Silver City, NM (542.7)
1,687. Carthage, TX (542.6)
1,687. Frostproof, FL (542.6)
1,689. Chester, IL (542.5)
1,689. Malone, NY (542.5)
1,691. Buena Vista, VA (542.3)
1,692. Chowchilla, CA (542.0)

1,693. Cornelia, GA (541.9)
1,693. DeRidder, LA (541.9)
1,695. Merced, CA (541.3)
1,696. Gustine, CA (541.1)
1,697. Los Banos, CA (540.9)
1,698. Whiteville, NC (540.7)
1,699. Mineral Wells, TX (540.6)
1,699. Mount Sterling, KY (540.6)
1,701. El Centro, CA (540.5)
1,702. Frankfort, IN (540.3)
1,703. Amite City, LA (540.2)
1,704. Dowagiac, MI (539.8)
1,705. Bay City, TX (539.7)
1,705. Hillsboro, TX (539.7)
1,707. Homesteads Addition, TX (539.6)
1,708. Farmington, NM (539.5)
1,709. Clifton Forge, VA (539.4)
1,710. Muleshoe, TX (539.1)
1,711. Carthage, MO (538.5)
1,711. Georgetown, DE (538.5)
1,711. Rocky Mount, NC (538.5)
1,714. Shamokin, PA (538.4)
1,715. Mayfield, KY (538.3)
1,715. Rantoul, IL (538.3)
1,717. Albany, GA (538.1)
1,718. Columbus, MS (537.4)
1,718. Richlands, VA (537.4)
1,718. Roanoke Rapids, NC (537.4)
1,721. Adel, GA (537.3)
1,722. Monett, MO (537.2)
1,723. Picayune, MS (537.1)
1,724. Hopkinsville, KY (537.0)
1,724. Point Pleasant, OH (537.0)
1,726. Sparta, TN (536.9)
1,727. Cambridge, MD (536.8)
1,728. Amory, MS (536.6)
1,728. Bolivar, TN (536.6)
1,730. Wynne, AR (536.4)
1,731. Pauls Valley, OK (536.0)
1,732. Watsonville, CA (535.9)
1,733. Dos Palos, CA (535.8)
1,734. Holly Springs, MS (535.6)

1,734. Luling, TX (535.6)

1,734. Rupert, ID (535.6)

1,737. Slaton, TX (535.5)

1,738. Harvard, IL (535.3)

1,739. Humboldt, TN (535.2)

1,740. Uvalde, TX (535.0)

1,741. Kenai, AK (534.9)

1,741. Logan, WV (534.9)

1,743. Nacogdoches, TX (534.8)

1,744. Union City, TN (534.3)

1,745. Yoakum, TX (534.1)

1,746. Valley, AL (532.9)

1,747. Middleport, OH (532.3)

1,748. Thomaston, GA (532.0)

1,749. Kaplan, LA (531.2)

1,750. Albion, MI (530.0)

1,750. Ocala Estates, FL (530.0)

1,752. Rockmart, GA (529.6)

1,753. Quincy, WA (529.4)

1,754. Sylacauga, AL (529.1)

1,755. Del Rio, TX (529.0)

1,756. Palestine, TX (528.9)

1,757. Williams, CA (528.7)

1,758. California City, CA (528.6)

1,759. Barnesville, GA (528.3)

1,759. Dalton, GA (528.3)

1,761. Weiser, ID (527.5)

1,762. Russellville, KY (527.1)

1,762. Salinas, CA (527.1)

1,764. Palatka, FL (526.9)

1,765. Andalusia, AL (526.8)

1,765. Walterboro, SC (526.8)

1,767. Salamanca, NY (526.6)

1,768. Coffeyville, KS (526.4)

1,768. Ingleside, TX (526.4)

1,770. Peru, IN (526.2)

1,771. Cleveland, TX (525.8)

1,772. Blackwell, OK (525.4)

1,773. Sallisaw, OK (524.7)

1,774. Vidalia, GA (524.6)

1,775. Barstow, CA (524.3)

1,776. Crooksville, OH (524.0)

1,777. Marion, VA (523.9)

1,778. Roswell, NM (523.8)

1,779. LaGrange, GA (523.5)

1,780. Clovis, NM (523.4)

1,780. Douglas, GA (523.4)

1,782. Atlanta, TX (523.3)

1,782. Jerome, ID (523.3)

1,784. Poplar Bluff, MO (523.2)

1,785. Eden, NC (522.5)

1,786. Milledgeville, GA (522.0)

1,787. Mena, AR (521.9)

1,788. Brady, TX (521.5)

1,788. Lafayette, TN (521.5)

1,790. Vicksburg, MS (521.4)

1,791. Gonzales, TX (521.1)

1,792. Pinckneyville, IL (520.8)

1,793. Harlingen, TX (520.4)

1,794. Rogersville, TN (520.3)

1,795. Marion, IN (520.2)

1,796. Troy, AL (519.8)

1,797. Clearlake, CA (519.5)

1,798. Middlesborough, KY (519.3)

1,799. Globe, AZ (519.1)

1,799. Jasper, TX (519.1)

1,801. Taylorsville, NC (518.4)

1,802. Holtville, CA (517.9)

1,803. Corning, CA (517.7)

1,803. McMinnville, TN (517.7)

1,805. Wharton, TX (517.6)

1,806. Prestonsburg, KY (517.4)

1,807. Mineola, TX (517.1)

1,808. Demopolis, AL (517.0)

1,809. Chester, SC (516.9)

1,809. Levelland, TX (516.9)

1,809. Winslow, AZ (516.9)

1,812. Muldrow, OK (516.7)

1,813. Kinston, NC (516.4)

1,814. Gainesville, TX (516.0)

1,814. Mount Pleasant, TX (516.0)

1,816. Alexander City, AL (515.9)

1,817. Eunice, LA (515.7)

1,818. Tifton, GA (515.6)

1,819. Pampa, TX (515.5)

1,820. Bloomfield, NM (515.4)

1,821. Meridian, MS (515.2)

1,822. Dayton, TN (515.0)
1,823. Marksville, LA (514.7)
1,823. Snyder, TX (514.7)
1,825. Denison, IA (514.4)
1,826. Vernon, TX (513.9)
1,827. Santa Paula, CA (513.8)
1,828. Jennings, LA (513.0)
1,829. Fayetteville, TN (512.9)
1,830. Borger, TX (512.7)
1,831. Lexington, NE (512.4)
1,832. Newport, AR (512.3)
1,833. Bainbridge, GA (511.9)
1,834. Colorado City, TX (511.8)
1,835. Trenton, MO (510.9)
1,836. Shenandoah, PA (510.8)
1,837. Perryton, TX (510.3)
1,838. Kerman, CA (510.1)
1,839. Siler City, NC (509.9)
1,840. Cleveland, MS (509.7)
1,840. Leitchfield, KY (509.7)
1,842. Miami, OK (509.6)
1,843. Franklin, LA (509.0)
1,844. Schuyler, NE (508.9)
1,845. Hartwell, GA (507.9)
1,845. Laughlin, NV (507.9)
1,845. Laurel, MS (507.9)
1,848. Cheraw, SC (507.7)
1,848. El Dorado, AR (507.7)
1,850. Marianna, FL (507.2)
1,851. Abbeville, LA (507.0)
1,852. Nogales, AZ (506.7)
1,853. Cynthiana, KY (506.2)
1,853. Douglas, AZ (506.2)
1,855. Las Vegas, NM (505.7)
1,856. Reedley, CA (505.6)
1,857. Othello, WA (505.5)
1,858. Morganfield, KY (505.1)
1,859. Mexia, TX (504.4)
1,860. Covington, TN (504.2)
1,861. Henderson, TX (504.0)
1,862. Newberry, SC (503.3)
1,863. Union, SC (503.2)
1,864. Clinton, SC (503.1)
1,865. Magnolia, AR (502.9)

1,866. Americus, GA (502.7)
1,867. Vinita, OK (502.5)
1,868. Idabel, OK (502.2)
1,869. Pearsall, TX (502.0)
1,870. Baxley, GA (501.6)
1,871. Rockingham, NC (501.1)
1,872. West Point, MS (501.0)
1,873. Guadalupe, CA (500.7)
1,873. Nelsonville, OH (500.7)
1,875. Hereford, TX (500.6)
1,876. Sunnyside, WA (500.0)
1,877. Crystal City, TX (499.9)
1,878. Beardstown, IL (499.7)
1,878. Kodiak, AK (499.7)
1,880. Roxboro, NC (499.6)
1,881. Porterville, CA (499.5)
1,882. Sandersville, GA (499.4)
1,883. Perry, FL (499.1)
1,884. Clanton, AL (499.0)
1,885. Pembroke, NC (497.2)
1,886. Kingsville, TX (496.9)
1,886. Marshall, TX (496.9)
1,888. Anadarko, OK (496.7)
1,888. South Boston, VA (496.7)
1,890. Opelousas, LA (496.3)
1,891. LaBelle, FL (496.1)
1,892. Mathis, TX (495.7)
1,893. Littlefield, TX (495.5)
1,894. Cedartown, GA (495.2)
1,894. Fort Payne, AL (495.2)
1,896. Morrilton, AR (494.7)
1,896. Sanger, CA (494.7)
1,898. Gaffney, SC (494.6)
1,899. Natchez, MS (494.3)
1,899. Navasota, TX (494.3)
1,901. Brewton, AL (493.7)
1,902. Lumberton, NC (493.6)
1,902. Ozark, AL (493.6)
1,902. Soledad, CA (493.6)
1,905. Pine Bluff, AR (493.0)
1,906. Truth or Consequences, NM (491.9)
1,907. Aztec, NM (491.8)
1,907. Indiantown, FL (491.8)

1,909. LaFayette, GA (491.5)
1,910. Swainsboro, GA (491.4)
1,911. Plainview, TX (491.3)
1,912. Cochran, GA (491.0)
1,912. New Roads, LA (491.0)
1,914. Columbia, MS (490.7)
1,915. Center, TX (490.5)
1,916. Shelbyville, TN (490.1)
1,917. Ferriday, LA (490.0)
1,917. Kirtland, NM (490.0)
1,919. Espanola, NM (489.7)
1,920. Philadelphia, MS (488.8)
1,921. Booneville, MS (488.6)
1,922. Toppenish, WA (488.2)
1,923. Madera, CA (487.9)
1,924. Big Stone Gap, VA (487.7)
1,924. Zuni Pueblo, NM (487.7)
1,926. Clewiston, FL (487.0)
1,927. Starke, FL (486.7)
1,928. Orosi, CA (486.6)
1,928. Summerville, GA (486.6)
1,930. Portales, NM (486.5)
1,931. Henryetta, OK (486.4)
1,932. Poteau, OK (486.2)
1,933. Canton, MS (485.8)
1,934. Eagle Pass, TX (485.5)
1,934. Morgan City, LA (485.5)
1,936. Prairie View, TX (485.2)
1,937. Colorado City, AZ (485.0)
1,938. Jacksonville, TX (484.9)
1,939. Crossett, AR (484.6)
1,940. Grayson, KY (484.3)
1,941. Talladega, AL (484.1)
1,942. Rio Grande City, TX (483.3)
1,943. Moultrie, GA (482.7)
1,944. Warren, AR (482.3)
1,945. Dillon, SC (481.8)
1,946. Oakdale, LA (481.2)
1,947. Thomson, GA (481.1)
1,948. Rayne, LA (481.0)
1,949. Grants, NM (479.1)
1,950. Brawley, CA (479.0)
1,950. Jasper, FL (479.0)
1,952. Reidsville, NC (478.7)

1,953. Gonzales, CA (478.3)
1,954. Taft, CA (477.9)
1,955. Henderson, NC (477.6)
1,955. Rockdale, TX (477.6)
1,955. Williamston, NC (477.6)
1,958. Blytheville, AR (477.4)
1,959. Metropolis, IL (477.2)
1,960. Monticello, KY (477.1)
1,961. Lamesa, TX (476.5)
1,961. Liberal, KS (476.5)
1,961. Mount Olive, NC (476.5)
1,964. Okmulgee, OK (476.1)
1,965. Shafter, CA (475.4)
1,966. Greenville, AL (474.7)
1,967. Guymon, OK (474.5)
1,968. King City, CA (474.2)
1,969. Interlachen, FL (473.5)
1,970. San Luis, AZ (473.0)
1,971. Mattawa, WA (472.3)
1,972. Immokalee, FL (472.2)
1,973. Florence, AZ (472.0)
1,974. Sinton, TX (471.1)
1,975. Somerton, AZ (469.8)
1,976. Mullins, SC (469.7)
1,977. Bridgeton, NJ (469.4)
1,978. Brownsville, TN (469.1)
1,979. Newport, TN (468.5)
1,980. Caruthersville, MO (465.9)
1,980. Crockett, TX (465.9)
1,982. Deming, NM (464.7)
1,983. Osceola, AR (464.6)
1,983. Sullivan City, TX (464.6)
1,983. Union City, IN (464.6)
1,986. Marion, SC (464.2)
1,987. Crowley, LA (464.1)
1,988. Chaparral, NM (463.6)
1,989. Raymondville, TX (463.5)
1,990. Beeville, TX (462.9)
1,991. Arcadia, FL (462.0)
1,992. Clarksville, AR (461.8)
1,993. Delano, CA (461.6)
1,994. Kosciusko, MS (461.3)
1,995. Eufaula, AL (460.7)
1,995. Harlan, KY (460.7)

1,997. Tarboro, NC (460.5)
1,998. Camden, AR (460.4)
1,999. Eastman, GA (459.9)
1,999. Seminole, OK (459.9)
2,001. Greenwood, MS (459.3)
2,002. Laurinburg, NC (458.8)
2,003. Minden, LA (458.0)
2,004. St. Martinville, LA (457.0)
2,005. Barbourville, KY (454.6)
2,006. Sylvester, GA (454.1)
2,007. Natchitoches, LA (453.5)
2,008. Greenville, MS (451.8)
2,009. Kinross, MI (451.0)
2,010. Wapato, WA (450.6)
2,011. Bogalusa, LA (450.4)
2,011. Cordele, GA (450.4)
2,013. Robstown, TX (449.9)
2,013. Russellville, AL (449.9)
2,015. Alice, TX (449.8)
2,015. Leesville, LA (449.8)
2,017. Forest, MS (449.5)
2,018. Folkston, GA (449.0)
2,019. McComb, MS (448.7)
2,020. Brownfield, TX (446.6)
2,021. Springhill, LA (446.3)
2,022. Lake Butler, FL (446.2)
2,023. Woodlake, CA (445.9)
2,024. Indianola, MS (445.6)
2,025. Wauchula, FL (444.8)
2,026. Cameron, TX (444.0)
2,027. Cairo, GA (442.9)
2,028. Clarksdale, MS (442.1)
2,029. Ripley, TN (441.7)
2,029. Wadesboro, NC (441.7)
2,031. Charleston, MO (441.5)
2,031. Laurens, SC (441.5)
2,033. Holdenville, OK (441.2)
2,034. Belle Glade, FL (441.1)
2,035. Kingstree, SC (439.8)
2,036. Firebaugh, CA (438.1)
2,037. Whiteriver, AZ (437.5)
2,038. Camilla, GA (437.4)
2,039. McFarland, CA (437.3)
2,040. Wasco, CA (437.0)

2,041. Greenfield, CA (436.7)
2,042. Jeanerette, LA (436.1)
2,043. Salem, NJ (435.4)
2,044. Pahokee, FL (434.3)
2,045. Fort Valley, GA (434.2)
2,046. Hazlehurst, MS (434.0)
2,047. Bennettsville, SC (431.8)
2,048. Corcoran, CA (430.7)
2,049. Elberton, GA (430.6)
2,050. Forrest City, AR (430.5)
2,051. Kayenta, AZ (429.1)
2,052. Selma, AL (429.0)
2,053. Fitzgerald, GA (426.5)
2,054. Earlimart, CA (423.2)
2,055. Ville Platte, LA (422.1)
2,056. Montezuma, GA (421.9)
2,057. De Queen, AR (421.4)
2,058. Eloy, AZ (420.9)
2,059. Quincy, FL (420.6)
2,060. Princess Anne, MD (420.3)
2,061. Lindsay, CA (418.7)
2,061. Shiprock, NM (418.7)
2,063. Atmore, AL (417.1)
2,064. Mansfield, LA (416.7)
2,065. Hope, AR (415.7)
2,066. Arvin, CA (414.2)
2,067. Parlier, CA (413.1)
2,068. Carrizo Springs, TX (410.1)
2,069. Jonesboro, LA (409.5)
2,070. Fabens, TX (408.4)
2,071. Avenal, CA (403.4)
2,072. Marlin, TX (400.2)
2,073. Orange Cove, CA (400.0)
2,074. Mendota, CA (397.3)
2,075. Zapata, TX (393.9)
2,076. Rio Bravo, TX (393.2)
2,077. Helena, AR (390.8)
2,078. Huron, CA (387.6)
2,079. Yazoo City, MS (387.1)
2,080. Tallulah, LA (380.9)
2,081. Mecca, CA (380.3)
2,082. Tuskegee, AL (377.3)
2,083. Bastrop, LA (374.7)
2,084. McRae, GA (288.5)

State by State

All 2,084 small towns are listed alphabetically by state, with their ranks in parentheses. You'll find listings for 49 states. Rhode Island is excluded because it does not contain any urbanized areas or urban clusters with populations between 5,000 and 199,999.

Alabama

Albertville (1,294)
Alexander City (1,816)
Andalusia (1,765)
Anniston (1,558)
Arab (662)
Athens (916)
Atmore (2,063)
Auburn (427)
Bay Minette (1,014)
Brewton (1,901)
Clanton (1,884)
Cullman (876)
Daphne (110)
Decatur (1,262)
Demopolis (1,808)
Dothan (1,221)
Enterprise (1,013)
Eufaula (1,995)
Florence (1,157)
Foley (701)
Fort Payne (1,894)
Gadsden (1,482)
Greenville (1,966)
Jasper (1,316)
Ozark (1,902)
Pell City (1,169)
Robertsdale (764)
Russellville (2,013)
Scottsboro (1,628)
Selma (2,052)
Sylacauga (1,754)
Talladega (1,941)
Troy (1,796)
Tuscaloosa (918)
Tuskegee (2,082)

Valley (1,746)
Wetumpka (1,313)

Alaska

Anchorage Northeast (864)
Fairbanks (1,470)
Juneau (712)
Kenai (1,741)
Ketchikan (1,074)
Kodiak (1,878)
Lakes (862)
Sitka (883)
Soldotna (691)

Arizona

Arizona City (1,536)
Bisbee (1,466)
Buckeye (1,274)
Bullhead City (1,409)
Camp Verde (1,230)
Casa Grande (1,385)
Chino Valley (740)
Colorado City (1,937)
Coolidge (1,407)
Corona de Tucson (98)
Cottonwood (533)
Douglas (1,853)
Eagar (1,622)
Eloy (2,058)
Estrella (211)
Flagstaff (378)
Florence (1,973)
Globe (1,799)
Kayenta (2,051)
Kingman (1,068)
Lake Havasu City (693)

Lake of the Woods (874)
Marana West (247)
Maricopa (537)
Nogales (1,852)
Page (1,148)
Parker (1,525)
Payson (804)
Prescott Valley (277)
Safford (1,038)
Sahuarita (260)
San Luis (1,970)
Sedona (130)
Show Low (1,405)
Sierra Vista (1,068)
Snowflake (1,182)
Somerton (1,975)
Tuba City (1,440)
Vail (92)
Village of Oak Creek (Big Park) (370)
Vistancia (9)
Whiteriver (2,037)
Winslow (1,809)
Yuma (1,586)

Arkansas

Arkadelphia (1,469)
Batesville (1,053)
Beebe (1,175)
Blytheville (1,958)
Camden (1,998)
Clarksville (1,992)
Conway (738)
Crossett (1,939)
De Queen (2,057)
El Dorado (1,848)
Forrest City (2,050)
Fort Smith (1,489)
Greenwood (851)
Harrison (1,259)
Heber Springs (1,153)
Helena (2,077)
Hope (2,065)
Hot Springs (1,008)
Hot Springs Village (590)

Jonesboro (625)
Magnolia (1,865)
Malvern (1,518)
Mena (1,787)
Monticello (1,282)
Morrilton (1,896)
Mountain Home (616)
Newport (1,832)
Osceola (1,983)
Paragould (906)
Pine Bluff (1,905)
Pocahontas (1,232)
Russellville (1,557)
Searcy (1,111)
Siloam Springs (802)
Stuttgart (1,544)
Trumann (1,622)
Walnut Ridge (1,487)
Warren (1,944)
Wynne (1,730)

California

Arcata (770)
Arroyo Grande (264)
Arvin (2,066)
Auburn (155)
Avenal (2,071)
Barstow (1,775)
Big Bear City (675)
Bishop (177)
Blythe (1,669)
Bonadelle Ranchos (434)
Brawley (1,950)
California City (1,758)
Calistoga (575)
Camarillo (218)
Cambria (198)
Chico (440)
Chowchilla (1,692)
Clearlake (1,797)
Cloverdale (506)
Coalinga (1,555)
Colusa (1,433)
Corcoran (2,048)

Corning (1,803)
Crescent City (1,562)
Davis (154)
Delano (1,993)
Desert Hot Springs (1,668)
Discovery Bay (161)
Dixon (936)
Dos Palos (1,733)
Earlimart (2,054)
El Centro (1,701)
Escalon (474)
Eureka (883)
Fairfield (684)
Fillmore (1,503)
Firebaugh (2,036)
Forestville (273)
Fort Bragg (914)
Fortuna (1,030)
Galt (830)
Gilroy (234)
Gonzales (1,953)
Grass Valley (288)
Greenfield (2,041)
Gridley (1,353)
Guadalupe (1,873)
Gustine (1,696)
Half Moon Bay (99)
Hanford (1,485)
Hemet (1,156)
Hilmar (875)
Hollister (1,269)
Holtville (1,802)
Huron (2,078)
Ione (595)
Jackson (353)
Kerman (1,838)
King City (1,968)
Lake Arrowhead (560)
Lake Los Angeles (1,601)
Lake of the Pines (32)
Lakeport (668)
Lake Wildwood (259)
Lindsay (2,061)
Live Oak (Sutter County) (1,663)

Livermore (102)
Lodi (1,135)
Lompoc (1,466)
Los Banos (1,697)
Madera (1,923)
Mammoth Lakes (242)
Manteca (926)
McFarland (2,039)
Mecca (2,081)
Mendota (2,074)
Merced (1,695)
Morro Bay (174)
Mountain House (87)
Mount Shasta (1,164)
Napa (531)
Needles (1,347)
Newman (1,446)
Nipomo (537)
Orange Cove (2,073)
Orland (1,540)
Orosi (1,928)
Oroville (1,152)
Paradise (655)
Parlier (2,067)
Paso Robles (283)
Patterson (1,608)
Petaluma (124)
Phelan (914)
Placerville (220)
Plumas Lake (186)
Porterville (1,881)
Ramona (575)
Rancho Calaveras (404)
Rancho Murieta (36)
Red Bluff (1,516)
Redding (515)
Reedley (1,856)
Ridgecrest (889)
Rio Vista (228)
Rosamond (1,672)
St. Helena (211)
Salinas (1,762)
Sanger (1,896)
San Luis Obispo (342)

Santa Cruz (170)
Santa Maria (1,630)
Santa Paula (1,827)
Seaside (562)
Selma (1,636)
Shafter (1,965)
Silver Lakes (336)
Simi Valley (376)
Soledad (1,902)
Solvang (197)
Sonoma (325)
Sonora (315)
South Lake Tahoe (425)
Susanville (1,640)
Taft (1,954)
Tehachapi (1,107)
Tracy (699)
Truckee (39)
Turlock (1,226)
Twentynine Palms (1,341)
Ukiah (1,184)
Vacaville (515)
Vallejo (687)
Wasco (2,040)
Waterford (1,614)
Watsonville (1,732)
Williams (1,757)
Willits (1,208)
Willows (1,108)
Winters (856)
Woodlake (2,023)
Woodland (734)
Yreka (830)
Yuba City (1,291)
Yucca Valley (889)

Colorado

Alamosa (1,098)
Aspen (13)
Basalt (72)
Battlement Mesa (572)
Boulder (37)
Breckenridge (25)
Brush (664)

Canon City (457)
Carbondale (321)
Cortez (1,053)
Craig (1,271)
Delta (1,572)
Durango (210)
Eagle (142)
Eaton (132)
Edwards (145)
Estes Park (76)
Evergreen (7)
Firestone (90)
Florence (1,241)
Fort Lupton (720)
Fort Morgan (1,271)
Glenwood Springs (617)
Grand Junction (558)
Greeley (495)
Gunnison (97)
Gypsum (131)
Johnstown (58)
Lafayette (11)
La Junta (1,426)
Lamar (1,397)
Leadville (283)
Longmont (165)
Montrose (492)
New Castle (304)
Pagosa Springs (335)
Pueblo (1,081)
Rifle (570)
Roxborough Park (5)
Salida (46)
Silverthorne (27)
Steamboat Springs (34)
Sterling (641)
Trinidad (1,471)
Vail (31)
Wellington (26)
Woodland Park (59)

Connecticut

Colchester (166)
Danbury (215)

Jewett City (688)
Lake Pocotopaug (74)
Stafford Springs (1,071)
Torrington (688)
Waterbury (795)
Willimantic (1,317)

Delaware

Dover (524)
Georgetown (1,711)
Lewes (41)
Long Neck (326)
Middletown (113)
Milford (603)
Millsboro (615)
Ocean View (53)

Florida

Alachua (361)
Arcadia (1,991)
Belle Glade (2,034)
Big Pine Key (156)
Blountstown (1,572)
Clewiston (1,926)
Crawfordville (498)
Crestview (673)
De Funiak Springs (1,090)
Deltona (565)
Fellsmere (1,642)
Fernandina Beach (61)
Fort Meade (1,114)
Four Corners (752)
Frostproof (1,687)
Homosassa Springs (825)
Immokalee (1,972)
Indiantown (1,907)
Interlachen (1,969)
Jasper (1,950)
Jupiter Farms (38)
Key Largo (157)
Keystone Heights (501)
Key West (533)
LaBelle (1,891)
Lady Lake (442)

Lake Butler (2,022)
Lake City (1,075)
Lake Placid (1,514)
Leesburg (424)
Live Oak (1,585)
Macclenny (1,227)
Marathon (400)
Marianna (1,850)
Marion Oaks (774)
Nassau Village (726)
North Port (355)
Ocala (825)
Ocala Estates (1,750)
Okeechobee (1,135)
Orangetree (79)
Pahokee (2,044)
Palatka (1,764)
Panama City (932)
Panama City Northeast (1,221)
Perry (1,883)
Poinciana (1,105)
Poinciana Southwest (1,180)
Quincy (2,059)
Rainbow Lakes Estates (608)
St. Augustine (95)
Santa Rosa Beach (70)
Sebastian (307)
Sebring (1,208)
Spring Hill (397)
Starke (1,927)
Sugarmill Woods (222)
Titusville (447)
Wauchula (2,025)
Wedgefield (230)
World Golf Village (4)
Yulee (312)
Zephyrhills (940)

Georgia

Adel (1,721)
Albany (1,717)
Americus (1,866)
Athens (469)
Bainbridge (1,833)

Barnesville (1,759)
Baxley (1,870)
Bremen (578)
Brunswick (1,144)
Buckhead (Bryan County) (10)
Cairo (2,027)
Calhoun (1,603)
Camilla (2,038)
Carrollton (838)
Cartersville (572)
Cedartown (1,894)
Cochran (1,912)
Commerce (816)
Cordele (2,011)
Cornelia (1,693)
Dahlonega (1,164)
Dalton (1,759)
Douglas (1,780)
Dublin (1,652)
Eastman (1,999)
Elberton (2,049)
Fitzgerald (2,053)
Folkston (2,018)
Fort Valley (2,045)
Gainesville (943)
Hartwell (1,845)
Hinesville (1,610)
Jackson (1,471)
Jasper (976)
Jefferson (235)
Jesup (1,580)
LaFayette (1,909)
LaGrange (1,779)
Macon (1,507)
McRae (2,084)
Milledgeville (1,786)
Monroe (1,664)
Montezuma (2,056)
Moultrie (1,943)
Rincon (391)
Rockmart (1,752)
Rome (1,214)
St. Marys (828)
St. Simons (16)

Sandersville (1,882)
Statesboro (1,338)
Summerville (1,928)
Swainsboro (1,910)
Sylvester (2,006)
Thomaston (1,748)
Thomasville (1,033)
Thomson (1,947)
Tifton (1,818)
Toccoa (1,447)
Valdosta (1,591)
Vidalia (1,774)
Warner Robins (487)
Waycross (1,577)
Waynesboro (1,550)
Winder (478)

Hawaii

Haleiwa (1,175)
Hawaiian Paradise Park (1,599)
Hilo (1,259)
Kahului (1,022)
Kailua (Hawaii County) (1,225)
Kailua (Honolulu County) (732)
Kalaheo (722)
Kapaa (551)
Kekaha (863)
Kihei (1,103)
Lahaina (1,571)
Laie (1,293)
Lihue (822)
Pukalani (697)
Waimea (Hawaii County) (1,194)

Idaho

Blackfoot (813)
Burley (853)
Coeur d'Alene (183)
Emmett (1,031)
Hailey (302)
Idaho Falls (207)
Jerome (1,782)
Kuna (169)
Lewiston (559)

Moscow (174)
Mountain Home (1,022)
Nampa (589)
Pocatello (334)
Rathdrum (374)
Rexburg (806)
Rigby (73)
Rupert (1,734)
Sandpoint (343)
Star (104)
Twin Falls (427)
Weiser (1,761)

Illinois

Alton (902)
Anna (1,333)
Beardstown (1,878)
Benton (1,510)
Bloomington (370)
Braidwood (490)
Breese (168)
Byron (341)
Canton (1,203)
Carbondale (1,050)
Carlinville (808)
Carmi (1,216)
Centralia (1,442)
Champaign (567)
Charleston (1,132)
Chester (1,689)
Clinton (1,078)
Danville (1,649)
Decatur (1,281)
DeKalb (820)
Dixon (593)
Du Quoin (1,680)
Effingham (273)
Eureka (647)
Fairfield (1,595)
Freeport (1,521)
Galesburg (1,540)
Geneseo (647)
Genoa (971)
Gillespie (1,489)

Greenville (1,311)
Harrisburg (1,412)
Harvard (1,738)
Highland (377)
Hillsboro (1,198)
Jacksonville (979)
Jerseyville (420)
Kankakee (911)
Kewanee (1,644)
Lake Holiday (501)
Lawrenceville (1,438)
Lincoln (1,113)
Litchfield (1,150)
Macomb (1,346)
Mahomet (257)
Marengo (640)
Mascoutah (447)
Mattoon (1,301)
Mendota (1,327)
Metropolis (1,959)
Monmouth (1,072)
Monticello (149)
Morris (414)
Mount Carmel (978)
Mount Vernon (960)
Murphysboro (1,254)
Olney (1,268)
Ottawa (746)
Pana (1,526)
Paris (1,008)
Peru (775)
Pinckneyville (1,792)
Pontiac (1,527)
Princeton (894)
Quincy (708)
Rantoul (1,715)
Robinson (1,123)
Rochelle (1,237)
St. Joseph (294)
Salem (1,264)
Springfield (436)
Staunton (664)
Sterling (1,313)
Streator (1,202)

Taylorville (1,035)
Vandalia (921)
Waterloo (217)
West Frankfort (1,619)
Woodstock (595)

Indiana

Anderson (1,374)
Angola (495)
Attica (1,216)
Auburn (1,078)
Batesville (467)
Bedford (1,027)
Berne (710)
Bloomington (380)
Bluffton (1,090)
Boonville (945)
Charlestown (1,114)
Clinton (1,510)
Columbia City (445)
Columbus (319)
Connersville (1,639)
Corydon (1,494)
Crawfordsville (1,182)
Decatur (1,212)
Elkhart (1,135)
Elwood (1,501)
Frankfort (1,702)
Greencastle (760)
Greensburg (681)
Hartford City (1,350)
Huntingburg (1,252)
Huntington (1,277)
Jasper (295)
Kendallville (1,513)
Kokomo (1,016)
Lafayette (441)
Lawrenceburg (1,353)
Lebanon (365)
Linton (1,518)
Logansport (1,679)
Lowell (533)
Madison (1,171)
Marion (1,795)

Martinsville (1,477)
Michigan City (1,385)
Monticello (929)
Mount Vernon (790)
Muncie (1,116)
Nappanee (1,218)
New Castle (1,444)
North Manchester (1,065)
North Vernon (1,621)
Peru (1,770)
Plymouth (1,545)
Portland (1,659)
Princeton (1,334)
Rensselaer (601)
Richmond (1,484)
Rochester (854)
Rushville (1,361)
Salem (1,288)
Scottsburg (1,656)
Seymour (885)
Shelbyville (1,153)
Syracuse (979)
Tell City (1,322)
Terre Haute (1,434)
Tipton (613)
Union City (1,983)
Vincennes (1,457)
Wabash (1,324)
Warsaw (511)
Washington (1,224)
Westville (1,537)

Iowa

Algona (419)
Ames (250)
Anamosa (1,055)
Atlantic (822)
Boone (664)
Burlington (1,252)
Carroll (108)
Cedar Rapids (286)
Centerville (1,574)
Charles City (1,125)
Clarinda (729)

Clear Lake (213)
Clinton (1,361)
Creston (964)
Decorah (105)
Denison (1,825)
Dubuque (387)
Estherville (1,266)
Fairfield (416)
Fort Dodge (1,047)
Fort Madison (1,148)
Glenwood (623)
Grinnell (411)
Humboldt (607)
Independence (457)
Indianola (244)
Iowa City (159)
Keokuk (1,198)
Knoxville (715)
Le Mars (279)
Maquoketa (797)
Marshalltown (1,488)
Mason City (477)
Mount Pleasant (1,020)
Mount Vernon (143)
Muscatine (768)
Nevada (456)
Newton (1,304)
Oelwein (1,177)
Orange City (77)
Oskaloosa (787)
Ottumwa (1,286)
Pella (107)
Perry (930)
Red Oak (954)
Sioux Center (129)
Sioux City (1,118)
Spencer (460)
Spirit Lake (62)
Storm Lake (1,627)
Washington (906)
Waterloo (848)
Waverly (309)
Webster City (1,119)
Winterset (246)

Kansas

Abilene (937)
Arkansas City (1,377)
Atchison (1,043)
Augusta (539)
Chanute (1,367)
Coffeyville (1,768)
Colby (187)
Concordia (803)
De Soto (771)
Dodge City (1,566)
El Dorado (409)
Emporia (827)
Eudora (263)
Fort Scott (1,411)
Garden City (1,450)
Great Bend (1,379)
Hays (526)
Hutchinson (937)
Independence (1,479)
Iola (1,371)
Junction City (1,569)
Lawrence (308)
Leavenworth (650)
Liberal (1,961)
Manhattan (759)
McPherson (133)
Newton (529)
Ottawa (966)
Paola (587)
Parsons (1,427)
Pittsburg (888)
Pratt (373)
Salina (940)
Spring Hill (254)
Tonganoxie (382)
Topeka (859)
Ulysses (1,335)
Wamego (354)
Wellington (1,168)
Winfield (1,249)

Kentucky

Barbourville (2,005)
Bardstown (724)
Beaver Dam (1,562)
Berea (931)
Bowling Green (669)
Campbellsville (1,425)
Central City (1,619)
Cynthiana (1,853)
Danville (1,063)
Elizabethtown (1,247)
Frankfort (972)
Franklin (1,339)
Georgetown (518)
Glasgow (1,540)
Grayson (1,940)
Harlan (1,995)
Harrodsburg (1,640)
Hazard (1,632)
Hopkinsville (1,724)
Lawrenceburg (954)
Lebanon (1,605)
Leitchfield (1,840)
London (1,485)
Madisonville (1,614)
Mayfield (1,715)
Maysville (1,561)
Middlesborough (1,798)
Monticello (1,960)
Morehead (1,278)
Morganfield (1,858)
Mount Sterling (1,699)
Murray (1,247)
Nicholasville (1,045)
Owensboro (947)
Paducah (649)
Paintsville (1,534)
Paris (1,301)
Pikeville (1,612)
Prestonsburg (1,806)
Princeton (1,292)
Richmond (1,111)
Russellville (1,762)
Shelbyville (542)

Somerset (1,100)
Versailles (394)
Williamsburg (1,586)
Wilmore (625)
Winchester (1,075)

Louisiana

Abbeville (1,851)
Alexandria (1,454)
Amite City (1,703)
Bastrop (2,083)
Benton (557)
Bogalusa (2,011)
Breaux Bridge (1,317)
Crowley (1,987)
DeRidder (1,693)
Donaldsonville (1,630)
Eunice (1,817)
Ferriday (1,917)
Fort Polk (1,564)
Franklin (1,843)
Galliano (1,537)
Gramercy (1,088)
Hammond (947)
Houma (1,385)
Jeanerette (2,042)
Jennings (1,828)
Jonesboro (2,069)
Kaplan (1,749)
Lake Charles (595)
Leesville (2,015)
Mandeville (64)
Mansfield (2,064)
Marksville (1,823)
Minden (2,003)
Monroe (1,653)
Morgan City (1,934)
Natchitoches (2,007)
New Roads (1,912)
Oakdale (1,946)
Opelousas (1,890)
Rayne (1,948)
Ruston (1,588)
St. Martinville (2,004)

Slidell (289)
Springhill (2,021)
Tallulah (2,080)
Ville Platte (2,055)

Maine

Augusta (864)
Bangor (746)
Brunswick (179)
Kennebunk (43)
Lewiston (954)
Presque Isle (1,565)
Rockland (545)
Sanford (1,108)
Waterville (846)

Maryland

Brunswick (203)
Cambridge (1,727)
Chesapeake Beach (147)
Chestertown (630)
Cumberland (1,173)
Easton (218)
Emmitsburg (320)
Frederick (137)
Hagerstown (927)
Leonardtown (135)
Lexington Park (336)
Long Beach (363)
Manchester (300)
Ocean Pines (71)
Prince Frederick (841)
Princess Anne (2,060)
Salisbury (905)
Shady Side (262)
Taneytown (625)
Thurmont (360)
Waldorf (437)
Westernport (1,578)
Westminster (120)

Massachusetts

Athol (846)
Greenfield (540)

Lee (280)
Leominster (585)
Nantucket (6)
New Bedford (858)
North Adams (555)
North Brookfield (411)
Pittsfield (500)
South Deerfield (183)
Vineyard Haven (23)
Ware (1,085)

Michigan

Adrian (848)
Albion (1,750)
Allegan (784)
Alma (1,126)
Alpena (549)
Au Sable (807)
Battle Creek (1,257)
Bay City (999)
Belding (1,416)
Benton Harbor (554)
Berrien Springs (701)
Big Rapids (1,171)
Cadillac (756)
Charlotte (612)
Chelsea (52)
Clare (743)
Coldwater (1,027)
Dorr (190)
Dowagiac (1,704)
Eaton Rapids (752)
Escanaba (909)
Frankenmuth (96)
Gaylord (530)
Goodrich (176)
Greenville (1,282)
Hastings (466)
Hillsdale (947)
Holland (231)
Holly (442)
Houghton (714)
Houghton Lake (1,257)
Ionia (1,193)

Iron Mountain (661)
Ironwood (1,416)
Ishpeming (1,018)
Jackson (1,093)
Kinross (2,009)
Lapeer (764)
Laurium (1,393)
Lowell (282)
Ludington (584)
Manistee (843)
Marquette (760)
Marshall (610)
Midland (182)
Milan (256)
Monroe (976)
Mount Pleasant (1,502)
Muskegon (703)
Otsego (574)
Owosso (1,105)
Paw Paw (984)
Paw Paw Lake (1,307)
Petoskey (172)
Port Huron (808)
Portland (760)
Richmond (520)
Saginaw (1,234)
St. Johns (695)
Sault Ste. Marie (1,523)
South Haven (426)
South Lyon (62)
Sturgis (1,607)
Three Rivers (1,242)
Traverse City (116)
Whitehall (793)
Williamston (224)

Minnesota

Albert Lea (1,017)
Alexandria (150)
Austin (1,290)
Belle Plaine (179)
Bemidji (841)
Brainerd (494)
Buffalo (139)

Byron (24)
Cambridge (439)
Cloquet (742)
Crookston (1,303)
Delano (122)
Detroit Lakes (622)
Duluth (476)
Fairmont (405)
Faribault (764)
Fergus Falls (391)
Forest Lake (160)
Glencoe (650)
Grand Rapids (745)
Hastings (268)
Hibbing (744)
Hutchinson (367)
International Falls (749)
Jordan (192)
Kasson (206)
Lake City (305)
Lindstrom (146)
Litchfield (473)
Little Falls (878)
Mankato (338)
Marshall (550)
Montevideo (749)
Monticello (178)
New Prague (185)
New Ulm (204)
North Branch (295)
Northfield (198)
Owatonna (231)
Red Wing (562)
Rochester (33)
St. Cloud (380)
St. Francis (363)
St. Peter (368)
Stewartville (258)
Thief River Falls (681)
Virginia (1,214)
Waconia (30)
Waseca (923)
Willmar (587)
Winona (580)

Worthington (1,610)
Zimmerman (189)

Mississippi

Amory (1,728)
Batesville (1,497)
Booneville (1,921)
Brookhaven (1,600)
Canton (1,933)
Clarksdale (2,028)
Cleveland (1,840)
Columbia (1,914)
Columbus (1,718)
Corinth (1,450)
Diamondhead (216)
Forest (2,017)
Greenville (2,008)
Greenwood (2,001)
Grenada (1,566)
Hattiesburg (1,108)
Hazlehurst (2,046)
Holly Springs (1,734)
Indianola (2,024)
Kosciusko (1,994)
Laurel (1,845)
McComb (2,019)
Meridian (1,821)
Natchez (1,899)
New Albany (1,489)
Oxford (111)
Pascagoula (1,671)
Philadelphia (1,920)
Picayune (1,723)
Pontotoc (1,616)
Senatobia (1,535)
Starkville (850)
Tupelo (993)
Vicksburg (1,790)
West Point (1,872)
Yazoo City (2,079)

Missouri

Aurora (1,466)
Bolivar (869)

Boonville (1,510)
Bowling Green (1,622)
Branson (783)
Cameron (1,266)
Cape Girardeau (514)
Carthage (1,711)
Caruthersville (1,980)
Charleston (2,031)
Chillicothe (1,288)
Clinton (1,207)
Columbia (295)
De Soto (1,493)
Dexter (1,475)
Eureka (67)
Excelsior Springs (777)
Farmington (1,163)
Forsyth (1,099)
Fort Leonard Wood (1,518)
Fulton (1,391)
Hannibal (969)
Harrisonville (1,047)
Jefferson City (568)
Joplin (791)
Kearney (276)
Kennett (1,439)
Kirksville (1,211)
Lebanon (1,245)
Lee's Summit (86)
Marshall (1,503)
Marshfield (1,383)
Maryville (1,085)
Mexico (1,654)
Moberly (1,545)
Monett (1,722)
Neosho (1,545)
Nevada (1,651)
Odessa (1,234)
Pacific (824)
Perryville (861)
Platte City (82)
Pleasant Hill (351)
Poplar Bluff (1,784)
Richmond (1,391)
Rolla (655)

St. Clair (1,634)
St. Joseph (1,396)
Savannah (873)
Scott City (1,477)
Sedalia (1,304)
Sikeston (1,404)
Sullivan (1,584)
Trenton (1,835)
Troy (1,197)
Union (819)
Warrensburg (785)
Warrenton (1,393)
Washington (323)
West Plains (1,187)
Whiteman AFB (642)
Willard (318)

Montana

Anaconda (1,413)
Belgrade (202)
Billings (670)
Bozeman (89)
Butte (988)
Columbia Falls (382)
Glendive (959)
Great Falls (1,218)
Hamilton (748)
Havre (1,095)
Helena (357)
Kalispell (245)
Laurel (1,061)
Lewistown (866)
Livingston (225)
Miles City (1,254)
Missoula (343)
Sidney (1,169)
Whitefish (54)

Nebraska

Alliance (617)
Beatrice (547)
Blair (479)
Chadron (760)
Columbus (510)

Crete (1,341)
Fremont (897)
Grand Island (1,229)
Hastings (856)
Holdrege (332)
Kearney (366)
Lexington (1,831)
McCook (532)
Nebraska City (812)
Norfolk (658)
North Platte (932)
Plattsmouth (673)
Schuyler (1,844)
Scottsbluff (1,061)
Seward (329)
Sidney (533)
Wayne (248)
York (362)

Nevada

Boulder City (509)
Carson City (972)
Dayton (617)
Elko (968)
Fallon (944)
Fernley (1,482)
Gardnerville Ranchos (610)
Incline Village (181)
Johnson Lane (114)
Laughlin (1,845)
Mesquite (894)
Moapa Valley (327)
Pahrump (1,035)
Winnemucca (1,177)

New Hampshire

Berlin (851)
Claremont (1,274)
Concord (298)
Dover (452)
Franklin (1,129)
Keene (421)
Laconia (278)
Lebanon (87)

Manchester (397)
Portsmouth (40)

New Jersey

Bridgeton (1,977)
Browns Mills (695)
Franklin (395)
Hammonton (830)
Jefferson Township North (84)
Mystic Island (431)
Newton (603)
Salem (2,043)
Twin Rivers (90)
Villas (229)
Vineland (1,393)
Washington (464)

New Mexico

Alamogordo (1,596)
Artesia (543)
Aztec (1,907)
Bloomfield (1,820)
Carlsbad (498)
Chaparral (1,988)
Clovis (1,780)
Deming (1,982)
Espanola (1,919)
Farmington (1,708)
Gallup (1,681)
Grants (1,949)
Hobbs (1,418)
Kirtland (1,917)
Las Cruces (1,499)
Las Vegas (1,855)
Los Alamos (28)
Los Lunas (1,380)
Lovington (1,657)
Portales (1,930)
Raton (1,684)
Roswell (1,778)
Ruidoso (987)
Santa Fe (513)
Shiprock (2,061)
Silver City (1,685)

Socorro (1,682)
Taos (1,350)
Truth or Consequences (1,906)
White Rock (21)
Zuni Pueblo (1,924)

New York

Albion (1,406)
Amsterdam (1,452)
Attica (1,043)
Auburn (1,092)
Batavia (951)
Bath (1,415)
Binghamton (793)
Brockport (678)
Canton (343)
Catskill (1,420)
Chester (136)
Clifton Springs (488)
Cobleskill (1,194)
Corning (459)
Cortland (1,045)
Coxsackie (1,239)
Dunkirk (957)
East Aurora (173)
Ellenville (820)
Elmira (927)
Geneseo (1,320)
Geneva (445)
Glens Falls (358)
Gloversville (1,306)
Gowanda (998)
Honeoye Falls (311)
Hornell (1,295)
Hudson (1,228)
Ilion (1,189)
Ithaca (266)
Jamestown (1,343)
Kingston (481)
Lockport (1,027)
Malone (1,689)
Massena (1,051)
Medina (756)
Middletown (617)

Monticello (1,675)
Newark (1,010)
Newfane (450)
Norwich (1,381)
Ogdensburg (1,221)
Olean (958)
Oneida (740)
Oneonta (568)
Oswego (1,140)
Penn Yan (1,051)
Plattsburgh (885)
Port Jervis (678)
Potsdam (690)
Ravena (982)
Red Hook (152)
Rome (1,038)
Salamanca (1,767)
Saranac Lake (917)
Saratoga Springs (68)
Sidney (1,245)
Southold (167)
Springs (240)
Utica (813)
Walden (422)
Warwick (112)
Watertown (1,201)
Wellsville (1,324)
West Point (109)

North Carolina

Albemarle (1,231)
Archer Lodge (19)
Asheboro (1,604)
Boiling Spring Lakes (650)
Boone (562)
Brevard (347)
Buies Creek (1,242)
Burlington (670)
Butner (519)
Cherryville (989)
Clinton (1,674)
Cullowhee (984)
Dunn (1,530)
Eden (1,785)

Elizabeth City (1,505)
Elkin (1,685)
Forest City (1,617)
Franklin (463)
Gastonia (828)
Goldsboro (1,575)
Greenville (912)
Hampstead (48)
Havelock (1,166)
Henderson (1,955)
High Point (854)
Jacksonville (1,296)
Kill Devil Hills (75)
Kinston (1,813)
Lake Norman of Catawba (93)
Laurinburg (2,002)
Lincolnton (1,004)
Lumberton (1,902)
Manteo (80)
Marion (1,358)
Mocksville (583)
Morehead City (194)
Mount Airy (1,356)
Mount Olive (1,961)
New Bern (1,063)
North Wilkesboro (1,278)
Oak Island (191)
Oxford (1,402)
Pembroke (1,885)
Pinehurst (152)
Reidsville (1,952)
Richlands South (617)
Roanoke Rapids (1,718)
Rockingham (1,871)
Rocky Mount (1,711)
Roxboro (1,880)
Sanford (1,280)
Shelby (1,601)
Siler City (1,839)
Smithfield (897)
Spout Springs (486)
Spruce Pine (1,135)
Swansboro (964)
Tarboro (1,997)

Taylorsville (1,801)
Wadesboro (2,029)
Washington (1,429)
Wendell (265)
Whiteville (1,698)
Williamston (1,955)
Wilson (1,539)

North Dakota

Bismarck (565)
Devils Lake (658)
Dickinson (1,403)
Grand Forks (837)
Jamestown (830)
Minot (1,286)
Valley City (561)
Wahpeton (650)
Williston (1,296)

Ohio

Ada (1,144)
Alliance (1,474)
Ashland (811)
Ashtabula (1,459)
Ashville (903)
Athens (1,035)
Bellefontaine (1,213)
Bellevue (801)
Bowling Green (897)
Bryan (685)
Bucyrus (1,330)
Caldwell (836)
Cambridge (1,551)
Celina (385)
Chardon (306)
Chillicothe (962)
Circleville (1,194)
Clyde (1,147)
Columbiana (710)
Conneaut (1,307)
Coshocton (1,548)
Crooksville (1,776)
Darbydale (962)
Defiance (989)

Delphos (813)
East Liverpool (1,605)
Eaton (838)
Findlay (402)
Fostoria (1,554)
Fremont (1,317)
Galion (1,385)
Garrettsville (1,307)
Geneva (1,508)
Greenville (1,372)
Harrison (551)
Hillsboro (1,551)
Jackson (1,430)
Johnstown (506)
Kenton (1,580)
Lancaster (947)
Lima (1,198)
Lisbon (1,464)
Logan (1,116)
London (1,085)
Lorain (1,369)
Mansfield (1,335)
Marietta (779)
Marion (1,540)
Marysville (119)
Middleport (1,747)
Middletown (866)
Mount Vernon (878)
Napoleon (1,075)
Nelsonville (1,873)
Newark (470)
New Bremen (77)
New Lexington (1,476)
New Philadelphia (779)
Norwalk (1,375)
Oberlin (939)
Orrville (474)
Ottawa (384)
Oxford (400)
Piqua (1,185)
Point Pleasant (1,724)
Port Clinton (286)
Portsmouth (1,618)
Russells Point (1,155)

St. Marys (497)
Salem (1,034)
Sandusky (951)
Seville (303)
Shelby (1,457)
Sidney (1,271)
Springfield (1,583)
Tiffin (1,191)
Upper Sandusky (792)
Urbana (1,549)
Van Wert (796)
Wapakoneta (582)
Washington Court House (786)
Wauseon (470)
Waverly City (1,343)
Wellington (1,381)
Willard (1,589)
Wilmington (1,158)
Wooster (482)
Zanesville (1,527)

Oklahoma

Ada (1,158)
Altus (1,530)
Alva (1,018)
Anadarko (1,888)
Ardmore (1,454)
Bartlesville (878)
Blackwell (1,772)
Chickasha (1,269)
Claremore (1,205)
Clinton (1,187)
Cushing (1,645)
Duncan (1,560)
Durant (1,350)
Elk City (1,578)
El Reno (1,232)
Enid (1,208)
Grove (1,104)
Guthrie (1,340)
Guymon (1,967)
Henryetta (1,931)
Holdenville (2,033)
Idabel (1,868)

Lawton (1,553)
McAlester (1,527)
Miami (1,842)
Muldrow (1,812)
Muskogee (1,655)
Norman (431)
Okmulgee (1,964)
Pauls Valley (1,731)
Ponca City (1,496)
Poteau (1,932)
Pryor Creek (1,592)
Purcell (1,177)
Sallisaw (1,773)
Seminole (1,999)
Shawnee (1,420)
Skiatook (1,647)
Stillwater (804)
Tahlequah (1,672)
Vinita (1,867)
Wagoner (1,410)
Weatherford (756)
Woodward (1,330)

Oregon

Albany (339)
Astoria (144)
Baker City (348)
Bend (15)
Brookings (662)
Canby (252)
Coos Bay (723)
Corvallis (188)
Cottage Grove (1,132)
Creswell (859)
Dallas (405)
Florence (706)
Grants Pass (731)
Hermiston (1,576)
Hood River (45)
Junction City (885)
Klamath Falls (1,056)
La Grande (645)
Lebanon (544)
Lincoln City (505)

Madras (1,353)
McMinnville (527)
Medford (504)
Molalla (540)
Monmouth (764)
Newberg (415)
Newport (431)
Ontario (1,322)
Pendleton (1,236)
Prineville (1,041)
Redmond (196)
Roseburg (591)
St. Helens (467)
Sandy (240)
Seaside (162)
Sheridan (986)
Silverton (208)
Stayton (960)
Sutherlin (775)
Sweet Home (1,465)
The Dalles (658)
Tillamook (634)
Tri-City (1,461)
Veneta (598)
Woodburn (1,274)

Pennsylvania

Altoona (736)
Ashland (1,661)
Bellefonte (629)
Blairsville (1,597)
Bloomsburg (838)
Bradford (1,072)
Butler (386)
Chambersburg (650)
Clarion (991)
Clearfield (1,093)
Corry (1,327)
Cresson (1,020)
DuBois (1,006)
East Stroudsburg (600)
Edinboro (704)
Ellwood City (818)
Erie (1,003)

Franklin (Venango County)
 (1,000)
Greenville (921)
Grove City (403)
Hanover (681)
Hazleton (1,566)
Honesdale (1,401)
Huntingdon (1,307)
Indiana (1,119)
Jersey Shore (1,570)
Jim Thorpe (891)
Johnstown (1,203)
Kittanning (1,158)
Kutztown (777)
Lebanon (1,070)
Lewistown (1,131)
Littlestown (614)
Lock Haven (1,041)
Meadville (752)
Milton (628)
Monessen (918)
Mount Pocono (718)
Muncy (1,047)
New Castle (913)
New Freedom (225)
North East (868)
Northern Cambria (1,348)
Oil City (897)
Orwigsburg (374)
Philipsburg (1,497)
Pocono Woodland Lakes (214)
Portage (993)
Pottstown (313)
Pottsville (1,130)
Punxsutawney (1,435)
Quarryville (1,100)
Roaring Spring (1,480)
St. Marys (454)
Saw Creek (482)
Sayre (1,002)
Shamokin (1,714)
Shenandoah (1,836)
Shippensburg (876)
Sierra View (585)

Slippery Rock (893)
Somerset (1,144)
State College (204)
Sunbury (808)
Tamaqua (1,480)
Titusville (1,399)
Tyrone (1,132)
Uniontown (800)
Warren (755)
Waynesboro (1,150)
Waynesburg (1,282)
Williamsport (1,095)

South Carolina

Anderson (501)
Batesburg (1,256)
Beaufort (300)
Belton (1,407)
Bennettsville (2,047)
Camden (720)
Cheraw (1,848)
Chester (1,809)
Clinton (1,864)
Clover (639)
Dillon (1,945)
Florence (918)
Gaffney (1,898)
Georgetown (1,580)
Greenwood (1,348)
Hartsville (940)
Hilton Head Island (138)
Kingstree (2,035)
Lake City (1,675)
Lancaster (993)
Laurens (2,031)
Marion (1,986)
Mauldin (50)
Mullins (1,976)
Newberry (1,862)
Orangeburg (1,677)
Pawleys Island (56)
Rock Hill (291)
Seneca (1,161)
Spartanburg (489)

Sumter (1,345)
Sun City Hilton Head (47)
Union (1,863)
Walterboro (1,765)
York (735)

South Dakota

Aberdeen (601)
Belle Fourche (1,250)
Box Elder (1,126)
Brandon (222)
Brookings (321)
Huron (1,428)
Madison (438)
Mitchell (545)
Pierre (521)
Rapid City (697)
Sioux Falls (340)
Spearfish (298)
Sturgis (981)
Tea (17)
Vermillion (453)
Watertown (409)
Yankton (261)

Tennessee

Arlington (227)
Athens (1,296)
Atoka (713)
Bolivar (1,728)
Bristol (909)
Brownsville (1,978)
Clarksville (642)
Cleveland (1,142)
Columbia (484)
Cookeville (634)
Covington (1,860)
Crossville (1,191)
Dandridge (330)
Dayton (1,822)
Dickson (982)
Dyersburg (1,364)
Erwin (1,626)
Fairfield Glade (598)

Fairview (106)
Fayetteville (1,829)
Greeneville (1,296)
Harriman (1,358)
Henderson (1,435)
Humboldt (1,739)
Jackson (1,015)
Johnson City (706)
Kingsport (830)
Lafayette (1,788)
La Follette (1,665)
Lawrenceburg (1,142)
Lebanon (290)
Lewisburg (1,369)
Lexington (1,648)
Madisonville (1,244)
Manchester (1,400)
Martin (1,445)
McMinnville (1,803)
Milan (736)
Morristown (1,262)
Murfreesboro (192)
Newport (1,979)
Oakland (323)
Paris (1,590)
Portland (797)
Pulaski (1,670)
Ripley (2,029)
Rogersville (1,794)
Savannah (1,452)
Sevierville (844)
Shelbyville (1,916)
South Pittsburg (1,638)
Sparta (1,726)
Springfield (1,461)
Spring Hill (14)
Sweetwater (1,454)
Tullahoma (1,081)
Union City (1,744)
Winchester (906)

Texas

Abilene (966)
Aledo (42)

Alice (2,015)
Alpine (881)
Andrews (1,360)
Anna (115)
Athens (1,205)
Atlanta (1,782)
Bastrop (390)
Bay City (1,705)
Beaumont (1,366)
Beeville (1,990)
Belterra (3)
Big Spring (1,300)
Boerne (29)
Bonham (638)
Borger (1,830)
Brady (1,788)
Breckenridge (1,459)
Brenham (1,119)
Bridgeport (1,523)
Brownfield (2,020)
Brownwood (1,173)
Burkburnett (1,625)
Cameron (2,026)
Canyon (591)
Canyon Lake (133)
Carrizo Springs (2,068)
Carthage (1,687)
Center (1,915)
Cleburne (1,441)
Cleveland (1,771)
College Station (637)
Colorado City (1,834)
Commerce (1,499)
Corsicana (1,592)
Crockett (1,980)
Crystal City (1,877)
Cuero (1,558)
Dalhart (1,010)
Dayton (1,083)
Decatur (1,650)
Del Rio (1,755)
Denver City (675)
Devine (1,357)
Dumas (1,637)

Eagle Pass (1,934)
Edna (1,522)
El Campo (1,613)
Elgin (997)
Ennis (904)
Fabens (2,070)
Floresville (730)
Forney (125)
Fort Stockton (1,646)
Fredericksburg (238)
Gainesville (1,814)
Galveston (1,024)
Gatesville (1,592)
Giddings (1,533)
Gilmer (1,662)
Gonzales (1,791)
Graham (935)
Granbury (411)
Grangerland (1,321)
Granite Shoals (255)
Greenville (1,420)
Gun Barrel City (1,330)
Harlingen (1,793)
Hempstead (1,430)
Henderson (1,861)
Hereford (1,875)
Hillsboro (1,705)
Homesteads Addition (1,707)
Hondo (1,509)
Huntsville (1,683)
Ingleside (1,768)
Iowa Park (738)
Jacksonville (1,938)
Jasper (1,799)
Kaufman (1,489)
Kenedy (1,313)
Kermit (781)
Kerrville (631)
Kilgore (1,449)
Kingsland (1,161)
Kingsville (1,886)
Lago Vista (122)
La Grange (992)
Lake Conroe Eastshore (22)

Lake Conroe Westshore (35)
Lake Jackson (644)
Lamesa (1,961)
Lampasas (1,102)
Levelland (1,809)
Liberty (677)
Lindale (462)
Littlefield (1,893)
Livingston (1,667)
Lockhart (1,556)
Longview (1,326)
Lufkin (1,516)
Luling (1,734)
Manor (60)
Marble Falls (250)
Marlin (2,072)
Marshall (1,886)
Mathis (1,892)
McGregor (1,659)
Mexia (1,859)
Midland (356)
Mineola (1,807)
Mineral Wells (1,699)
Monahans (633)
Mount Pleasant (1,814)
Muleshoe (1,710)
Nacogdoches (1,743)
Navasota (1,899)
Odessa (1,608)
Palestine (1,756)
Paloma Creek South (44)
Pampa (1,819)
Paris (1,437)
Pearsall (1,869)
Pecan Acres (1,375)
Pecan Plantation (140)
Pecos (693)
Perryton (1,837)
Plainview (1,911)
Pleasanton (1,180)
Port Arthur (1,413)
Port Isabel (1,530)
Port Lavaca (1,312)
Prairie View (1,936)

Raymondville (1,989)
Rio Bravo (2,076)
Rio Grande City (1,942)
Robstown (2,013)
Rockdale (1,955)
Rockport (1,634)
San Angelo (1,124)
Sanger (391)
San Marcos (768)
Sealy (969)
Seguin (1,447)
Seminole (830)
Sherman (1,024)
Silsbee (1,265)
Sinton (1,974)
Slaton (1,737)
Snyder (1,823)
Stephenville (771)
Sullivan City (1,983)
Sulphur Springs (1,377)
Sweetwater (1,665)
Taylor (781)
Temple (605)
Terrell (1,031)
Texarkana (1,432)
Texas City (869)
Tyler (1,007)
Uvalde (1,740)
Vernon (1,826)
Victoria (1,389)
Waco (1,237)
Weatherford (201)
West Columbia (657)
West Tawakoni (1,633)
Wharton (1,805)
Wichita Falls (1,218)
Woodcreek (51)
Yoakum (1,745)
Zapata (2,075)

Utah

Cedar City (163)
Eagle Mountain South (49)
Ephraim (194)

Grantsville (416)
Heber (8)
Hurricane (315)
Logan (148)
Moab (128)
Nephi (208)
Park City (2)
Price (1,078)
Richfield (423)
Roosevelt (923)
St. George (85)
Santaquin (81)
Stansbury Park (65)
Summit Park (1)
Tooele (427)
Tremonton (378)
Vernal (1,420)

Vermont

Barre (511)
Bellows Falls (725)
Bennington (577)
Brattleboro (670)
Burlington (171)
Middlebury (359)
Milton (271)
Rutland (523)
St. Albans (686)

Virginia

Bealeton (728)
Bedford (1,057)
Big Stone Gap (1,924)
Blacksburg (517)
Broadway (1,057)
Buena Vista (1,691)
Charlottesville (117)
Clifton Forge (1,709)
Covington (871)
Crozet (20)
Culpeper (901)
Danville (1,282)
Emporia (1,327)
Farmville (1,597)

Franklin (1,383)
Fredericksburg (198)
Front Royal (891)
Galax (1,059)
Harrisonburg (717)
Lake Land'Or (726)
Lake Monticello (99)
Lake of the Woods (141)
Lexington (447)
Lynchburg (521)
Marion (1,777)
Martinsville (1,643)
Norton (1,250)
Pulaski (1,398)
Purcellville (12)
Richlands (1,718)
Rocky Mount (1,364)
Ruckersville (65)
Smithfield (369)
South Boston (1,888)
Staunton (692)
Strasburg (1,135)
Stuarts Draft (578)
Williamsburg (101)
Winchester (285)
Woodstock (1,471)
Wytheville (953)

Washington

Aberdeen (1,119)
Anacortes (102)
Bellingham (151)
Birch Bay (121)
Camano (280)
Centralia (636)
Cheney (788)
Colville (292)
Connell (1,463)
Ellensburg (267)
Ephrata (1,372)
Everson (450)
Grandview (1,678)
Granite Falls (490)
Indianola (239)

Longview (1,024)
Lynden (231)
Marysville (293)
Mattawa (1,971)
Montesano (1,089)
Moses Lake (881)
Mount Vernon (479)
Oak Harbor (399)
Ocean Shores (1,389)
Olympia (157)
Omak (1,189)
Othello (1,857)
Port Angeles (732)
Port Townsend (55)
Pullman (464)
Quincy (1,753)
Sequim (248)
Shelton (1,367)
Snoqualmie (18)
Stanwood (271)
Sultan (528)
Sunnyside (1,876)
Toppenish (1,922)
Walla Walla (624)
Wapato (2,010)
Wenatchee (571)
Woodland (771)
Yakima (1,361)
Yelm (485)

West Virginia

Beckley (1,443)
Bluefield (1,506)
Buckhannon (1,335)
Charleston (1,167)
Charles Town (389)
Clarksburg (593)
Elkins (1,418)
Fairmont (1,185)
Grafton (1,658)
Huntington (1,140)
Keyser (1,629)
Lewisburg (972)
Logan (1,741)

Morgantown (268)
New Martinsville (1,515)
Parkersburg (1,000)
Weirton (1,261)
Wheeling (845)

Wisconsin

Antigo (945)
Ashland (1,060)
Baldwin (275)
Baraboo (348)
Beaver Dam (817)
Beloit (1,012)
Black River Falls (1,240)
Burlington (460)
Columbus (220)
Delavan (645)
Eau Claire (327)
Edgerton (314)
Elkhorn (370)
Evansville (330)
Fond du Lac (716)
Fort Atkinson (472)
Hudson (69)
Janesville (427)
Kenosha (547)
Kiel (555)
La Crosse (348)
Lake Delton (387)
Lake Geneva (237)
Lake Mills (164)
Manitowoc (749)
Marinette (1,097)
Marshfield (242)
Menomonie (705)
Merrill (581)
Monroe (317)
Mount Horeb (127)
Mukwonago (83)
New London (1,067)
New Richmond (270)
Oregon (94)
Oshkosh (608)
Platteville (524)

Plymouth (346)
Portage (667)
Prairie du Chien (894)
Prairie du Sac (117)
Racine (1,038)
Reedsburg (416)
Rhinelander (508)
Rice Lake (444)
Ripon (925)
River Falls (333)
Shawano (1,066)
Sheboygan (455)
Sparta (718)
Stevens Point (253)
Sturgeon Bay (126)
Tomah (631)
Union Grove (1,004)
Watertown (678)
Waupaca (699)
Waupun (709)
Wausau (352)
West Bend (235)
Whitewater (1,126)
Wisconsin Rapids (605)

Wyoming

Casper (871)
Cheyenne (407)
Cody (309)
Douglas (799)
Evanston (434)
Gillette (996)
Green River (972)
Jackson (57)
Lander (408)
Laramie (492)
Powell (553)
Rawlins (934)
Riverton (1,494)
Rock Springs (788)
Sheridan (396)
Torrington (1,083)
Worland (1,424)

SOURCES

Each source is initially noted with a full citation; subsequent mentions are accompanied by shortened citations. A book is listed with full author name, full title, publisher, and publication date only on first reference. The same is true for full author name, full title, newspaper or magazine name, date, and web address (if applicable) for a published article, and full author name, full title, posting date (if available), and web address for other online material.

Abbreviations

ACS 2014: 2014 American Community Survey, Five-Year Estimates (December 1, 2015), U.S. Census Bureau, census.gov.

ACS 2019: 2019 American Community Survey, Five-Year Estimates (December 10, 2020), U.S. Census Bureau, census.gov.

BEA: U.S. Bureau of Economic Analysis, bea.gov.

BLS: U.S. Bureau of Labor Statistics, bls.gov.

USCB: U.S. Census Bureau, census.gov.

1. Thinking Small

Creekside Chalets and Redfin study: Vicky Collins, "Covid-19 Brings Unexpected Boon to Small Colorado Town," NBC News (November 1, 2020), nbcnews.com.

Harris Poll: Arianne Cohen, "Should You Flee Your City? Almost 40% Have Considered It During the Pandemic," *Fast Company* (May 4, 2020), fastcompany.com; "The American Dream, Remodeled," Harris Poll (May 8-10, 2020), theharrispoll.com.

Housing boom: Nicole Friedman, "Pandemic Fueled a Rush to Buy Homes in 2020," *Wall Street Journal* (January 23-24, 2021), p. A3; Ryan

Bieber, "Zoom Town: Could Ithaca Become the Place Remote Workers Abandon Cities For?" *Ithaca Times* (January 20, 2021), ithaca.com.

Home values: ACS 2019.

Work at home: Jonathan Dingel and Brent Neiman, "How Many Jobs Can Be Done at Home?" National Bureau of Economic Research (June 2020), nber.org; Trevor Bach, "What the Surge in Working From Home Means for Big Cities," *U.S. News and World Report* (June 29, 2020), usnews.com.

Exodus to small towns: Greg Shepard, "How Remote Work Can Transform Smaller Cities," *U.S. News and World Report* (September 28, 2020), usnews.com; ACS 2019; Brad Cartier, "The Rising Interest in Rural and Small-Town Real Estate," *Millionacres* (May 14, 2020), fool.com/millionacres.

Maine: Michael Braga, "Are We in Another Housing Bubble?" *USA Today* (February 5, 2021), p. 2B.

Jefferson: G. Scott Thomas, *The United States of Suburbia* (Buffalo: Prometheus Books, 1998), p. 110.

Rural-urban population: "Urban and Rural Areas: History," USCB (December 17, 2020); USCB, *Historical Statistics of the United States: Colonial Times to 1970* (Washington: U.S. Government Printing Office, 1975), pp. 11-12.

1949 Gallup Poll: Thomas, *United States of Suburbia*, p. 110.

1978-2001 polls: G. Scott Thomas, *The Rating Guide to Life in America's Small Cities* (Buffalo: Prometheus Books, 1990), pp. 7-8; Humphrey Taylor, "Half of All Those Who Live in Cities Would Prefer to Move Somewhere Else," Harris Poll (September 6, 1992), theharrispoll.com; Lydia Saad, "Country Living Enjoys Renewed Appeal in U.S.," Gallup (January 5, 2021), gallup.com.

2020 Gallup Poll: Saad, "Country Living."

Urban population: ACS 2019.

Definitions of urban and rural: "Urban and Rural Areas: History," USCB.

Suburban explosion: Thomas, *United States of Suburbia*, pp. 35-37; William Manchester, *The Glory and the Dream* (Boston: Little, Brown, and Co.), pp. 431-432.

Metropolitan areas: "Metropolitan Areas: History," USCB (December 17, 2020); "Population of Standard Metropolitan Areas: April 1, 1950," USCB (November 5, 1950).

Urbanized areas: "2010 Census Urban Area FAQs," USCB (December 2, 2019); "2010 Census Urban and Rural Classification and Urban Area Criteria," USCB (December 2, 2019).

Current situation: "Metropolitan and Micropolitan," USCB (April 1, 2020); G. Scott Thomas, *Micropolitan America* (Buffalo: Niawanda Books, 2017), pp. 15-18; "2010 Census Urban and Rural Classification," USCB.

Major urban hubs: ACS 2019; "2019 Gazetteer Files," USCB.

Strengths of small towns (points 1-6): ACS 2019; "2019 Gazetteer Files," USCB; "Regional Price Parities by State and Metro Area," BEA (December 15, 2020); "Census Bureau Releases New Data on Community Resilience," USCB (June 22, 2020).

Weaknesses of small towns (points 1-6): ACS 2014; ACS 2019; Kurt Schindler, "People Count: Population Growth Causes Basic Economic Growth," Michigan State University (January 19, 2017), msu.edu; Katherine Phillips, "How Diversity Makes Us Smarter," *Scientific American* (October 1, 2014), scientificamerican.com; Shepard, "How Remote Work Can Transform."

Lending Tree: Steve Brown, "Pandemic Has Few Dallas Homeowners Fleeing for Small Towns," *Dallas Morning News* (December 21, 2020), dallasnews.com.

2. The Tests

Resilience: "New Data on Community Resilience," USCB.

Short commutes: ACS 2019; "United States Commuting at a Glance," USCB (January 4, 2021).

Living with two parents: ACS 2019; "Religion and Living Arrangements Around the World," Pew Research Center (December 12, 2019), pewforum.org; Robert Pondiscio, "The School Success Sequence," *Philanthropy Magazine* (Fall 2019), philanthropyroundtable.org; "Two Out of Three Kids in America Are Living With Both Parents," Annie E. Casey Foundation (November 7, 2017), datacenter.kidscount.org.

Occupied homes: ACS 2019; Rachel Dovey, "Dollar Amount Put on Cost of Blight to Neighbors," *Next City* (January 17, 2017), nextcity.org.

Population growth: ACS 2014; ACS 2019; Igor Derysh, "U.S. on Pace for Slowest Population Growth Since Spanish Flu and Economic Impact is Already Evident," *Salon* (December 19, 2020), salon.com.

Economic growth: "Gross Domestic Product by County," BEA (December 9, 2020); Elvis Picardo, "The Importance of GDP," *Investopedia* (October 20, 2020), investopedia.com.

High school graduates: ACS 2019; Eric Hanushek and Ludger Woessmann, "The Economic Impacts of Learning Losses," Organization for Economic Cooperation and Development (September 2020), oced.org; "Usual Weekly Earnings of Wage and Salary Workers, Fourth Quarter 2020," BLS (January 21, 2021).

College graduates: ACS 2019; Russell Flannery, "Tough Choices: Falling Enrollment, Covid Pressure College Cities and Towns," *Forbes* (February 16, 2021), forbes.com.

MBSA workers: ACS 2019; Kaia Hubbard, "A New Report Paints a Complicated Picture of Distress and Prosperity in U.S. Cities," *U.S. News and World Report* (October 14, 2020), usnews.com.

Private-sector job growth: "Quarterly Census of Employment and Wages," BLS (June 3, 2020); "Employment, Hours, and Earnings — National," BLS (February 22, 2021).

Small business growth: "County Business Patterns," USCB (June 25, 2020); Shannon Pettypiece, "Biden Announces Changes in Loan Program Aimed at Aiding Small and Minority-Owned Businesses," NBC News (February 22, 2021), nbcnews.com; Maneet Ahuja, "Small Business Strikes Back: The Numbers Behind the Next 1,000," *Forbes* (February 16, 2021), forbes.com.

Self-employed workers: ACS 2019; N.F. Mendoza, "You're Your Own Boss: The State of the Self-Employed," *TechRepublic* (February 10, 2021), techrepublic.com; Shobhit Seth, "Why Entrepreneurship is Important to the Economy," *Investopedia* (January 4, 2021), investopedia.com.

Median annual earnings: ACS 2019; G. Scott Thomas, "4 Cities Where Just About Everyone Earns 'Passive Income,'" *The Business Journals* (November 23, 2015), bizjournals.com; "Consumer Price Index," BLS (February 10, 2021).

Living in poverty: ACS 2019; "Poverty Data Tables," USCB (September 15, 2020); "Many Rural Americans Are Still 'Left Behind,'" Institute for Research on Poverty, University of Wisconsin (January 2020), irp.wisc.edu.

Home ownership: ACS 2019; George Morris, "Advantages and Disadvantages of Owning a Home," InCharge Debt Solutions, incharge.org; "Preliminary Analysis of Homeownership Trends for Nine Cities," U.S. Government Accountability Office (June 25, 2020), gao.gov; "Quarterly

Residential Vacancies and Homeownership," USCB (February 2, 2021).

Monthly housing costs: ACS 2019; "Homeownership Trends for Nine Cities," U.S. Government Accountability Office; Brenda Richardson, "Housing Market Gains More Value in 2020 Than in Any Year Since 2005," *Forbes* (January 26, 2021), forbes.com; "Median Selected Monthly Owner Costs," USCB.

Health care workers: ACS 2019; Robin Warshaw, "Health Disparities Affect Millions in Rural U.S. Communities," Association of American Medical Colleges (October 31, 2017), aamc.org; Evan Comen, "The 25 Least Healthy Cities in America," *24/7 Wall Street* (January 13, 2020), 247wallst.com.

Fair or poor health: "Poor or Fair Health," County Health Rankings and Roadmaps, countyhealthrankings.org; "Health-Related Quality of Life," Centers for Disease Control (October 31, 2018), cdc.gov.

Stores per 10,000: "County Business Patterns," USCB; Daphne Howland, "Anchors, Away: How Department Stores Are Ditching Malls," *Retail Dive* (November 12, 2020), retaildive.com; "Advance Monthly Sales for Retail and Food Services, January 2021," USCB (February 17, 2021); Michael Powe and Hanna Love, "Proximity Doesn't Benefit Just Big Cities — It's Helping Rural Communities Weather the Economic Crisis, Too," Brookings Institution (October 8, 2020), brookings.edu.

Restaurants per 10,000: "County Business Patterns," USCB; "Total Restaurant Industry Sales," National Restaurant Association (February 23, 2021), restaurant.org; Nick Kokonas, "What's Next for Restaurants," *Food & Wine* (June 15, 2020), foodandwine.com.

Broadband subscriptions: ACS 2019; Emily Vogels, Andrew Perrin, Lee Rainie, and Monica Anderson, "53% of Americans Say the Internet Has Been Essential During the Covid-19 Outbreak," Pew Research Center (April 30, 2020), pewresearch.org; Jessica Farrish, "West Virginia Lawmaker Calls for State Broadband Regulation," *Government Technology* (February 8, 2021), govtech.com.

Smartphone access: ACS 2019; Bret Swanson, "The Economic Impact of Mobile and Cloud Computing is Greater Than Previously Thought," American Enterprise Institute (August 10, 2018), aei.org.

Major hub miles: "2019 Gazetteer Files," USCB; Ed Quioco, "Oldsmar Growth Still Booming," *Tampa Bay Times* (September 14, 2005), tampabay.com.

Major or mid-major miles: "2019 Gazetteer Files," USCB.

3. The Winners

Summit Park, Utah: Shelly Hagan and Wei Lu, "These Are the Best Places to Own a Vacation Home in the U.S.," *Bloomberg* (April 2, 2019), bloomberg.com.

Park City, Utah: "Park City, Utah," *Encyclopedia Britannica*, britannica. com; Hagan and Lu, "Best Places to Own a Vacation Home."

Belterra, Texas: Emily Varnell, "The Origins of Founder's Day," *Texas Monthly* (April 21, 2017), texasmonthly.com; "Belterra Neighborhood Guide," *Austin Texas Insider*, austintexasinsider.com.

World Golf Village, Florida: Stuart Korfhage, "Growing Pains and Gains," *St. Augustine Record* (February 16, 2019), staugustine.com; Colleen Jones, "See Inside Author Steve Berry's World Golf Village Home," *St. Augustine Record* (July 31, 2019), staugustine.com.

Roxborough Park, Colorado: "History in Our Own Backyard," Roxborough Area Historical Society, roxhistory.com; Jordan Steffen, "Roxborough Park Visitors Get a Glimpse into Past Populations," *Denver Post* (October 20, 2012), denverpost.com.

Nantucket, Massachusetts: "Nantucket, Massachusetts," *Encyclopedia Britannica*, britannica.com; Ann Binlot, "10 Reasons For a Nantucket Road Trip," *Forbes* (October 15, 2020), forbes.com.

Evergreen, Colorado: Amy Sward, "5 Must-Visit Towns Near Denver, Colorado," *Travel Awaits* (June 10, 2020), travelawaits.com; Evergreen Area Chamber of Commerce, evergreenchamber.com.

Heber, Utah: Scott Pierce, "Expedia Declares Heber City is One of America's Most Beautiful Towns," *Salt Lake Tribune* (June 12, 2018), sltrib.com.

Vistancia, Arizona: "West Valley History Shaped by Pioneers, World Events," *Arizona Republic* (May 14, 2015), azcentral.com; David Brown, "Vistancia's Final Phase Begins," *Arizona Republic* (June 25, 2014), azcentral.com.

Buckhead (Bryan County), Georgia: Buckhead Homeowners Association, buckheadhoa.com.

Lafayette, Colorado: "The Coal Mining Heritage of Lafayette," City of Lafayette, lafayetteco.gov.

Purcellville, Virginia: "Purcellville, Virginia, History," History of Loudoun County, Virginia, loudounhistory.org; "Purcellville," Commonwealth of Virginia Tourism, virginia.org.

Aspen, Colorado: Bryan Hood, "Jackson Hole vs. Aspen: Which Is America's Best Ski Destination?" *Robb Report* (February 7, 2021), robbreport.com; ACS 2019; Sarah Kuta, "Where to Eat, Stay, and Play in Aspen, Colorado," *Conde Nast Traveler* (December 21, 2020), cntraveler.com.

Spring Hill, Tennessee: "City History," City of Spring Hill, springhilltn.org; Jamie LaReau, "GM Idles Shifts at 4 Factories Amid Arctic Blast," *Detroit Free Press* (February 15, 2021), freep.com; Eric Snyder, "GM Laying Off Hundreds in Spring Hill," *Nashville Business Journal* (June 25, 2020), bizjournals.com/nashville.

Bend, Oregon: ACS 2019; Zach Urness, "Bend Asks Tourists to Stay Away Through Labor Day Following Covid-19 Rise," *Salem Statesman Journal* (July 17, 2020), statesmanjournal.com.

St. Simons, Georgia: David Brown, "Georgia's Sea Islands: A Destination Worth the Paddle," *Washington Post* (February 27, 2020), washingtonpost.com; Lisa Wilson, "Yay! Conde Nast Readers Say Hilton Head is Best Island in U.S. for 4th Year in a Row," *Island Packet* (October 6, 2020), islandpacket.com.

Tea, South Dakota: Colman Andrews, "50 Strangest Town Names in America (and Where They Came From)," *24/7 Wall Street* (August 23, 2020), 247wallst.com; ACS 2019.

Snoqualmie, Washington: "Snoqualmie Historical Closures and Snowfall Records," Washington State Department of Transportation, wsdot.com; Paige Cornwell, "Snoqualmie Tribe Buys Salish Lodge and Adjacent Land for $125 Million, Halting Nearby Development," *Seattle Times* (November 1, 2019), seattletimes.com; ACS 2019.

Archer Lodge, North Carolina: Drew Jackson, "Archer Lodge Sells Its First Cold One," *News and Observer* (September 26, 2016), newsobserver.com; Jeff Reeves, "Johnston County Adapting to Recent Explosive Growth," WNCN (December 21, 2017), cbs17.com; ACS 2019.

Crozet, Virginia: "The New Rules of Adventure: Mid-Atlantic," *Outside* (January 29, 2021), outsideonline.com.

White Rock, New Mexico: Scott Wyland, "Los Alamos County Seeks Over 3,000 Acres from Energy Department," *Santa Fe New Mexican*, santafenewmexican.com; Gaby Galvin, "America's Healthiest Community: Los Alamos County," *U.S. News and World Report* (September 22, 2020), usnews.com.

Lake Conroe Eastshore, Texas: "History of Lake Conroe," San Jacinto River Authority, sjra.net.

Vineyard Haven, Massachusetts: "Martha's Vineyard," *Encyclopedia Britannica*, britannica.com; Mike Benjamin, "Martha's Vineyard, Off-Season," *New York Times* (November 14, 2016), nytimes.com.

Byron, Minnesota: ACS 2019; "History," City of Byron, byronmn.com.

Breckenridge, Colorado: Aimee Heckel, "Road Trip Loop: A Unique Denver/Las Vegas Itinerary," *USA Today 10 Best* (February 5, 2021), 10best.com; Amy Piper, "8 Best Restaurants in Breckenridge," *Travel Awaits* (February 8, 2021), travelawaits.com.

4. The Dreamtowns

Small-town weaknesses and Dreamtowns (points 1-6): ACS 2014; ACS 2019.

Additional strengths of Dreamtowns: ACS 2019; "Poor or Fair Health," County Health Rankings and Roadmaps; "County Business Patterns," USCB.

Basic stats (scorecards): ACS 2019; "2019 Gazetteer Files," USCB.

Race (scorecards): ACS 2019.

Household income ladder (scorecards): ACS 2019.

Home value ladder (scorecards): ACS 2019.

Resilience (scorecards): "New Data on Community Resilience," USCB.

Short commutes (scorecards): ACS 2019.

Living with two parents (scorecards): ACS 2019.

Occupied homes (scorecards): ACS 2019.

Population growth (scorecards): ACS 2014; ACS 2019.

Economic growth (scorecards): "Gross Domestic Product by County," BEA.

High school graduates (scorecards): ACS 2019.

College graduates (scorecards): ACS 2019.

MBSA workers (scorecards): ACS 2019.

Private-sector job growth (scorecards): "Quarterly Census of Employment and Wages," BLS.

Small business growth (scorecards): "County Business Patterns," USCB.

Self-employed workers (scorecards): ACS 2019.

Median annual earnings (scorecards): ACS 2019.

Living in poverty (scorecards): ACS 2019.

Home ownership (scorecards): ACS 2019.

Monthly housing costs (scorecards): ACS 2019.

Health care workers (scorecards): ACS 2019.
Fair or poor health (scorecards): "Poor or Fair Health," County Health Rankings and Roadmaps.
Stores per 10,000 (scorecards): "County Business Patterns," USCB.
Restaurants per 10,000 (scorecards): "County Business Patterns," USCB.
Broadband subscriptions (scorecards): ACS 2019.
Smartphone access (scorecards): ACS 2019.
Major hub miles (scorecards): "2019 Gazetteer Files," USCB.
Major or mid-major miles (scorecards): "2019 Gazetteer Files," USCB.

5. Made to Order

States: ACS 2019.
Regions: ACS 2019.
Population: ACS 2019.
Population density: ACS 2019; "2019 Gazetteer Files," USCB.
Latitude: "Geographic Mobility: 2019 to 2020," USCB (December 2020); "2019 Gazetteer Files," USCB.
Closest major hub: "2019 Gazetteer Files," USCB.
Diversions: "County Business Patterns," USCB.
Commuting: ACS 2019.
Population growth: ACS 2014; ACS 2019.
Education: ACS 2019.
Money: ACS 2019.
Age: ACS 2019.
Diversity: ACS 2019.
Housing: "Geographic Mobility: 2019 to 2020," USCB; ACS 2019.

6. Escape Routes

Kelman forecast: Cartier, "The Rising Interest."
2019-2020 moves: "Geographic Mobility: 2019 to 2020," USCB; "CPS Historical Migration/Geographic Mobility Tables," USCB (December 2020).
Air mileage: "2019 Gazetteer Files," USCB.

7. Full Standings

Rhode Island urbanized areas: ACS 2019.